Triumph Acclaim Owners Workshop Manual

AK Legg T Eng MIMI

Models covered
All Triumph Acclaim models, 1335 cc

(792-4T3)

ABCDE FGHIJ KLMNO PQRS 2

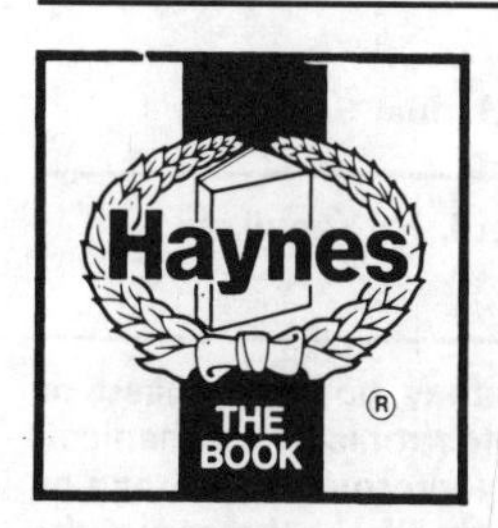

Haynes Publishing
Sparkford Nr Yeovi
Somerset BA22 7J

Haynes Publications, Inc
861 Lawrence Drive
Newbury Park
California 91320 USA

Acknowledgements
Thanks are due to the Champion Sparking Plug Company Limited, who supplied the illustrations showing spark plug conditions, to Holt Lloyd Limited who supplied the illustrations showing bodywork repair, and to Duckhams Oils who provided lubrication data. BL Cars Limited supplied technical information. Thanks are also due to Sykes-Pickavant, who provided some of the workshop tools, and to all those people at Sparkford who helped in the production of this Manual.

A book in the **Haynes Owners Workshop Manual Series**

Printed by J. H. Haynes & Co. Ltd, Sparkford, Nr Yeovil, Somerset BA22 7JJ, England

ISBN 1 85010 057 8

Contents

Triumph Acclaim CD model

About this manual

Its aim

The aim of this manual is to help you get the best value from your vehicle. It can do so in several ways. It can help you decide what work must be done (even should you choose to get it done by a garage), provide information on routine maintenance and servicing, and give a logical course of action and diagnosis when random faults occur. However, it is hoped that you will use the manual by tackling the work yourself. On simpler jobs it may even be quicker than booking the car into a garage and going there twice, to leave and collect it. Perhaps most important, a lot of money can be saved by avoiding the costs a garage must charge to cover its labour and overheads.

The manual has drawings and descriptions to show the function of the various components so that their layout can be understood. Then the tasks are described and photographed in a step-by-step sequence so that even a novice can do the work.

Its arrangement

The manual is divided into thirteen Chapters, each covering a logical sub-division of the vehicle. The Chapters are each divided into Sections, numbered with single figures, eg 5; and the Sections into paragraphs (or sub-sections), with decimal numbers following on from the Section they are in, eg 5.1, 5.2, 5.3 etc.

It is freely illustrated, especially in those parts where there is a detailed sequence of operations to be carried out. There are two forms of illustration: figures and photographs. The figures are numbered in sequence with decimal numbers, according to their position in the Chapter – eg Fig. 6.4 is the fourth drawing/illustration in Chapter 6. Photographs carry the same number (either individually or in related groups) as the Section or sub-section to which they relate.

There is an alphabetical index at the back of the manual as well as a contents list at the front. Each Chapter is also preceded by its own individual contents list.

References to the 'left' or 'right' of the vehicle are in the sense of a person in the driver's seat facing forwards.

Unless otherwise stated, nuts and bolts are removed by turning anti-clockwise, and tightened by turning clockwise.

Vehicle manufacturers continually make changes to specifications and recommendations, and these, when notified, are incorporated into our manuals at the earliest opportunity.

Whilst every care is taken to ensure that the information in this manual is correct, no liability can be accepted by the authors or publishers for loss, damage or injury caused by any errors in, or omissions from, the information given.

Introduction to the Triumph Acclaim

Introduced in October 1981, the Triumph Acclaim is the first mass-produced car to be manufactured in Britain in collaboration with the Japanese Honda Motor Company. Being of identical design to the Honda Ballade, the Acclaim is fitted with an all-alloy 1335 cc four-cylinder engine mounted transversely and driving the front wheels through either a five-speed manual gearbox or three-speed semi-automatic transmission.

The lightweight body results in a high power-to-weight ratio, giving excellent fuel consumption figures together with sporting performance. The independent suspension has been specially developed for European conditions. Power-assisted dual line brakes are fitted, with discs at the front and drums at the rear, and the steering is of rack-and-pinion design.

The Acclaim is extremely well equipped and all models are fitted with headlamp levelling, a tachometer, radio, digital clock and an interior boot release.

Working on the Acclaim is well within the scope of the DIY home mechanic. The mechanical design is straightforward and simple, and does not incorporate the complexities of early transverse-mounted engines.

General dimensions, weights and capacities

Dimensions

Overall height	52.7 in (1.340 m)
Overall width	63.0 in (1.600 m)
Overall length	161.2 in (4.095 m)
Ground clearance	6.5 in (165 mm)
Turning circle	32.75 ft (9.98 m)
Wheelbase	91.3 in (2.320 m)
Track:	
Front	53.5 in (1.360 m)
Rear	54.3 in (1.380 m)

Weights

Kerb weight* (with full fuel tank):	
HL (manual)	1784 lb (809 kg)
HL (Trio-matic)	1808 lb (820 kg)
HLS (manual)	1797 lb (815 kg)
HLS (Trio-matic)	1821 lb (826 kg)
CD (manual)	1819 lb (825 kg)
CD (Trio-matic)	1843 lb (836 kg)
For models with air conditioner add 66 lb (30 kg)	
Maximum gross vehicle weight	2822 lb (1280 kg)
Power unit weight:	
With manual gearbox	289 lb (131 kg)
With Trio-matic transmission	306 lb (139 kg)
Maximum roof rack load	110 lb (50 kg)
Maximum towing weight	1545 lb (700 kg)

Capacities

Engine oil (with filter)	
From dry	7 pints (4.0 litres)
Service	6.25 pints (3.5 litres)
Manual gearbox oil:	
From dry	4.75 pints (2.7 litres)
Service	4.5 pints (2.5 litres)
Trio-matic transmission fluid:	
From dry	8.75 pints (4.9 litres)
Service	4.5 pints (2.5 litres)
Cooling system coolant:	
From dry	8.5 pints (4.8 litres)
Service	7 pints (4.0 litres)
Fuel tank	10 gallons (46 litres)

Buying spare parts and vehicle identification numbers

Buying spare parts

Spare parts are available from many sources, for example: BL garages, other garages and accessory shops, and motor factors. Our advice regarding spare part sources is as follows:

Officially appointed BL garages – There are the best source of parts which are peculiar to your car and are otherwise not generally available (eg complete cylinder heads, internal gearbox components, badges, interior trim etc). It is also the only place at which you should buy parts if your car is still under warranty; non-BL components may invalidate the warranty. To be sure of obtaining the correct parts it will always be necessary to give the storeman your car's engine and chassis number, and if possible, to take the 'old' parts along for positive identification. Remember that many parts are available on a factory exchange scheme – any parts returned should always be clean! It obviously makes good sense to go straight to the specialists on your car for this type of part for they are best equipped to supply you.

Other garages and accessory shops – These are often very good places to buy materials and components needed for the maintenance of your car (eg filters, spark plugs, bulbs, drivebelts, oils and greases, touch-up paint, filler paste, etc). They also sell general accessories, usually have convenient opening hours, charge lower prices and can often be found not far from home.

Motor factors – Good factors will stock all of the more important components which wear out relatively quickly (eg clutch components, pistons, valves, exhaust systems, brake cylinders/pipes/hoses/seals/shoes and pads etc). Motor factors will often provide new or reconditioned components on a part exchange basis – this can save a considerable amount of money.

Vehicle identification numbers

Modifications are a continuing and unpublicised process in vehicle manufacture quite apart from major model changes. Spare parts manuals and lists are compiled upon a numerical basis, the individual vehicle numbers being essential for correct identification of the component required.

When ordering spare parts, always give as much information as possible. Quote the car model, year of manufacture, body and engine numbers as appropriate.

The vehicle identification plate carries the main vehicle identification number and is located on the engine bulkhead (photo).

The body number is stamped on the front upper crossmember.

The engine number is stamped on the rear of the crankcase next to the flywheel housing (photo).

The gearbox number is on a label attached to the top of the gearbox.

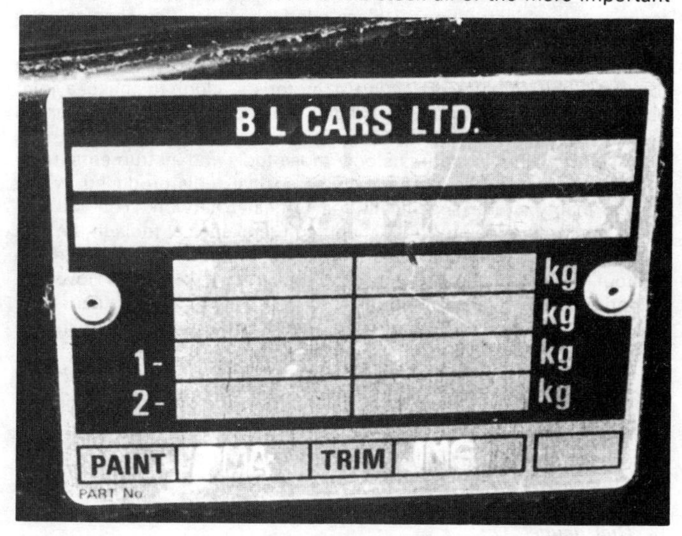

Vehicle identification plate

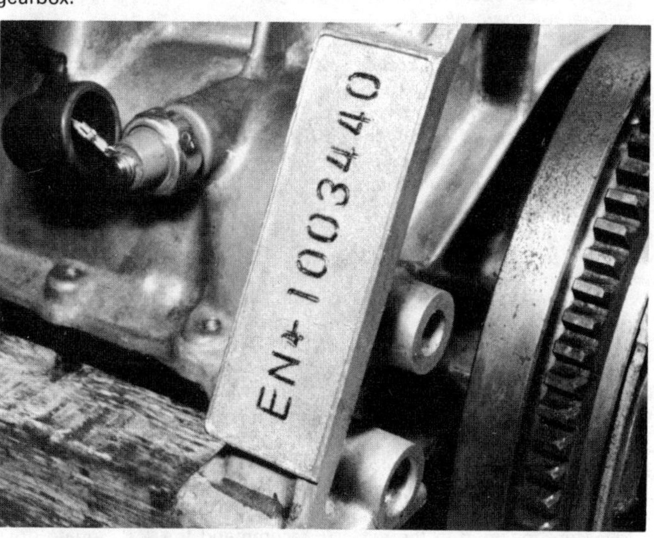

Engine number location

Tools and working facilities

Introduction

A selection of good tools is a fundamental requirement for anyone contemplating the maintenance and repair of a motor vehicle. For the owner who does not possess any, their purchase will prove a considerable expense, offsetting some of the savings made by doing-it-yourself. However, provided that the tools purchased meet the relevant national safety standards and are of good quality, they will last for many years and prove an extremely worthwhile investment.

To help the average owner to decide which tools are needed to carry out the various tasks detailed in this manual, we have compiled three lists of tools under the following headings: *Maintenance and minor repair, Repair and overhaul,* and *Special.* The newcomer to practical mechanics should start off with the *Maintenance and minor repair* tool kit and confine himself to the simpler jobs around the vehicle. Then, as his confidence and experience grow, he can undertake more difficult tasks, buying extra tools as, and when, they are needed. In this way, a *Maintenance and minor repair* tool kit can be built-up into a *Repair and overhaul* tool kit over a considerable period of time without any major cash outlays. The experienced do-it-yourselfer will have a tool kit good enough for most repair and overhaul procedures and will add tools from the *Special* category when he feels the expense is justified by the amount of use to which these tools will be put.

It is obviously not possible to cover the subject of tools fully here. For those who wish to learn more about tools and their use there is a book entitled *How to Choose and Use Car Tools* available from the publishers of this manual.

Maintenance and minor repair tool kit

The tools given in this list should be considered as a minimum requirement if routine maintenance, servicing and minor repair operations are to be undertaken. We recommend the purchase of combination spanners (ring one end, open-ended the other); although more expensive than open-ended ones, they do give the advantages of both types of spanner.

Combination spanners - 10, 11, 12, 13, 14 & 17 mm
Adjustable spanner - 9 inch
Gearbox drain plug key
Spark plug spanner (with rubber insert)
Spark plug gap adjustment tool
Set of feeler gauges
Brake bleed nipple spanner
Screwdriver - 4 in long x $\frac{1}{4}$ in dia (flat blade)
Screwdriver - 4 in long x $\frac{1}{4}$ in dia (cross blade)
Combination pliers - 6 inch
Hacksaw (junior)
Tyre pump
Tyre pressure gauge
Oil can
Fine emery cloth (1 sheet)
Wire brush (small)
Funnel (medium size)

Repair and overhaul tool kit

These tools are virtually essential for anyone undertaking any major repairs to a motor vehicle, and are additional to those given in the *Maintenance and minor repair* list. Included in this list is a comprehensive set of sockets. Although these are expensive they will be found invaluable as they are so versatile - particularly if various drives are included in the set. We recommend the $\frac{1}{2}$ in square-drive type, as this can be used with most proprietary torque wrenches. If you cannot afford a socket set, even bought piecemeal, then inexpensive tubular box spanners are a useful alternative.

The tools in this list will occasionally need to be supplemented by tools from the *Special* list.

Sockets (or box spanners) to cover range in previous list
Reversible ratchet drive (for use with sockets)
Extension piece, 10 inch (for use with sockets)
Universal joint (for use with sockets)
Torque wrench (for use with sockets)
'Mole' wrench - 8 inch
Ball pein hammer
Soft-faced hammer, plastic or rubber
Screwdriver - 6 in long x $\frac{5}{16}$ in dia (flat blade)
Screwdriver - 2 in long x $\frac{5}{16}$ in square (flat blade)
Screwdriver - $1\frac{1}{2}$ in long x $\frac{1}{4}$ in dia (cross blade)
Screwdriver - 3 in long x $\frac{1}{8}$ in dia (electricians)
Pliers - electricians side cutters
Pliers - needle nosed
Pliers - circlip (internal and external)
Cold chisel - $\frac{1}{2}$ inch
Scriber
Scraper
Centre punch
Pin punch
Hacksaw
Valve grinding tool
Steel rule/straight-edge
Allen keys
Selection of files
Wire brush (large)
Axle-stands
Jack (strong scissor or hydraulic type)

Special tools

The tools in this list are those which are not used regularly, are expensive to buy, or which need to be used in accordance with their manufacturers' instructions. Unless relatively difficult mechanical jobs are undertaken frequently, it will not be economic to buy many of these tools. Where this is the case, you could consider clubbing together with friends (or joining a motorists' club) to make a joint purchase, or borrowing the tools against a deposit from a local garage or tool hire specialist.

The following list contains only those tools and instruments freely available to the public, and not those special tools produced by the vehicle manufacturer specifically for its dealer network. You will find occasional references to these manufacturers' special tools in the text of this manual. Generally, an alternative method of doing the job without the vehicle manufacturers' special tool is given. However, sometimes, there is no alternative to using them. Where this is the case and the relevant tool cannot be bought or borrowed, you will have to entrust the work to a franchised garage.

Valve spring compressor (where applicable)
Piston ring compressor
Balljoint separator
Universal hub/bearing puller
Impact screwdriver
Micrometer and/or vernier gauge
Dial gauge
Stroboscopic timing light

Dwell angle meter/tachometer
Universal electrical multi-meter
Cylinder compression gauge
Lifting tackle (photo)
Trolley jack
Light with extension lead

Buying tools

For practically all tools, a tool factor is the best source since he will have a very comprehensive range compared with the average garage or accessory shop. Having said that, accessory shops often offer excellent quality tools at discount prices, so it pays to shop around.

There are plenty of good tools around at reasonable prices, but always aim to purchase items which meet the relevant national safety standards. If in doubt, ask the proprietor or manager of the shop for advice before making a purchase.

Care and maintenance of tools

Having purchased a reasonable tool kit, it is necessary to keep the tools in a clean serviceable condition. After use, always wipe off any dirt, grease and metal particles using a clean, dry cloth, before putting the tools away. Never leave them lying around after they have been used. A simple tool rack on the garage or workshop wall, for items such as screwdrivers and pliers is a good idea. Store all normal wrenches and sockets in a metal box. Any measuring instruments, gauges, meters, etc, must be carefully stored where they cannot be damaged or become rusty.

Take a little care when tools are used. Hammer heads inevitably become marked and screwdrivers lose the keen edge on their blades from time to time. A little timely attention with emery cloth or a file will soon restore items like this to a good serviceable finish.

Working facilities

Not to be forgotten when discussing tools, is the workshop itself. If anything more than routine maintenance is to be carried out, some form of suitable working area becomes essential.

It is appreciated that many an owner mechanic is forced by circumstances to remove an engine or similar item, without the benefit of a garage or workshop. Having done this, any repairs should always be done under the cover of a roof.

Wherever possible, any dismantling should be done on a clean, flat workbench or table at a suitable working height.

Any workbench needs a vice: one with a jaw opening of 4 in (100 mm) is suitable for most jobs. As mentioned previously, some clean dry storage space is also required for tools, as well as for lubricants, cleaning fluids, touch-up paints and so on, which become necessary.

Another item which may be required, and which has a much more general usage, is an electric drill with a chuck capacity of at least $\frac{5}{16}$ in (8 mm). This, together with a good range of twist drills, is virtually essential for fitting accessories such as mirrors and reversing lights.

Last, but not least, always keep a supply of old newspapers and clean, lint-free rags available, and try to keep any working area as clean as possible.

Spanner jaw gap comparison table

Jaw gap (in)	Spanner size
0.250	$\frac{1}{4}$ in AF
0.276	7 mm
0.313	$\frac{5}{16}$ in AF
0.315	8 mm
0.344	$\frac{11}{32}$ in AF; $\frac{1}{8}$ in Whitworth
0.354	9 mm
0.375	$\frac{3}{8}$ in AF
0.394	10 mm
0.433	11 mm
0.438	$\frac{7}{16}$ in AF
0.445	$\frac{3}{16}$ in Whitworth; $\frac{1}{4}$ in BSF
0.472	12 mm
0.500	$\frac{1}{2}$ in AF
0.512	13 mm
0.525	$\frac{1}{4}$ in Whitworth; $\frac{5}{16}$ in BSF
0.551	14 mm
0.563	$\frac{9}{16}$ in AF
0.591	15 mm
0.600	$\frac{5}{16}$ in Whitworth; $\frac{3}{8}$ in BSF
0.625	$\frac{5}{8}$ in AF
0.630	16 mm
0.669	17 mm
0.686	$\frac{11}{16}$ in AF
0.709	18 mm
0.710	$\frac{3}{8}$ in Whitworth; $\frac{7}{16}$ in BSF
0.748	19 mm
0.750	$\frac{3}{4}$ in AF
0.813	$\frac{13}{16}$ in AF
0.820	$\frac{7}{16}$ in Whitworth; $\frac{1}{2}$ in BSF
0.866	22 mm
0.875	$\frac{7}{8}$ in AF
0.920	$\frac{1}{2}$ in Whitworth; $\frac{9}{16}$ in BSF
0.938	$\frac{15}{16}$ in AF
0.945	24 mm
1.000	1 in AF
1.010	$\frac{9}{16}$ in Whitworth; $\frac{5}{8}$ in BSF
1.024	26 mm
1.063	$1\frac{1}{16}$ in AF; 27 mm
1.100	$\frac{5}{8}$ in Whitworth; $\frac{11}{16}$ in BSF
1.125	$1\frac{1}{8}$ in AF
1.181	30 mm
1.200	$\frac{11}{16}$ in Whitworth; $\frac{3}{4}$ in BSF
1.250	$1\frac{1}{4}$ in AF
1.260	32 mm
1.300	$\frac{3}{4}$ in Whitworth; $\frac{7}{8}$ in BSF
1.313	$1\frac{5}{16}$ in AF
1.390	$\frac{13}{16}$ in Whitworth; $\frac{15}{16}$ in BSF
1.417	36 mm
1.438	$1\frac{7}{16}$ in AF
1.480	$\frac{7}{8}$ in Whitworth; 1 in BSF
1.500	$1\frac{1}{2}$ in AF
1.575	40 mm; $\frac{15}{16}$ in Whitworth
1.614	41 mm
1.625	$1\frac{5}{8}$ in AF
1.670	1 in Whitworth; $1\frac{1}{8}$ in BSF
1.688	$1\frac{11}{16}$ in AF
1.811	46 mm
1.813	$1\frac{13}{16}$ in AF
1.860	$1\frac{1}{8}$ in Whitworth; $1\frac{1}{4}$ in BSF
1.875	$1\frac{7}{8}$ in AF
1.969	50 mm
2.000	2 in AF
2.050	$1\frac{1}{4}$ in Whitworth; $1\frac{3}{8}$ in BSF
2.165	55 mm
2.362	60 mm

Jacking and towing

For modifications, and information applicable to later models, see Supplement at end of manual

Jacking

To change a roadwheel, remove the spare wheel and jack from the luggage compartment (photos). Apply the handbrake and check the wheel diagonally opposite the one to be changed. Make sure that the car is located on firm level ground, then raise the jack and locate it under the reinforced flange nearest the wheel being removed. Note that the jack head must straddle the flange – **do not** jack beneath the floor. Slightly loosen the wheel nuts with the spanner provided, then using the handle raise the jack until the wheel is free of the ground. Remove the wheel nuts and trim, and lift off the wheel.

Fit the spare wheel and trim. Lightly tighten the wheel nuts, making sure that their tapered ends face the wheel. Lower the jack and finally tighten the wheel nuts in diagonal sequence. Remove the chock and refit the wheel and jack to the luggage compartment. Have a punctured tyre repaired or renewed at the earliest opportunity.

When jacking up the car with a trolley jack, lift under the towing/lashing eyes so that the eye is located in the jack head (photos). Axle stands should be placed under the reinforced flanges used for the jack supplied with the car.

Never venture under the car when it is supported by a jack alone, whether it is the vehicle jack or a workshop jack. Supplement the jack with axle stands, ramps or suitable blocks.

Towing

The car may be towed provided the gearbox and driveshafts are not faulty. If Trio-matic transmission is fitted, do not tow the car for more than 50 miles (80 km). The two front lashing eyes may be used to raise the front wheels if required, or the front towing eye may be used with all four wheels on the ground. When being towed the transmission should be in neutral and the ignition key in position 'I'. Remember that the brake servo will not be working. Use of the rear lashing eye for towing other vehicles is not recommended.

Spare wheel located in the luggage compartment

Using the jack

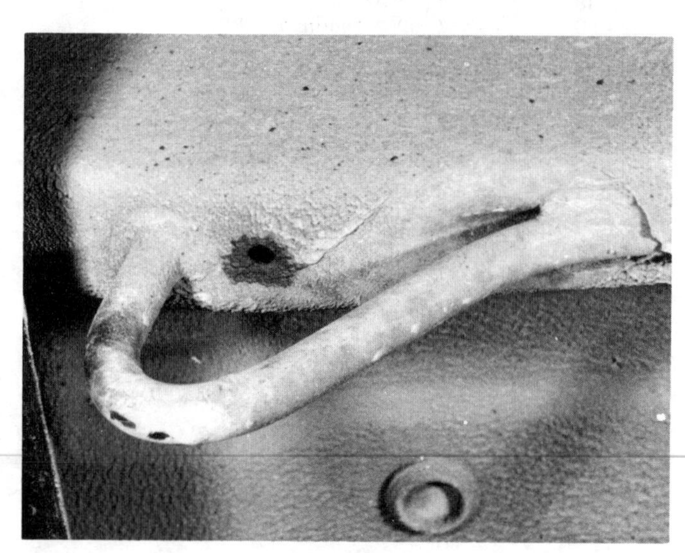

Rear lashing eye

A front lashing eye

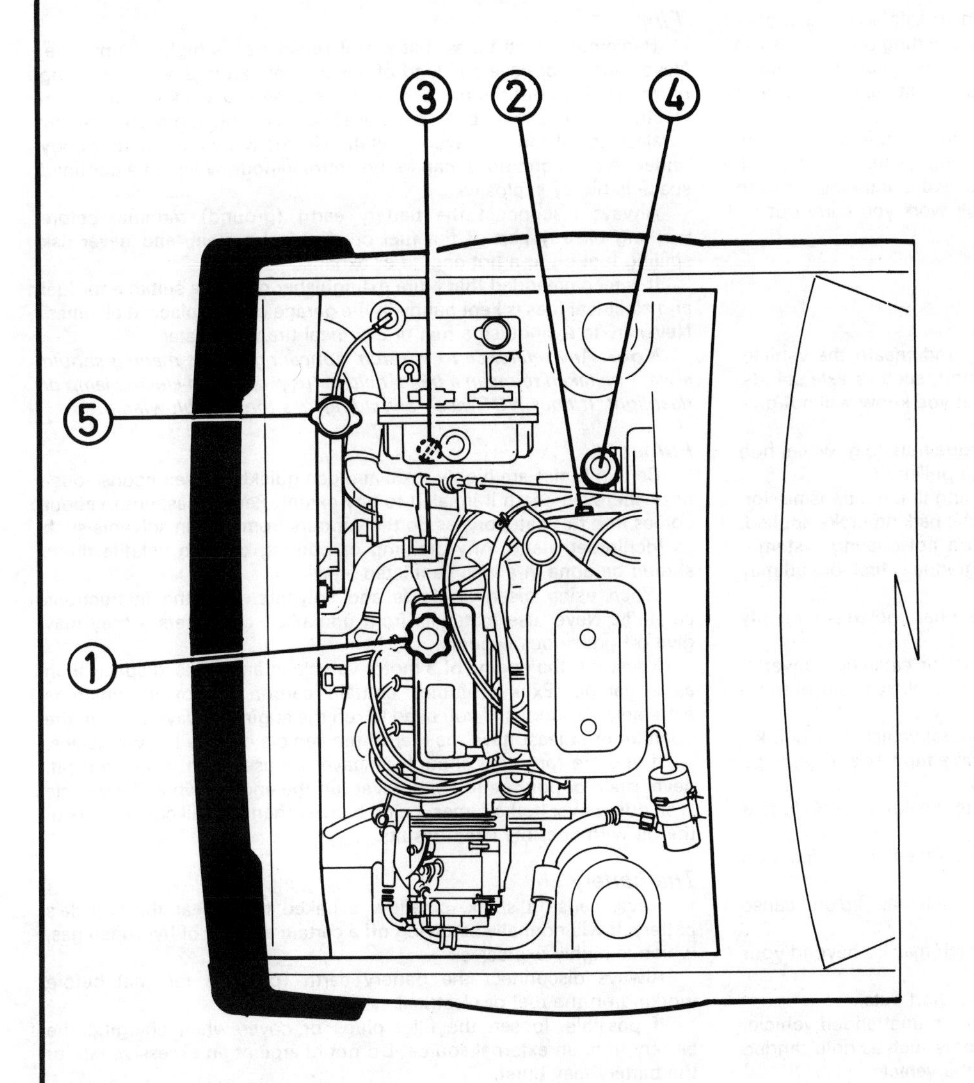

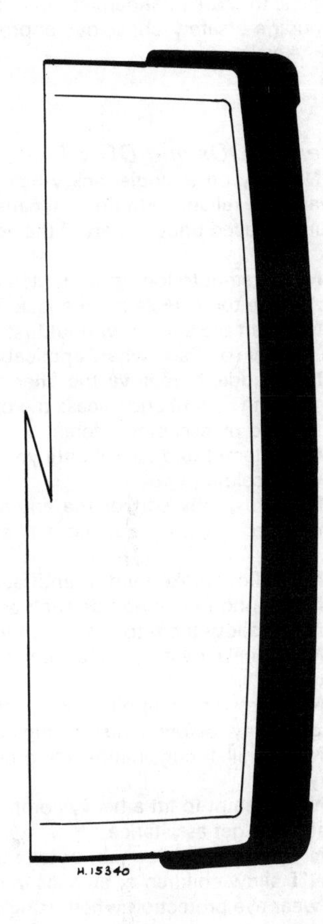

Recommended lubricants and fluids

Component or system	Lubricant type/specification	Duckhams recommendation
1 **Engine***	Multigrade engine oil, viscosity SAE 10W/40 or 15W/50	Duckhams QXR, Hypergrade or 10W/40 Motor Oil
2 **Manual gearbox***	Multigrade engine oil, viscosity SAE 10W/30 or 10W/40	Duckhams QXR, Hypergrade or 10W/40 Motor Oil
3 **Trio-matic transmission**	Dexron II type automatic transmission fluid	Duckhams D-Matic
4 **Brake fluid reservoir**	Hydraulic fluid to SAE J1703 or FMVSS 116 DOT 3	Duckhams Universal Brake and Clutch Fluid
5 **Cooling system**	Antifreeze to BS 3151, 3152 or 6580	Duckhams Universal Antifreeze and Summer Coolant
6 **Steering gear and all grease points**	Multi-purpose lithium-based grease	Duckhams LB 10

* **Note:** *The vehicle manufacturer specifies a 10W/40 oil to meet warranty requirements for models produced after August 1983. Duckhams QXR and 10W/40 Motor Oil are available to meet these requirements*

Safety first!

Professional motor mechanics are trained in safe working procedures. However enthusiastic you may be about getting on with the job in hand, do take the time to ensure that your safety is not put at risk. A moment's lack of attention can result in an accident, as can failure to observe certain elementary precautions.

There will always be new ways of having accidents, and the following points do not pretend to be a comprehensive list of all dangers; they are intended rather to make you aware of the risks and to encourage a safety-conscious approach to all work you carry out on your vehicle.

Essential DOs and DON'Ts

DON'T rely on a single jack when working underneath the vehicle. Always use reliable additional means of support, such as axle stands, securely placed under a part of the vehicle that you know will not give way.
DON'T attempt to loosen or tighten high-torque nuts (e.g. wheel hub nuts) while the vehicle is on a jack; it may be pulled off.
DON'T start the engine without first ascertaining that the transmission is in neutral (or 'Park' where applicable) and the parking brake applied.
DON'T suddenly remove the filler cap from a hot cooling system – cover it with a cloth and release the pressure gradually first, or you may get scalded by escaping coolant.
DON'T attempt to drain oil until you are sure it has cooled sufficiently to avoid scalding you.
DON'T grasp any part of the engine, exhaust or catalytic converter without first ascertaining that it is sufficiently cool to avoid burning you.
DON'T allow brake fluid or antifreeze to contact vehicle paintwork.
DON'T syphon toxic liquids such as fuel, brake fluid or antifreeze by mouth, or allow them to remain on your skin.
DON'T inhale dust – it may be injurious to health (see *Asbestos* below).
DON'T allow any spilt oil or grease to remain on the floor – wipe it up straight away, before someone slips on it.
DON'T use ill-fitting spanners or other tools which may slip and cause injury.
DON'T attempt to lift a heavy component which may be beyond your capability – get assistance.
DON'T rush to finish a job, or take unverified short cuts.
DON'T allow children or animals in or around an unattended vehicle.
DO wear eye protection when using power tools such as drill, sander, bench grinder etc, and when working under the vehicle.
DO use a barrier cream on your hands prior to undertaking dirty jobs – it will protect your skin from infection as well as making the dirt easier to remove afterwards; but make sure your hands aren't left slippery. Note that long-term contact with used engine oil can be a health hazard.
DO keep loose clothing (cuffs, tie etc) and long hair well out of the way of moving mechanical parts.
DO remove rings, wristwatch etc, before working on the vehicle – especially the electrical system.
DO ensure that any lifting tackle used has a safe working load rating adequate for the job.
DO keep your work area tidy – it is only too easy to fall over articles left lying around.
DO get someone to check periodically that all is well, when working alone on the vehicle.
DO carry out work in a logical sequence and check that everything is correctly assembled and tightened afterwards.
DO remember that your vehicle's safety affects that of yourself and others. If in doubt on any point, get specialist advice.
IF, in spite of following these precautions, you are unfortunate enough to injure yourself, seek medical attention as soon as possible.

Fire

Remember at all times that petrol (gasoline) is highly flammable. Never smoke, or have any kind of naked flame around, when working on the vehicle. But the risk does not end there – a spark caused by an electrical short-circuit, by two metal surfaces contacting each other, by careless use of tools, or even by static electricity built up in your body under certain conditions, can ignite petrol vapour, which in a confined space is highly explosive.

Always disconnect the battery earth (ground) terminal before working on any part of the fuel or electrical system, and never risk spilling fuel on to a hot engine or exhaust.

It is recommended that a fire extinguisher of a type suitable for fuel and electrical fires is kept handy in the garage or workplace at all times. Never try to extinguish a fuel or electrical fire with water.

Note: *Any reference to a 'torch' appearing in this manual should always be taken to mean a hand-held battery-operated electric lamp or flashlight. It does NOT mean a welding/gas torch or blowlamp.*

Fumes

Certain fumes are highly toxic and can quickly cause unconsciousness and even death if inhaled to any extent. Petrol (gasoline) vapour comes into this category, as do the vapours from certain solvents such as trichloroethylene. Any draining or pouring of such volatile fluids should be done in a well ventilated area.

When using cleaning fluids and solvents, read the instructions carefully. Never use materials from unmarked containers – they may give off poisonous vapours.

Never run the engine of a motor vehicle in an enclosed space such as a garage. Exhaust fumes contain carbon monoxide which is extremely poisonous; if you need to run the engine, always do so in the open air or at least have the rear of the vehicle outside the workplace.

If you are fortunate enough to have the use of an inspection pit, never drain or pour petrol, and never run the engine, while the vehicle is standing over it; the fumes, being heavier than air, will concentrate in the pit with possibly lethal results.

The battery

Never cause a spark, or allow a naked light, near the vehicle's battery. It will normally be giving off a certain amount of hydrogen gas, which is highly explosive.

Always disconnect the battery earth (ground) terminal before working on the fuel or electrical systems.

If possible, loosen the filler plugs or cover when charging the battery from an external source. Do not charge at an excessive rate or the battery may burst.

Take care when topping up and when carrying the battery. The acid electrolyte, even when diluted, is very corrosive and should not be allowed to contact the eyes or skin.

If you ever need to prepare electrolyte yourself, always add the acid slowly to the water, and never the other way round. Protect against splashes by wearing rubber gloves and goggles.

When jump starting a car using a booster battery, for negative earth (ground) vehicles, connect the jump leads in the following sequence: First connect one jump lead between the positive (+) terminals of the two batteries. Then connect the other jump lead first to the negative (-) terminal of the booster battery, and then to a good earthing (ground) point on the vehicle to be started, at least 18 in (45 cm) from the battery if possible. Ensure that hands and jump leads are clear of any moving parts, and that the two vehicles do not touch. Disconnect the leads in the reverse order.

Mains electricity and electrical equipment

When using an electric power tool, inspection light etc, always ensure that the appliance is correctly connected to its plug and that, where necessary, it is properly earthed (grounded). Do not use such appliances in damp conditions and, again, beware of creating a spark or applying excessive heat in the vicinity of fuel or fuel vapour. Also ensure that the appliances meet the relevant national safety standards.

Asbestos

Certain friction, insulating, sealing, and other products – such as brake linings, brake bands, clutch linings, torque converters, gaskets, etc – contain asbestos. *Extreme care must be taken to avoid inhalation of dust from such products since it is hazardous to health.* If in doubt, assume that they *do* contain asbestos.

Ignition HT voltage

A severe electric shock can result from touching certain parts of the ignition system, such as the HT leads, when the engine is running or being cranked, particularly if components are damp or the insulation is defective. Where an electronic ignition system is fitted, the HT voltage is much higher and could prove fatal.

Routine maintenance

Maintenance is essential for ensuring safety and desirable for the purpose of getting the best in terms of performance and economy from the car. Over the years the need for periodic lubrication – oiling, greasing and so on – has been drastically reduced if not totally eliminated. This has unfortunately tended to lead some owners to think that because no such action is required the items either no longer exist or will last for ever. This is a serious delusion. It follows therefore that the largest initial element of maintenance is visual examination. This may lead to repairs or renewals.

If operating under adverse conditions, more frequent oil and/or oil filter changes may be necessary. If in doubt, consult your BL dealer.

Every 250 miles (400 km) or weekly – whichever comes first

Engine

Check the level of oil and top up if necessary (photos)
Check the coolant level and top up if necessary
Check the level of electrolyte in the battery and top up as necessary (photo)

Brakes

Check the level of fluid in the brake master cylinder reservoir, and top up as necessary. Investigate any sudden fall in level

Lights and wipers

Check that all the lights work
Clean the headlamps
Check the windscreen washer fluid level, and top up if necessary, adding a screen wash additive such as Turtle Wax High Tech Screen Wash

Tyres

Check the tyre pressures (photo)
Visually examine the tyres for wear and damage

Every 7500 miles (12 000 km) or 6 months – whichever comes first

Engine

Check the drivebelt(s) and adjust or renew
Renew the engine oil (warm engine) (photo)
Renew the oil filter
Check all fuel pipes and hoses for damage and leaks
Check exhaust system for security and leaks
Check air conditioning refrigerant (where applicable)
Adjust engine idle speed if necessary
Check engine for oil leaks

Transmission

Check and if necessary top up the level of oil or fluid in the Triomatic transmission or manual gearbox
Check the condition of the driveshaft gaiters
Check and adjust the clutch cable

Brakes

Check all brake lines and hoses for corrosion, damage and leaks
Lubricate the handbrake linkage and cables
Check operation of the foot and hand brakes

Electrical equipment

Check the operation of all electrical equipment including the horn

Suspension and steering

Check and adjust spare wheel tyre pressure, and check tyre for wear and damage
Check and adjust all tyre pressures, and check them for wear and damage
Check the wheels for damage and for tightness of nuts
Check steering gear for security, and joints for wear

Engine oil level dipstick location

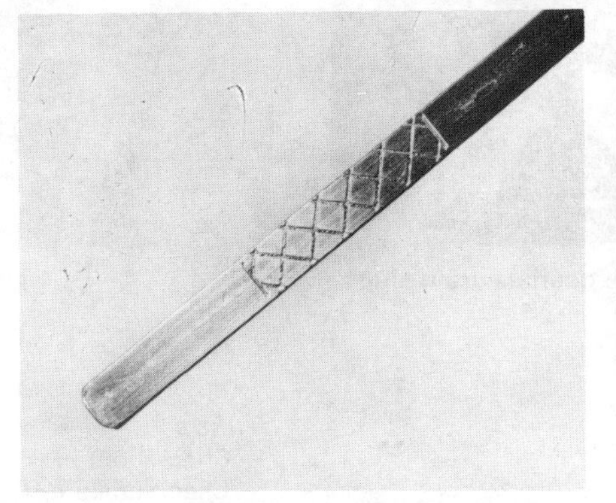

Dipstick markings. To raise level from low to high, add $1\frac{1}{4}$ pints

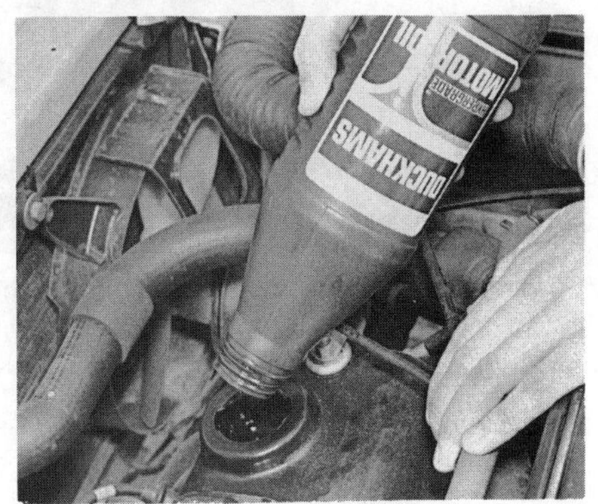

Topping up the engine oil

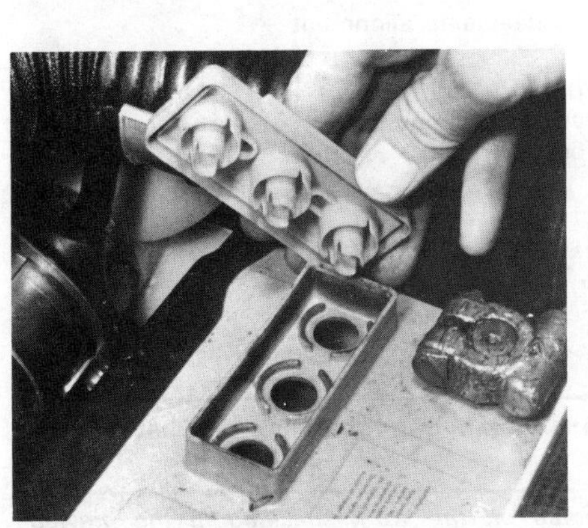

Checking battery electrolyte level

Topping up coolant level

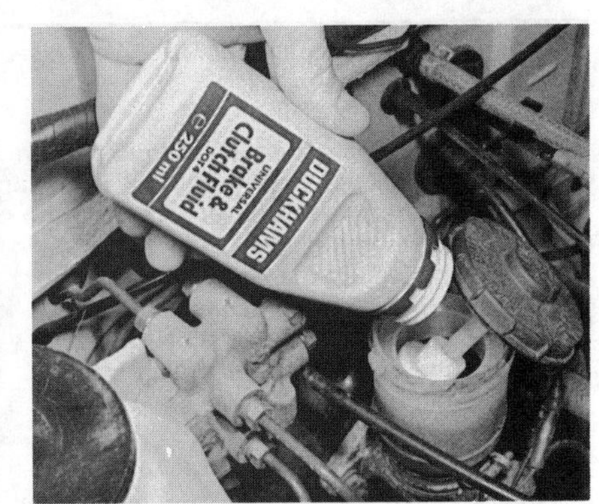

Topping up brake fluid level

Engine sump drain plug

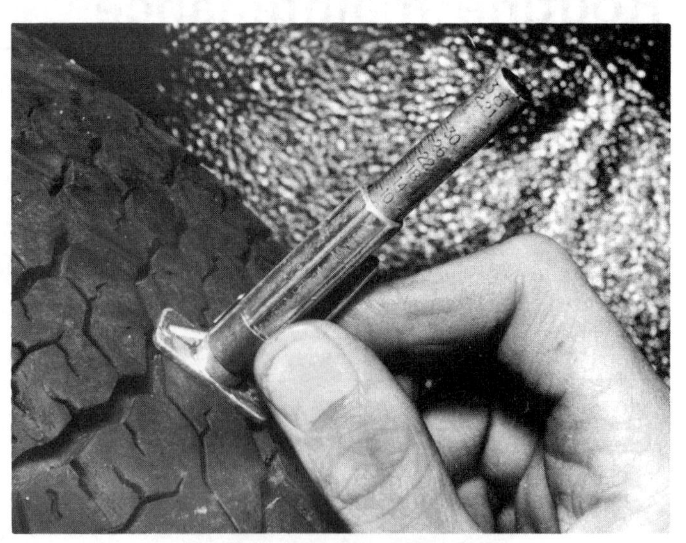
Checking the tyre tread depth

Using a $\frac{3}{8}$ in square drive tool to remove the gearbox drain plug

Filling the gearbox with oil

Bodywork
Check seats and seat belts for security and wear

Every 15 000 miles (24 000 km) or 12 months – whichever comes first

In addition to, or instead of, the work specified in the previous schedule

Engine
Check the camshaft drivebelt for condition, and adjust or renew
Check the cooling system for leaks and condition of hoses
Clean the battery terminals and coat with petroleum jelly
Renew the spark plugs
Check and adjust the valve clearances
Renew the air cleaner element
Check throttle and choke cable operation
Adjust the carburettor fast idling setting
Adjust the engine idling speed

Transmission
Check clutch and gearbox operation
Check gearbox for oil leaks

Brakes
Check front brake pads and discs for wear and renew if necessary
Check brake operation, including servo

Electrical equipment
Check and adjust the headlamp alignment

Suspension and steering
Check front and rear wheel alignment
Check shock absorber operation

Bodywork
Lubricate all locks and hinges (except steering lock)

Every 30 000 miles (48 000 km) or 24 months – whichever comes first

In addition to, or instead of, the work specified in the previous schedules

Engine

Renew the fuel filter
Check and adjust the ignition timing and distributor characteristics

Transmission

Renew the gearbox/transmission oil or fluid (photos)

Brakes

Renew the brake fluid
Check the rear brake linings and drums for wear and renew if necessary

Every 45 000 miles (72 000 km) or 36 months – whichever comes first

In addition to, or instead of, the work specified in the previous schedules

Engine

Renew the camshaft drivebelt (if not previously done)
Renew the engine coolant
Clean the radiator matrix

Every 60 000 miles (96 000 km) or 48 months – whichever comes first

In addition to, or instead of, the work specified in the previous schedules

Suspension and steering

Renew the rear wheel bearing grease and check condition of bearings and oil seals

Under-bonnet view of Acclaim. Air filter has been removed for clarity

1 Radiator filler cap
2 Coolant expansion tank
3 Windscreen washer reservoir
4 Battery
5 Brake fluid reservoir
6 Fuel pump
7 Bonnet catch
8 Carburettors
9 Ignition coil
10 Distributor
11 Coolant bleed nipple
12 Thermostat housing
13 Engine oil dipstick
14 Radiator top hose
15 Oil filler cap
16 Radiator cooling fan

Fault diagnosis

Introduction

The vehicle owner who does his or her own maintenance according to the recommended schedules should not have to use this section of the manual very often. Modern component reliability is such that, provided those items subject to wear or deterioration are inspected or renewed at the specified intervals, sudden failure is comparatively rare. Faults do not usually just happen as a result of sudden failure, but develop over a period of time. Major mechanical failures in particular are usually preceded by characteristic symptoms over hundreds or even thousands of miles. Those components which do occasionally fail without warning are often small and easily carried in the vehicle.

With any fault finding, the first step is to decide where to begin investigations. Sometimes this is obvious, but on other occasions a little detective work will be necessary. The owner who makes half a dozen haphazard adjustments or replacements may be successful in curing a fault (or its symptoms), but he will be none the wiser if the fault recurs and he may well have spent more time and money than was necessary. A calm and logical approach will be found to be more satisfactory in the long run. Always take into account any warning signs or abnormalities that may have been noticed in the period preceding the fault – power loss, high or low gauge readings, unusual noises or smells, etc – and remember that failure of components such as fuses or spark plugs may only be pointers to some underlying fault.

The pages which follow here are intended to help in cases of failure to start or breakdown on the road. There is also a Fault Diagnosis Section at the end of each Chapter which should be consulted if the preliminary checks prove unfruitful. Whatever the fault, certain basic principles apply. These are as follows:

Verify the fault. This is simply a matter of being sure that you know what the symptoms are before starting work. This is particularly important if you are investigating a fault for someone else who may not have described it very accurately.

Don't overlook the obvious. For example, if the vehicle won't start, is there petrol in the tank? (Don't take anyone else's word on this particular point, and don't trust the fuel gauge either!) If an electrical fault is indicated, look for loose or broken wires before digging out the test gear.

Cure the disease, not the symptom. Substituting a flat battery with a fully charged one will get you off the hard shoulder, but if the underlying cause is not attended to, the new battery will go the same way. Similarly, changing oil-fouled spark plugs for a new set will get you moving again, but remember that the reason for the fouling (if it wasn't simply an incorrect grade of plug) will have to be established and corrected.

Don't take anything for granted. Particularly, don't forget that a 'new' component may itself be defective (especially if it's been rattling round in the boot for months), and don't leave components out of a fault diagnosis sequence just because they are new or recently fitted. When you do finally diagnose a difficult fault, you'll probably realise that all the evidence was there from the start.

Electrical faults

Electrical faults can be more puzzling than straightforward mechanical failures, but they are no less susceptible to logical analysis if the basic principles of operation are understood. Vehicle electrical wiring exists in extremely unfavourable conditions – heat, vibration and chemical attack – and the first things to look for are loose or corroded connections and broken or chafed wires, especially where the wires pass through holes in the bodywork or are subject to vibration.

All metal-bodied vehicles in current production have one pole of the battery 'earthed', ie connected to the vehicle bodywork, and in nearly all modern vehicles it is the negative (–) terminal. The various electrical components – motors, bulb holders etc – are also connected to earth, either by means of a lead or directly by their mountings. Electric current flows through the component and then back to the battery via the bodywork. If the component mounting is loose or corroded, or if a good path back to the battery is not available, the circuit will be incomplete and malfunction will result. The engine and/or gearbox are also earthed by means of flexible metal straps to the body or subframe; if these straps are loose or missing, starter motor, generator and ignition trouble may result.

Assuming the earth return to be satisfactory, electrical faults will be due either to component malfunction or to defects in the current supply. Individual components are dealt with in Chapter 10. If supply wires are broken or cracked internally this results in an open-circuit, and the easiest way to check for this is to bypass the suspect wire temporarily with a length of wire having a crocodile clip or suitable connector at each end. Alternatively, a 12V test lamp can be used to verify the presence of supply voltage at various points along the wire and the break can be thus isolated.

If a bare portion of a live wire touches the bodywork or other earthed metal part, the electricity will take the low-resistance path thus formed back to the battery: this is known as a short-circuit. Hopefully a short-circuit will blow a fuse, but otherwise it may cause burning of the insulation (and possibly further short-circuits) or even a fire. This is why it is inadvisable to bypass persistently blowing fuses with silver foil or wire.

Spares and tool kit

Most vehicles are supplied only with sufficient tools for wheel changing; the *Maintenance and minor repair* tool kit detailed in *Tools*

Carrying a few spares can save you a long walk!

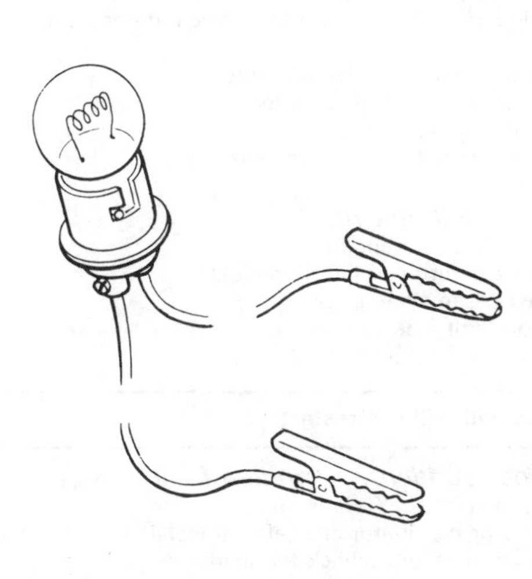

A simple test lamp is useful for checking electrical faults

and working facilities, with the addition of a hammer, is probably sufficient for those repairs that most motorists would consider attempting at the roadside. In addition a few items which can be fitted without too much trouble in the event of a breakdown should be carried. Experience and available space will modify the list below, but the following may save having to call on professional assistance:

Spark plugs, clean and correctly gapped
HT lead and plug cap – long enough to reach the plug furthest from the distributor
Distributor rotor
Drivebelt(s) – emergency type may suffice
Spare fuses
Set of principal light bulbs
Tin of radiator sealer and hose bandage
Exhaust bandage
Roll of insulating tape
Length of soft iron wire
Length of electrical flex
Torch or inspection lamp (can double as test lamp)
Battery jump leads
Tow-rope

NEGATIVE
18 in. MIN
DISCHARGED BATTERY
BOOSTER BATTERY
POSITIVE
H16299

Jump start lead connections for negative earth vehicles – connect leads in order shown

Ignition water dispersant aerosol
Litre of engine oil
Sealed can of hydraulic fluid
Emergency windscreen
Worm drive clips

If spare fuel is carried, a can designed for the purpose should be used to minimise risks of leakage and collision damage. A first aid kit and a warning triangle, whilst not at present compulsory in the UK, are obviously sensible items to carry in addition to the above.

When touring abroad it may be advisable to carry additional spares which, even if you cannot fit them yourself, could save having to wait while parts are obtained. The items below may be worth considering:

Clutch and throttle cables
Cylinder head gasket
Alternator brushes
Tyre valve core

One of the motoring organisations will be able to advise on availability of fuel etc in foreign countries.

Crank engine and check for a spark. Hold the lead with an insulated tool!

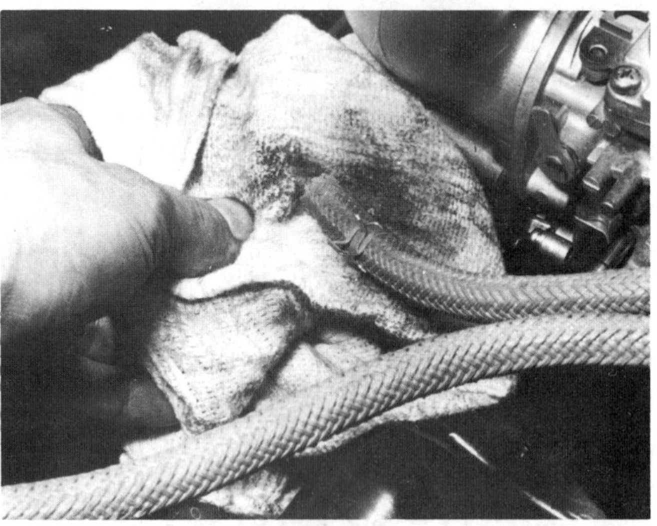

Checking for fuel delivery while cranking the engine. Disable the ignition system first

Checking the alternator drivebelt tension

Engine will not start

Engine fails to turn when starter operated

Flat battery (recharge, use jump leads, or push start manual gearbox models)
Battery terminals loose or corroded
Battery earth to body defective
Engine earth strap loose or broken
Starter motor (or solenoid) wiring loose or broken
Trio-matic transmission selector in wrong position, or inhibitor switch faulty
Ignition/starter switch faulty
Major mechanical failure (seizure)
Starter or solenoid internal fault (see Chapter 10)

Starter motor turns engine slowly

Partially discharged battery (recharge, use jump leads, or push start manual gearbox models)
Battery terminals loose or corroded
Battery earth to body defective
Engine earth strap loose
Starter motor (or solenoid) wiring loose
Starter motor internal fault (see Chapter 10)

Engine turns normally but fails to start

Damp or dirty HT leads and distributor cap – crank engine and check for spark (photo), or try a moisture dispersant such as Holts Wet Start
No fuel in tank (check for delivery at carburettor) (photo)
Excessive choke (hot engine) or insufficient choke (cold engine)
Fouled or incorrectly gapped spark plugs (remove, clean and regap)
Other ignition system fault (see Chapter 4)
Other fuel system fault (see Chapter 3)
Poor compression (see Chapter 1)
Major mechanical failure (eg camshaft drive)

Engine fires but will not run

Insufficient choke (cold engine)
Air leaks at carburettor or inlet manifold
Fuel starvation (see Chapter 3)
Other ignition fault (see Chapter 4)

Engine cuts out and will not restart

Engine cuts out suddenly – ignition fault

Loose or disconnected LT wires
Wet HT leads or distributor cap (after traversing water splash)
Coil or condenser failure (check for spark)
Other ignition fault (see Chapter 4)

Engine misfires before cutting out – fuel fault

Fuel tank empty
Fuel pump defective or filter blocked (check for delivery)
Fuel tank filler vent blocked (suction will be evident on releasing cap)
Carburettor needle valve sticking
Carburettor jets blocked (fuel contaminated)
Other fuel system fault (see Chapter 3)

Engine cuts out – other causes

Serious overheating
Major mechanical failure (eg camshaft drive)

Engine overheats

Ignition (no-charge) warning light illuminated

Slack or broken drivebelt – retension or renew (Chapter 2) (photo)

Ignition warning light not illuminated

Coolant loss due to internal or external leakage (see Chapter 2)
Thermostat defective

Low oil level
Brakes binding
Radiator clogged externally or internally
Electric cooling fan not operating correctly
Engine waterways clogged
Ignition timing incorrect or automatic advance malfunctioning
Mixture too weak

Note: *Do not add cold water to an overheated engine or damage may result*

Low engine oil pressure

Warning light illuminated with engine running

Oil level low or incorrect grade
Defective sender unit
Wire to sender unit earthed
Engine overheating
Oil filter clogged or bypass valve defective
Oil pressure relief valve defective
Oil pick-up strainer clogged
Oil pump worn or mountings loose
Worn main or big-end bearings

Note: *Low oil pressure in a high-mileage engine at tickover is not necessarily a cause for concern. Sudden pressure loss at speed is far more significant. In any event, check the gauge or warning light sender before condemning the engine.*

Engine noises

Pre-ignition (pinking) on acceleration

Incorrect grade of fuel
Ignition timing incorrect
Distributor faulty or worn
Worn or maladjusted carburettor
Excessive carbon build-up in engine

Whistling or wheezing noises

Leaking vacuum hose
Leaking carburettor or manifold gasket
Blowing head gasket

Tapping or rattling

Incorrect valve clearances
Worn valve gear
Broken piston ring (ticking noise)

Knocking or thumping

Unintentional mechanical contact (eg fan blades)
Peripheral component fault (generator, water pump etc)
Worn big-end bearings (regular heavy knocking, perhaps less under load)
Worn main bearings (rumbling and knocking, perhaps worsening under load)
Piston slap (most noticeable when cold)

Chapter 1 Engine

For modifications, and information applicable to later models, see Supplement at end of manual

Contents

Specifications

General

Engine type	Four-cylinder in-line, overhead camshaft, transverse mounting
Bore	72 mm (2.83 in)
Stroke	82 mm (3.23 in)
Capacity	1335 cc (81.5 cu in)
Firing order	1 - 3 - 4 - 2
Crankshaft rotation	Anti-clockwise (viewed from crankshaft pulley end)
Compression ratio	8.4 to 1

Crankshaft and bearings

Main journal diameter	49.976 to 50.000 mm (1.9676 to 1.9685 in)
Main journal code tolerances from nominal diameter of 50 mm (1.9685 in):	
Code	**Tolerance**
1	0 to -0.006 mm (0 to -0.0002 in)
2	-0.006 to -0.012 mm (-0.0002 to -0.0005 in)
3	-0.012 to -0.018 mm (-0.0005 to -0.0007 in)
4	-0.018 to -0.024 mm (-0.0007 to -0.0009 in)
Crankpin journal diameter	39.976 to 40.000 mm (1.5739 to 1.5748 in)
Crankpin journal code tolerances from nominal diameter of 40 mm (1.5748 in):	
Code	**Tolerance**
A	0 to -0.006 mm (0 to -0.0002 in)
B	-0.006 to -0.012 mm (-0.0002 to -0.0005 in)
C	-0.012 to -0.018 mm (-0.0005 to -0.0007 in)
D	-0.018 to -0.024 mm (-0.0007 to -0.0009 in)
Crankshaft main bearing bore diameter in cylinder block:	
Bearings 1, 2, 4 and 5	53.976 to 54.0 mm (2.125 to 2.1260 in)
Bearing 3	53.990 to 54.014 mm (2.1256 to 2.1266 in)

Crankshaft main bearing bore code tolerances from nominal diameter of 54 mm (2.126 in):

Bearings 1, 2, 4 and 5	As crankpin journal code
Bearing 3:	
Code	**Tolerance**
A	-0.010 to -0.004 mm (-0.0004 to -0.0002 in)
B	-0.004 to +0.002 mm (-0.0002 to +0.0001 in)
C	+0.002 to +0.008 mm (+0.0001 to +0.0003 in)
D	+0.008 to +0.014 mm (+0.0003 to +0.0006 in)

Main bearing colour code:

Crankshaft code number	**Bearing bore code**			
	A	**B**	**C**	**D**
1	Red	Pink	Yellow	Green
2	Pink	Yellow	Green	Brown
3	Yellow	Green	Brown	Black
4	Green	Brown	Black	Blue

Main bearing colour code tolerances:	
Red	-0.002 to -0.005 mm (-0.0001 to -0.0002 in)
Pink	+0.001 to -0.002 mm (+0.00004 to -0.0001 in)
Yellow	+0.004 to +0.001 mm (+0.0002 to +0.00004 in)
Green	+0.007 to +0.004 mm (+0.0003 to +0.0002 in)
Brown	+0.010 to +0.007 mm (+0.0004 to +0.0003 in)
Black	+0.013 to +0.010 mm (+0.0005 to +0.0004 in)
Blue	+0.016 to +0.013 mm (+0.0006 to +0.0005 in)
Main bearing running clearance	0.024 to 0.07 mm (0.0009 to 0.0030 in)

Big-end bearing colour code:

Crankpin code	**Connecting rod code**			
	1	**2**	**3**	**4**
A	Red	Pink	Yellow	Green
B	Pink	Yellow	Green	Brown
C	Yellow	Green	Brown	Black
D	Green	Brown	Black	Blue

Big-end bearing colour code tolerances:	
Red	-0.008 to -0.011 mm (-0.0003 to -0.0004 in)
Pink	-0.005 to -0.008 mm (-0.0002 to -0.0003 in)
Yellow	-0.002 to -0.005 mm (-0.0001 to -0.0002 in)
Green	+0.001 to -0.002 mm (+0.00004 to -0.0001 in)
Brown	+0.004 to +0.001 mm (+0.0002 to +0.00004 in)
Black	+0.007 to +0.004 mm (+0.0003 to +0.0002 in)
Blue	+0.010 to +0.007 mm (+0.0004 to +0.0003 in)
Big-end bearing running clearance	0.026 to 0.07 mm (0.001 to 0.003 in)
Crankshaft endfloat	0.10 to 0.45 mm (0.004 to 0.018 in)

Connecting rods

Length between centres	125.85 to 125.95 mm (4.955 to 4.959 in)

Pistons

Clearance in cylinder	0 to 0.10 mm (0 to 0.004 in)
Skirt outside diameter measured at 22 mm (0.87 in) from bottom of piston	71.95 to 72.00 mm (2.833 to 2.835 in)

Piston rings

Compression rings groove clearance	0.02 to 0.13 mm (0.0008 to 0.005 in)
End gap:	
Compression rings	0.15 to 0.55 mm (0.006 to 0.022 in)
Oil control ring (rails)	0.30 to 1.10 mm (0.012 to 0.043 in)

Gudgeon pins

Diameter	16.947 to 16.978 mm (0.6672 to 0.6684 in)
Interference fit in connecting rod	0.016 to 0.039 mm (0.0006 to 0.0015 in)

Cylinder block

Bore diameter	72.00 to 72.10 mm (2.835 to 2.839 in)
Maximum bore taper	0.05 mm (0.002 in)
Reboring limit	0.25 mm (0.010 in)

Flywheel

Maximum run-out	0.15 mm (0.006 in)

Camshaft and rocker arms

Bearing running clearance	0.05 to 0.15 mm (0.002 to 0.006 in)
Endfloat	0.05 to 0.50 mm (0.002 to 0.020 in)
Rocker arm bearing running clearance (maximum)	0.08 mm (0.003 in)

Valves

Seat angle	45°

Head diameter:	
Inlet	35.9 to 36.1 mm (1.413 to 1.421 in)
Exhaust	31.9 to 32.1 mm (1.256 to 1.264 in)
Stem diameter:	
Inlet	6.55 to 6.59 mm (0.258 to 0.259 in)
Exhaust	6.52 to 6.56 mm (0.257 to 0.2583 in)
Valve clearance in guide:	
Inlet	0.02 to 0.08 mm (0.0008 to 0.003 in)
Exhaust	0.05 to 0.21 mm (0.002 to 0.005 in)
Seat width (inlet and exhaust)	1.40 to 2.00 mm (0.055 to 0.080 in)

Valve guides

Inside diameter (inlet and exhaust)	6.55 to 6.63 mm (0.258 to 0.261 in)

Valve springs

Free length:	
Inner	44.4 mm (1.75 in)
Outer	45.3 mm (1.78 in)

Valve timing

At valve clearance of 0.15 mm (0.006 in), and between points where valve lift is 1.0 mm (0.039 in)

Inlet opens	10° ATDC
Inlet closes	30° ABDC
Exhaust opens	40° BBDC
Exhaust closes	10° BTDC

Valve clearances (cold)

Inlet	0.12 to 0.17 mm (0.005 to 0.007 in)
Exhaust	0.17 to 0.22 mm (0.007 to 0.009 in)

Lubrication system

Oil pump:	
Type	Bi-rotor
Outer rotor endfloat	0.15 mm (0.006 in)
Inner rotor endfloat	0.15 mm (0.006 in)
Rotor-to-housing clearance	0.20 mm (0.008 in)
Rotor lobe clearance	0.20 mm (0.008 in)
Drivegear endfloat	0.05 to 0.30 mm (0.002 to 0.012 in)
Drivegear backlash	0.05 to 0.10 mm (0.002 to 0.004 in)
Oil pressure (hot):	
At 3000 rpm	54 to 65 lbf/in^2 (3.8 to 4.6 kgf/cm^2)
At 800 rpm	21 lbf/in^2 (1/5 kgf/cm^2)
Pressure relief valve opens	54 to 65 lbf/in^2 (3.8 to 4.6 kgf/cm^2)
Oil filter	Champion E101
Lubricant type/specification*	Multigrade engine oil, viscosity SAE 10W/40 or 15W/50 (Duckhams QXR, Hypergrade or 10W/40 Motor Oil)

***Note**: *The vehicle manufacturer specifies a 10W/40 oil to meet warranty requirements for models produced after August 1983. Duckhams QXR and 10W/40 Motor Oil are available to meet these requirements*

Torque wrench settings

	lbf ft	Nm
Engine front and rear mounting nuts	15	20
Engine LH mounting setscrews	21	29
Engine LH mounting-to-body bolt	29	39
Engine LH mounting bracket to engine bolts	26	35
Front and rear torque rod bolts	55	75
Rear torque rod bracket bolts	29	39
Centre beam bolts	38	51
Damper bracket	15	20
Timing belt tensioner bolts	32	43
Timing cover bolts	7	10
Valve cover nuts	7	10
Cylinder head bolts and nuts:		
Pre-tighten	22	30
Final	40	55
Oil pump drivegear retainer	9	12
Rocker shaft bolts	16	22
Valve clearance adjuster locknuts	14	20
Camshaft gear bolt	22	30
Crankshaft pulley bolt	85	115
Big-end nuts	19	26
Main bearing cap bolts	30	40
Flywheel bolts (manual transmission)	52	71
Driveplate bolts (Trio-matic transmission)	37	50
Oil pump bolts	9	12
Sump bolts	9	12
Sump nuts	7	10
Drain plug	33	45
Oil pressure switch	13	18

1 General description

The engine is of four-cylinder, in-line, overhead camshaft type, and is designated type EN4 by the manufacturers. It is mounted transversely at the front of the car with the gearbox attached to the right-hand side, enabling sump and gearbox removal with the engine *in situ.*

The cylinder head and cylinder block are of aluminium alloy. Cast iron cylinder liners are fitted. The crankshaft is of five bearing type; No 4 main bearing incorporates thrust washers to control crankshaft endfloat. The main bearing caps are retained in a monoblock aluminium casting.

Engine rotation is anti-clockwise when viewed from the crankshaft pulley end.

Each piston incorporates an offset gudgeon pin which is an interference fit in the connecting rod. Two compression rings and a 3-piece oil control ring are fitted.

The cylinder head incorporates hemispherical combustion chambers, and inclined valves operated by a belt-driven camshaft. Skew gears on the camshaft drive the distributor and oil pump driveshaft, and an eccentric cam operates the fuel pump. The camshaft is supported in five bearings.

The timing belt is tensioned by an adjustable pulley.

The lubrication system incorporates a bi-rotor oil pump and a full flow cartridge oil filter containing a bypass valve. The engine oil gallery is incorporated in the monoblock main bearing cap casting. The camshaft and rocker shafts are supplied with oil via a drilling in the oil pump driveshaft.

Crankcase ventilation is via a hose from the rocker cover to an oil separator mounted under the air cleaner body, and a hose from the oil separator to the inlet manifold. Blow-by fumes from the engine crankcase are drawn into the inlet manifold and bonnet in the combustion chambers. Oil from the separator drains back into the engine through the rocker cover.

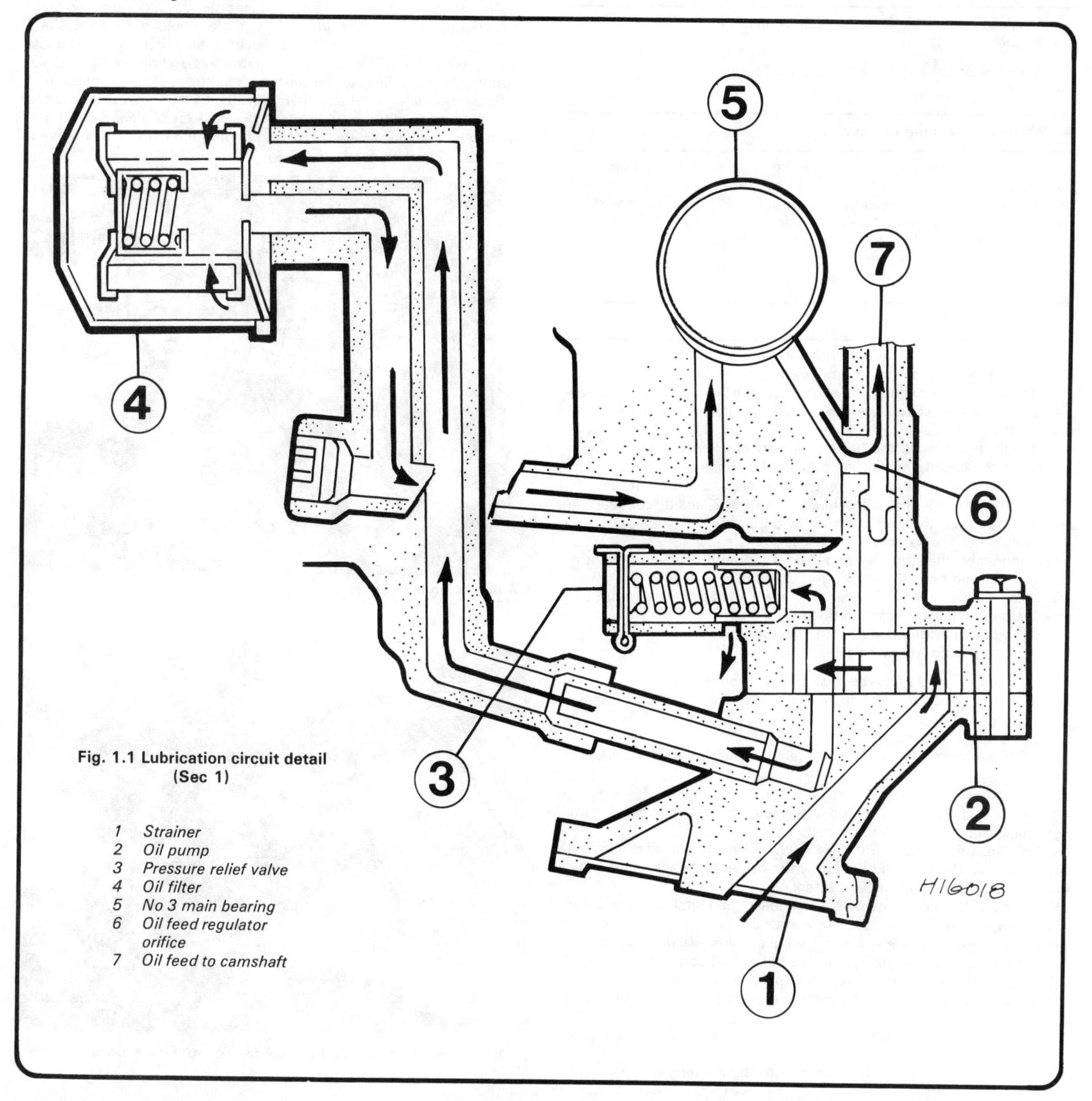

Fig. 1.1 Lubrication circuit detail (Sec 1)

1 *Strainer*
2 *Oil pump*
3 *Pressure relief valve*
4 *Oil filter*
5 *No 3 main bearing*
6 *Oil feed regulator orifice*
7 *Oil feed to camshaft*

2 Major operations possible with the engine in the car

The following operations can be carried out without having to remove the engine from the car:

(a) Removal and servicing of the cylinder head, camshaft, and valve gear
(b) Renewal of the timing belt
(c) Removal of the flywheel or driveplate
(d) Renewal of the engine mountings
(e) Removal of the oil pump
(f) Removal of the piston/connecting rod assemblies
(g) Renewal of the big-end bearings

3 Major operations only possible after removal of the engine from the car

The following operations can only be carried out after removal of the engine from the car:

Removal of the crankshaft and main bearings.

4 Method of engine removal

The best method is to remove the engine and gearbox as a complete unit, then separate the gearbox from the engine on the bench. This method is described in the following Section. However, should the lifting equipment be suitable for the combined weight of the engine and gearbox, the gearbox may be removed first as described in Chapter 6 or 7 as applicable.

5 Engine – removal

1 Remove the bonnet as described in Chapter 12.
2 If fitted, remove the headlamp washer reservoir.
3 Disconnect the negative then the positive battery leads. Loosen the clamp nuts, then remove the clamp and lift out the battery and plastic tray.
4 Unbolt and remove the battery support bracket (photo).
5 Drain the cooling system as described in Chapter 2.
6 Remove the air cleaner complete as described in Chapter 3.
7 Remove the radiator as described in Chapter 2, and disconnect the bottom base from the engine water pipe (photo).
8 Disconnect the servo vacuum hose.
9 Disconnect the throttle and mixture control cables from the carburettors and bracket, referring to Chapter 3.
10 Unscrew the domed nut and disconnect the earth cable from the rocker cover (photo). Loosely refit the nut.
11 Unbolt the earth cable from the gearbox (photo).
12 Disconnect the following wiring:

(a) Coil HT and LT wires (also release from clips)
(b) Engine harness connector (also press the tab and release from clip)
(c) Starter motor cables
(d) Reversing lamp switch and temperature transmitter wires

13 Unscrew the cable nut and detach the tachometer cable from the right-hand side of the cylinder head.
14 Pull the rubber boot from the gearbox end of the speedometer cable, remove the clip, and withdraw the cable. Disconnect the cable from the support spring (where fitted).
15 On manual gearbox models, disconnect the clutch release cable from the gearbox as described in Chapter 5.
16 On Trio-matic models, disconnect the transmission fluid cooler hoses from the transmission. Plug the hoses and connectors.
17 Disconnect and plug the fuel feed pipe from the carburettors.
18 Disconnect the top hose from the thermostat housing and remove the hose.
19 Disconnect the heater outlet hose from the engine water pipe (photo).
20 Disconnect the heater inlet hose from the heater valve.
21 On models equipped with air conditioning, remove the compressor belt cover and idler pulley nut, then remove the mounting bolts and lift the compressor from the bracket. Secure the compressor to one side, leaving the refrigerant hoses still attached. Unbolt the compressor bracket. Disconnect the idle boost vacuum pipes.
22 Jack up the front of the car and support it on axle stands. Apply the handbrake. Alternatively, position the car over a pit or on car ramps.
23 Remove the front exhaust pipe mounting and disconnect the downpipe from the exhaust manifold, referring to Chapter 3. Remove the sealing ring.
24 On manual gearbox models, disconnect the gearchange rod from the gearbox selector shaft by prising off the clip and driving out the roll pin (photo). If the pin is seized in position, it may be necessary to heat the rod in order to remove it.
25 Also on manual gearbox models, unscrew the mounting bolt and detach the gearchange torsion rod from the gearbox. Tie the rod to one side and remove the large washer.
26 On Trio-matic models, working inside the car pull the knob from the headlamp adjuster and prise off the plate. Remove the screws and withdraw the console, then select reverse and prise out the cable retaining pin and clip. Unbolt the cable bracket and pull out the cable. Alternatively the cable can be disconnected from the transmission.
27 Place a suitable container beneath the engine, then unscrew the driven plug and drain the oil. Wipe away the excess oil and check the condition of the washer, then refit and tighten the plug. Similarly drain the gearbox oil or transmission fluid.

5.4 Removing the battery support bracket

5.7 Bottom hose and heater hose connection to the engine water pipe

5.10 Disconnecting the earth cable from the rocker cover

5.11 Disconnecting the earth cable from the gearbox

5.19 Disconnecting the heater outlet hose

5.24 Gearchange rod roll pin location and covering clip (arrowed)

28 Using a flat metal bar, lever both inner drive shaft joints from the differential gears far enough to release the internal retaining circlips from their grooves.
29 Attach a suitable hoist to the engine and gearbox and lightly take the weight of the assembly. On models equipped with air conditioning it will be necessary to refit the lifting bracket removed when removing the compressor.
30 Using a long extension and socket through the centre beam, unscrew the lower mounting nuts from the engine front and rear mountings.
31 Unscrew the left-hand side mounting bolts and through-bolt, and prise the mounting away from the engine and into the bracket.
32 Unscrew and remove the bolts securing the front and rear torque rod mountings to the engine. Loosen the remaining torque rod mounting bolts and swivel the rods away from the engine (photos).
33 Raise the engine and gearbox slightly, then disconnect the right-hand driveshaft from the differential. Turn the assembly and disconnect the left-hand driveshaft. Take care not to extend the driveshafts.
34 Check that all hoses, cables etc have been disconnected, then lift the engine and gearbox from the engine compartment. Take care not to damage the brake master cylinder or any other components mounted on the bulkhead or side panels (photo).
35 Lower the assembly onto a workbench or a large piece of wood placed on the floor.

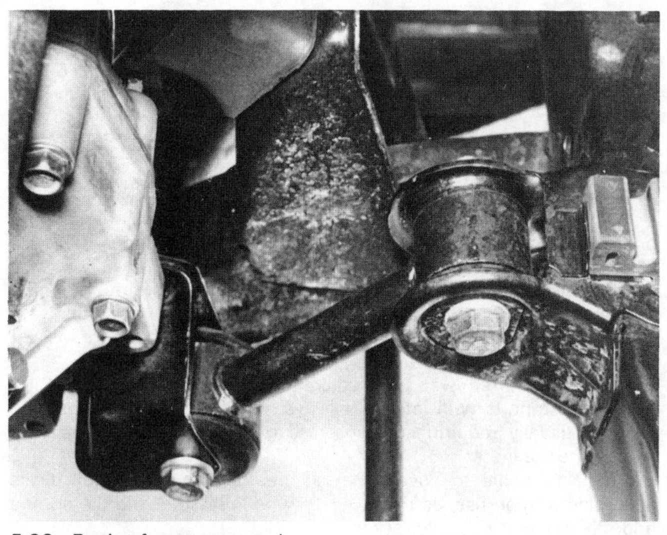
5.32a Engine front torque rod

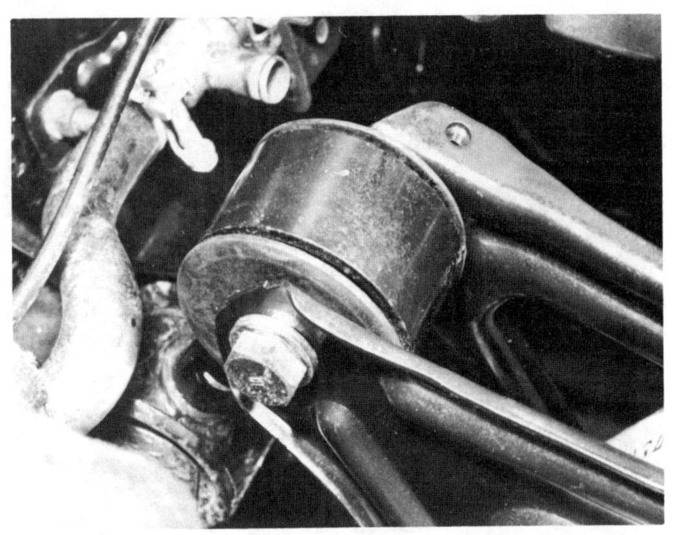

5.32b Engine rear torque rod and bracket

5.32c Engine rear torque rod and mounting (engine removed)

5.34 Removing the engine and gearbox

5.36 Separating the manual gearbox from the engine

36 Separate the gearbox from the engine, referring to Chapter 6 or 7 as applicable (photo).

6 Engine dismantling – general

1 If possible mount the engine on a stand for the dismantling procedure, but failing this, support it in an upright position with blocks of wood.
2 Cleanliness is most important, and if the engine is dirty, it should be cleaned with paraffin while keeping it in an upright position.
3 Avoid working with the engine directly on a concrete floor, as grit presents a real source of trouble.
4 As parts are removed, clean them in a paraffin bath. However, do not immerse parts with internal oilways in paraffin as it is difficult to remove, usually requiring a high pressure hose. Clean oilways with nylon pipe cleaners.
5 It is advisable to have suitable containers to hold small items according to their use, as this will help when reassembling the engine and also prevent possible losses.
6 Always obtain complete sets of gaskets when the engine is being dismantled, but retain the old gaskets with a view to using them as a pattern to make a replacement if a new one is not available.
7 When possible, refit nuts, bolts, and washers in their location after being removed, as this helps to protect the threads and will also be helpful when reassembling the engine.
8 Retain unserviceable components in order to compare them with the new parts supplied.

7 Ancillary components – removal

With the engine removed and the gearbox separated, the externally-mounted ancillary components, as given in the following list, can be removed:

(a) Distributor (Chapter 4) – must be removed before inlet manifold
(b) Carburettors and inlet manifold (Chapter 3)
(c) Exhaust manifold (Chapter 3)
(d) Fuel pump (Chapter 3)
(e) Alternator (Chapter 10)
(f) Thermostat (Chapter 2)
(g) Wiring harness (photos)

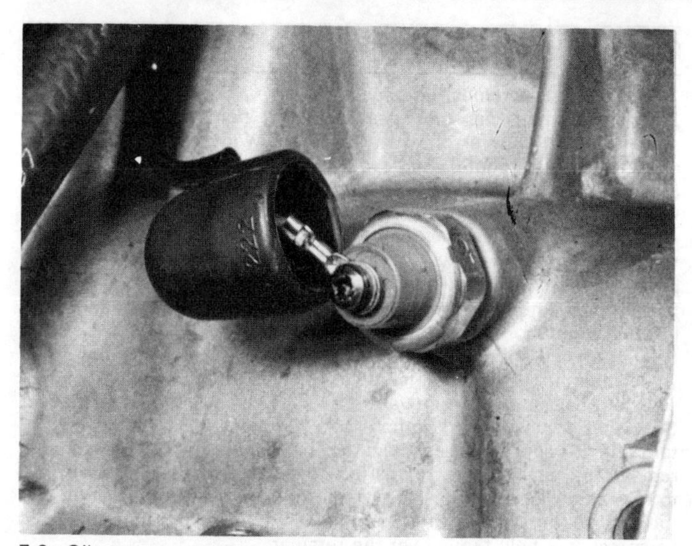
7.0a Oil pressure switch and wiring

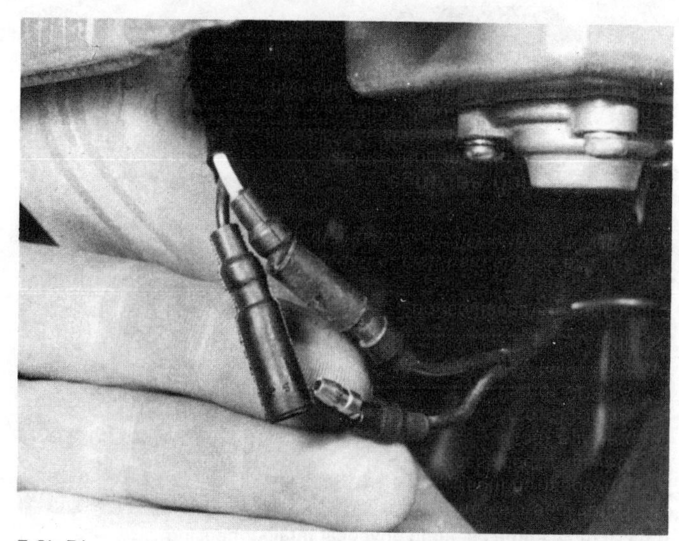
7.0b Disconnecting part of the wiring harness on the engine

8 Cylinder head – removal

If the engine is still in the car, first carry out the following operations:

(a) *Disconnect the battery negative lead*
(b) *Remove the bonnet (Chapter 12)*
(c) *Drain the cooling system (Chapter 3)*
(d) *Remove the inlet and exhaust manifolds (Chapter 3). (This work may be carried out after removing the cylinder head, in which case the exhaust downpipe must be disconnected together with wiring harness cables and carburettor control cables.) Also disconnect all hoses*
(e) *On models equipped with air conditioning, remove the compression belt cover and idler pulley nut, then remove the mounting bolts and lift the compressor from the bracket. Secure the compressor to one side leaving the refrigerant hoses still attached. Unbolt the compressor bracket. Disconnect the idle boost vacuum pipes*
(f) *Remove the fuel pump (Chapter 3)*
(g) *Disconnect the tachometer drive cable*
(h) *Disconnect the HT lead from the coil*

1 Disconnect the HT leads from the spark plugs and bracket, and unbolt and remove the distributor (photo).

2 Unscrew the domed nuts and remove the valve cover and gasket (photo). Note the location of the brackets.

3 Unbolt and remove the timing belt upper cover and gasket.

4 Turn the crankshaft by means of the pulley bolt until the notches on the camshaft gear are aligned with the upper face of the cylinder head. The white (TDC) line on the crankshaft pulley should also be aligned with the rib on the lower timing cover.

5 Loosen the timing belt tensioner bolts protruding through the lower timing cover, then ease the timing belt off the camshaft gear. Take care not to damage the belt or contaminate it with oil.

6 Unbolt and remove the retainer housing from the oil pump drivegear and shaft, then withdraw the shaft from the cylinder head (photos).

7 Unscrew the cylinder head nuts and bolts a third of a turn at a time, in the reverse order to that shown in Fig. 1.12.

8 Lift the cylinder head from the block, making sure that the timing belt is held free of the gear (photo). If the head is stuck, tap it free with a wooden mallet or lever between the special flanges provided. **Do not** lever between the mating faces of the cylinder head and block.

9 Remove the cylinder head gasket from the block using a scraper if necessary, but take care not to damage the mating face.

8.1 Spark plug HT lead retainer

8.2 Removing the valve cover

8.6a Removing the oil pump drivegear retainer housing

8.6b Removing the oil pump drivegear and shaft

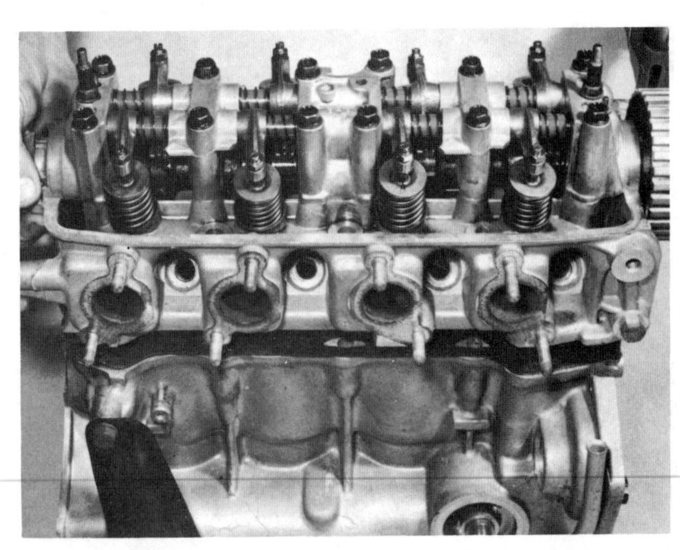
8.8 Lifting the cylinder head from the block

9 Cylinder head – dismantling

1 Unscrew and remove the spark plugs.
2 Unscrew the camshaft gear retaining bolt, holding the gear stationary with a lever or wide-bladed screwdriver inserted through one of the holes (photo). Remove the washer.
3 Withdraw the camshaft gear from the camshaft and extract the Woodruff key (photos).
4 Remove the cross-head screws from the tachometer drive end of the rocker shaft assembly. Also extract the tachometer drive retaining pin using a pair of grips (photos).
5 Unscrew the bolts from the camshaft bearing caps, noting their location in relation to length.
6 Lift off the bearing caps and rocker shaft assembly (photo).
7 Withdraw the tachometer drive and lift the camshaft from the cylinder head (photo). Remove the oil seal.
8 Using a valve spring compressor, compress the valve springs in turn until the split collets can be removed. Release the compressor and remove the retainer and springs (photos). If the retainers are difficult to release, do not continue to tighten the compressor, but gently tap the top of the tool with a hammer. Always make sure that the compressor is held firmly over the retainer.
9 Remove the valves from the combustion chambers, keeping them in their order of removal together with the respective valve springs and retainers (photo). Identify each valve according to the cylinder, remembering that No 1 cylinder is at the timing bolt end of the cylinder head.
10 Prise the valve seals from the valve guides and remove the spring seats (photo).

10 Timing belt and tensioner – removal

If the engine is still in the car, first carry out the following operations:

(a) Disconnect the battery negative liftedlead
(b) On models equipped with air conditioning, remove the compressor belt cover and idler pulley nut, then remove the mounting bolts and lift the compressor from the bracket. Secure the compressor to one side, leaving the refrigerant hoses still attached. Unbolt the compressor bracket
(c) Disconnect the crankcase ventilation hose from the rocker arm cover (photo)
(d) Remove the water pump/alternator drivebelt (Chapter 2) and unbolt the water pump pulley
(e) Unscrew the left-hand side engine mounting bolts and through-bolt and prise the mounting away from the engine into the bracket
(f) Remove the starter motor (Chapter 10) in order to restrain the ring gear in the subsequent procedure

1 Disconnect the HT leads from the spark plugs and bracket.
2 Unscrew the domed nuts and remove the valve cover and gasket. Note the location of the brackets.
3 Unbolt and remove the timing belt upper cover and gasket (photo).
4 Turn the crankshaft pulley bolt until the notches on the camshaft gear are aligned with the upper face of the cylinder head. The white (TDC) line on the crankshaft pulley should also be aligned with the rib on the lower timing cover (photos).
5 Hold the crankshaft stationary using a lever in the starter ring gear. Alternatively, if the engine is removed from the car, the left-hand lifting hanger may be bolted to the flywheel/driveplate (photo).
6 Unscrew the crankshaft pulley bolt, remove the washer, and withdraw the pulley (photo).
7 Extract the rubber seals from the timing belt tensioner bolts in the centre of the lower timing cover. Do not loosen the bolts at this stage (photo).
8 Unbolt and remove the lower timing cover together with the gasket (photo).
9 Check that the crankshaft is still positioned as described in paragraph 4, then remove the outer guide plate from the crankshaft together with the key (photo).
10 Loosen the timing belt tensioner bolts, pivot the tensioner away from the belt, then tighten the bolts to hold the tensioner. Unbolt the engine left-hand mounting bracket (photo).

9.2 Removing the camshaft gear retaining bolt

9.3a Removing the camshaft gear

9.3b Camshaft gear Woodruff key

9.4a Remove the cross-head screws ...

9.4b ... and the tachometer drive retaining pin (arrowed)

9.6 Removing the rocker shafts and camshaft bearing cap assembly

9.7 Removing the camshaft

9.8a Compressing a valve spring to remove the split collets

9.8b Removing the retainer ...

9.8c ... and valve springs

9.9 Removing a valve

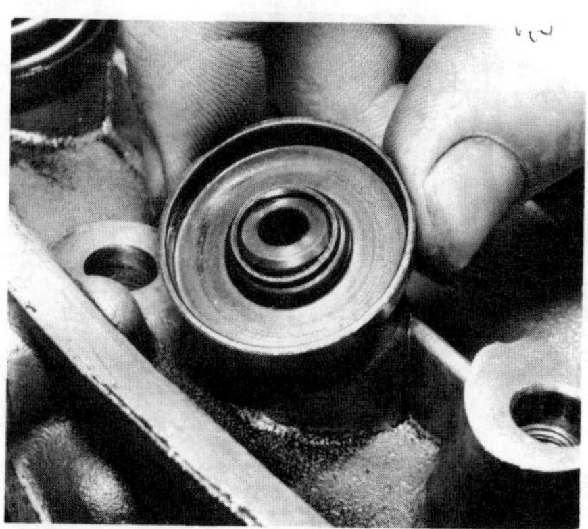
9.10 Removing a valve spring seat

10.0 Valve cover crankcase ventilation hose location

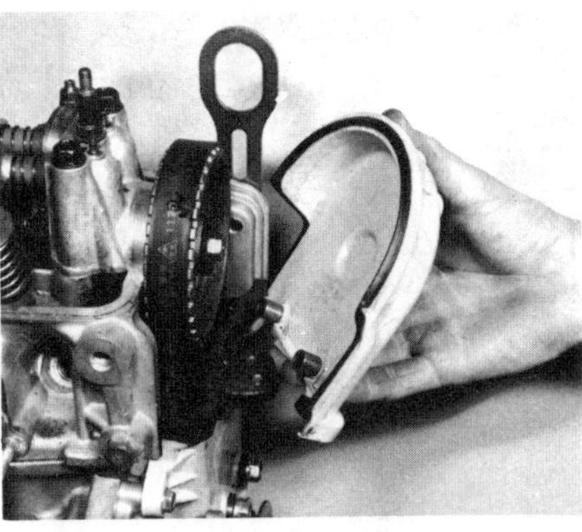
10.3 Removing the timing belt upper cover

10.4a TDC (No 1 cylinder) alignment marks (arrowed) on the camshaft gear. Central lobe is uppermost

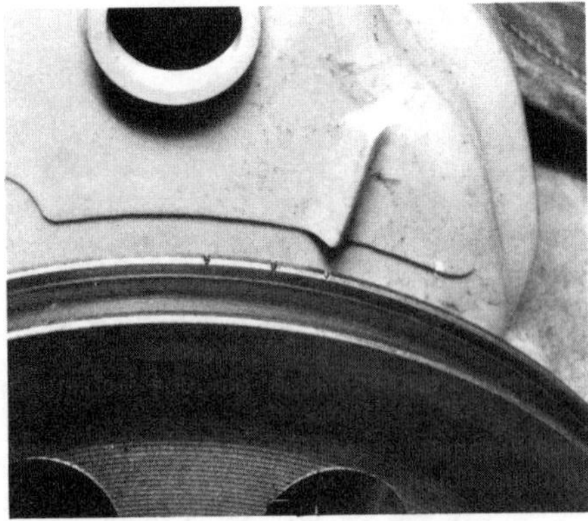
10.4b TDC alignment marks on the crankshaft pulley and lower timing cover

10.5 Using the engine left-hand lifting hanger to hold the flywheel stationary

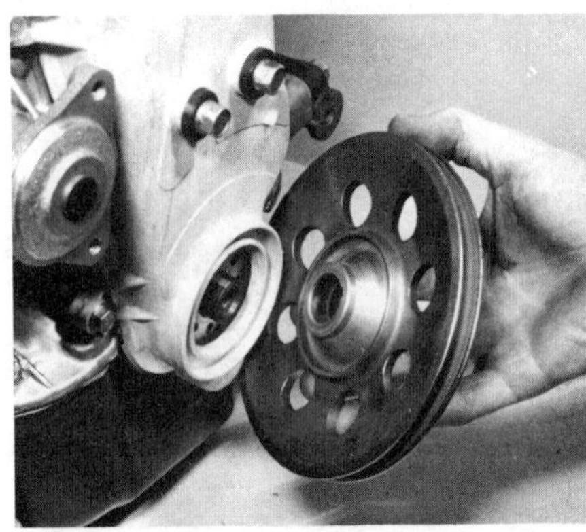
10.6 Removing the crankshaft pulley

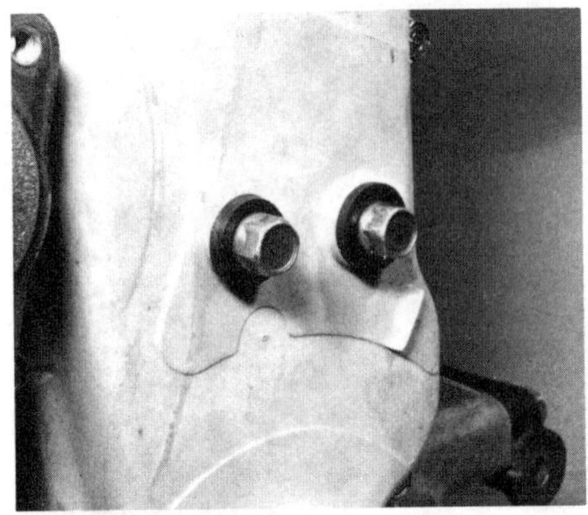
10.7 Rubber seal locations on the timing belt tensioner bolts

10.8 The lower timing cover

10.9 Timing belt outer guide plate

10.10 Engine left-hand mounting bracket

10.12 Timing belt tensioner assembly

10.13a Remove the crankshaft gear ...

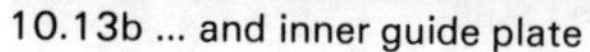
10.13b ... and inner guide plate

11.2 Removing the flywheel

12.1 Oil filter cartridge

11 Slide the timing belt from the crankshaft and camshaft gears. Note that the outer edge of the belt should be identified if the belt is to be re-used. Keep the belt free of oil and do not bend or otherwise stress it.
12 Remove the timing belt tensioner bolts, withdraw the tensioner, and unhook the spring (photo).
13 Withdraw the crankshaft gear and inner guide plate from the crankshaft (photos).

11 Flywheel/driveplate – removal

If the engine is still in the car first carry out the following operations:

(a) *Remove the manual gearbox or semi-automatic transmission as described in Chapter 6 or 7*
(b) *On manual gearbox models, remove the clutch as described in Chapter 5*

1 Hold the flywheel/driveplate stationary using the method described in Section 10.
2 Mark the flywheel/driveplate in relation to the crankshaft, then unscrew the mounting bolts. Remove the restraining device and withdraw the flywheel or driveplate and centreplate (photo). Take care not to drop the flywheel, it is heavy.

12 Oil filter – removal

1 Wipe clean the oil filter and surrounding area of the engine (photo).
2 Position a suitable container beneath the oil filter, then unscrew it from the cylinder block using a strap wrench. Discard the filter cartridge.

13 Sump – removal

If the engine is still in the car, first follow the procedure described in paragraphs 1 to 9 inclusive.
1 Jack up the front of the car and support it on axle stands. Apply the handbrake.
2 Place a suitable container beneath the engine, then unscrew the drain plug and drain the oil. Check the condition of the washer, then refit and tighten the plug.
3 Using a hoist connected to the right-hand engine hanger, take the weight of the engine and gearbox.
4 Using a long extension and socket, unscrew the nuts from the engine front and rear mountings to release the mountings from the centre beam.
5 On semi-automatic models, remove the selector cable bracket from the centre beam.
6 Unbolt the anti-roll bar brackets from the body.
7 Unbolt the centre beam from the body.
8 Unbolt the front torque rod bracket from the engine and remove the stud.
9 On semi-automatic models, remove the screws holding the driveplate cover to the transmission.
10 Unbolt the sump from the cylinder block, noting that the flywheel/driveplate cover is located on the end bolts (photos).
11 Remove the gasket (photo).

14 Oil pump – removal

1 With the sump removed, unscrew the bolts retaining the oil pump and by-pass tube to the main bearing cap monoblock.
2 Withdraw the oil pump assembly (photo).

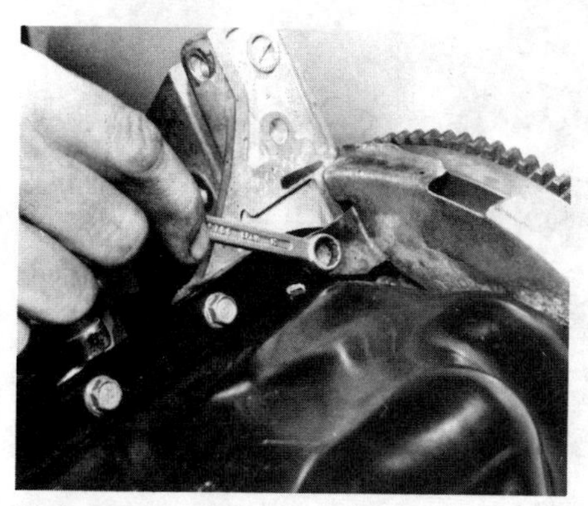
13.10a Removing the flywheel cover ...

13.10b ... and the sump

13.11 Removing the sump gasket

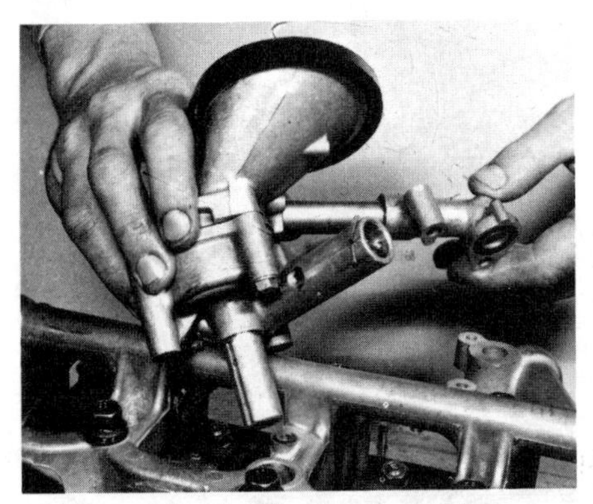
14.2 Removing the oil pump assembly

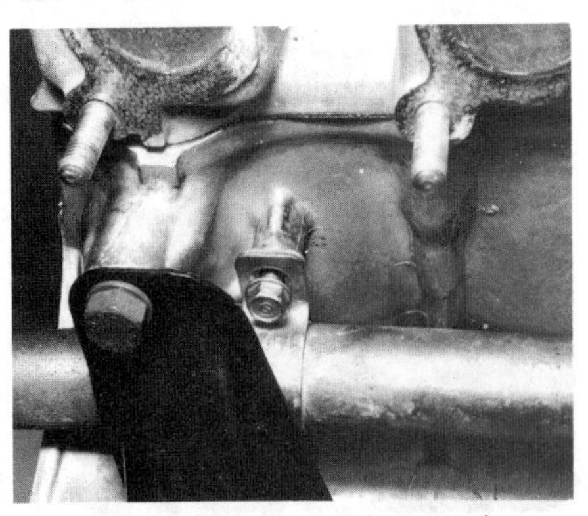
15.2a Engine water supply tube mounting bolt ...

15.2b ... and end seal

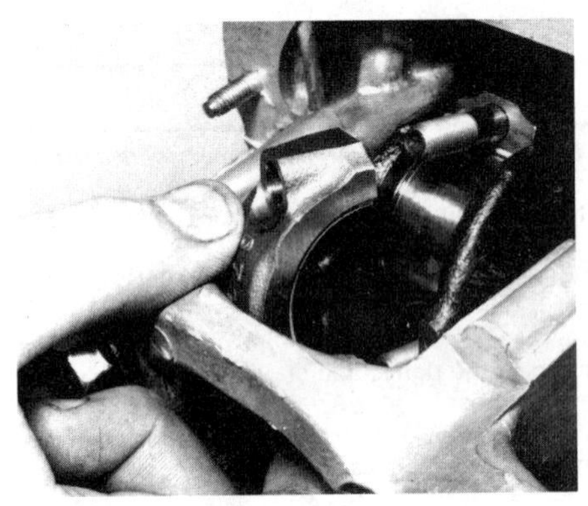
15.6 Removing a big-end bearing cap

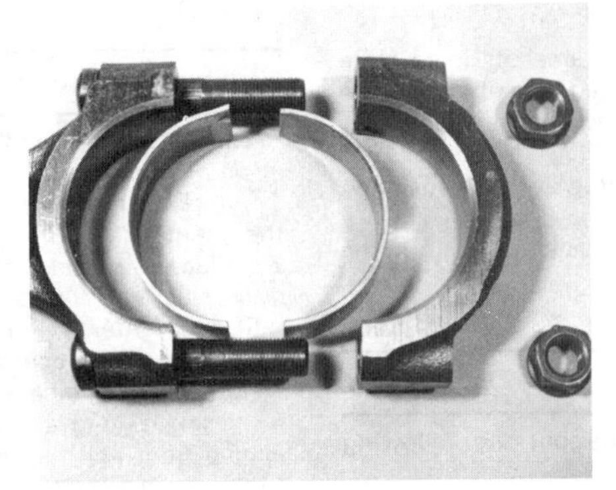
15.8a Big-end bearing components

15.8b A piston and rings

15 Pistons and connecting rods – removal

1 Remove the cylinder head as described in Section 8, and the sump as described in Section 13.
2 If the engine is removed from the car, unbolt and remove the water supply tube from the water pump housing (photos). Place the engine on its side.
3 Turn the crankshaft until No 1 piston halfway down its bore. In order to turn the crankshaft with the engine removed, insert two bolts in the flange and use a lever.
4 If the bores are worn excessively and there is a ridge or ring of carbon at the top of the base, remove the ridge or carbon with a scraper or ridge reamer.
5 Check the big-end caps for identification marks. If necessary use a centre-punch on the caps and connecting rods to identify them.
6 Remove the big-end bearing cap nuts from No 1 piston assembly and withdraw the cap complete with the bearing shell (photo).
7 Using the handle of a hammer, tap the piston and connecting rod up through the base and withdraw them from the top of the cylinder block.
8 Loosely refit the cap and bearing to the connecting rod (photos).
9 Repeat the procedure on the remaining piston and connecting rod assemblies.

16 Crankshaft and main bearings – removal

1 With the engine out of the car, remove the timing belt (Section 10), the flywheel/driveplate (Section 11), the sump (Section 13) and the oil pump (Section 14).
2 Disconnect the big-end bearing caps as described in Section 15 – there is no need to remove the pistons.
3 Before removing the crankshaft, check its endfloat using a dial gauge or feeler blades. This will indicate whether new thrust washers are required.
4 Mark the main bearing cap monoblock for position, then unscrew the bolts evenly and in diagonal sequence.
5 Lift the monoblock from the crankcase, making sure that the bearing shells remain in position (photo).
6 Lift the crankshaft from the crankcase and remove the front and rear oil seals (photo).
7 Remove the thrust washers from No 4 main bearing in the crankcase.
8 Extract the bearing shells from the crankcase recesses and monoblock, keeping them identified for location (photo).

16.5 Removing the main bearing cap monoblock

Are your plugs trying to tell you something?

Normal.
Grey-brown deposits, lightly coated core nose. Plugs ideally suited to engine, and engine in good condition.

Heavy Deposits.
A build up of crusty deposits, light-grey sandy colour in appearance.
Fault: Often caused by worn valve guides, excessive use of upper cylinder lubricant, or idling for long periods.

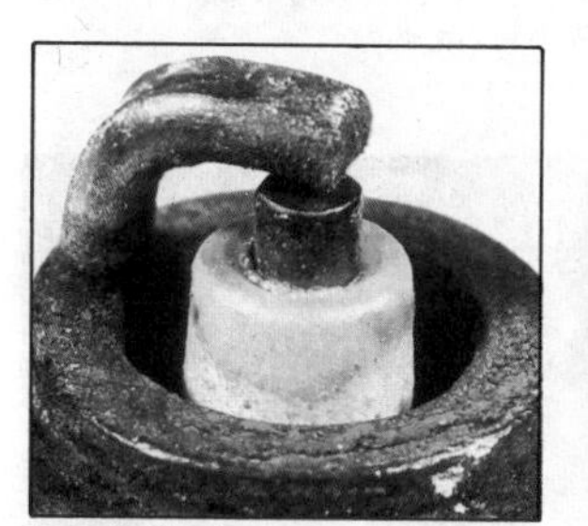

Lead Glazing.
Plug insulator firing tip appears yellow or green/yellow and shiny in appearance.
Fault: Often caused by incorrect carburation, excessive idling followed by sharp acceleration. Also check ignition timing.

Carbon fouling.
Dry, black, sooty deposits.
Fault: over-rich fuel mixture.
Check: carburettor mixture settings, float level, choke operation, air filter.

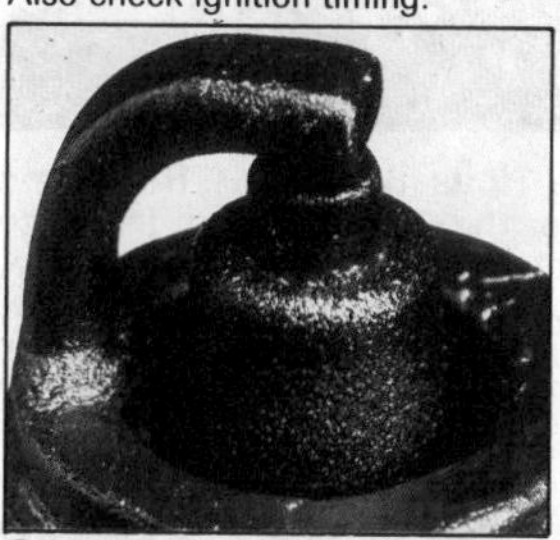

Oil fouling.
Wet, oily deposits. Fault: worn bores/piston rings or valve guides; sometimes occurs (temporarily) during running-in period.

Overheating.
Electrodes have glazed appearance, core nose very white – few deposits. Fault: plug overheating. Check: plug value, ignition timing, fuel octane rating (too low) and fuel mixture (too weak).

Electrode damage.
Electrodes burned away; core nose has burned, glazed appearance. Fault: pre-ignition. Check: for correct heat range and as for 'overheating'.

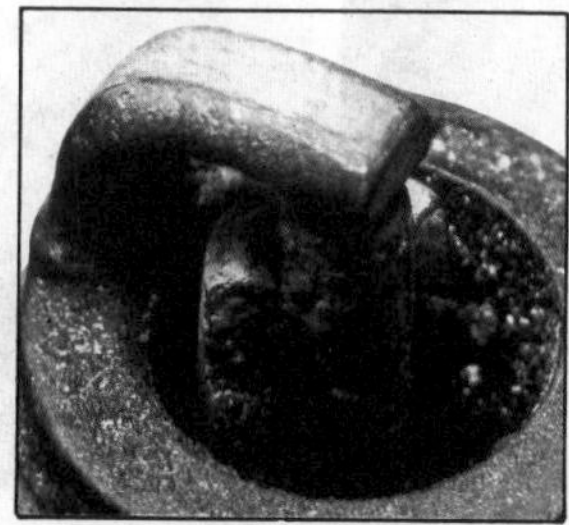

Split core nose.
(May appear initially as a crack). Fault: detonation or wrong gap-setting technique. Check: ignition timing, cooling system, fuel mixture (too weak).

WHY DOUBLE COPPER IS BETTER FOR YOUR ENGINE.

Unique Trapezoidal Copper Cored Earth Electrode
50% Larger Spark Area
Copper Cored Centre Electrode

Champion Double Copper plugs are the first in the world to have copper core in both centre and earth electrode. This innovative design means that they run cooler by up to 100°C – giving greater efficiency and longer life. These double copper cores transfer heat away from the tip of the plug faster and more efficiently. Therefore, Double Copper runs at cooler temperatures than conventional plugs giving improved acceleration response and high speed performance with no fear of pre-ignition.

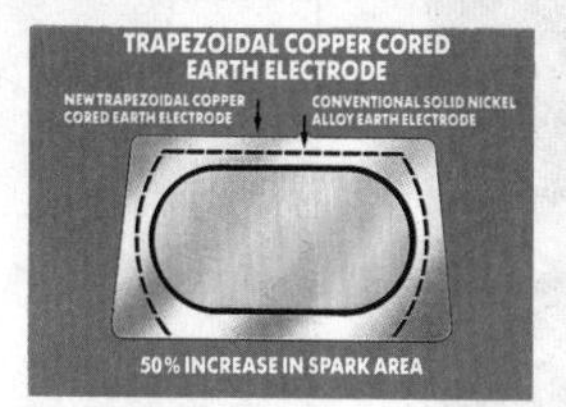

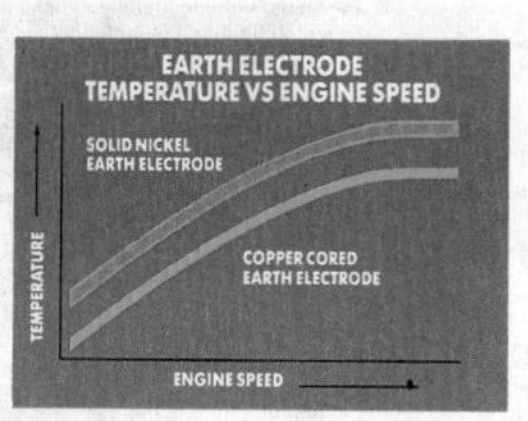

Champion Double Copper plugs also feature a unique trapezoidal earth electrode giving a 50% increase in spark area. This, together with the double copper cores, offers greatly reduced electrode wear, so the spark stays stronger for longer.

 **FASTER COLD STARTING**

 **FOR UNLEADED OR LEADED FUEL**

 **ELECTRODES UP TO 100°C COOLER**

 **BETTER ACCELERATION RESPONSE**

 **LOWER EMISSIONS**

 **50% BIGGER SPARK AREA**

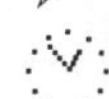 **THE LONGER LIFE PLUG**

Plug Tips/Hot and Cold.
Spark plugs must operate within well-defined temperature limits to avoid cold fouling at one extreme and overheating at the other.
Champion and the car manufacturers work out the best plugs for an engine to give optimum performance under all conditions, from freezing cold starts to sustained high speed motorway cruising.
Plugs are often referred to as hot or cold. With Champion, the higher the number on its body, the hotter the plug, and the lower the number the cooler the plug.

Plug Cleaning
Modern plug design and materials mean that Champion no longer recommends periodic plug cleaning. Certainly don't clean your plugs with a wire brush as this can cause metal conductive paths across the nose of the insulator so impairing its performance and resulting in loss of acceleration and reduced m.p.g.
However, if plugs are removed, always carefully clean the area where the plug seats in the cylinder head as grit and dirt can sometimes cause gas leakage.
Also wipe any traces of oil or grease from plug leads as this may lead to arcing.

DOUBLE COPPER

This photographic sequence shows the steps taken to repair the dent and paintwork damage shown above. In general, the procedure for repairing a hole will be similar; where there are substantial differences, the procedure is clearly described and shown in a separate photograph.

First remove any trim around the dent, then hammer out the dent where access is possible. This will minimise filling. Here, after the large dent has been hammered out, the damaged area is being made slightly concave.

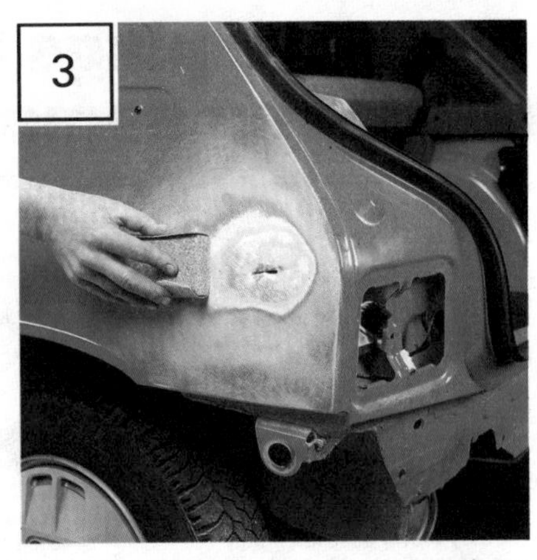

Next, remove all paint from the damaged area by rubbing with coarse abrasive paper or using a power drill fitted with a wire brush or abrasive pad. 'Feather' the edge of the boundary with good paintwork using a finer grade of abrasive paper.

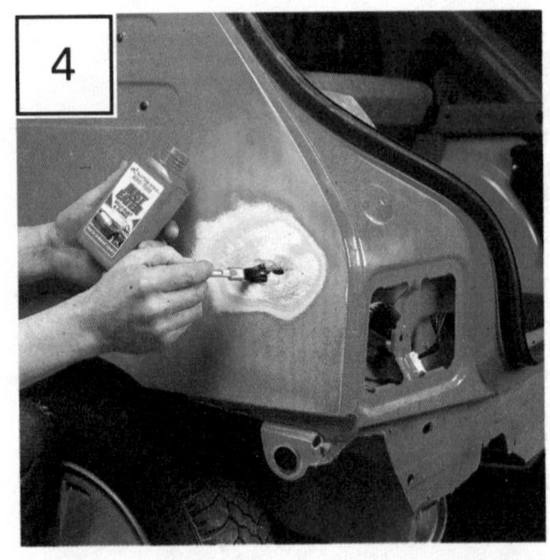

Where there are holes or other damage, the sheet metal should be cut away before proceeding further. The damaged area and any signs of rust should be treated with Turtle Wax Hi-Tech Rust Eater, which will also inhibit further rust formation.

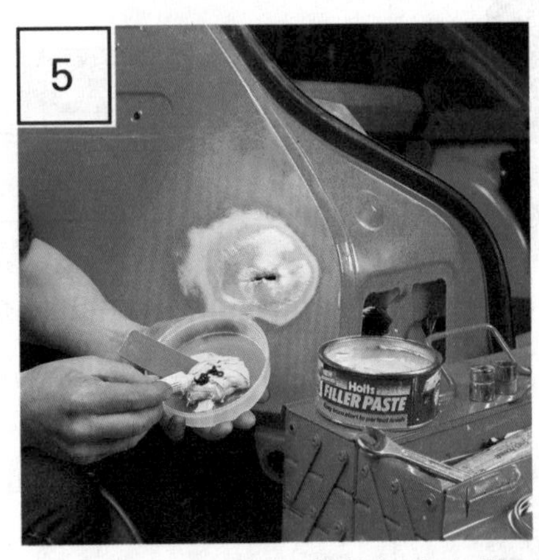

For a large dent or hole mix Holts Body Plus Resin and Hardener according to the manufacturer's instructions and apply around the edge of the repair. Press Glass Fibre Matting over the repair area and leave for 20-30 minutes to harden. Then ...

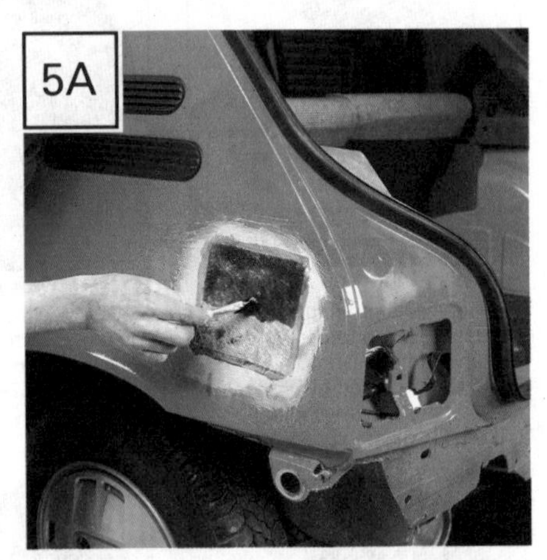

... brush more Holts Body Plus Resin and Hardener onto the matting and leave to harden. Repeat the sequence with two or three layers of matting, checking that the final layer is lower than the surrounding area. Apply Holts Body Plus Filler Paste as shown in Step 5B.

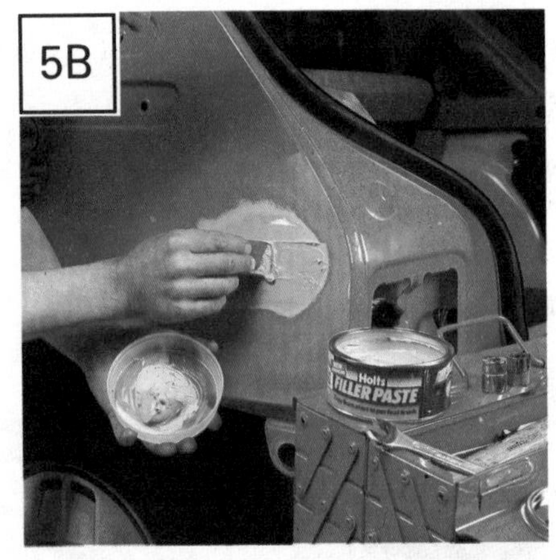

For a medium dent, mix Holts Body Plus Filler Paste and Hardener according to the manufacturer's instructions and apply it with a flexible applicator. Apply thin layers of filler at 20-minute intervals, until the filler surface is slightly proud of the surrounding bodywork.

For small dents and scratches use Holts No Mix Filler Paste straight from the tube. Apply it according to the instructions in thin layers, using the spatula provided. It will harden in minutes if applied outdoors and may then be used as its own knifing putty.

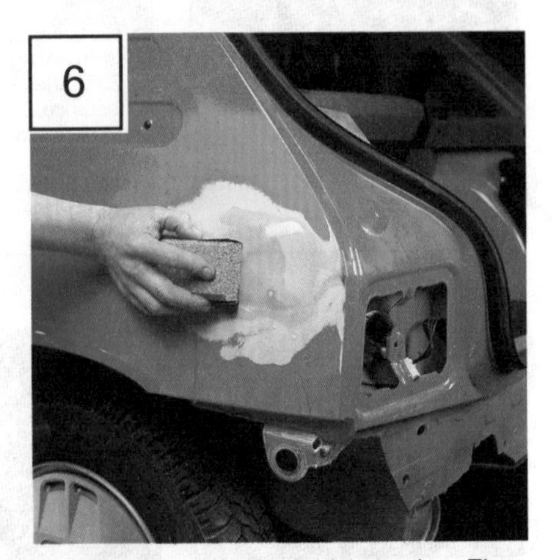

Use a plane or file for initial shaping. Then, using progressively finer grades of wet-and-dry paper, wrapped round a sanding block, and copious amounts of clean water, rub down the filler until glass smooth. 'Feather' the edges of adjoining paintwork.

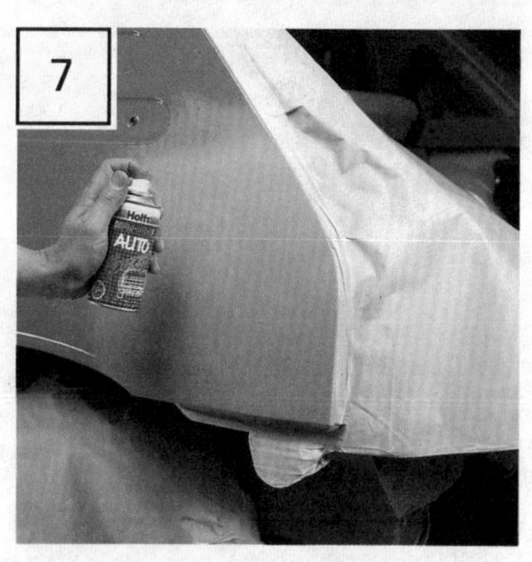

Protect adjoining areas before spraying the whole repair area and at least one inch of the surrounding sound paintwork with Holts Dupli-Color primer.

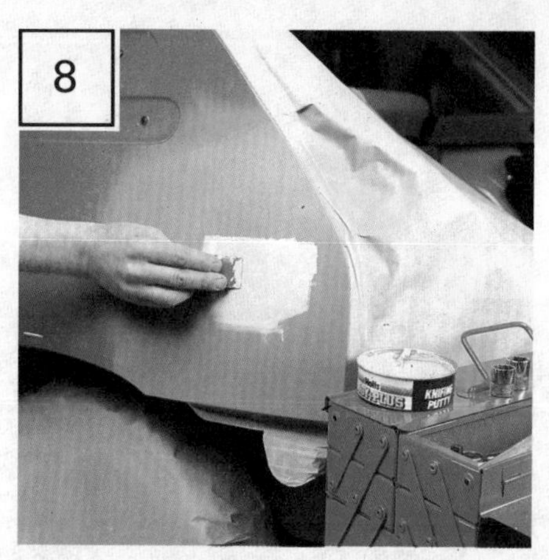

Fill any imperfections in the filler surface with a small amount of Holts Body Plus Knifing Putty. Using plenty of clean water, rub down the surface with a fine grade wet-and-dry paper – 400 grade is recommended – until it is really smooth.

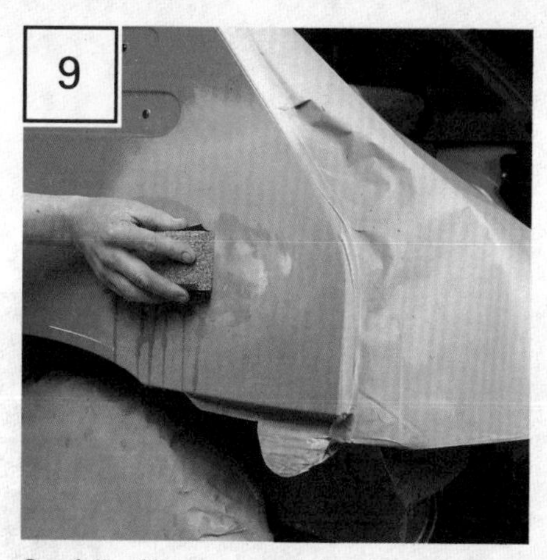

Carefully fill any remaining imperfections with knifing putty before applying the last coat of primer. Then rub down the surface with Holts Body Plus Rubbing Compound to ensure a really smooth surface.

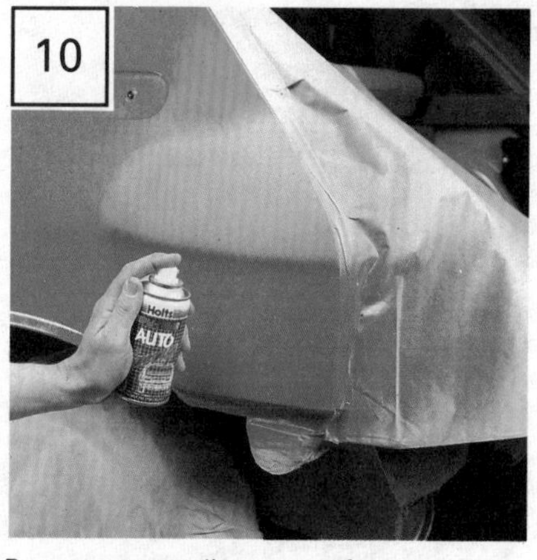

Protect surrounding areas from overspray before applying the topcoat in several thin layers. Agitate Holts Dupli-Color aerosol thoroughly. Start at the repair centre, spraying outwards with a side-to-side motion.

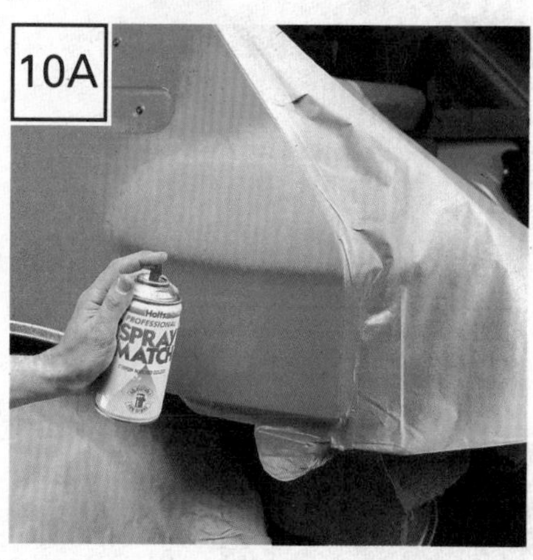

If the exact colour is not available off the shelf, local Holts Professional Spraymatch Centres will custom fill an aerosol to match perfectly.

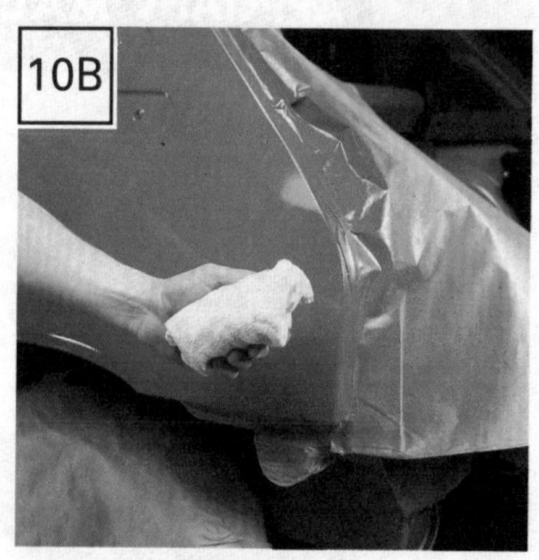

To identify whether a lacquer finish is required, rub a painted unrepaired part of the body with wax and a clean cloth.

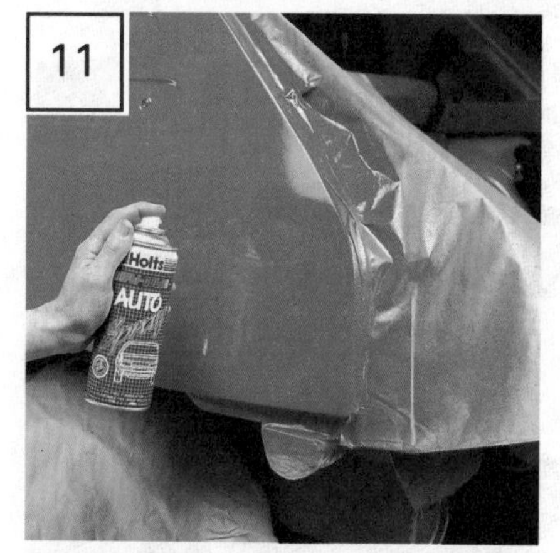

If *no* traces of paint appear on the cloth, spray Holts Dupli-Color clear lacquer over the repaired area to achieve the correct gloss level.

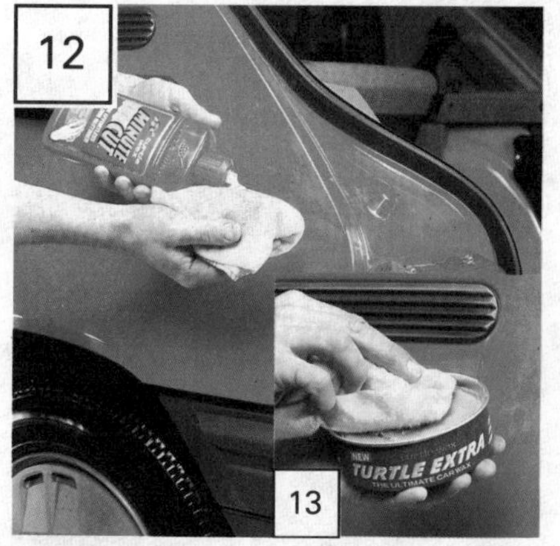

The paint will take about two weeks to harden fully. After this time it can be 'cut' with a mild cutting compound such as Turtle Wax Minute Cut prior to polishing with a final coating of Turtle Wax Extra.

When carrying out bodywork repairs, remember that the quality of the finished job is proportional to the time and effort expended.

16.6 Removing the crankshaft

16.8 Removing a main bearing shell

17 Camshaft front oil seal – renewal

1 Disconnect the battery negative lead.
2 On models equipped with air conditioning, remove the compressor belt cover and idler pulley nut, then remove the mounting bolts and lift the compressor from the bracket. Secure the compressor to one side, leaving the refrigerant hoses still attached. Unbolt the compressor bracket.
3 Disconnect the HT leads from the spark plugs and bracket.
4 Disconnect the crankcase ventilation hose from the valve cover.
5 Unscrew the domed nuts and remove the valve cover and gasket. Note the location of the brackets and earth lead.
6 Unbolt and remove the timing belt upper cover and gasket.
7 Turn the crankshaft pulley bolt until the notches on the camshaft gear are aligned with the upper face of the cylinder head. The white (TDC) line on the crankshaft pulley should also be aligned with the rib on the lower timing cover.
8 Loosen the timing belt tensioner bolts protruding through the lower timing cover, then ease the timing belt off the camshaft gear. Take care not to damage the bolt or contaminate it with oil.
9 Unscrew the camshaft gear retaining bolt, holding the gear stationary with a lever or wide-bladed screwdriver inserted through one of the holes. Remove the washer.
10 Withdraw the camshaft gear from the camshaft and extract the Woodruff key.
11 Using a hooked instrument, extract the camshaft front oil seal. Wipe clean the recess.
12 Apply a little silicone sealant to the housing joints in the recess.
13 Smear a little engine oil on the lip of the new oil seal, then locate it on the camshaft with the lip facing inwards (photo).
14 Using a suitable metal tube, drive the oil seal fully into position. Wipe away any excess oil.
15 Refit the removed components using a reversal of the removal procedure. When fitting the timing belt to the camshaft gear, make sure that the marks on the camshaft gear and crankshaft pulley are correctly aligned as in paragraph 7. Tension the belt by turning the crankshaft anti-clockwise 90°, then tighten the tensioner bolts.

18 Crankshaft front oil seal – renewal

1 Remove the timing belt and crankshaft gear as described in Section 10.
2 Using a hooked instrument, extract the crankshaft front oil seal. Wipe clean the recess.
3 Apply a little non-hardening sealant to the recess.
4 Smear a little engine oil on the lip of the new oil seal, then locate it on the crankshaft with the lip facing inwards.
5 Using a suitable metal tube, drive the oil seal fully into position. Wipe away any excess oil.

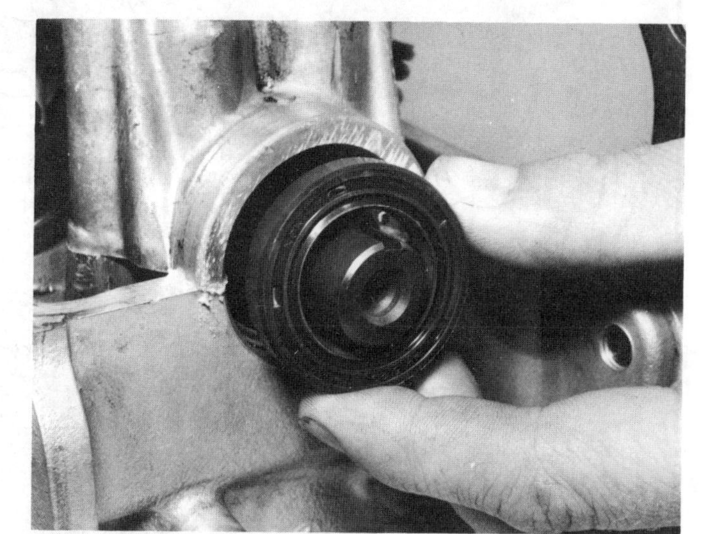

17.13 Inserting the camshaft oil seal

6 Refit the timing belt and crankshaft gear as described in Section 36.

19 Engine mountings – renewal

Left-hand mounting

1 On models equipped with air conditioning, remove the compressor belt cover and idler pulley nut, then remove the mounting bolts and lift the compressor from the bracket. Secure the compressor to one side, leaving the refrigerant hoses still attached. Unbolt the compressor bracket.
2 Unscrew the small mounting bolts and remove the washer, then unscrew the through-bolt and remove the washers (photo).
3 Push the mounting into the body cavity, then lever the mounting bracket under the engine bracket (photo). The mounting can now be removed.
4 Fit the new mounting using a reversal of the removal procedure.

Front mounting

5 Jack up the front of the car and support it on axle stands. Apply the handbrake.
6 Connect a hoist to the engine and gearbox assembly and take its weight.

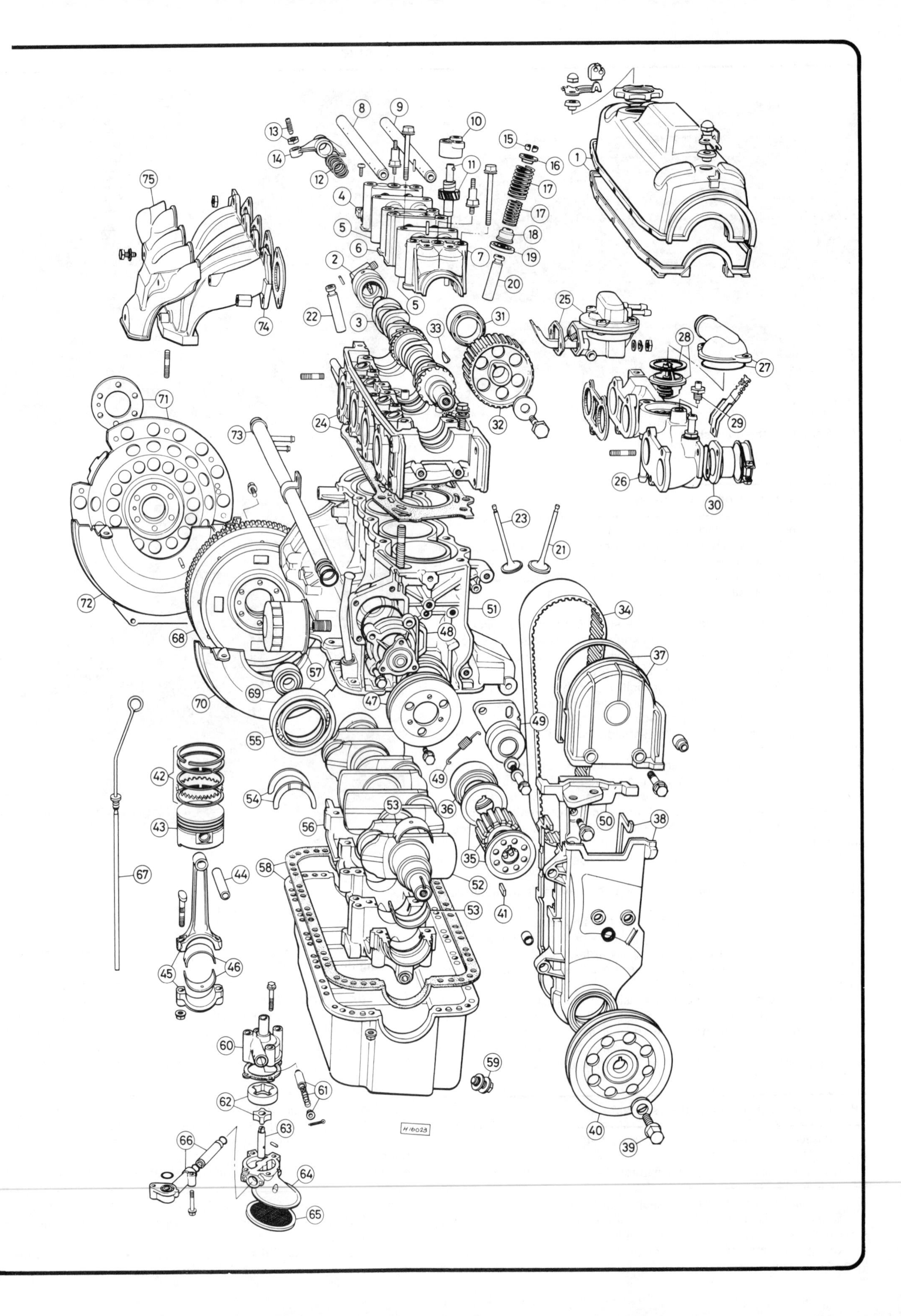

1
2
3
4
5
5
5
6
7
8
9
10
11
12
13
14
15
16
17
17
18
19
20
21
22
23
24
25
26
27
28
29
30
31
32
33
34
35
36
37
38
39
40
41
42
43
44
45
46
47
48
49
49
50
51
52
53
53
54
55
56
57
58
59
60
61
62
63
64
65
66
67
68
69
70
71
72
73
74
75
H16023

Fig. 1.2 Exploded view of the engine (Secs 7 to 18)

1 Rocker cover and gasket
2 Tachometer drivegear
3 Camshaft
4 Camshaft bearing cap
5 Rocker shaft support bracket
6 Camshaft bearing cap – centre
7 Camshaft bearing cap
8 Rocker shaft – exhaust
9 Rocker shaft – inlet
10 Oil pump drivegear retainer
11 Oil pump drivegear and shaft
12 Rocker arm tension spring
13 Adjusting screw and locknut
14 Rocker arm
15 Valve cotters
16 Valve spring retainer
17 Valve spring
18 Oil seal – inlet valve
19 Valve spring seat
20 Valve guide – inlet
21 Inlet valve
22 Valve guide – exhaust
23 Exhaust valve
24 Cylinder head and gasket
25 Fuel pump and insulator
26 Inlet manifold
27 Thermostat housing and O-ring
28 Thermostat and mounting seal
29 Bleed screw
30 Insulator
31 Camshaft oil seal
32 Camshaft sprocket
33 Woodruff key
34 Timing belt
35 Crankshaft sprocket and guide plates
36 Crankshaft oil seal
37 Upper cover and gasket – timing belt
38 Lower cover and gasket – timing belt
39 Pulley bolt
40 Crankshaft pulley
41 Woodruff key
42 Piston rings
43 Piston
44 Gudgeon pin
45 Connecting rod and cap
46 Big-end bearing shells
47 Water pump pulley
48 Water pump
49 Tensioner pulley and spring – timing belt
50 Engine mounting bracket LH
51 Cylinder block
52 Crankshaft
53 Main bearing shells
54 Thrust washers
55 Oil seal
56 Main bearing cap and oil gallery
57 Oil filter
58 Sump and gasket
59 Drain plug
60 Oil pump body
61 Oil pressure relief valve
62 Inner and outer rotors
63 Pump shaft
64 Pick-up body
65 Oil strainer
66 Oil pipe and connecting block
67 Dipstick
68 Flywheel
69 Spigot bearing
70 Cover – clutch housing
71 Driveplate and washer – Trio-matic
72 Cover – converter housing
73 Connecting pipe – coolant
74 Exhaust manifold
75 Hot air cover

7 Using a long extension and socket, unscrew the nuts retaining the front and rear mountings to the centre beam (photo).
8 Unbolt the anti-roll bar brackets from the body.
9 On Trio-matic models, detach the selector cable bracket from the centre beam.
10 Unbolt and remove the centre beam (photo).
11 Unbolt the mounting bracket from the engine, then remove the nut and separate the mounting rubber and shield.
12 Fit the new mounting using a reversal of the removal procedure, but before tightening the nuts all the nuts and bolts shown in Fig. 1.4 should be loosened, then tightened in the sequence shown.

Rear mounting

13 Jack up the front of the car and support it on axle stands. Apply the handbrake.
14 Connect a hoist to the engine and gearbox assembly and take its weight.
15 Using a long extension and socket, unscrew the nut retaining the rear mounting to the centre beam.
16 On Trio-matic models, detach the selector cable bracket from the centre beam.
17 Loosen the front bolts of the centre beam, and remove the rear bolts. Lower the centre beam from the mounting.
18 Unscrew the nut and remove the rear mounting from its bracket (photo).
19 Fit the new mounting using a reversal of the removal procedure, but before tightening the nuts all the nuts and bolts shown in Fig 1.4 should be loosened, then tightened in the sequence shown.

20 Examination and renovation – general

With the engine completely stripped, clean all the components and examine them for wear. Each part should be checked, and where necessary renewed or renovated as described in the following Sections. Renew main and big-end shell bearings as a matter of course, unless you know that they have had little wear and are in perfect condition.

19.2 Engine left-hand mounting bolts

19.3 Pushing the left-hand mounting into the body cavity

19.7a Unscrewing the engine mounting lower nuts

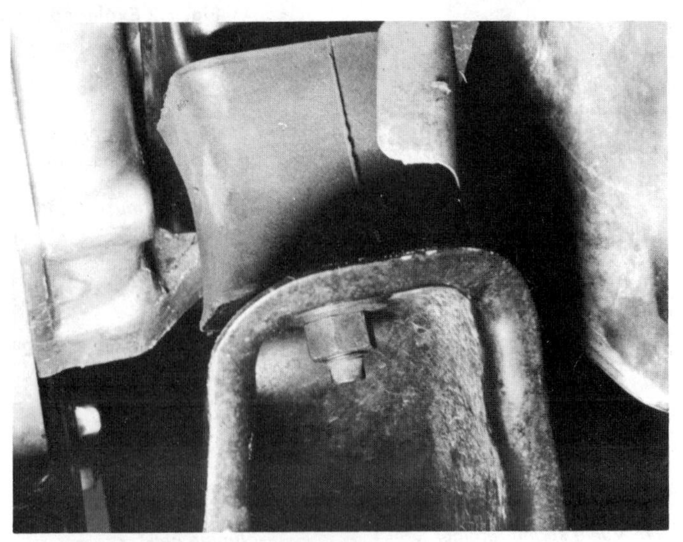
19.7b The engine front mounting lower nut

19.10 The engine mounting centre beam

19.18 Engine rear mounting

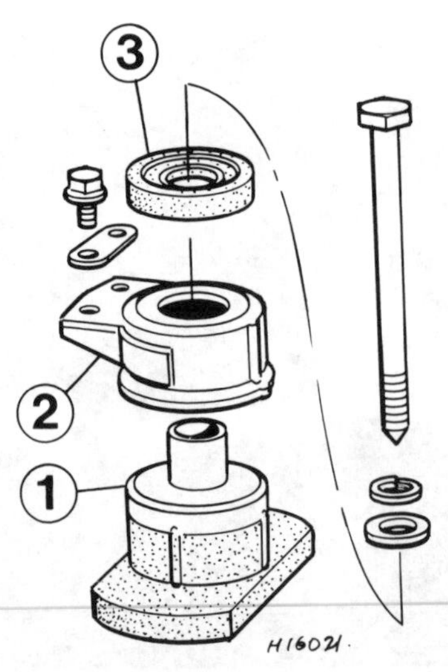

Fig. 1.3 Engine left-hand mounting components (Sec 19)

1 *Mounting rubber*
2 *Bracket*
3 *Bumper rubber*

21 Oil pump – examination and renovation

1 Pull out the bypass tube and remove the seal (photo).
2 Prise off the strainer (photo).
3 Extract the split pin and withdraw the collar, spring, and pressure relief valve (photos).
4 Unbolt and remove the pump cover. Remove the gasket.
5 Clean all the components with paraffin and wipe dry.
6 Using a feeler blade, and where necessary a straight-edge, check that the rotor clearances are as given in the Specifications (photos). If any clearance is outside that specified, or if damage is evident on any component, renew the components concerned. Note that the rotor endfloat must be checked with the gasket in position.
7 Reassemble the oil pump in the reverse order, using a new gasket and lubricating the rotors with engine oil. Also renew the seals on the by-pass tube.

22 Crankshaft and bearings – examination and renovation

1 Examine the bearing surfaces of the crankshaft for scratches or scoring and, using a micrometer, check each journal and crankpin for ovality and taper. Where this is found to be in excess of 0.010 mm

Fig. 1.4 Engine mounting tightening sequence. Encircled numbers indicate light tightening (Sec 19)

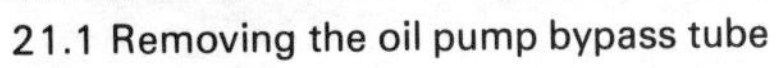

21.1 Removing the oil pump bypass tube

21.2 Prising off the oil pump strainer

21.3a Remove the pressure relief valve split pin ...

21.3b ... the collar ...

21.3c ... and the spring and plunger

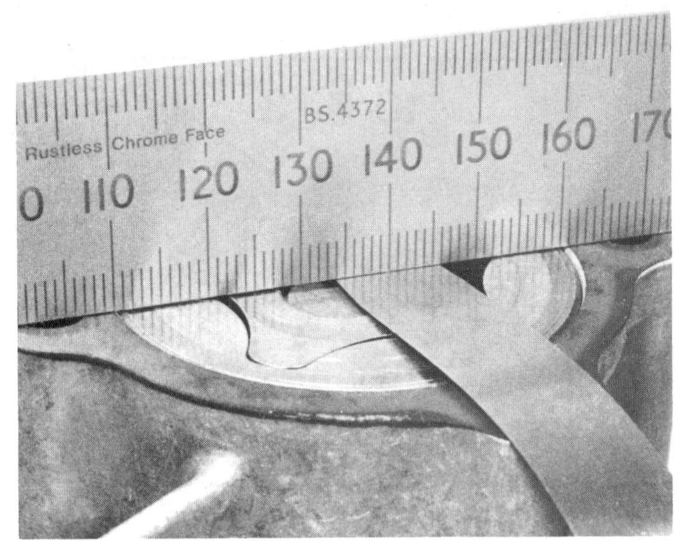

21.6a Checking the oil pump rotor endfloat ...

21.6b ... rotor-to-housing clearance ..

21.6c ... and rotor lobe clearance

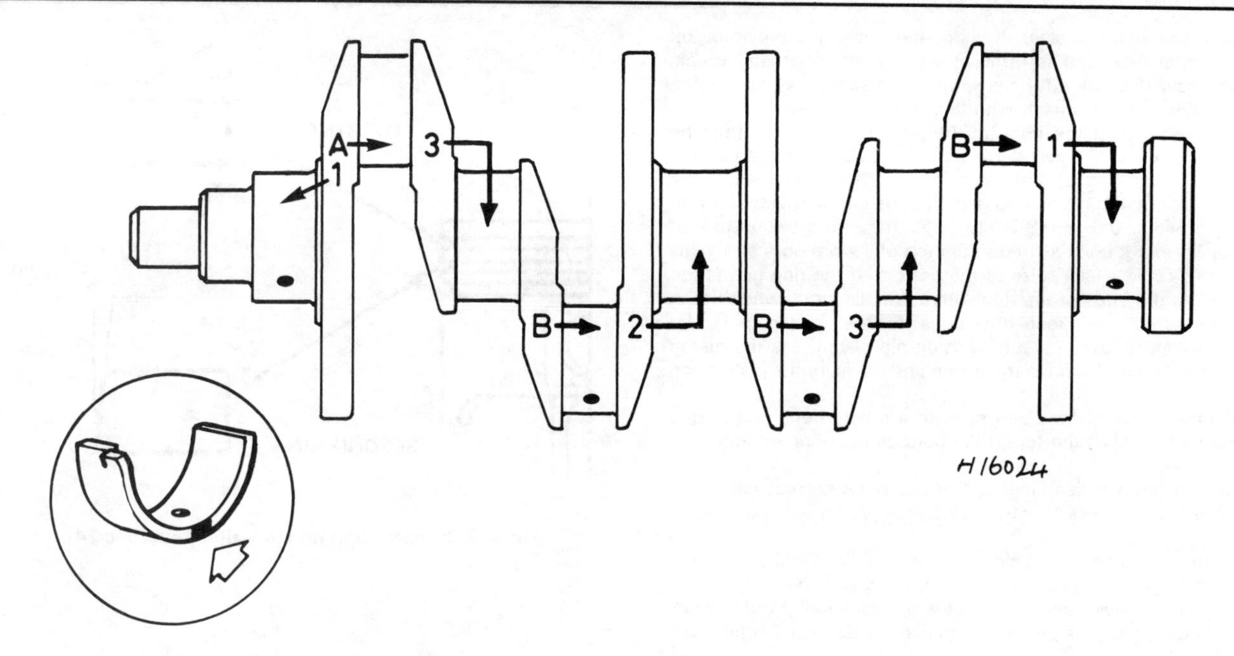

Fig. 1.5 Example of crankshaft journal and crankpin size coding. Inset shows bearing shell colour code location (Sec 22)

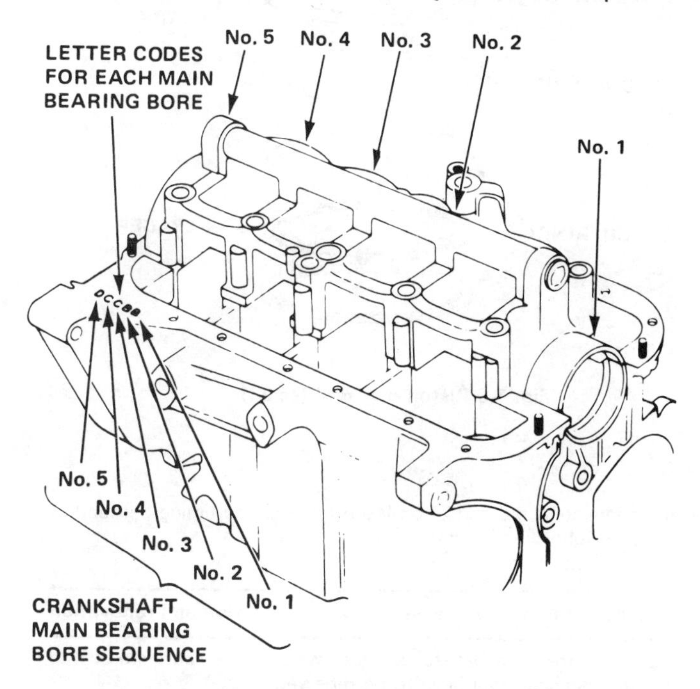

Fig. 1.6 Crankshaft main bearing bore coding (Sec 22)

(0.0004 in), a new crankshaft must be obtained. Alternatively, it may be possible to have the crankshaft reground and undersize bearings fitted. Note however that regrinding is not recommended by the manufacturers.

2 If Plastigage is available, the running clearances of the bearings can be checked and compared with those given in the Specifications. If the crankshaft journals are in good condition but the running clearances are excessive, fit new bearing shells having the same colour as those removed. The colour coding of the bearing is derived from a combination of a letter and a number as shown in the Specifications. For the main bearings, letters stamped on the cylinder block lower face indicate the bearing bore tolerance in the monoblock cap and crankcase, and a number stamped on the crankshaft webs indicates the main bearing journal tolerances. For the big-end bearings a number stamped on the connecting rod and cap indicates the bearing bore tolerance in the connecting rod and cap, and a letter stamped on the crankshaft web indicates the crankpin tolerance.

3 It is permissible to fit new bearing shells one colour smaller than those originally fitted, provided that the correct running clearances are maintained. Seek professional advice if in doubt on this point.

4 If the crankshaft endfloat is more than the amount given in the Specifications, new thrust washers should be fitted to No 4 main bearing.

23 Cylinder block – examination and renovation

1 Check that all the internal oilways and waterways are clear of any obstruction. Thoroughly check the cylinder block for damage and cracking (where applicable, remove the water pump).

2 The cylinder bores must be examined for taper, ovality, scoring and scratches. Start by examining the top of the bores: if these are worn, a slight ridge will be found which marks the top of the piston ring travel. If the wear is excessive, the engine will have had a high oil consumption rate accompanied by blue smoke from the exhaust.

3 If available, use an inside dial gauge to measure the bore diameter just below the ridge and compare it with the diameter at the bottom of the bore, which is not subject to wear. If the difference is more than the specified amount, the cylinder will normally require reboring with new oversize pistons fitted.

4 Provided the cylinder bore wear does not exceed 0.008 in (0.2 mm), however, special oil control rings may be available to restore compression and stop the engine burning oil.

5 If new pistons are being fitted to old bores, it is essential to roughen the bore walls slightly with fine glasspaper to enable the new piston rings to bed in properly.

6 Where applicable, fit the water pump to the cylinder block as described in Chapter 2, but do not fit the upper mounting bolt or pulley.

24 Pistons and connecting rods – examination and renovation

1 Examine the pistons for ovality, scoring, and scratches. Check the connecting rods and caps for damage and incorrect alignment. Check the gudgeon pin for wear.

2 If new pistons are to be fitted to the existing connecting rods, this work should be entrusted to a BL garage or suitably equipped engineering works.

3 If the old pistons are to be refitted, carefully remove the piston rings and thoroughly clean the pistons. Take particular care to clean out the piston ring grooves. At the same time do not scratch the aluminium. If new rings are to be fitted to the old pistons, then the top

ring should be stepped to clear the ridge left above the previous top ring. If a normal new ring is fitted, it will hit the ridge and break, because the new ring will not have worn in the same way as the old, which will have worn in unison with the ridge.

4 Prior to assembling the rings to the pistons, each ring must be inserted into its respective cylinder bore and the gap measured with a feeler gauge. It is essential that each ring gap is as specified at the beginning of this Chapter. The ring gap must be checked with the ring positioned to within 0.5 to 0.8 in (13 to 20 mm) from the bottom of the cylinder bore. If it is measured at the top of a worn bore and gives a perfect fit, it could easily seize at the bottom. If the ring gap is too small rub down the ends of the ring with a fine file, until, when fitted, the gap is correct. To keep the rings square in the bore for measurement, line each up in turn with an old piston; use the piston to push the ring down. Remove the piston and measure the piston ring gap.

5 When fitting new pistons and rings to a rebored engine the ring gap can be measured at the top of the bore as the bore will now not taper.

6 Piston ring groove clearance will normally be correct with new pistons but even so, check it with a feeler gauge and see that it is as specified.

7 The piston-to-cylinder bore clearance should also be checked, and must be within the tolerance given in the Specifications.

8 If new pistons have been fitted to the old connecting rods, check that the indentation on the piston crown is towards the oil squirt hole in the connecting rod and also biased towards the timing belt end of the engine (photo).

24.8a Indentation in piston crown (arrowed) – scratched arrow indicates timing belt end of engine

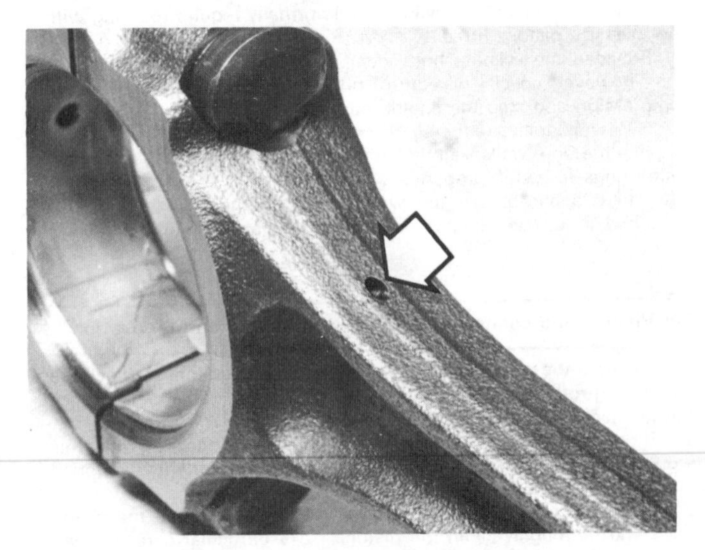
24.8b Oil squirt hole (arrowed) in the connecting rod

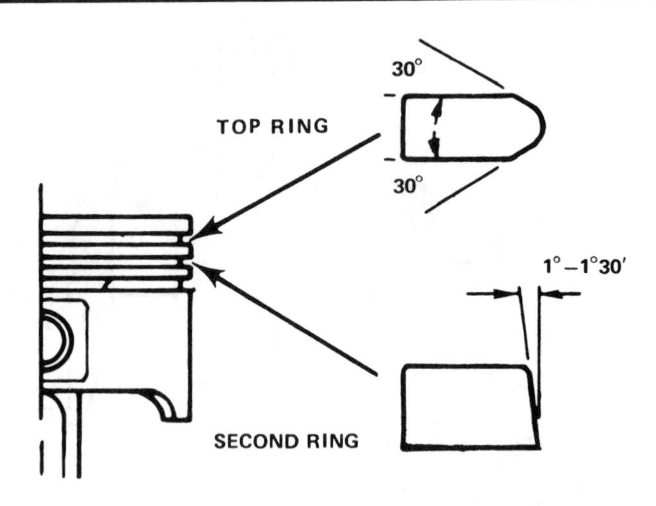

Fig. 1.7 Compression ring identification (Sec 24)

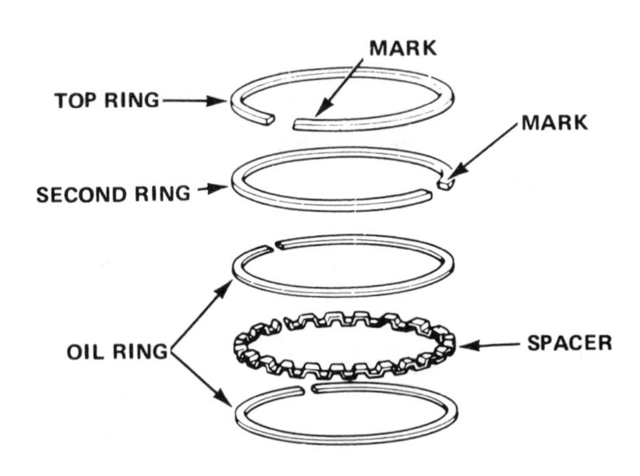

Fig. 1.8 Piston ring set (Sec 24)

25 Camshaft and rocker assembly – examination and renovation

1 Examine the camshaft for signs of wear. If the cams are scored badly, the camshaft will have to be renewed.

2 Place the camshaft in V-blocks and, using a dial gauge, rotate the shaft and check the bearing journals for wear. The total indicated run-out should not exceed 0.06 mm (0.002 in).

3 If the camshaft is to be renewed then the oil pump drivegear and shaft should be renewed also, since it is not good practice to mesh a new gear with a worn one.

4 If the camshaft bearing surfaces in the cylinder head are worn, the cylinder head must be renewed as no repair is possible. If Plastigage is available, the running clearances of the bearings can be checked and compared with those given in the Specifications.

5 Check the rocker arms for wear by attempting to rock them on their shafts. If necessary the assembly may be dismantled by extracting the dowel pins and sliding off the brackets, springs, and rocker arms, but place each item in its order of removal to ensure correct reassembly (photos).

6 Clean all the components in paraffin and wipe dry, then check them for wear.

7 Renew the components as necessary, then reassemble the rocker assembly in the reverse order to dismantling.

25.5a Rocker shaft dowel pins on the left-hand bearing cap

25.5b Dismantling the rocker shaft assembly

25.5c Rocker shaft dowel pin on the right-hand bearing cap

26 Timing components – examination and renovation

1 The timing belt should be renewed every 45 000 miles (72 500 km). However, if signs of wear are evident or if the belt is contaminated with oil, it should be renewed regardless of mileage.
2 Check the camshaft and crankshaft gears for wear, and the tensioner for roughness. Renew the components as necessary.

27 Flywheel (manual gearbox models) – examination and renovation

1 Examine the clutch driven plate mating surface of the flywheel, referring to Chapter 5.
2 Check the starter ring gear teeth and if they are chipped and worn, renew the flywheel – the ring gear is not supplied separately.
3 Check the spigot bearing in the flywheel for roughness. If necessary, drive out the old bearing and drive in a new bearing using a suitable metal tube (photo).

27.3 Spigot bearing in the flywheel

28 Cylinder head – decarbonising, valve grinding and renovation

1 The operation will normally only be required at comparatively high mileages. However, if persistent pinking occurs and performance has deteriorated even though the engine adjustments are correct, decarbonising and valve grinding may be required.
2 With the cylinder head removed and dismantled use a scraper to remove the carbon from the cylinder head surface, then wash it thoroughly with paraffin.
3 Use a straight-edge and feeler blade to check that the cylinder head surface is not distorted. If it is, it must be resurfaced by a suitably equipped engineering works. Also check the cylinder block surface.
4 If the engine is still in the car, clean the piston crowns and cylinder bore upper edges, but make sure that no carbon drops between the pistons and bores. To do this, locate two of the pistons at the top of their bores and seal off the remaining bores with paper and masking tape. Press a little grease between the two pistons and their bores to collect any carbon dust; this can be wiped away when the piston is lowered. To prevent carbon build-up, polish the piston crown with metal polish, but remove all traces of the polish afterwards.
5 Examine the heads of the valves for pitting and burning, especially the exhaust valve heads. Renew any valve which is badly burnt. Examine the valve seats at the same time. If the pitting is very slight, it can be removed by grinding the valve heads and seats together with coarse, then fine, grinding paste.
6 Where excessive pitting has occurred, the valve seats must be recut or renewed by a suitably equipped engineering works.
7 Valve grinding is carried out as follows. Place the cylinder head upside down on a bench with a block of wood at each end to give clearance for the valve stems.
8 Smear a trace of coarse carborundum paste on the seat face and press a suction grinding tool onto the valve head. With a semi-rotary action, grind the valve head to its seat, lifting the valve occasionally to redistribute the grinding paste. When a dull matt even surface is produced on both the valve seat and the valve, wipe off the paste and repeat the process with fine carborundum paste as before. A light spring placed under the valve head will greatly ease this operation. When a smooth unbroken ring of light grey matt finish is produced on both the valve and seat, the grinding operation is complete.
9 Scrape away all carbon from the valve head and stem, and clean away all traces of grinding compound. Clean the valves and seats with a paraffin soaked rag, then wipe with a clean rag.
10 If the valve guides are worn, indicated by a side to side motion of the valve, new guides must be fitted. This work must be entrusted to a BL garage or engineering works, as it involves the use of special tools.
11 Check the free length of the valve springs. Renew them as a set if any are less than the specified length; renew them in any case at time of major overhaul.
12 Obtain a set of new valve seals.

29 Engine reassembly – general

1 To ensure maximum life with minimum trouble from a rebuilt engine, not only must everything be correctly assembled, but it must also be spotlessly clean. All oilways must be clear, and locking washers and spring washers must be fitted where indicated. Oil all bearings and other working surfaces thoroughly with engine oil during assembly.
2 Before assembly begins, renew any bolts or studs with damaged threads.
3 Gather together a torque wrench, oil can, clean rag, and a set of engine gaskets and oil seals, together with a new oil filter cartridge.

30.2a Installing No 4 main bearing shell

30.2b Lubricating the main bearing shells

30.4 Installing the crankshaft

30.5 Inserting the crankshaft thrust washers

30.6 Checking the crankshaft endfloat

30.8 Tightening the main bearing monoblock bolts

30 Crankshaft and main bearings – refitting

1 Clean the backs of the bearing shells, and the bearing recess in the cylinder block and the main bearing cap monoblock.
2 Press the bearing shells into the cylinder block and monoblock and oil them liberally (photo).
3 Smear a little engine oil onto the lips of the front and rear oil seals, then locate them on the ends of the crankshaft.
4 With the cylinder block upside-down, lower the crankshaft into position (photo).
5 Feed the thrust washers to each side of No 4 main bearing with the oilways facing away from the bearing (photo). Turn the crankshaft while doing this and make sure the washers are fully entered in the block.
6 Using a feeler gauge, check that the crankshaft endfloat is as given in the Specifications (photo).
7 Apply a little silicone sealant to the end joint faces of the monoblock and block valves where the oil seals are located.
8 Check that the oil seals are located correctly, then fit the main bearing monoblock to the crankcase. Insert the bolts and tighten them in a diagonal sequence to the specified torque (photo).
9 If the pistons are already in position, re-connect the big-end bearing caps as described in Section 31.
10 Refit the oil pump (Section 32), the sump (Section 33), the flywheel/driveplate (Section 35), and the timing belt (Section 36).

31 Pistons and connecting rods – refitting

1 With the engine on its side, turn the crankshaft so that the crankpins are level with the bottom face of the cylinder block.
2 Clean the backs of the bearing shells and the recesses in the connecting rods and big-end caps.
3 Press the big-end bearing shells into the connecting rods and caps in their correct positions and oil them liberally.
4 Position the compression ring gaps 90° from each other and facing the thrust side of the pistons (see Fig. 1.9). Position the oil control ring spacer ends opposite the 2nd compression ring gap with the oil ring gaps 15° to each side.
5 Lubricate the cylinder bores and crankpins liberally with oil.
6 Fit a ring compressor to No 1 piston, then insert the piston and connecting rod into No 1 cylinder. Drive the piston carefully into the cylinder with the wooden handle of a hammer, and at the same time guide the connecting rod onto the crankpin (photo). Make sure that the indentation on the piston crown is facing the timing belt end of the engine.
7 Fit the big-end bearing cap in its previously noted position, then tighten the nuts evenly to the specified torque (photo).
8 Check that the crankshaft turns freely, using a lever and two bolts in the crankshaft flange where necessary.
9 Repeat the procedure given in paragraphs 6 to 8 on the remaining piston and connecting rod assemblies.
10 If the engine is removed from the car, fit a new seal to the end of the water supply tube, then locate the tube in the water pump housing and tighten the retaining bolt.
11 Refit the sump (Section 33) and cylinder head (Section 38).

32 Oil pump – refitting

1 Align the oil pump shaft with the slot in the driveshaft (if already fitted), then locate the oil pump and bypass tube on the main bearing cap monoblock. Tighten the bolts evenly to the specified torque.
2 Refit the sump (Section 33).

33 Sump – refitting

1 Clean and degrease the mating faces of the sump, crankcase and gasket. Any oil remaining will cause the gasket to slip from position as the sump retaining bolts are tightened. Apply silicone sealant only to

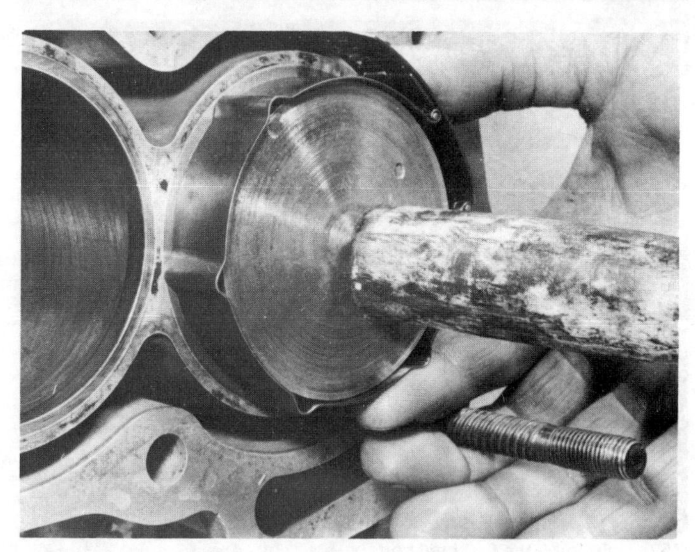
31.6 Installing a piston

31.7 Tightening the big-end bearing cap nuts

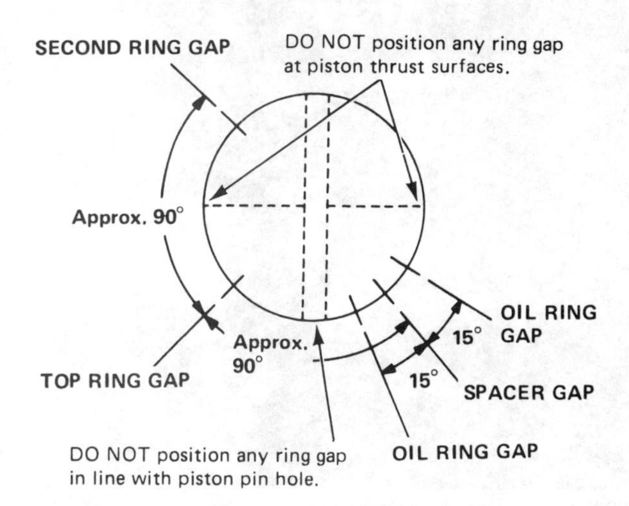

Fig. 1.9 Piston ring gap positions (Sec 31)

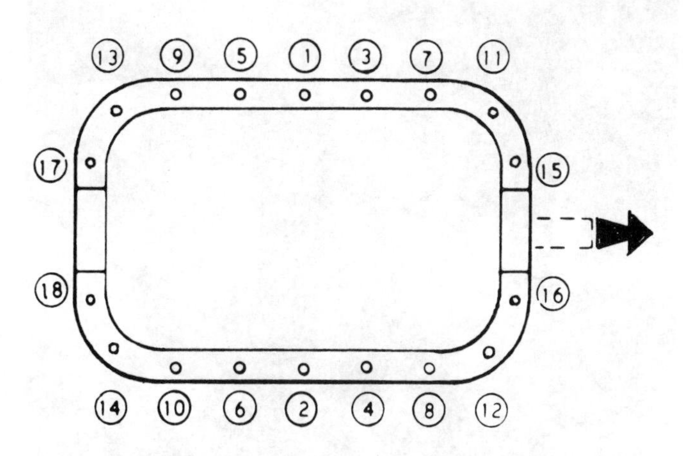

Fig. 1.10 Sump tightening sequence (Sec 33)

the points of the gasket shown in Fig. 1.11, spreading it thinly.

2 Locate the new gasket on the crankcase and over the studs.

3 Position the sump on the gasket, together with the flywheel/driveplate cover, and insert all the bolts and nuts loosely.

4 Tighten the nuts and bolts evenly in the sequence shown in Fig. 1.10 to the specified torque.

5 If the engine is already in the car, reverse the procedure given in Section 13, paragraphs 1 to 9. However note that the engine mountings must be tightened as described in Section 19. Refill the engine with oil.

34 Oil filter – refitting

1 Wipe clean the filter sealing face on the cylinder block.

2 Smear a little engine oil on the sealing rubber of the new filter cartridge, then screw it into position until it just touches the sealing face. Tighten the filter a further half turn by hand.

3 The filter should be checked for leakage at the earliest opportunity when the engine is next run.

35 Flywheel/driveplate – refitting

1 Wipe clean the mating faces of the flywheel/driveplate and crankshaft, then fit the flywheel/driveplate in its previously noted

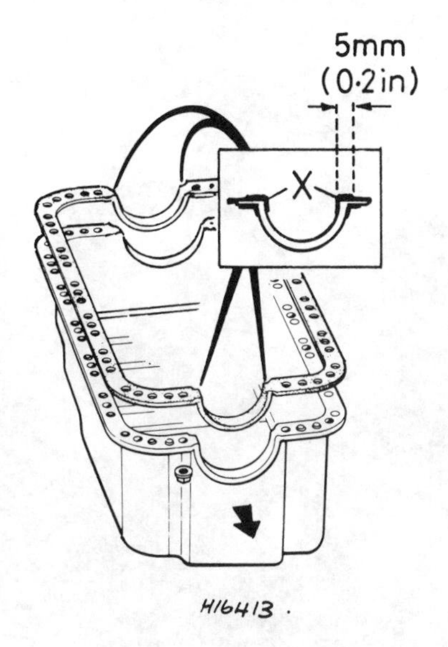

Fig. 1.11 Sump gasket sealant application (Sec 33)

X indicates points of application

position and insert the bolts, having previously coated the threads with a liquid locking agent.

2 Tighten the bolts evenly in diagonal sequence to the specified torque, holding the crankshaft stationary either by using a lever in the starter ring gear or by bolting the left-hand lifting hanger to the flywheel/driveplate (see Section 10) (photo).

3 If the engine is in the car, reverse the preliminary procedures given in Section 11.

36 Timing belt and tensioner – refitting

1 Turn the crankshaft so that Nos 1 and 4 pistons are at TDC.

2 With the engine upright, fit the inner guide plate (concave side first) and crankshaft gear.

3 Hook the tensioner spring on the bracket, then locate the tensioner on the front of the cylinder block and attach the free end of the spring to it (photo). Insert the tensioner bolts loosely.

4 Pull the tensioner against the spring tension and temporarily retain it in this position by tightening the bolts.

5 If necessary, refit the cylinder head (Section 38). Check that the notches on the camshaft gear are aligned with the upper face of the cylinder head. Check that the crankshaft is at TDC on Nos 1 and 4 pistons by temporarily fitting the lower timing cover, key and crankshaft pulley, and aligning the TDC marks.

35.2 Tightening the flywheel bolts

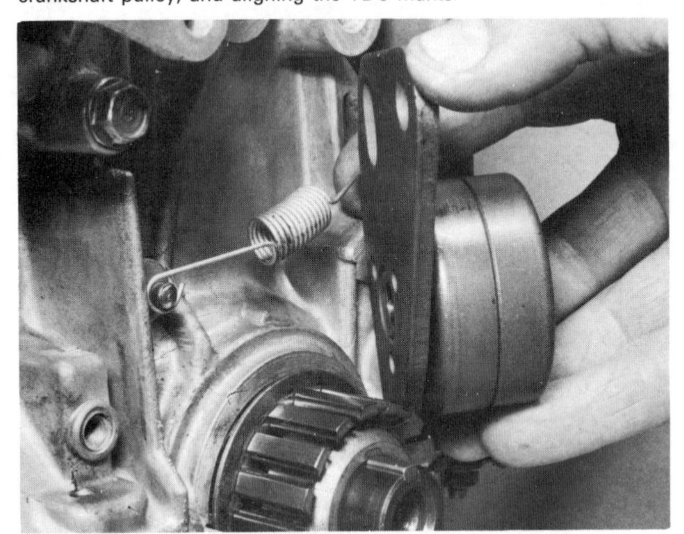

36.3 Installing the timing belt tensioner

36.6 Fitted position of the timing belt

36.8 Key location on the crankshaft

36.12 Tightening the crankshaft pulley bolt

6 Slide the timing belt onto the crankshaft and camshaft gears, with the flat (non-toothed) side on the tensioner pulley (photo). If the original belt is being refitted, make sure that it is fitted in its previously noted position.
7 Locate the left-hand mounting bracket on the cylinder block, insert the bolts and tighten them.
8 Fit the outer guide plate (convex side first) to the crankshaft. Make sure the key is in position (photo).
9 Fit the lower timing cover, together with a new gasket, and tighten the bolts.
10 Press the rubber seals onto the tensioner adjusting bolts.
11 Locate the pulley on the front of the crankshaft making sure that it engages the key correctly. Insert the pulley bolt together with the washer.
12 Tighten the pulley bolt to the specified torque while holding the crankshaft stationary, either using a lever in the starter ring gear or by bolting the left-hand lifting hanger to the flywheel/driveplate (see Section 10) (photo).
13 Tension the timing belt by loosening the tensioner bolts and turning the crankshaft anti-clockwise through 90°, then tighten the tensioner bolts.
14 Fit the timing belt upper cover, together with a new gasket, and tighten the bolts.
15 Fit the valve cover together with a new gasket, install the brackets and domed nuts and tighten the nuts.
16 Fit the HT leads to the spark plugs and bracket.
17 If the engine is already in the car, reverse the preliminary procedures given in Section 10. Tension the water pump/alternator drivebelt as described in Chapter 2.

37 Cylinder head – reassembly

1 Locate the spring seats over the valve guides and press the new valve seals onto the valve guides, noting that the inlet and exhaust valve seals are different (photos).
2 Fit the valves in their original sequence or, if new valves have been obtained, to the seat to which they have been ground.
3 Working on one valve fit the springs and retainer, then compress the springs with the compressor and insert the split collets. Carefully release the compressor and remove it.
4 Repeat the procedure given in paragraph 3 on the remaining valves. Tap the end of each valve stem with a non-metallic mallet to settle the collets.
5 Lubricate the bearing surfaces of the camshaft with engine oil. Smear a little oil onto the lip of the oil seal. The oil seal can be located on the end of the camshaft at this stage, or alternatively installed later as described in Section 17.
6 Lower the camshaft onto the cylinder head and position the tachometer drive and seal so that it engages the slot (photo).
7 Apply a little silicone at the points where the oil seals contact the upper face of the cylinder head (photo).
8 Fit the bearing caps and rocker shaft assembly over the camshaft, and insert the dowel pins loosely to align the tachometer drive. Insert the bolts and tighten them evenly in diagonal sequence to the specified torque (photos).
9 Fully drive in the tachometer drive dowel, then insert and tighten the cross-head screws on the end cap.
10 Locate the Woodruff key in the slot and fit the camshaft gear.
11 Insert the bolt and washer, and tighten the bolt to the specified torque while holding the gear stationary with a lever or wide-bladed screwdriver inserted through one of the holes.
12 Adjust the valve clearances as described in Section 41.

38 Cylinder head – refitting

1 Make sure that the faces of the cylinder head and block are perfectly clean and that the ring dowels are correctly located (photo).
2 Fit the new gasket over the dowels and studs. Do not use jointing compound (photo).
3 Lower the cylinder head onto the gasket, and fit the nuts and bolts loosely.
4 Pre-tighten the nuts and bolts to the first stage specified torque in the sequence shown in Fig. 1.12, then tighten them to the specified final torque using the same sequence (photo).

37.1a Installing a valve seal

37.1b Note the marking (arrowed) identifying inlet or exhaust valve seals

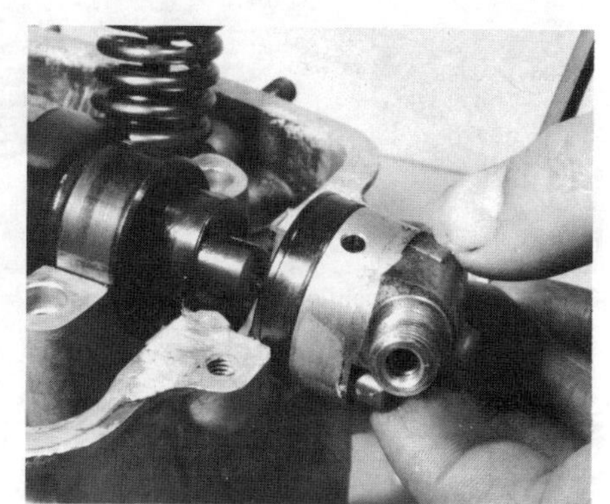
37.6 Fitting the tachometer drive

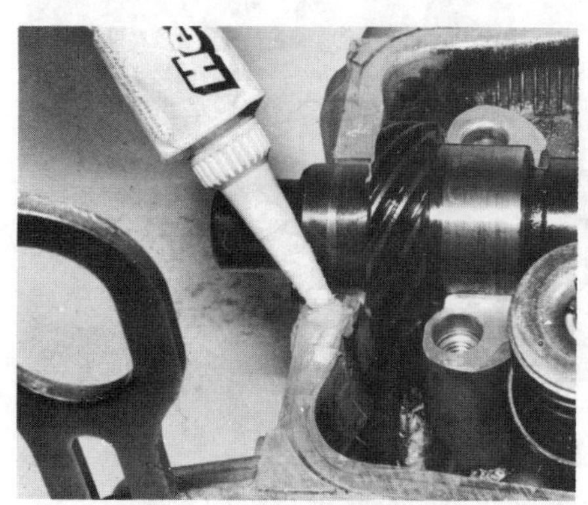
37.7 Applying silicone sealant to oil seal points on the cylinder head

37.8a Installing the rocker shaft assembly

37.8b Tightening the rocker shaft assembly bolts

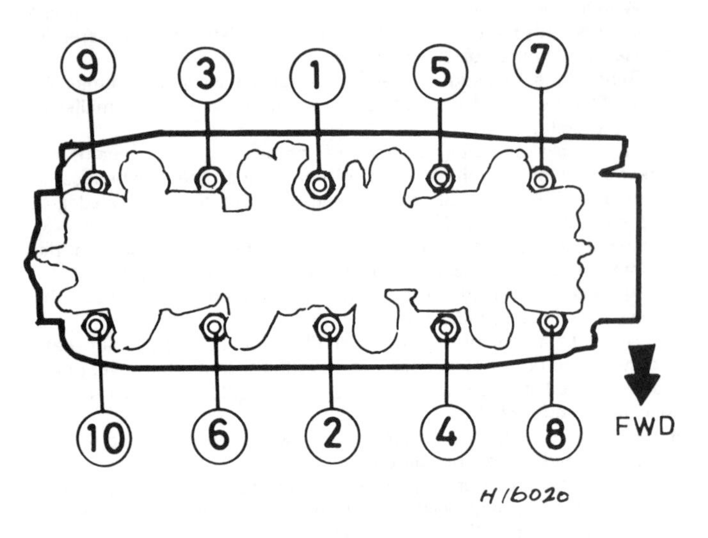

Fig. 1.12 Cylinder head tightening sequence (Sec 38)

5 Check that the white line on the crankshaft pulley is aligned with the rib on the lower timing cover, indicating that Nos 1 and 4 pistons are at TDC.

6 Check that the notches on the camshaft gear are aligned with the upper face of the cylinder head.

7 Slide the timing belt onto the camshaft gear. Tension the timing belt by loosening the tensioner bolts, turning the crankshaft anti-clockwise through 90°, then tightening the bolts.

8 Insert the oil pump drive gear and shaft through the cylinder head and into engagement with the oil pump and camshaft skew gear (photo).

9 Fit the retainer housing and tighten the bolts to the specified torque.

10 Fit the timing belt upper cover, together with a new gasket, and tighten the bolts.

11 Fit the valve cover together with a new gasket, install the brackets and domed nuts and tighten the nuts.

12 Refit and tighten the spark plugs. Fit the HT leads to the spark plugs and bracket.

13 If the engine is already in the car, reverse the preliminary procedures given in Section 8.

38.1 Ring dowel location in the cylinder block

38.2 Cylinder head gasket installed on the cylinder block

38.4 Tightening the cylinder head nuts and bolts

38.8 Oil pump drivegear and shaft located in the cylinder head

39 Ancillary components – refitting

Refer to Section 7 and refit the listed components with reference to the Chapters indicated.

40 Engine – refitting

Reverse the removal procedure given in Section 5, but note the following additional points:

(a) *Make sure that the driveshafts are fully entered (see Chapter 8)*
(b) *Tighten the engine mountings as described in Section 19, and make sure that the engine damper is mounted centrally*
(c) *Adjust the clutch cable (where applicable) as described in Chapter 5*
(d) *Fill the cooling system as described in Chapter 2*
(e) *Fill the engine and gearbox with oil*
(f) *Adjust the throttle and choke cables as described in Chapter 3*

41 Valve clearances – adjustment

1 With the valve cover removed, turn the crankshaft anti-clockwise until the notches on the camshaft gear are aligned with the upper face of the cylinder head. The centred lobe on the gear should be uppermost – see photo 10.4A. Use a socket on the crankshaft pulley bolt to turn the engine. (If the bolt becomes loose, select top gear or 'P' (as applicable) and re-tighten the bolt to the specified torque). With the camshaft in this position, No 1 cylinder valves are shut and the clearances may be adjusted on these valves. (Exhaust valves are on the front of the engine, inlet valves on the rear.)

2 Insert a feeler blade of the specified thickness between the rocker arm and valve stem. If the blade is not a firm sliding fit, loosen the locknut on the rocker arm with a ring spanner and turn the adjusting screw with a screwdriver as necessary. Tighten the locknut while holding the adjusting screw stationary, then recheck the adjustment (photo).

3 Rotate the crankshaft half a turn anti-clockwise so that one of the notches on the camshaft gear is aligned with the top web on the upper timing cover (or the centre of the camshaft bearing cap). The valves of No 3 cylinder are now shut and their clearances should be checked and adjusted as described in paragraph 2.

4 Rotate the crankshaft a further half a turn anti-clockwise (the camshaft will turn a quarter of a turn) and adjust the valve clearances of No 4 cylinder.

5 Finally rotate the crankshaft a further half a turn anti-clockwise and adjust the valve clearances of No 2 cylinder.

6 Check the valve cover gasket for damage and renew it if necessary, then refit the valve cover.

42 Engine – initial start-up and adjustment after major repair

1 With the engine refitted to the car make a final check to ensure that everything has been reconnected and that no rags or tools have been left in the engine compartment (photo).

2 If new pistons or crankshaft bearings have been fitted, turn the throttle stop screw in about half a turn to compensate for the initial tightness of the new components.

3 Pull the choke fully out and start the engine. This may take a little longer than usual as the fuel pump and carburettor float chambers may be empty.

4 As soon as the engine starts, push in the choke until the engine runs at a fast tickover. Check that the oil pressure light goes out.

5 Check the oil filter, fuel hoses, and water hoses for leaks.

6 Run the engine until normal operating temperature is reached, then adjust the slow running as described in Chapter 3.

7 If new pistons or crankshaft bearings have been fitted, the engine should be run-in for the first 500 miles (800 km). Do not operate the engine at full throttle or allow it to labour in any gear. Change the engine oil and filter at the end of the running-in period.

41.2 Adjusting the valve clearances

42.1 Correct routing of cables and hoses

'Fault diagnosis appears overleaf'

43 Fault diagnosis – engine

Symptom	Reason(s)
Engine fails to start	Discharged battery Loose battery connection Loose or broken ignition leads Moisture on spark plugs, distributor cap, or HT leads Incorrect spark plug gaps Cracked distributor cap or rotor Dirt or water in carburettor(s) Empty fuel tank Faulty fuel pump Faulty starter motor Low cylinder compressions
Engine idles erratically	Inlet manifold air leak Leaking cylinder head gasket Worn valvegear Faulty fuel pump Incorrect valve clearances Loose or broken crankcase ventilation hoses Slow running adjustment incorrect Uneven cylinder compressions Air cleaner choked
Engine misfires	Incorrect spark plug gap Faulty coil Dirt or water in carburettor(s) Carburettor adjustment incorrect Burnt out valve Leaking cylinder head gasket Distributor cap cracked Incorrect valve clearances Uneven cylinder compressions
Engine stalls	Carburettor adjustment incorrect Inlet manifold air leak Ignition timing incorrect
Excessive oil consumption	Worn pistons and cylinder bores Valve guides and inlet valve seals worn Oil leaking from valve cover, crankshaft oil seals, camshaft oil seal, or filter
Engine backfires	Carburettors adjusted incorrectly Ignition timing incorrect Incorrect valve clearances Exhaust system air leak Inlet manifold air leak Sticking valve
Engine lacks power	Incorrect ignition timing (check auto advance) Incorrectly adjusted spark plugs Low cylinder compression pressures Excessive carbon build up in engine Overheating

Chapter 2 Cooling system

For modifications, and information applicable to later models, see Supplement at end of manual

Contents

Specifications

System type
Pressurized with belt-driven pump, thermostatically-controlled electric cooling fan

Thermostat
Opening temperature ... 82°C (180°F)

Radiator cap pressure
13 lbf/in^2 (0.9 kgf/cm^2)

Drivebelt tension
0.5 to 0.7 in (12 to 17 mm) deflection between water pump and alternator pulleys under load of 20 to 24 lbf (9 to 11 kgf)

Electric cooling fan
Cut-in temperature ... 88.5° to 91.5°C (191° to 196°F)
Cut-out temperature ... 82° to 88°C (180° to 190°F)
Running current ... 6.0 to 7.5 amps

Coolant type/specification
Antifreeze to BS 3151, 3152 or 6580 (Duckhams Universal Antifreeze and Summer Coolant)

System capacity (including heater)
Total (from dry) ... 8.5 pints (4.9 litres)
Drain and refill ... 7.0 pints (3.9 litres)

Torque wrench settings

	lbf ft	Nm
Water pump	9	12
Water pump pulley	9	12
Inlet pipe to block	9	12
Thermostat cover	9	12
System bleed screw	9	12
Thermosensor (cooling fan)	17	23

1 General description

The cooling system is of pressurized type and includes a front-mounted radiator, a belt-driven water pump and an electric cooling fan. The thermostat is located on top of the inlet manifold. The radiator incorporates a drain plug at the bottom of the left-hand end tank; no drain plug is provided in the cylinder block. The radiator expansion tank is located on the right-hand side of the engine compartment and serves as an overflow container when the pressure in the cooling system exceeds the relief pressure of the radiator cap. Coolant is returned to the radiator as the pressure decreases. The expansion tank is not pressurized.

The system functions as follows. Cold water in the bottom of the radiator circulates through the bottom hose and the metal pipe to the water pump, where the pump impeller pushes the water around the cylinder block, cylinder head and inlet manifold. After cooling the cylinder bores, combustion surfaces and valve seats, the water enters the inlet manifold and, because the thermostat is initially closed, circulates through the bypass hose to the water pump inlet pipe. When the engine is cold, the thermostat remains closed and the water circulates only through the engine (and through the heater if it is set for heat). When the coolant reaches the predetermined temperature (see Specifications), the thermostat opens and the water passes through the top hose to the top of the radiator. As the water circulates down through the radiator, it is cooled by the inrush of air when the car is in forward motion, supplemented by the action of the electric cooling fan when necessary. Having reached the bottom of the radiator, the water is now cooled and the cycle is repeated.

The electric cooling fan is controlled by a thermosensor located near the bottom hose outlet on the right-hand side of the radiator. The coolant temperature gauge is served by a sender unit located beneath the inlet manifold.

2 Cooling system – draining

1 It is preferable to drain the cooling system when the engine has cooled. If this is not possible, place a cloth over the radiator filler cap and turn it **slowly** in an anti-clockwise direction until the first stop is reached, then wait until all the pressure has been released.
2 Remove the filler cap.
3 Move the heater temperature control on the facia fully to the right (ie maximum heat).
4 Place a suitable container beneath the left-hand side of the radiator.
5 Unscrew and remove the drain plug and washer, and drain the coolant into the container (photo).
6 Remove the windscreen washer bottle (1 screw), then lift out the expansion tank, remove the cap, and empty the contents into the container.

3 Cooling system – flushing

1 The cooling system should be flushed every 45 000 miles (72 000 km) in order to remove any scale or sediment which may restrict the engine waterways and reduce the efficiency of the system. In severe cases, when the coolant appears rusty and dark in colour, the system should be reverse flushed as described later.
2 Disconnect the inlet manifold-to-heater hose at the heater valve.
3 Insert a hose in the radiator filler neck, and allow water to circulate

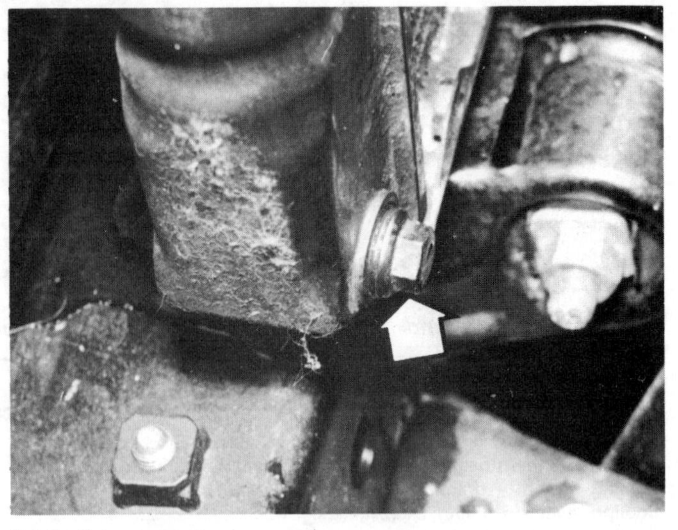

2.5 Radiator drain plug (arrowed)

through the radiator, engine and heater until it runs clear at the heater valve and hose.
4 Swill out the expansion tank and make sure that water runs freely

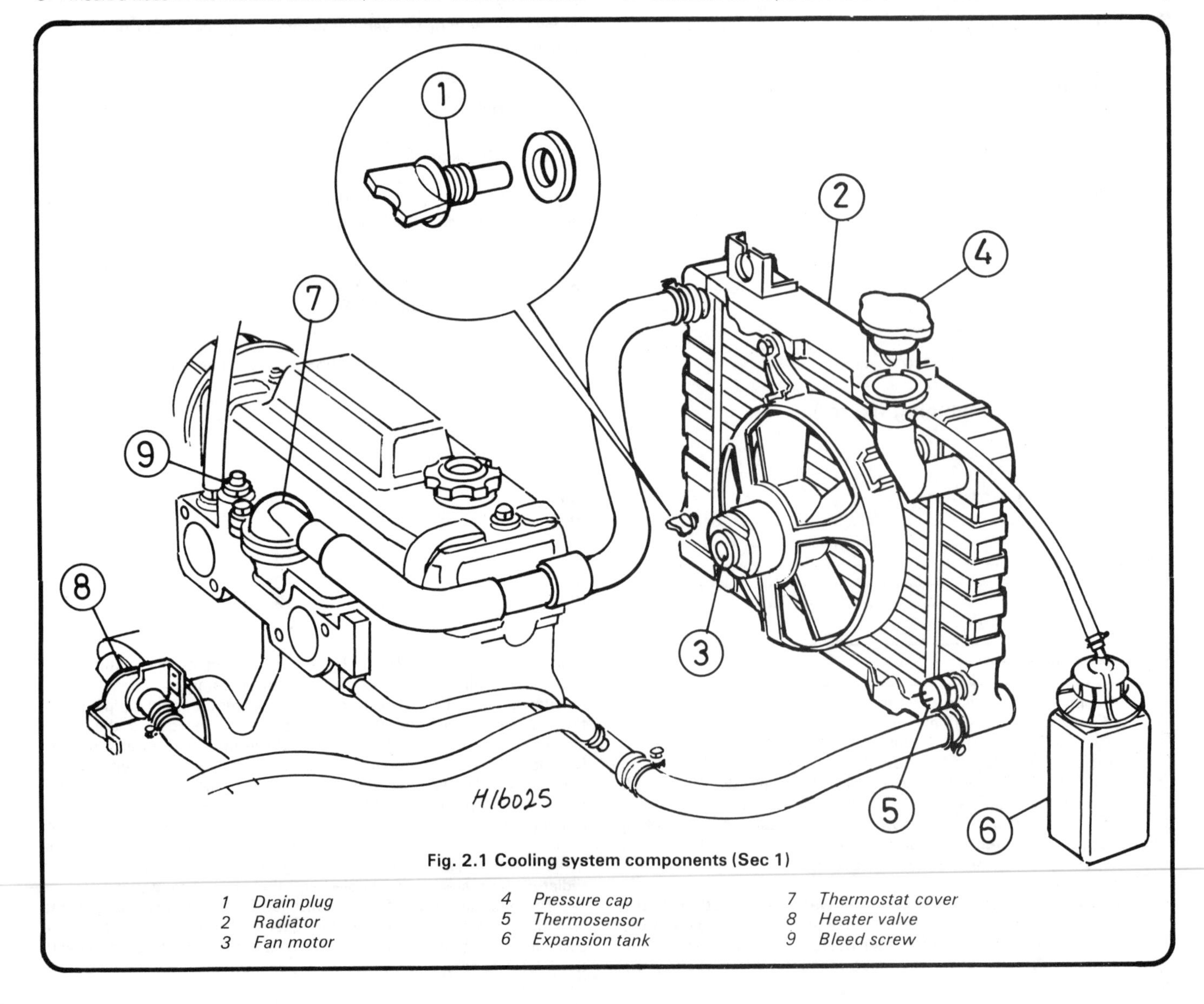

Fig. 2.1 Cooling system components (Sec 1)

1 Drain plug
2 Radiator
3 Fan motor
4 Pressure cap
5 Thermosensor
6 Expansion tank
7 Thermostat cover
8 Heater valve
9 Bleed screw

through the small hose to the radiator filler neck.
5 In severe cases of contamination the system should be reverse flushed. To do this, remove the radiator, invert it, and insert a hose in the bottom outlet. Continue flushing until clear water runs from the filler neck. Also reverse flush the engine by removing the thermostat, inserting a hose in the inlet manifold, and flushing until clear water runs from the bottom hose and heater hose.
6 If, after a reasonable period, the water still does not run clear, the radiator may be flushed with a good proprietary cleaning agent, such as Holts Radflush or Holts Speedflush. It is important that the manufacturer's instructions are followed carefully.
7 The regular renewal of antifreeze should prevent further scaling and contamination of the system.

4 Cooling system – filling

1 Refit the radiator and expansion tank, and thermostat if removed, then reconnect all hoses. Insert and tighten the radiator drain plug using a new washer if necessary.
2 Loosen the bleed screw located on top of the inlet manifold next to the thermostat housing (photo).
3 Pour coolant onto the radiator until it reaches the filler cap base sealing shoulder (photo).
4 When bubble-free coolant emerges from the bleed screw tighten it, then top up the radiator to the shoulder. Half-fill the expansion tank with coolant and refit the cap.
5 With the radiator cap removed, run the engine until normal operating temperature has been reached, indicated by the electric cooling fan having operated *twice*
6 Top up the radiator and refit the cap, then switch off the engine and allow it to cool.
7 Run the engine to operating temperature again and check the complete cooling system for leaks. If necessary top up the expansion tank to the maximum level mark (photo).

4.2 Cooling system bleed screw (arrowed)

4.3 Radiator filler cap showing the sealing shoulder

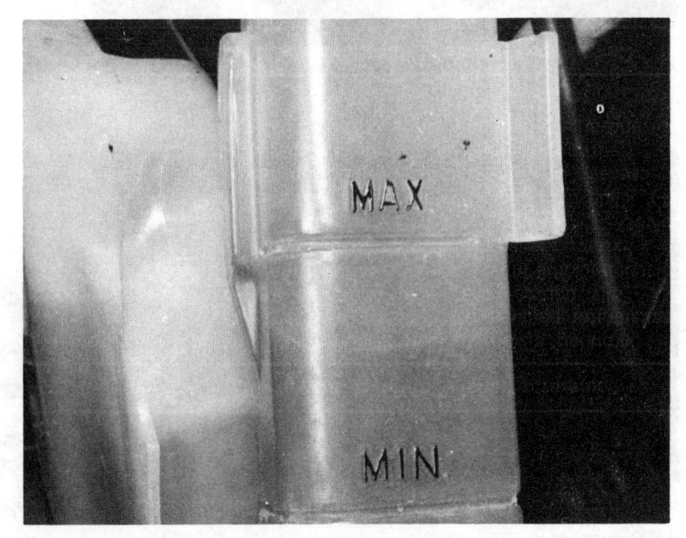

4.7 Radiator expansion tank markings

5 Antifreeze mixture

1 The antifreeze mixture should be renewed every 45 000 miles (72 000 km) or 3 years, whichever comes first. This is necessary not only to maintain the antifreeze properties, but also to prevent corrosion which would otherwise occur as the inhibitors become progressively less effective.
2 Always use an ethylene glycol based antifreeze (ie one containing no methanol) which also contains non-phosphate corrosion inhibitors suitable for use in aluminium alloy engines.
3 Before adding antifreeze, the cooling system should be completely drained and flushed, and all hose connections checked for tightness. Renew any doubtful hoses or clips.
4 The quantity of antifreeze and levels of protection are given in the following table. It is recommended that the antifreeze concentration should never fall below 50% by volume. Concentrations in excess of 60% by volume are not recommended since the efficiency of the cooling system is progressively reduced.

Concentration	Quantity	Commences freezing
50%	*4.25 pints (2.4 litres)*	*-36°C (-33°F)*
60%	*5.1 pints (2.9 litres)*	*-52°C (-62°F)*

5 After filling with antifreeze, a label should be attached to the radiator stating the type of antifreeze and the date installed. Any subsequent topping up should be made with the same type and concentration of antifreeze.

6 Radiator – removal, inspection, cleaning and refitting

Note: *If the reason for removing the radiator is concern over coolant loss, note that minor leaks may be repaired by using a radiator sealant, such as Holts Radweld, with the radiator* in situ.

1 Disconnect the battery negative lead.
2 Drain the cooling system as described in Section 2.
3 Disconnect the wiring from the electric cooling fan, and from the thermosensor located on the right-hand side of the radiator (photos).
4 On Trio-matic models disconnect the top and bottom oil cooler hoses from the radiator right-hand end tank. Plug the hoses and

6.3a Disconnecting the electric cooling fan wiring

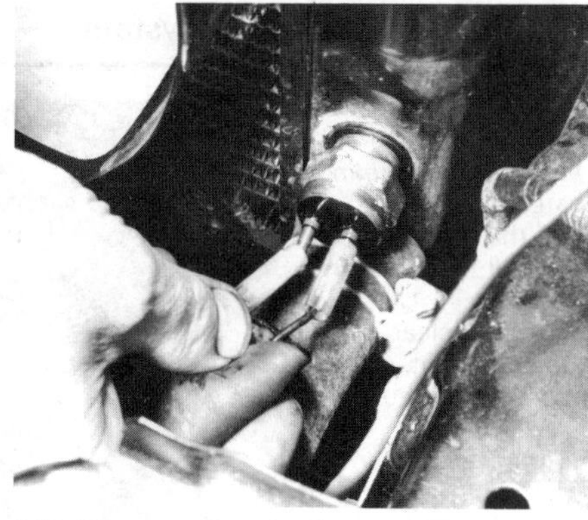

6.3b Disconnecting the thermosensor wiring

6.7 Radiator mounting bolt and air hose clip

6.9 Removing the radiator

6.10 The radiator and electric cooling fan assembly

6.11 Radiator rubber mounting

7.4 Removing the thermostat cover

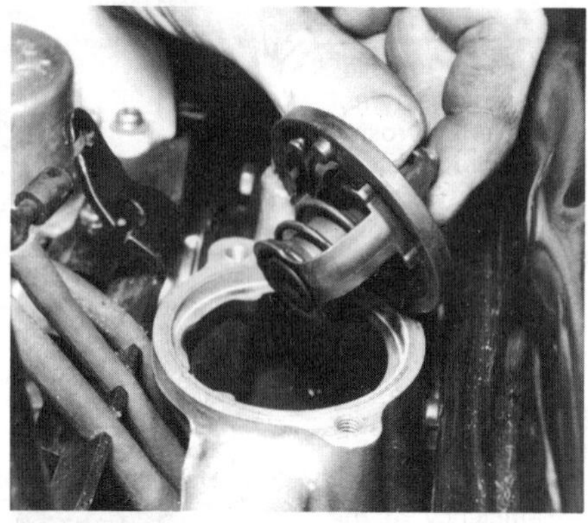

7.5a Removing the thermostat

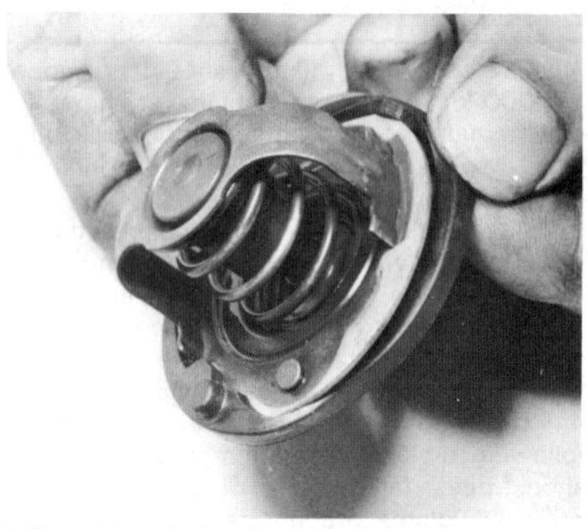

7.5b Prising the sealing ring from the thermostat

8.5 Removing the water pump pulley

8.6a Unscrew the mounting bolts ...

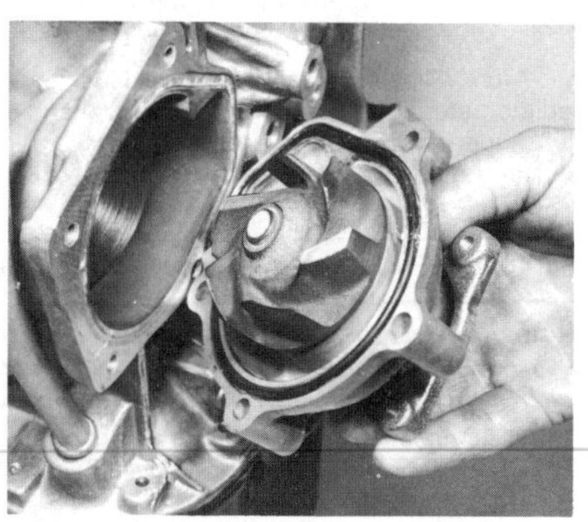

8.6b ... and withdraw the water pump

identify them for position to ensure correct refitting.
5 Loosen the clips and disconnect the top and bottom hoses from the radiator. Also disconnect the expansion tank hose (although this is unnecessary if the expansion tank cap is removed).
6 Unclip the air cleaner inlet hose from the clip on the radiator and move it to one side.
7 Unscrew and remove the radiator mounting bolts, noting the location of the air hose clip (photo).
8 On models equipped with air conditioning, unscrew the bolts and detach the additional cooling fan from the condenser.
9 On all models, lift the radiator from its location, taking care not to spill coolant on the bodywork (photo).
10 Unbolt the electric cooling fan assembly from the radiator (photo).
11 If necessary, prise out the rubber mountings from the top brackets and remove the thermosensor (photo).
12 Radiator repair is best left to a specialist, but minor leaks may be repaired or sealed using a proprietary coolant additive. Clear the radiator matrix of flies and small leaves with a soft brush or by hosing with water.
13 Reverse flush the radiator as described in Section 3. Renew the top and bottom hoses if they are damaged or have deteriorated, and also check the heater hoses and all hose clips. The wire hose clips fitted as original equipment tend to cut into the hoses after some time; use worm drive clips for preference.
14 Refitting is a reversal of removal. Fill the cooling system as described in Section 4.

7 Thermostat – removal, testing and refitting

1 Drain the cooling system as described in Section 2.
2 Remove the air cleaner complete as described in Chapter 3.
3 Disconnect the top hose from the thermostat cover – this is not essential but may be helpful if the gasket has to be cleaned from its surface.
4 Unbolt and remove the thermostat cover and gasket (photo).
5 Extract the thermostat and prise the O-ring seal from the housing. Also prise the sealing ring from the thermostat (photos).
6 To test whether the unit is servicable, suspend it with a piece of string in a container of water. Gradually heat the water and note the temperature at which the thermostat starts to open. Remove the thermostat from the water and check that it is fully closed when cold.
7 Renew the thermostat if the opening temperature is not as specified, or if the unit does not fully close when cold. Note that the opening temperature is usually stamped on the thermostat.
8 Clean all traces of gasket from the thermostat housing mating surfaces, and obtain a new gasket and O-ring seal.
9 Refitting is a reversal of removal, but use the new gasket and O-ring. Fill the cooling system as described in Section 4.

8 Water pump – removal and refitting

1 Disconnect the battery negative lead.
2 Drain the cooling system as described in Section 2.
3 On models equipped with air conditioning, remove the compressor and drivebelt as described in Chapter 12 and position the compressor to one side. **Do not** disconnect the refrigerant lines.
4 Remove the water pump/alternator drivebelt as described in Section 11.
5 Unbolt the water pump pulley from the flange, and remove the crankshaft pulley and upper and lower timing covers as described in Chapter 1 (photo).
6 Unscrew the mounting bolts and remove the water pump from the cylinder block together with the O-ring seal (photos).
7 If the water pump is faulty it must be renewed, as spares are not available to overhaul it. Remove the O-ring seal and clean the mating faces of the water pump and cylinder block.
8 Refitting is a reversal of removal, but use a new O-ring seal and tighten all bolts to the specified torque. Adjust the water pump/alternator drivebelt as described in Section 11. Where applicable refit the air conditioning compressor and adjust the drivebelt as described in Chapter 12. Fill the cooling system as described in Section 4.

9 Electric cooling fan and motor – removal, inspection and refitting

1 Disconnect the battery negative lead.
2 Unclip the air cleaner inlet hose from the clip on the radiator and move it to one side.
3 Disconnect the wiring from the fan motor.
4 Unbolt the electric cooling fan assembly from the radiator and carefully withdraw it from the engine compartment.
5 Extract the spring clip and withdraw the fan blades from the shaft.
6 Unscrew the bolts and separate the fan motor from the cage. Remove the bushes and spacers.
7 If the shaft bearings are worn excessively or if the motor is faulty, a new unit should be fitted. The motor can be checked for operation by connecting a 12 volt battery across the supply leads.
8 Refitting is a reversal of removal.

10 Cooling fan thermosensor – testing, removal and refitting

1 The thermosensor is located at the bottom right-hand side of the radiator. If it devlops a fault, it is most likely to fail open-circuited. This will cause the fan motor to remain stationary even though the coolant may reach boiling point.

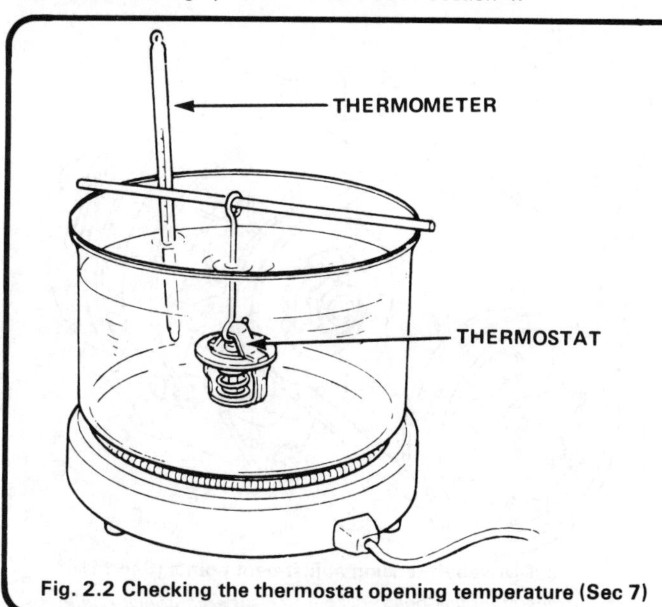

Fig. 2.2 Checking the thermostat opening temperature (Sec 7)

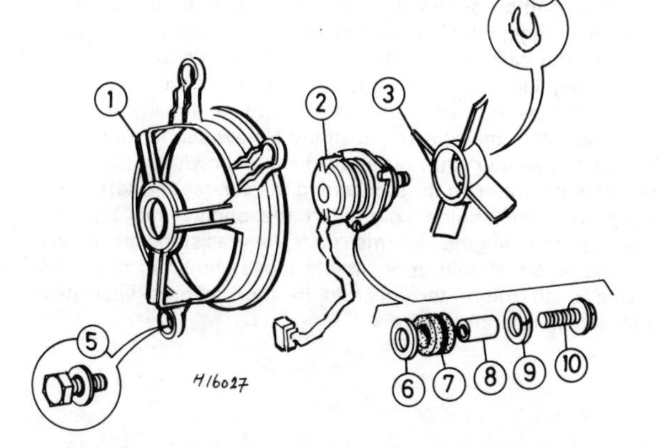

Fig. 2.3 Exploded view of the electric cooling fan (Sec 9)

1 *Fan cage*
2 *Electric motor*
3 *Fan blades*
4 *Spring clip*
5 *Bolt*
6 *Washer*
7 *Grommet*
8 *Spacer*
9 *Washer*
10 *Bolt*

2 To test for a faulty thermosensor, disconnect the supply wires and link them together. If the fan then operates with the ignition switched on, but refuses to operate normally within the cut-in and cut-out temperatures given in the Specifications, the thermosensor should be renewed. If the fan fails to operate with the ignition switched on and the thermosensor wires linked, check for a blown fuse, or on models with air conditioning for a faulty relay.
3 To remove the thermosensor, first drain the cooling system as described in Section 2.
4 Unscrew the thermosensor from the radiator and remove the washer.
5 Fit the new thermosensor using a new washer and tighten it to the specified torque.
6 Refill the cooling system as described in Section 4.

11 Drivebelt – renewal and adjustment

1 The water pump/alternator drivebelt should be checked for condition and tension every 7500 miles (12 000 km). Visually examine the complete drivebelt for cracking, then check that its tension is as given in the Specifications.
2 To remove the drivebelt, first disconnect the battery negative lead.
3 On models with air conditioning remove the compressor drivebelt as described in Chapter 12.
4 Loosen the alternator pivot and adjustment bolts, and swivel the alternator in towards the cylinder block.
5 Slip the drivebelt from the alternator pulley, water pump pulley and crankshaft pulley.
6 Fit the new drivebelt over the pulleys, then carefully lever the alternator away from the cylinder block until the specified tension is achieved (photo). The alternator must *only* be levered at the drive end bracket.
7 Tighten the adjustment bolt, then the pivot bolt.
8 Reconnect the battery negative lead, then run the engine for five minutes at 1000 rpm.
9 Recheck the drivebelt tension and adjust if necessary.
10 Where applicable, refit and tension the air conditioning compressor drivebelt.

11.6 Checking the drivebelt tension

12.5 Water temperature sender unit location on the inlet manifold

12 Water temperature gauge and sender unit – testing

1 If the water temperature gauge reads incorrectly, first check the gauge and wiring as follows. Disconnect the yellow/green wire at the sender unit (located beneath the inlet manifold) and connect it to a suitable earthing point.
2 Turn the ignition switch on for a few seconds and observe the needle of the gauge, which should move to the maximum (H) position. If this is not the case, renew the gauge, as described in Chapter 10.
3 If the foregoing test proves satisfactory, check the sender unit. An ohmmeter will be required and unless one is already owned, the cheaper alternative may be to substitute a new sender unit.
4 To test the sender unit, disconnect the yellow/green lead from it and having applied the ohmmeter lead to the sender unit terminal, take a reading with the engine cold. Start the engine and take further readings as the engine warms up. The resistances at various temperature levels should approximate those shown in the following table. Use a thermometer inserted in the radiator filler neck to establish the temperature levels.

Temperature	*122°F (50°C)*	*176°F (80°C)*	*212°F (100°C)*
Resistance (ohms)	154	52	27

5 If the sender unit fails to meet the resistance test, drain the cooling system and unscrew it from the inlet manifold (photo). Fit a new unit, then refill the cooling system and recheck the gauge.

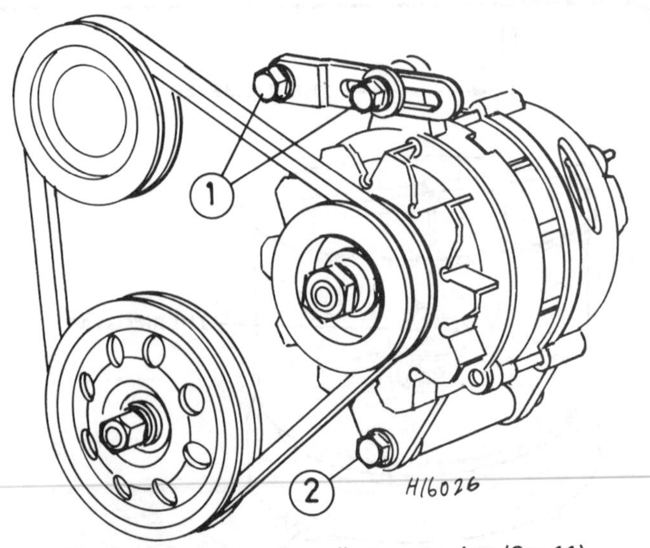

Fig. 2.4 Drivebelt tension adjustment points (Sec 11)

1 *Adjustment link bolts* 2 *Alternator pivot bolt*

13 Fault diagnosis – cooling system

Symptom	Reason(s)
Overheating	Low coolant level Faulty radiator pressure cap Thermostat sticking shut Drivebelt slipping Open-circuit thermosensor Faulty cooling fan motor Clogged radiator matrix Brakes binding Retarded ignition timing
Slow warm-up	Thermostat sticking open Incorrect thermostat
Coolant loss	Damaged or deteriorated hose Leaking cooling system gasket Blown cylinder head gasket Leaking radiator Faulty radiator pressure cap

Chapter 3 Fuel and exhaust systems

For modifications, and information applicable to later models, see Supplement at end of manual

Contents

Specifications

General

System type	Temperature-controlled air cleaner, twin sidedraught carburettors, mechanical fuel pump
Fuel octane rating	91 RON (UK 2-star)

Fuel tank

Capacity	10 gallons (46 litres)
Vent valve opening pressure:	
Vacuum side	0.02 kgf/cm^2 (0.28 lbf/in^2)
Pressure side	0.04 kgf/cm^2 (0.57 lbf/in^2)

Fuel pump

Type	Mechanical, diaphragm, driven by eccentric on camshaft
Delivery pressure	0.15 to 0.20 kgf/cm^2 (2 to 3 lbf/in^2)
Inlet suction	230 mm (9 in) Hg

Carburettors

Make and type	Twin Keihin, constant depression sidedraught
Float level	16 ± 1 mm (0.63 ± 0.04 in)
Jet sizes:	
Main jet - primary	85
Main jet - secondary	165
Main air jet - primary	130
Main air jet - secondary	60
Slow jet	38
Slow air jet	120

Air cleaner element

Air cleaner element	Champion W176

Adjustment data

Idle speed:	
Manual gearbox	800 ± 50 rpm
Trio-matic (in 'P')	900 ± 50 rpm
Fast idle speed	2400 ± 400 rpm
Exhaust gas CO level at idle	0.5 to 3.0%
Accelerator pump arm clearance	14 to 16 mm (0.55 to 0.63 in)

Torque wrench settings

	lbf ft	Nm
Inlet manifold - pre-tighten	7	10
Inlet manifold - final	16	22
Fuel pump	15	20
Fuel tank	16	22
Fuel tank drain plug	37	50
Exhaust manifold - pre-tighten	7	10
Exhaust manifold - final	16	22
Exhaust manifold flange nuts	37	50
Exhaust pipe clamp	16	22
Manifold shroud	9	12
Rear exhaust pipe joint	15	20

1 General description

The fuel system comprises a rear-mounted fuel tank, a camshaft-operated fuel pump, and twin Keihin constant depression sidedraught carburettors.

The air cleaner is of automatic air temperature control type, incorporating a disposable paper element and a condensation chamber which separates oil from the crankcase fumes. Hot air for the air cleaner is taken from an exhaust manifold shroud.

The inlet manifold is heated by engine coolant and incorporates the cooling system thermostat.

The exhaust system is in two sections, connected by butt flanges and a sealing ring. The front section incorporates the front silencer, and the downpipe is double-skinned in order to reduce exhaust noise. The rear section incorporates the rear silencer.

2 Air cleaner and element – removal and refitting

1 Unscrew the two wing nuts on top of the air cleaner and remove the washers (photo).

2 Release the spring clips and lift off the cover (photo).

3 Withdraw the element (photo) and discard it if it has completed 15 000 miles (24 000 km). Remove the gaskets.

4 Clean the interior of the air cleaner with a fuel-moistened cloth and wipe dry. Also clean the cover (photo).

5 To remove the air cleaner body, disconnect the cold and hot air inlet hoses (photo), the air temperature control vacuum pipe, and the crankcase ventilation hoses.

6 Release the brake servo pipe and the coil HT lead from the clips.

7 Unbolt the stay from the air cleaner.

8 Unscrew the mounting nuts from the inlet elbow studs and remove the washers. Withdraw the air cleaner and remove the two rubber insulators.

9 Clean all the components and wipe dry. The air temperature control flap is vacuum-operated by a temperature sensor located in the air cleaner body (photo). Check that the flap moves freely and that the vacuum pipes are in good condition (photo). The operation of the control flap is best checked with the air cleaner refitted but with the cold air supply hose disconnected. With the engine cold and idling, the flap should admit hot air from the exhaust manifold shroud, but with the engine hot it should admit only cold air.

10 Refitting of the air cleaner and element is a reversal of removal, but make sure that the sealing gaskets are correctly positioned and align the arrows on the air cleaner cover and body (photo).

3 Fuel pump – testing, removal and refitting

1 The fuel pump is located on the rear right-hand end of the cylinder head. Although the top cover may be removed, no fuel pump internal components are available from the manufacturers and in the event of faulty operation, the pump should be renewed complete.

2 To test the operation of the fuel pump *in situ*, first remove the air cleaner as described in Section 2, then disconnect the fuel outlet pipe. Disconnect one of the LT leads from the coil and spin the engine on the starter while holding a wad of rag near the outlet pipe. Well-defined spurts of fuel should be ejected if the pump is operating correctly, provided there is fuel in the fuel tank. **Take care** to avoid fire hazards during this test.

3 To remove the fuel pump, disconnect the battery negative lead. Identify the two pipes on the fuel pump, then disconnect and plug them (photo).

4 Note the location of the bypass hose bracket, then unscrew the mounting nuts and remove the washers and bracket (photo).

5 Withdraw the fuel pump, followed by the insulator block and gaskets (photo).

6 Clean the fuel pump and scrape all traces of gasket from the pump flange, insulator block, and cylinder head.

7 If necessary, the fuel pump can be dry tested using a pressure gauge and vacuum gauge. First connect the pressure gauge to the pump outlet and operate the pump lever through two full strokes. The specified delivery pressure should be obtained, with a maximum drop

2.1 Air cleaner cover showing wing nuts

2.2 Air cleaner cover spring clip and body stay

2.3 Air cleaner element

2.4 Interior of air cleaner body

2.5 Disconnecting the air cleaner cold air supply hose

2.9a Temperature-sensitive air bleed valve in the air cleaner body

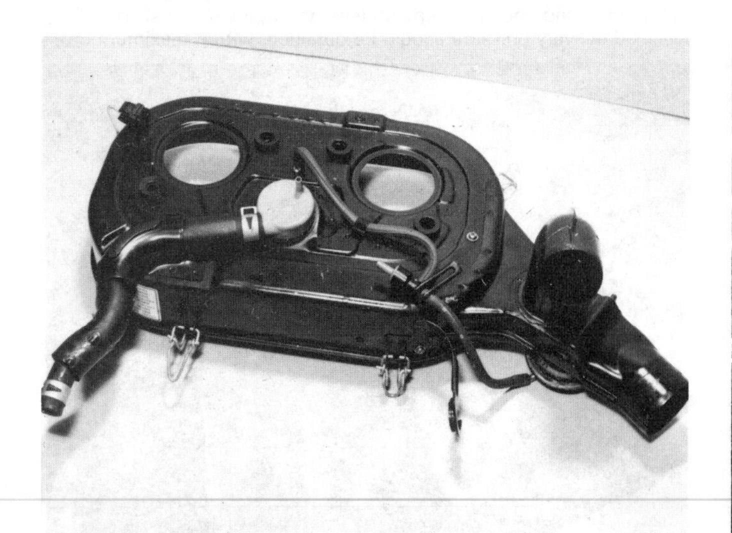

2.9b Air temperature control hoses (right) and crankcase ventilation oil separator (left on the bottom of the air cleaner)

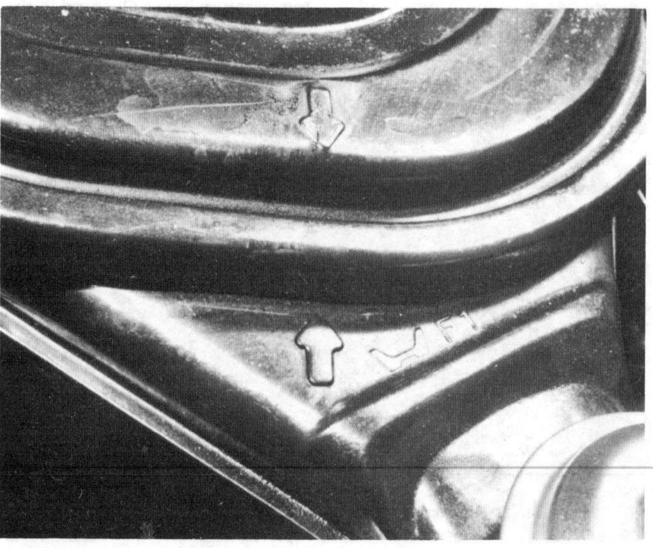

2.10 Alignment arrows on the air cleaner cover and body

3.3 Disconnecting the feed pipe from the fuel pump

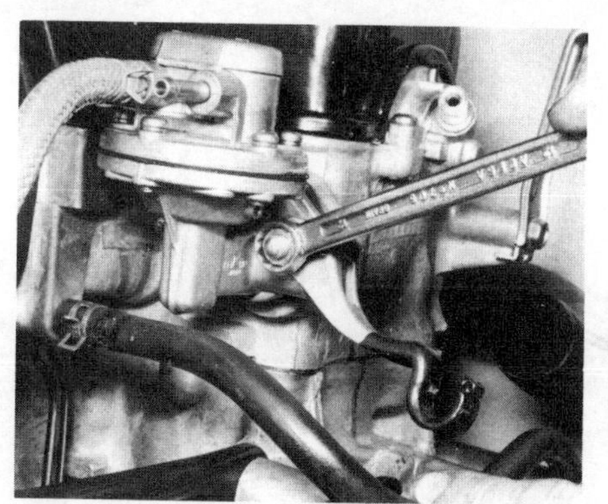
3.4 Removing the bypass hose bracket and fuel pump nuts

3.5 Removing the fuel pump

of 0.08 kgf/cm^2 (1 lbf/in^2) in five seconds. Now connect the vacuum gauge to the pump inlet and operate the pump lever through the full strokes. The specified minimum vacuum should be obtained, and it should not fall below 150 mm (6 in) Hg within five seconds.
8 Refitting is a reversal of removal, but use new gaskets.

4 Fuel tank – removal, servicing and refitting

Note: *For safety reasons the fuel tank must always be removed in a well ventilated area, never over a pit.*
1 Disconnect the battery negative lead.
2 Jack up the rear of the car and support it on axle stands. Chock the front roadwheels.
3 Remove the filler cap. Position a suitable container under the fuel tank, then unscrew the drain plug and drain the fuel (photos). Check the drain plug washer and renew it if necessary, then refit and tighten the plug.
4 Remove the left-hand rear roadwheel. Identify all the tank hoses for position.
5 Disconnect and plug the hoses from each end of the filter. Remove the filter from its mounting.
6 Disconnect the convoluted filler hose and the vent hose from the filler pipe.
7 Disconnect the breather hoses from the loop pipe, noting that the middle hose differs from the outer hoses.
8 Support the fuel tank with a trolley jack and remove the mounting bolts (photo).
9 Lower the fuel tank far enough to disconnect the wiring from the fuel gauge tank unit.
10 Remove the two-way vent valve hoses from the crossmember and separator, and unclip the valve from the top of the tank.
11 Lower the fuel tank and withdraw it from under the car.
12 Disconnect the remaining hoses, and remove the fuel gauge tank unit as described in Section 5.
13 If the tank is contaminated with sediment or water, swill it out with clean fuel. If it is damaged or leaks, it should be repaired by specialists or alternatively renewed. *Do not under any circumstances solder or weld a fuel tank.*
14 Refitting is a reversal of removal. Tighten the mounting bolts to the specified torque.

5 Fuel gauge tank unit – removal, testing and refitting

1 Remove the fuel tank as described in Section 4.
2 Using two crossed screwdrivers, turn the locking ring to release it from the tank, then carefully remove the fuel gauge tank unit and gasket.
3 Clean all traces of gasket from the tank and unit. Seal the tank aperture with a polythene sheet or similar if the unit is not to be refitted at once.
4 To test the tank unit, connect an ohmmeter between the live terminal and earth and check the resistances in various float positions as shown in Fig. 3.2. If incorrect readings are obtained, renew the unit.
5 Refitting is a reversal of removal, but use a new gasket and make sure that the unit is held stationary while the locking ring is tightened, otherwise the float may touch the internal pick-up pipe and give false readings. Refer to Section 4 for the fuel tank refitting procedure.

6 Choke control cable – removal and refitting

1 Remove the air cleaner as described in Section 2.
2 Pull the rubber dust cover from the engine end of the outer cable, and unscrew the locknut from the end of the ferrule (photo).
3 Pull out the outer cable and disconnect it from the bracket, then disconnect the inner cable and stop from the choke lever.
4 Remove the outer cable from the clip and push the cable grommet from the bulkhead.

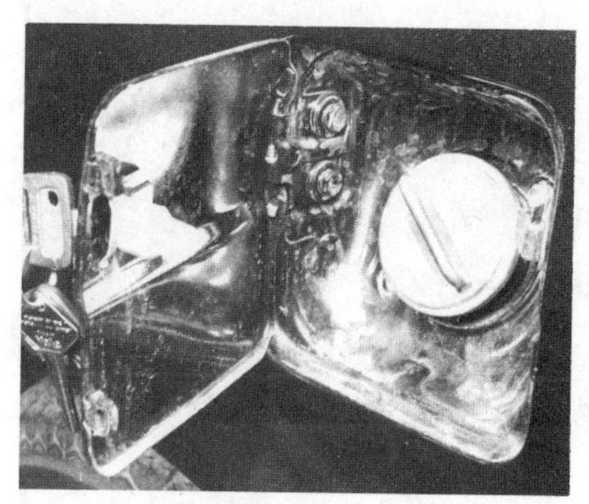
4.3a Fuel tank filler cap

4.3b Fuel tank drain plug

4.8 Fuel tank mounting bolts (only two visible)

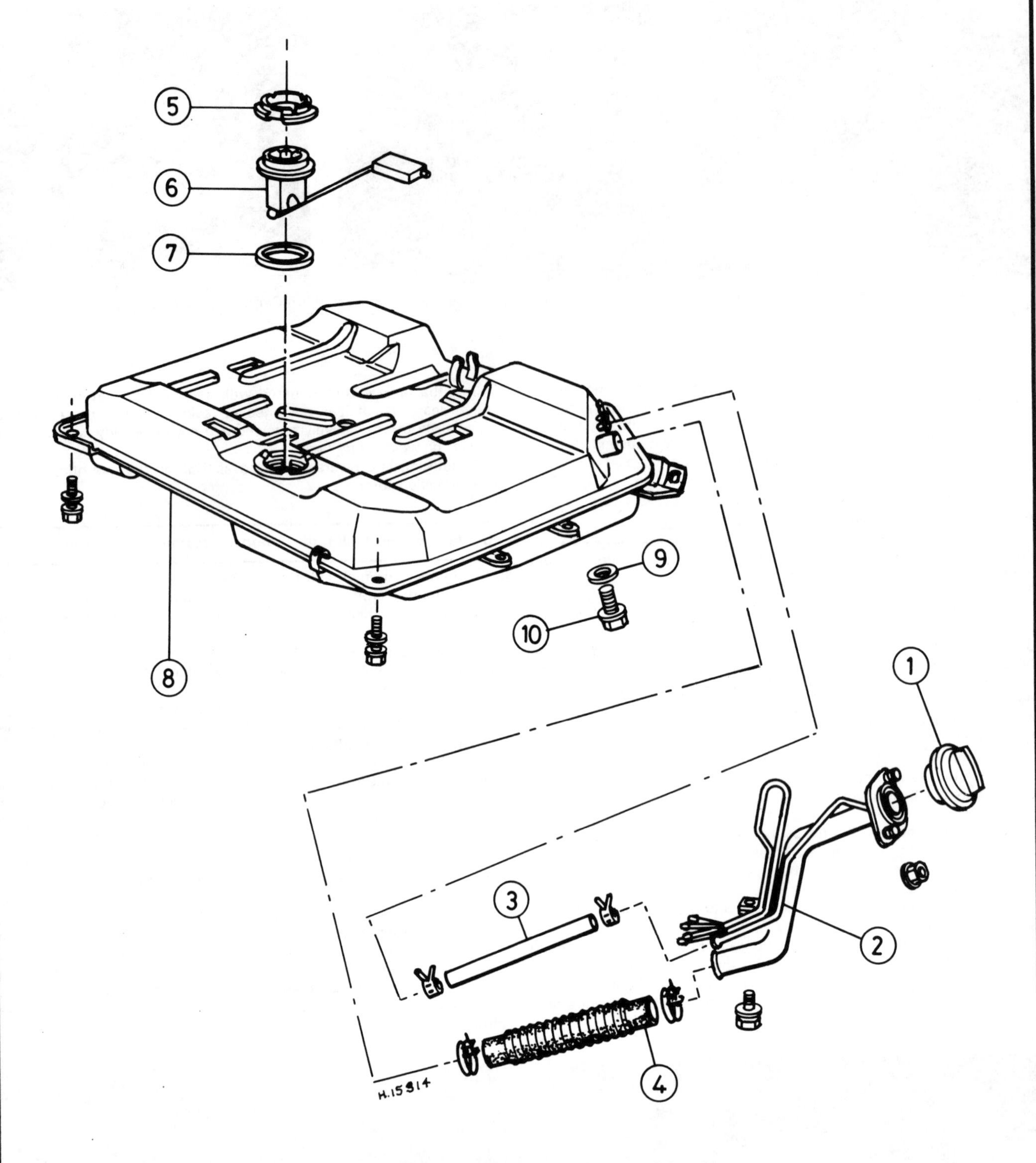

Fig. 3.1 Fuel tank components (Sec 4)

1 Filler cap
2 Filler pipe
3 Bleed hose
4 Filler hose
5 Ring
6 Fuel gauge tank unit
7 Gasket
8 Tank
9 Washer
10 Drain plug

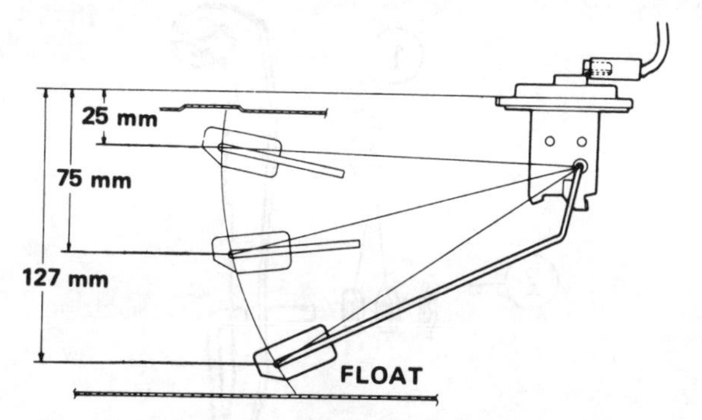

Fig. 3.2 Fuel gauge tank unit resistance test (Sec 5)

25 mm – 2 to 5 ohms
75 mm – 25.5 to 39.5 ohms
127 mm – 105 to 110 ohms

6.2 Choke cable fixing to carburettors. Adjuster is arrowed

5 Working inside the car, remove the lower panel from under the facia.
6 Loosen the small grub screw and remove the knob.
7 Unscrew the retaining ring and withdraw the cable from the facia.
8 Disconnect the choke warning switch wires and withdraw the cable into the passenger compartment.
9 Refitting is a reversal of removal, but adjust the position of the outer cable so that when the choke control knob is pulled out to the first detent, the line on the right-hand carburettor lever aligns with the line on the carburettor body.

7 Accelerator cable – removal and refitting

1 Remove the air cleaner as described in Section 2.
2 Pull the rubber dust cover from the engine end of the outer cable and unscrew the locknut from the end of the ferrule (photo).
3 Pull out the outer cable and disconnect it from the bracket, then disconnect the inner cable and stop from the throttle lever cam.

7.2 Removing the accelerator cable

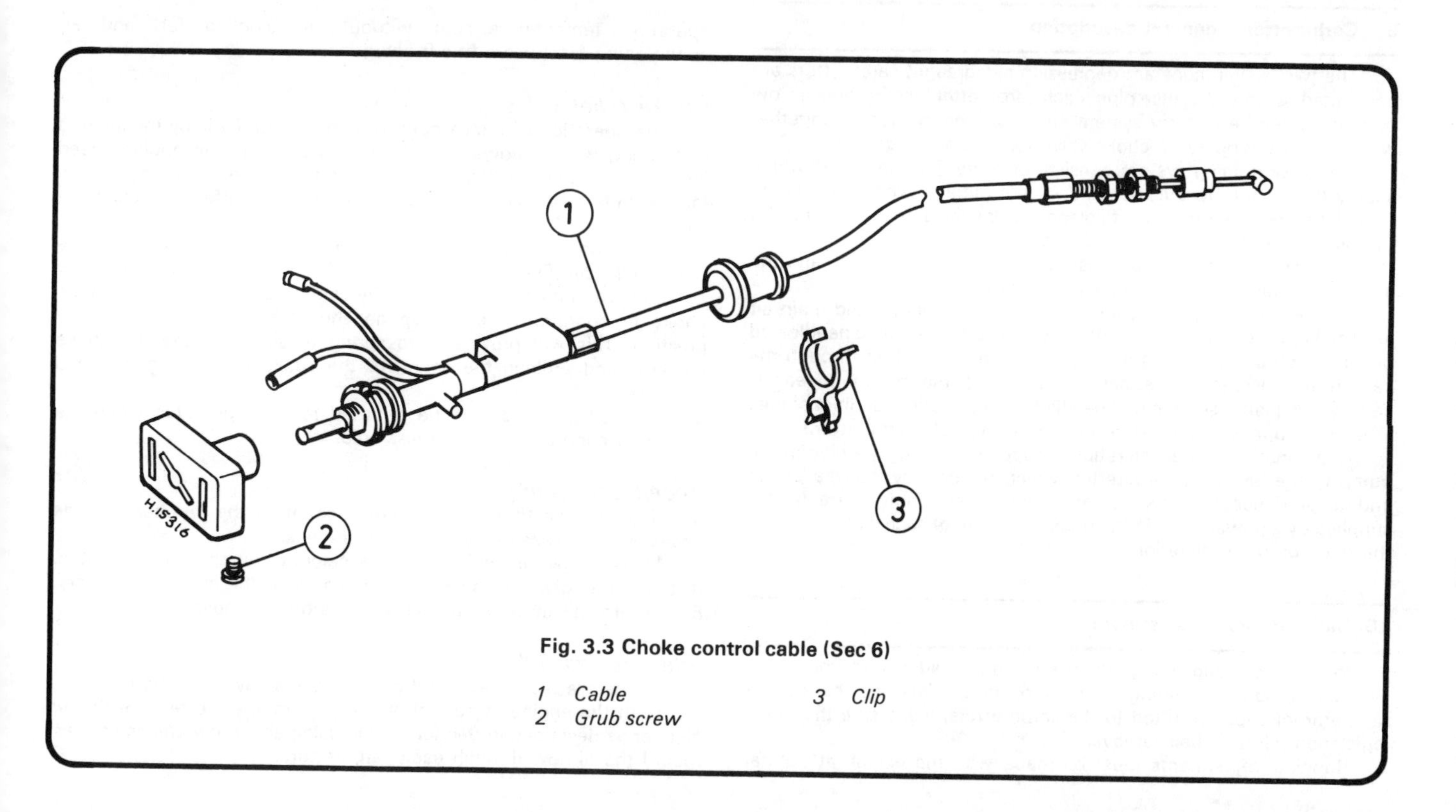

Fig. 3.3 Choke control cable (Sec 6)

1 Cable
2 Grub screw
3 Clip

4 Working inside the car, disconnect the inner cable and fitting from the top of the throttle pedal.
5 Remove the outer cable from the bulkhead and withdraw the complete cable into the engine compartment.
6 Refitting is a reversal of removal. Adjust the outer cable so that the inner cable has a deflection of 4 to 10 mm (0.2 to 0.4 in) midway between the end of the outer cable and the throttle lever cam.

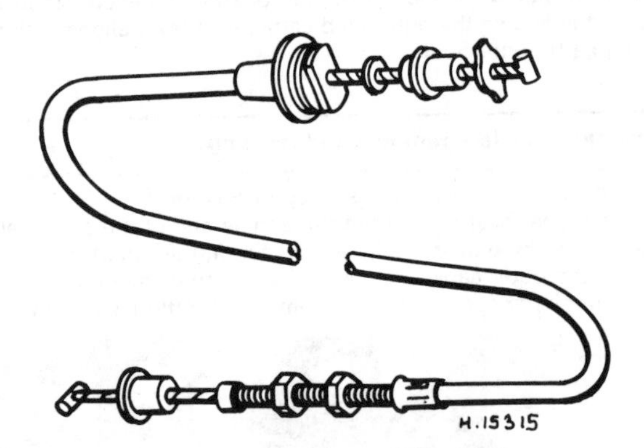

Fig. 3.4 Accelerator cable (Sec 7)

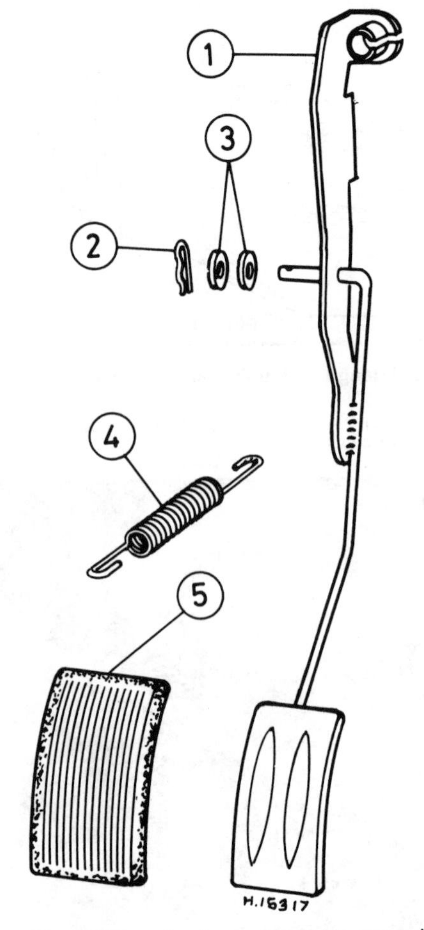

Fig. 3.5 Accelerator pedal components (Sec 8)

1 *Pedal*
2 *Spring clip*
3 *Washers*
4 *Return spring*
5 *Pad*

8 Accelerator pedal – removal and refitting

1 Working inside the car, disconnect the return spring from the accelerator pedal.
2 Fully depress the pedal and hold the inner cable extended, disconnect the inner cable and fitting and release the cable.
3 Extract the spring clip and remove the washer from the pedal pivot.
4 Slide the pedal from the bracket and remove the inner washer. If necessary, prise the pad from the bottom of the pedal.
5 Refitting is a reversal of removal. Lubricate the pivot with a little oil and adjust the cable as described in Section 7.

9 Carburettor – general description

The twin Keihin constant depression sidedraught carburettors are connected by an air balance pipe. Each carburettor incorporates a slow running system, a primary system and a secondary system, together with a manually-operated choke valve for cold starting.

The slow running system consists of a fuel jet and air jet which supply the mixture to the bypass and pilot outlets. When the ignition is switched off, the fuel cut-off solenoid stops the supply of mixture to the pilot outlet on the right-hand carburettor.

The primary system also consists of a fuel jet and air jet, and the mixture is supplied to the primary main nozzle.

The secondary system consists of the main fuel jet and main air jet. The supply of mixture is controlled by a vertical tapered needle and piston which act as a variable venturi. As the flow of air through the carburettor increases, the depression above the piston increases, causing the piston and tapered needle to rise and admit additional fuel. (The same principle is used in the well-known SU carburettor.)

Additional fuel for acceleration is supplied initially by a diaphragm pump in the left-hand carburettor, which temporarily lifts the piston and tapered needle. However after the initial supply, extra fuel is supplied by a power valve in the primary system of each carburettor for the duration of acceleration.

10 Carburettors – adjustments

1 Before adjusting the carburettors, make sure that the valve clearances, ignition timing and spark plug gaps are correct. If tamperproof caps are fitted to the carburettors, make sure that local legislation permits their removal.
2 Running adjustments must be made with the engine at normal operating temperature, but without the cooling fan and air conditioning fan (where fitted) operating.

Choke relief valve

3 The operation of the carburettor choke butterfly is by means of a coil spring which allows the butterfly to open as the engine speed increases, thus preventing an over-rich mixture. The coil spring may be located in two alternative positions which provide different choke relief settings.
4 Under normal conditions the coil spring should be located in the rear notch (see Fig. 3.6). If the engine is difficult to start in freezing conditions and misfiring occurs as the engine speed increases with the choke in operation, the coil spring should be moved to the front position. This will provide extra spring tension to close the choke butterfly and prolong the action of the choke as the engine speed increases.
5 The coil spring should be returned to the rear notch when the operating conditions become less cold.

Accelerator pump

6 Unscrew the throttle stop screw, counting the number of turns necessary to release its pressure on the link.
7 Measure the distance from the accelerator pump arm to the stop. If it is not as given in the Specifications, bend the arm as necessary.
8 Return the throttle stop screw to its original position.

Idle and fast idle

9 Connect a tachometer and exhaust gas analyser to the engine.
10 With the engine at normal operating temperature remove the air cleaner as described in Section 2, and using an airflow balance meter, record the airflow through each carburettor.

11 If the airflow is not equal on both carburettors, loosen the locknut on the right-hand carburettor and turn the airflow adjusting screw until the right-hand carburettor airflow equals the left-hand carburettor airflow. Tighten the locknut after making the adjustment.

12 Make sure that all electrical components are switched off. Increase the engine speed slowly to 2500 rpm and hold it at this speed for 30 seconds in order to clear the inlet manifold of excess fuel. During the remaining adjustment procedure, repeat this operation at three-minute intervals.

13 With the engine idling, check that the idle speed is as given in the Specifications. If not, turn the throttle stop screw located on the left-hand carburettor.

14 Switch off the engine and remove the tamperproof caps from the mixture adjustment screws.

15 Set the mixture adjusting screw on each carburettor to its initial setting by screwing it in until lightly contacting its seat, then backing it off two and a half turns. Do not screw it in hard.

16 Allow the engine to idle, then turn each mixture screw in or out by equal amounts to give the highest engine speed consistent with smooth running.

17 Readjust the throttle stop screw if necessary to regain the correct idling speed.

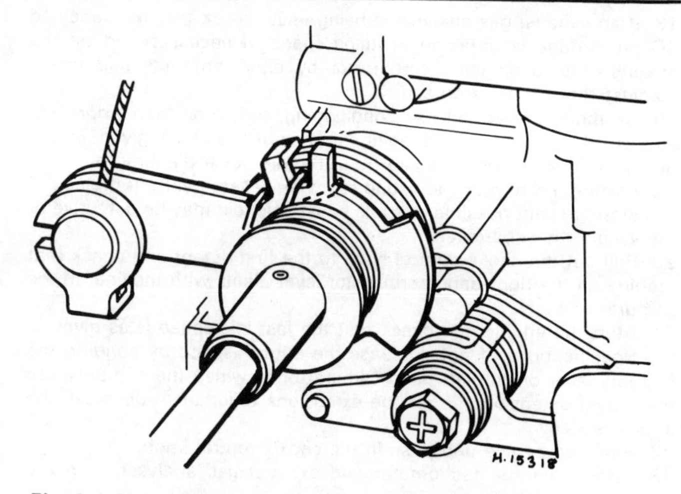

Fig. 3.6 Choke relief valve coil spring located in the rear notch – broken line indicates front position (Sec 10)

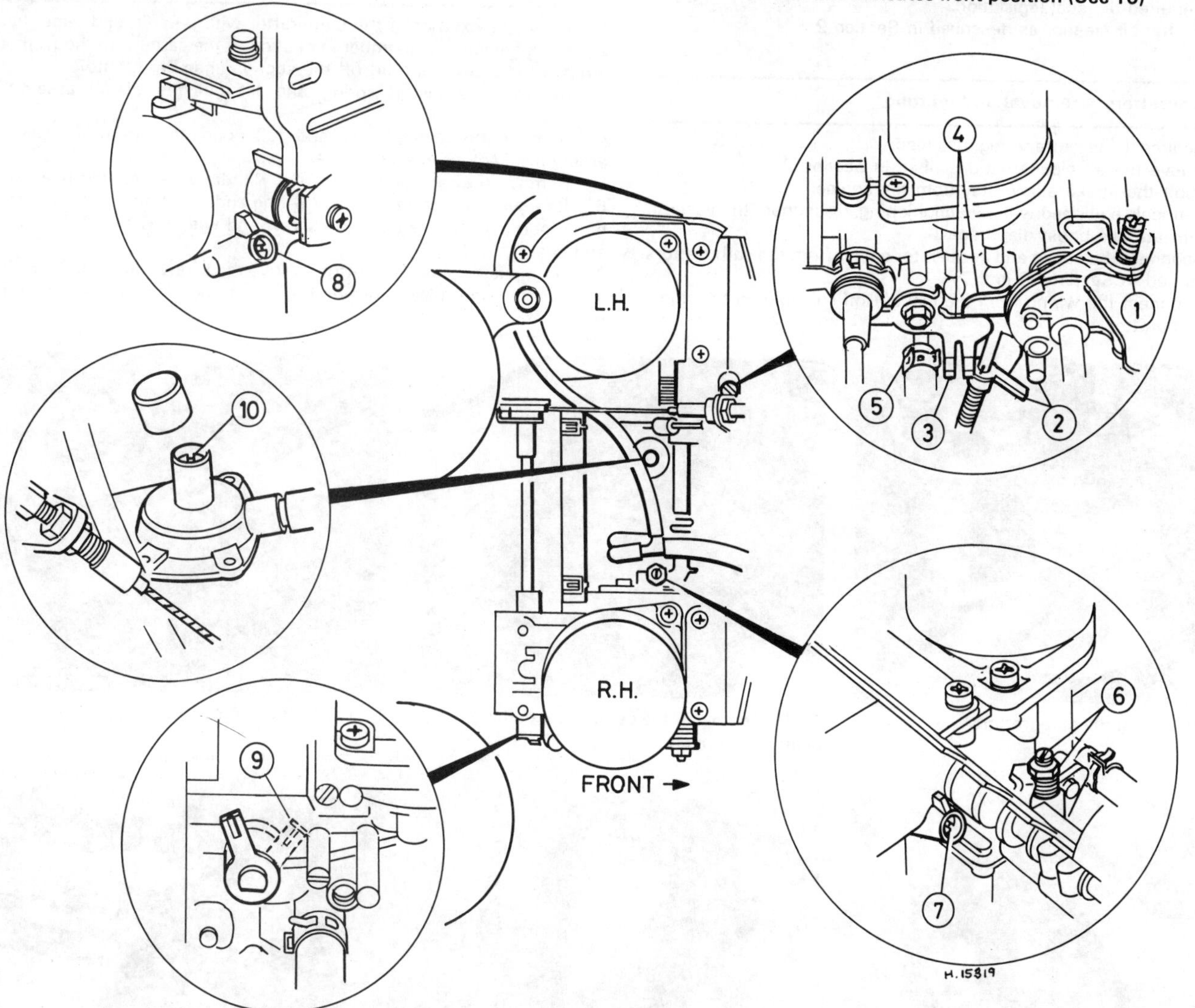

Fig. 3.7 Carburettor adjustment points (Sec 10)

1 *Throttle stop (idle speed) screw*
2 *Accelerator pump arm and stop*
3 *Fast idle adjustment slot*
4 *Fast idle and throttle levers*
5 *Fuel line*
6 *Airflow adjustment screw and locknut*
7 *Mixture adjustment screw (RH)*
8 *Mixture adjustment screw (LH)*
9 *Choke lever and alignment mark*
10 *Idle boost adjusting screw (air conditioned models only)*

18 If an exhaust gas analyser is being used, check that the specified CO percentage is obtained at idling speed. If necessary, adjust the mixture screws on each carburettor by equal amounts and finally readjust the throttle stop screw.
19 On models fitted with air conditioning, switch on the compressor and check the idle speed again. If it is not still as given in the Specifications, remove the cap from the idle boost diaphragm on the carburettor and turn the adjusting screw as necessary. Refit the cap. If adjustment is not possible, the idle boost solenoid may be defective or the vacuum hoses broken.
20 Pull out the choke control knob to the first detent and check that the line on the right-hand carburettor lever aligns with the line on the carburettor body.
21 Start the engine and check that the fast idle speed is as given in the Specifications. If not, increase the engine speed by bending the fast idle lever on the left-hand carburettor to widen the gap between the forked extensions. Press the extensions together to decrease the engine speed.
22 Stop the engine and push in the choke control knob.
23 Disconnect the tachometer and exhaust gas analyser from the engine.
24 Fit new tamperproof caps to the mixture adjustment screws where this is required by local legislation.
25 Refit the air cleaner as described in Section 2.

11 Carburettors – removal and refitting

1 Disconnect the battery negative lead.
2 Remove the air cleaner as described in Section 2.
3 Unbolt the intake elbow stay from the engine.
4 On models equipped with air conditioning, disconnect the vacuum pipe from the idle boost diaphragm.
5 Disconnect the choke and accelerator cables from the carburettors as described in Sections 6 and 7.
6 Disconnect the wiring from the fuel cut-off solenoid on the right-hand carburettor.
7 Where fitted, disconnect the vacuum advance pipe from the left-hand carburettor.
8 Disconnect and plug the fuel supply hose from the right-hand carburettor.
9 Loosen the screws on the retaining clips and withdraw the carburettors from the inlet manifold insulators (photo).
10 Remove the screws and withdraw the baffle plate and front stay (photo).
11 Remove the clamp screws and withdraw the intermediate fuel supply pipe from the carburettors together with the seals (photos).
12 Release the clips and remove the air balance pipe.
13 Unbolt the intake elbows and recover the sealing rings (photo).
14 Loosen the throttle link connection and separate the carburettors (photo).
15 Refitting is a reversal of removal. When connecting the carburettors together, make sure that the tongue on the choke link rod engages the slot. Adjust the choke and accelerator cables as described in Sections 6 and 7. When completed, adjust the carburettors as described in Section 10.

12 Carburettor – dismantling, overhaul and reassembly

1 Wash the exterior of the carburettor with paraffin and wipe dry.
2 Mark the suction chamber in relation to the carburettor body, then remove the screws and lift off the suction chamber (photo).
3 Remove the piston spring and lift out the piston assembly (photos).
4 Remove the spring seat and full open stop from the piston assembly. Remove the O-ring seal.
5 Remove the retaining screw and withdraw the tapered needle.
6 Remove the suction chamber O-ring and seat from the carburettor body (photos), then remove the screw and withdraw the air jet cover and seal.
7 On the left-hand carburettor remove the screws and withdraw the accelerator pump cover, followed by the spring, diaphragm and pump rod.

11.9 Removing the carburettors

11.10 Removing the carburettor baffle plate and front stay

11.11a Remove the clamp screws ...

11.11b ... the intermediate fuel supply pipe, and seals

11.13 Removing the intake elbow from the carburettors

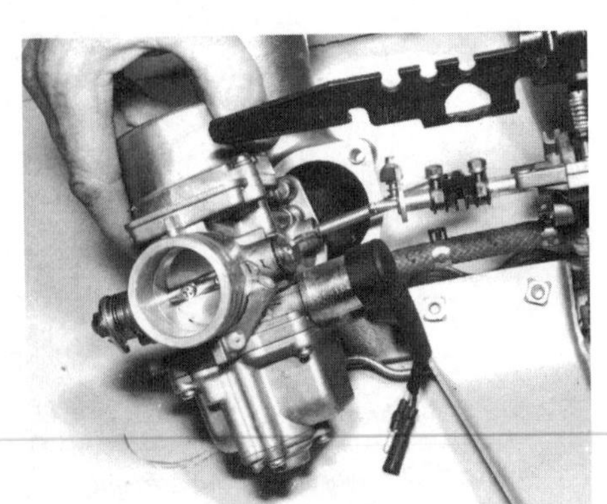
11.14 Separating the carburettors

8 Remove the screws and withdraw the power valve cover, followed by the spring, diaphragm and O-ring. Also remove the fuel cut-off solenoid from the right-hand carburettor (photos).
9 Remove the screws and withdraw the float chamber and gasket (photo).
10 Unscrew and remove the power valve, primary main jet, secondary main jet and jet needle holder, secondary main nozzle, primary main nozzle, and the slow jet.
11 Pull out the spindle, then remove the float and needle valve (photos).
12 Unscrew and remove the needle valve seat and O-ring seal.
13 Remove the mixture screw, noting the number of turns necessary to remove it.
14 Clean all the components in solvent and allow to dry. Thoroughly examine the components for damage and excessive wear. Check the carburettor body for cracks and security of brass items, and check the throttle spindle and bearings for wear – the main body is not supplied as a separate part and if faulty, a new carburettor will be required (photos). Check the needle valve and seating for excessive ridging. Shake the float and listen for any trapped fuel which may have entered through a small crack or fracture. Renew the components as necessary and obtain a complete set of gaskets and seals. Make sure that all jets and internal drillings are free of obstructions by using air pressure from an air line or tyre pump.
15 During reassembly all bearing surfaces should be lightly lubricated with engine oil.
16 Reassembly is a reversal of dismantling, but after fitting the float, adjust the float height as follows. Hold the carburettor so that the float hangs down and is lightly contacting the needle valve, then measure the distance from the carburettor face to the mid-point of the top of the float (photo). If the dimension is not as given in the Specifications, carefully bend the float tab as necessary.

12.2 Removing the suction chamber

12.3a Removing the spring ...

12.3b ... and piston

12.6a Removing the suction chamber O-ring ...

12.6b ... and the seat

12.8a Removing the power valve cover ...

12.8b ... the spring ...

12.8c ... the diaphragm ...

12.8d ... the O-ring (in foreground) ...

12.8e ... and the fuel cut-off solenoid

12.9 Removing the float chamber

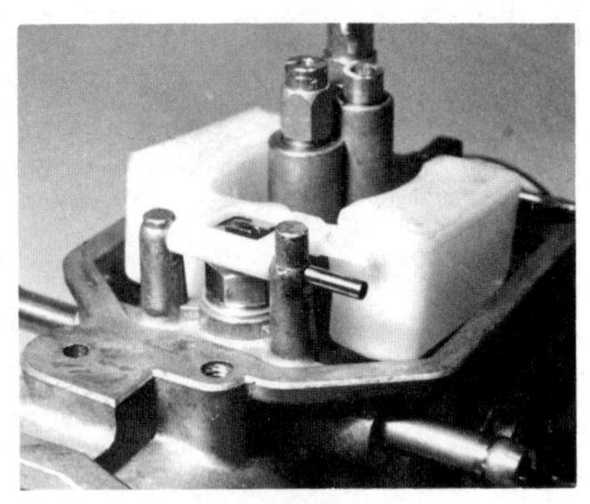
12.11a Pull out the spindle ...

12.11b ... and remove the float

12.14a Top view of the dismantled right-hand carburettor

12.14b Right-hand view of dismantled right-hand carburettor

12.14c Left-hand view of dismantled right-hand carburettor

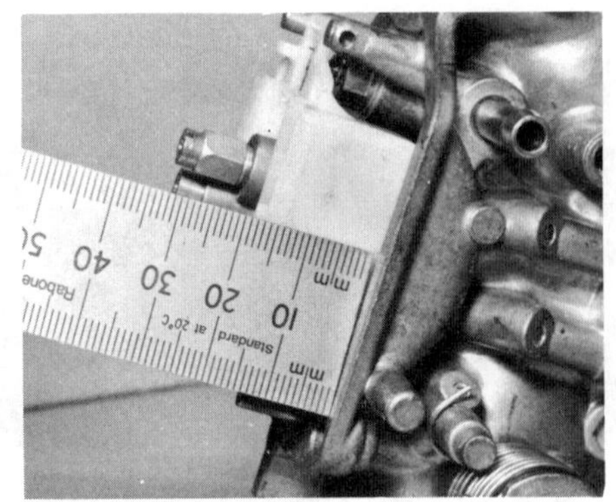
12.16 Checking the float height

13 Inlet manifold – removal and refitting

1 Remove the carburettors as described in Section 11.
2 Drain the cooling system as described in Chapter 2.
3 Disconnect the wiring from the temperature transmitter.
4 Remove the distributor as described in Chapter 4.
5 On models equipped with air conditioning, disconnect the idle boost solenoid vacuum pipes.
6 Disconnect the top hose from the thermostat housing and the heater return hose from the bottom of the inlet manifold. Disconnect the bypass hose and brake servo pipe.
7 Note the location of the HT lead bracket and pipe clip, then unscrew the mounting nuts and withdraw the inlet manifold from the studs on the cylinder head (photos).
8 Remove the gaskets and clean the mating faces of the inlet manifold and cylinder head (photo). Remove the thermostat as described in Chapter 2. Unbolt the carburettor insulators and remove the O-ring seals.
9 Refitting is a reversal of removal, but use new gaskets and tighten the mounting nuts in two stages to the specified torque, using the sequence shown in Fig. 3.11. Adjust the choke control and accelerator cables as described in Sections 6 and 7. Fill the cooling system as described in Chapter 2.

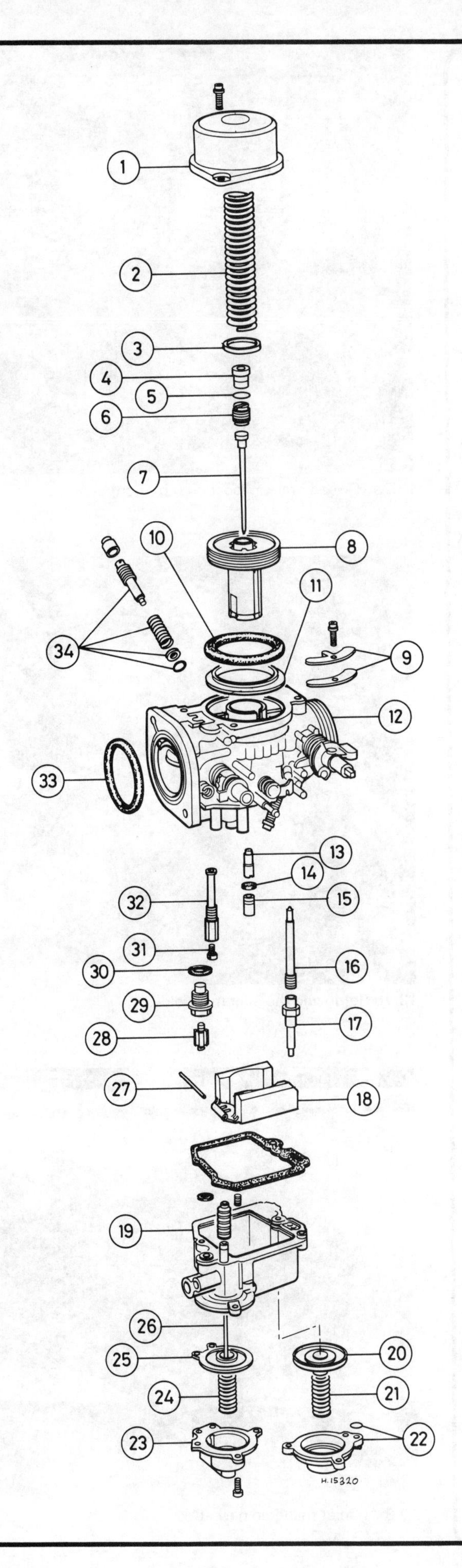

Fig. 3.8 Exploded view of the carburettor (Sec 12)

1 *Suction chamber*
2 *Piston spring*
3 *Spring seat*
4 *Full open stop*
5 *O-ring*
6 *Needle retaining screw*
7 *Needle*
8 *Piston*
9 *Air jet cover seal*
10 *O-ring*
11 *Seal seat*
12 *Carburettor body*
13 *Slow jet*
14 *O-ring*
15 *Primary main jet*
16 *Primary main nozzle*
17 *Power valve*
18 *Float*
19 *Float chamber*
20 *Power valve diaphragm*
21 *Power valve spring*
22 *Power valve cover*
23 *Accelerator pump cover**
24 *Accelerator pump spring**
25 *Accelerator pump diaphragm**
26 *Accelerator pump rod**
27 *Float spindle*
28 *Needle valve*
29 *Needle valve seat*
30 *O-ring*
31 *Secondary main jet*
32 *Jet needle holder*
33 *O-ring*
34 *Mixture control screw*
** LH carb only*

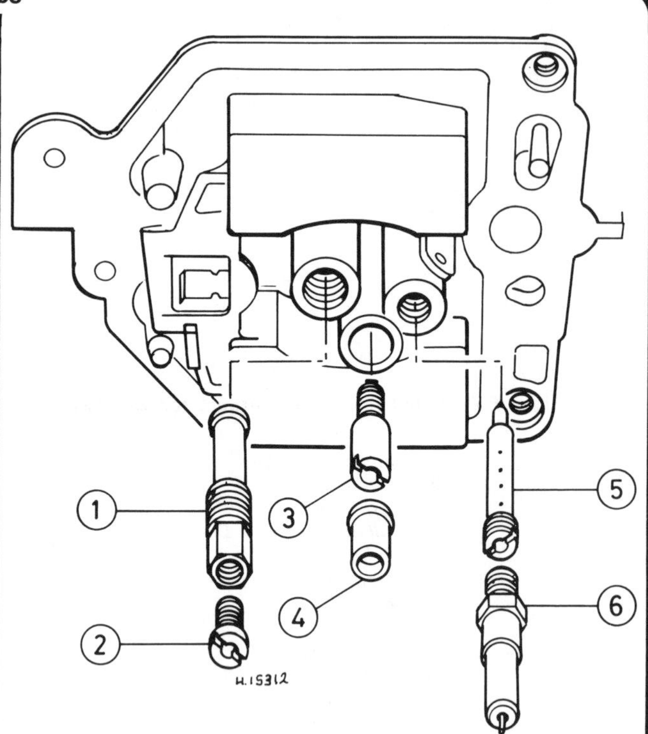

Fig. 3.9 Jet locations in the carburettor body (Sec 12)

1	*Jet needle holder*	4	*Primary main jet*
2	*Secondary main jet*	5	*Primary main nozzle*
3	*Slow jet*	6	*Power valve*

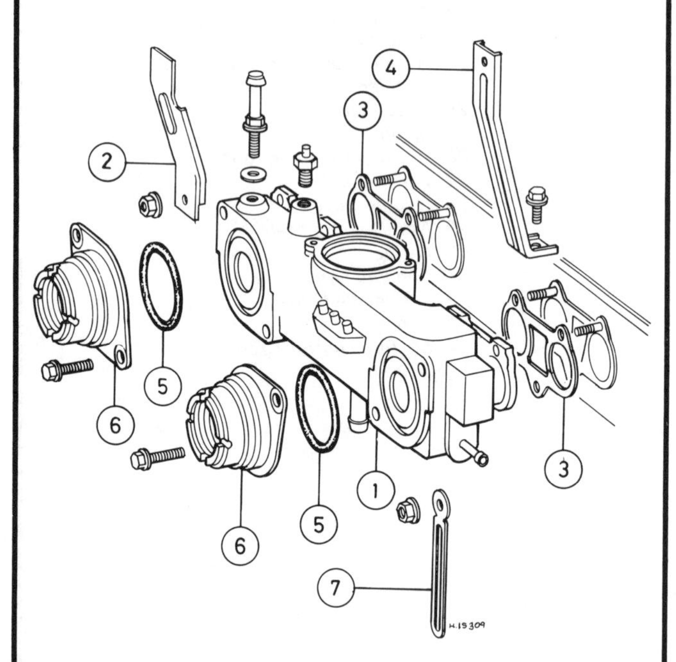

Fig. 3.10 Inlet manifold components (Sec 13)

1	*Inlet manifold*	5	*O-rings*
2	*HT lead bracket*	6	*Insulators*
3	*Gaskets*	7	*Pipe clip*
4	*Air cleaner bracket*		

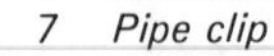

13.7a HT lead bracket location (arrowed)

13.7b Removing the inlet manifold

13.8 An inlet manifold gasket

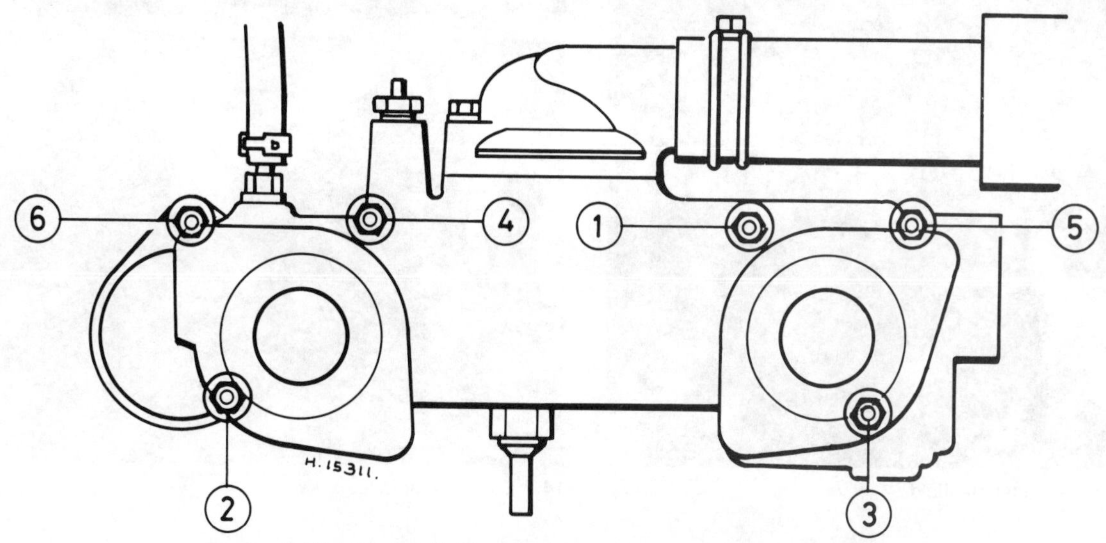

Fig. 3.11 Inlet manifold mounting nut tightening sequence (Sec 13)

14 Exhaust manifold – removal and refitting

1 Disconnect the battery negative lead.
2 Unbolt the exhaust pipe front mounting clamp located below the manifold.
3 Unscrew the flange nuts and lower the exhaust pipe from the manifold. Recover the sealing ring.
4 On models equipped with air conditioning, remove the cooling fan and support bracket, and the compressor support bracket.
5 Disconnect the hot air pipe from the manifold shroud, then unbolt the shroud from the manifold (photo).
6 Unscrew the mounting nuts, noting that the longer nuts are located on the left-hand studs. Withdraw the exhaust manifold from the studs on the cylinder head (photos).
7 Remove the gaskets and clean the mating faces of the exhaust manifold and cylinder head (photo). Also clean the flange faces of the manifold and exhaust pipe.
8 Refitting is a reversal of removal, but use new gaskets and, if necessary, a new sealing ring. Tighten the mounting nuts in two stages to the specified torque, using the sequence shown in Fig. 3.13 – on models equipped with air conditioning this must be carried out before tightening the compressor mounting bolts.

15 Exhaust system – checking, removal and refitting

1 The exhaust system should be examined for leaks and damage, and checked for security, every 7500 miles (12 000 km). To do this, apply the handbrake and allow the engine to idle. Check the full length of the exhaust system from each side while an assistant temporarily places a wad of cloth over the tailpipe. If a leak is evident, stop the engine, and use a good proprietary repair kit to seal it. Holts Flexiwrap and Holts Gun Gum exhaust repair systems can be used for effective repairs to exhaust pipes and silencer boxes, including ends and bends. Holts Flexiwrap is an MOT-approved permanent exhaust repair. If the leak is large, or if serious damage is evident, it may be better to renew the relevant exhaust section. Check the rubber mountings for deterioration, and renew if necessary.
2 To remove the exhaust system, jack up the front and rear of the car and support it on axle stands. Alternatively, locate the front wheels on car ramps, then jack up the rear and support with axle stands.
3 Unscrew the nuts from the flange connecting the front section to the rear section (photo).
4 Release the rubber mountings and withdraw the rear exhaust section (photo). Recover the flange sealing ring.
5 Unbolt the front exhaust pipe mounting clamp and bracket located below the exhaust manifold (photos).
6 Unscrew the flange nuts and lower the exhaust pipe from the manifold. Recover the sealing ring (photos).
7 Unscrew the nut, disconnect the mounting bracket from the

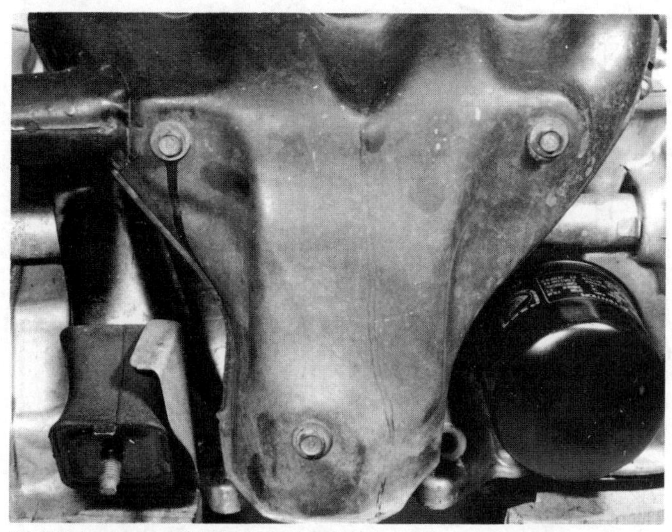
14.5 Exhaust manifold hot air shroud

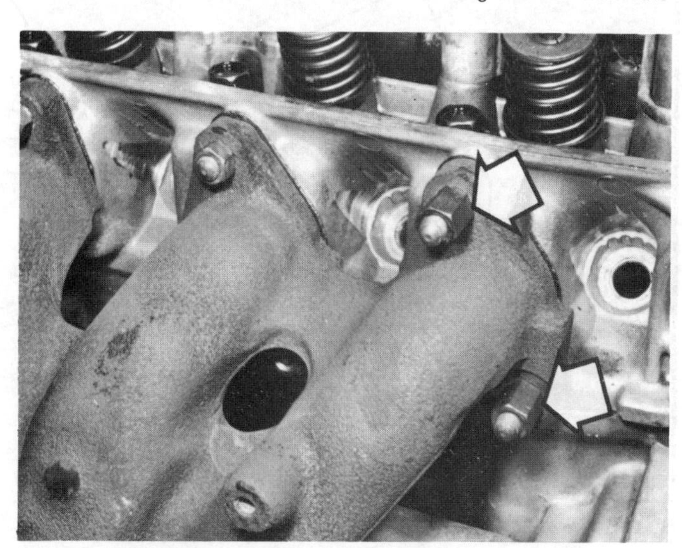
14.6a Note the location of the long nuts (arrowed)

14.6b Removing the exhaust manifold

14.7 Exhaust manifold gaskets

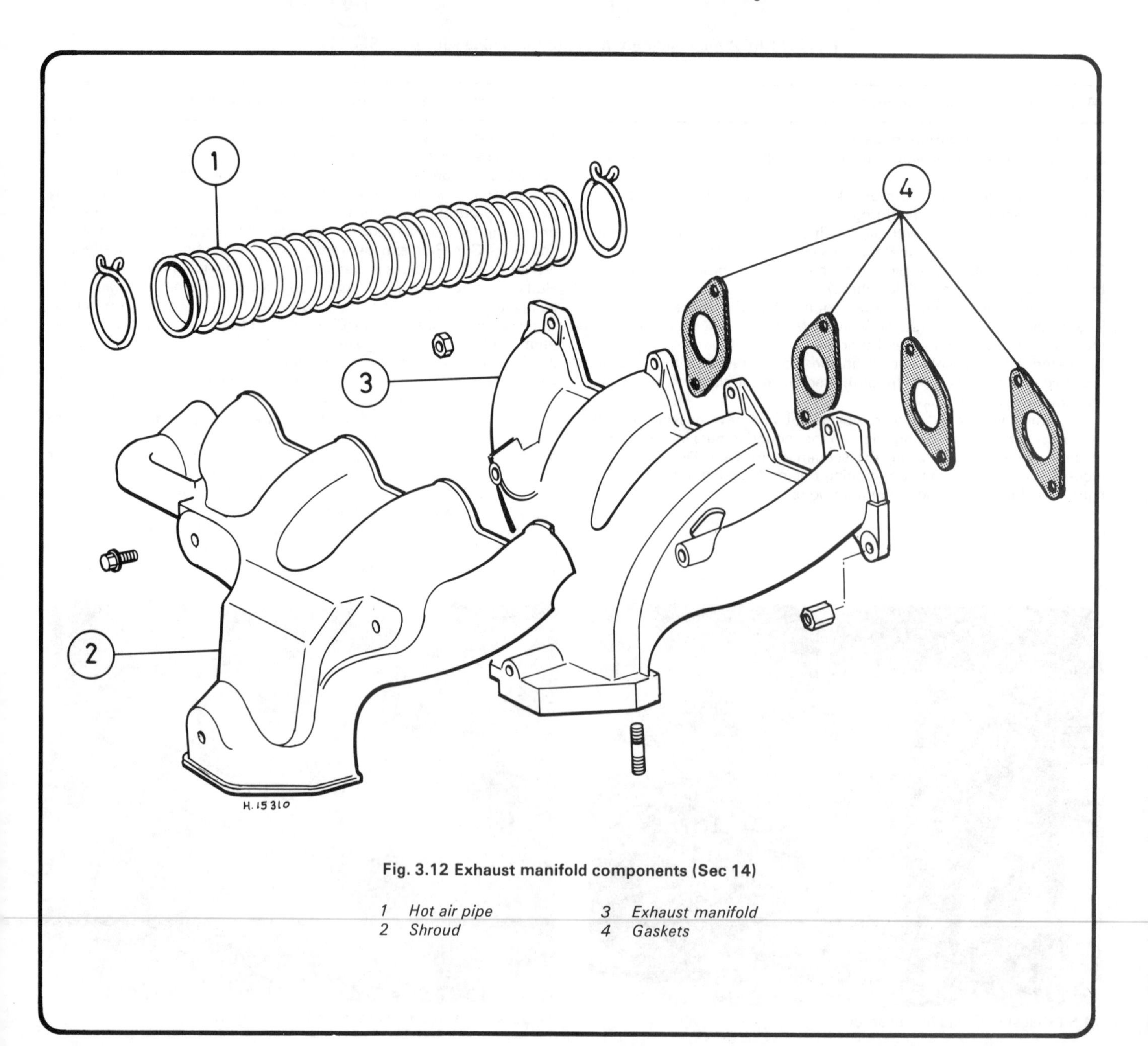

Fig. 3.12 Exhaust manifold components (Sec 14)

1 Hot air pipe
2 Shroud
3 Exhaust manifold
4 Gaskets

exhaust pipe, then withdraw the front exhaust section (photo).

8 Clean the mating faces of the flanges and renew the sealing rings if necessary.

9 Refitting is a reversal of removal. Before assembly, smear all joints with a good proprietary exhaust sealing compound, such as Holts Firegum. Loosely assemble the complete system before tightening the nuts and bolts to the specified torques, starting with the manifold flange joint and finishing at the rear of the car.

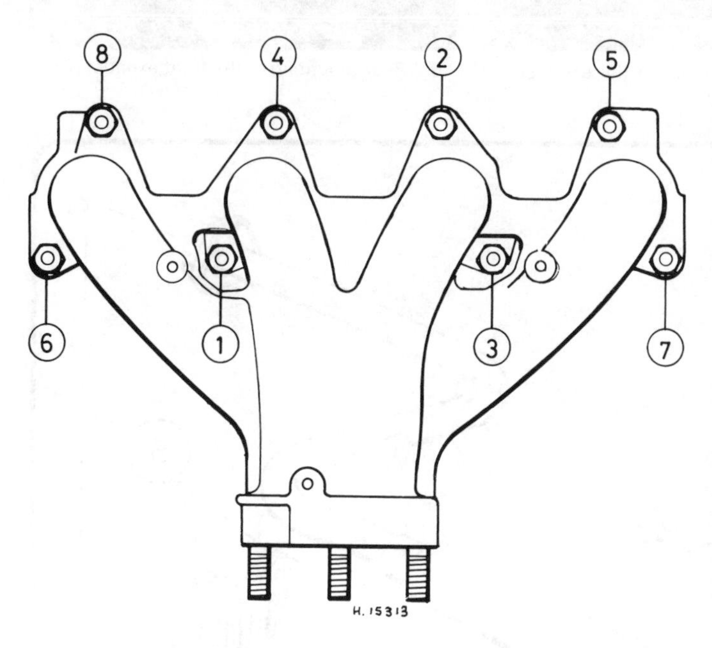

Fig. 3.13 Exhaust manifold mounting nut tightening sequence (Sec 14)

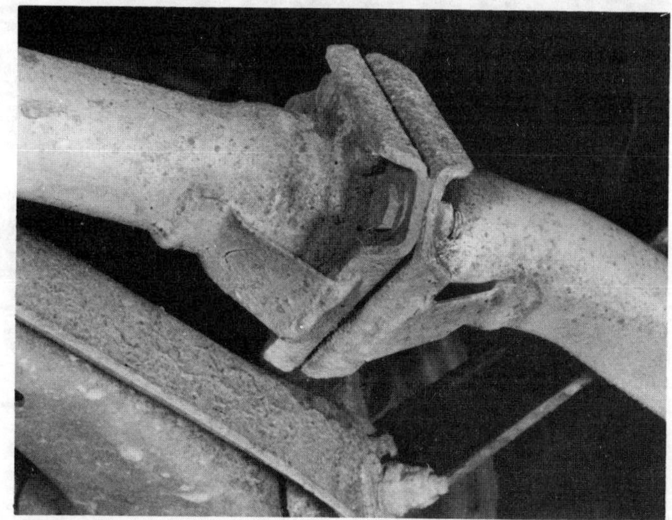

15.3 Exhaust front-to-rear section flange

15.4 Rear exhaust section rubber mountings

15.5a Remove the mounting clamp ...

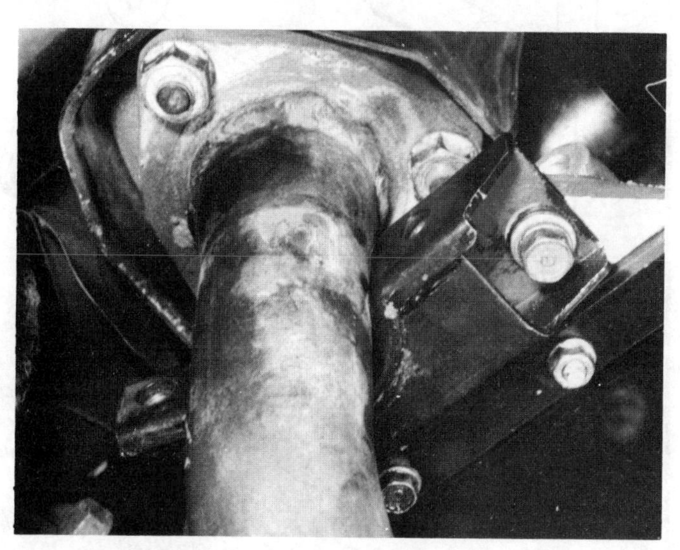

15.5b ... and bracket

15.6a Removing the exhaust pipe from the manifold

15.6b Sealing ring location in the exhaust downpipe

15.7 Rear mounting of the front exhaust pipe

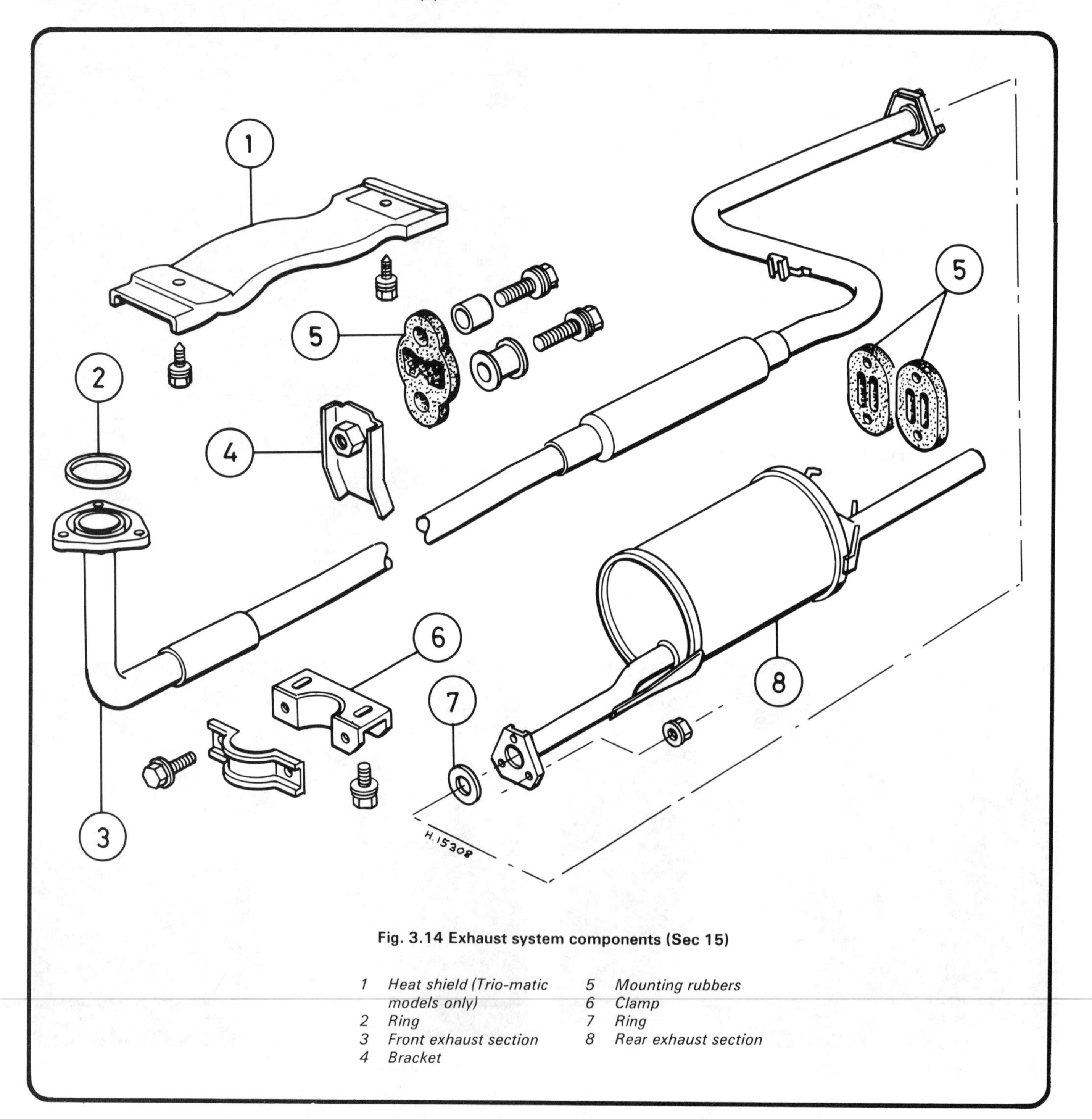

Fig. 3.14 Exhaust system components (Sec 15)

1 Heat shield (Trio-matic models only)
2 Ring
3 Front exhaust section
4 Bracket
5 Mounting rubbers
6 Clamp
7 Ring
8 Rear exhaust section

16 Fault diagnosis – fuel and exhaust systems

Symptom	Reason(s)
Excessive fuel consumption	Air cleaner element choked Leaks in fuel tank, carburettors, or fuel lines Float level incorrect Mixture adjustment incorrect Ignition timing incorrect, or other ignition fault Valve clearances incorrect Brakes binding Tyres underinflated Worn carburettor Sticking needle valve (open)
Insufficient fuel supply or weak mixture	Sticking needle valve (shut) Faulty fuel pump Leaking fuel line Leaking inlet manifold gaskets Mixture adjustment incorrect Clogged fuel filter (attached to fuel tank)
Engine will not idle	Fuel cut-off solenoid disconnected or defective

Chapter 4 Ignition system

Contents

Specifications

General

System type	Breakerless electronic ignition with conventional coil
Firing order	1-3-4-2
Location of No 1 cylinder	Timing belt end

Coil and HT leads

Primary winding resistance at 20°C (68°F)	1.8 to 2.1 ohms
Secondary winding resistance at 20°C	8800 to 12 200 ohms
HT lead resistance	25 000 ohms minimum

Distributor

Make and type	Toyodenso breakerless
Direction of rotor rotation	Anti-clockwise
Reluctor-to-stator air gaps	All equal
Pulse generator coil resistance	600 to 800 ohms

Ignition timing

At idle speed, vacuum advance connected:	
Manual gearbox models	5° BTDC (red mark)
Trio-matic models (P selected)	12° BTDC
Centrifugal advance (decelerating vacuum disconnected):	
4000 rpm	27° to 31°
3000 rpm	20° to 24°
2000 rpm	12° to 17°
1000 rpm	0° to 1°
Vacuum advance (maximum):	
Manual gearbox models	13° to 17° at 225 mm (8.9 in) Hg
Trio-matic models	4° to 8° at 275 mm (10.9 in) Hg

Spark plugs

Make and type	Champion RN9YCC or RN9YC
Electrode gap:	
Champion RN9YCC	0.8 mm (0.032 in)
Champion RN9YC	0.7 mm (0.028 in)

Torque wrench settings

	lbf ft	Nm
Distributor retaining bolt	9	12
Spark plugs	13	18

1 General description

A breakerless electronic ignition system is fitted, comprising the battery, coil, electronic module (photo), pulse generator (in the distributor), and spark plugs. The distributor is driven by a skew gear on the timing belt end of the camshaft.

In order that the engine can run correctly, it is necessary for an electrical spark to ignite the fuel/air mixture in the combustion chamber at exactly the right moment in relation to engine speed and load. The ignition system is based on feeding low tension voltage from the battery to the coil, where it is converted to high tension voltage. The high tension voltage is powerful enough to jump the spark plug gap in the cylinders many times a second under high compression, providing that the system is in good condition and that all adjustments are correct.

The ignition system is divided into two circuits, the low tension circuit and the high tension circuit. The low tension (sometimes known as the primary) circuit consists of the battery, lead to the ignition switch, lead from the ignition switch to the low tension or primary coil windings (terminal +), and the lead from the low tension coil windings (coil terminal -) to the electronic module. The module is also supplied with a main feed wire from the ignition switch and control switching wires from the pulse generator in the distributor. A condenser is fitted in the LT circuit (photo).

The high tension circuit consists of the high tension or secondary coil windings, the heavy ignition lead from the coil to the distributor cap, the rotor arm, and the spark plug leads and spark plugs.

The system functions in the following manner. Low tension voltage is changed in the coil into high tension voltage by the switching function of the electronic module, which is controlled by the pulse generator. High tension voltage is then fed via the carbon brush in the centre of the distributor cap to the rotor arm of the distributor, and each time it comes in line with one of the four metal segments in the cap, which are connected to the spark plug leads, the operation of the electronic module causes the high tension voltage to build up, jump the gap from the rotor arm to the appropriate metal segment, and so via the spark plug lead to the spark plug, where it finally jumps the spark plug gap before going to earth. The ignition is advanced and retarded automatically, to ensure that the spark occurs at just the right instant for the particular load at the prevailing engine speed.

The ignition advance is controlled both mechanically and by a vacuum-operated system. The mechanical governor mechanism comprises two weights which move out from the distributor shaft as the engine speed rises due to centrifugal force. As they move outwards they rotate the reluctor relative to the distributor shaft, and so advance the tension of the springs which is largely responsible for correct spark advancement.

The vacuum control consists of a diaphragm, one side of which is connected via a small bore tube to the carburettors and the other side to the pick-up base. Depression in the inlet manifold and carburettors, which varies with engine speed and throttle opening, causes the diaphragm to move, so moving the pick-up base and advancing or retarding the spark. A fine degree of control is achieved by a spring in the vacuum assembly.

2 Distributor – removal and refitting

1 Disconnect the battery negative lead.

2 Note the location of the No 1 cylinder (crankshaft pulley end) spark plug HT lead on the distributor cap. Remove the distributor cap, using a cross-head screwdriver or 7 mm spanner to remove the two screws, then rotate the engine in an anti-clockwise direction (viewed from the crankshaft pulley end) until the distributor rotor arm approaches the No 1 position.

3 Continue turning the engine (using a spanner on the crankshaft pulley bolt) until the *white* mark on the crankshaft pulley is aligned with the rib on the lower timing cover. No 1 piston is not at TDC on its compression stroke.

4 Disconnect the vacuum advance pipe and the radio suppressor earth wire from the distributor. Disconnect the pulse generator wires at the connector plug.

5 Mark the rim of the distributor body in line with the centre of the rotor arm tip. Also mark the distributor retaining plate in relation to the cylinder head.

6 Unscrew and remove the retaining bolt and withdraw the distributor direct from the cylinder head without turning it (photos). Mark the rim of the distributor body in line with the new position of the rotor arm tip, using two lines to distinguish it from the first mark.

7 Before refitting the distributor, check that the air gaps between the reluctor and stator are equal. Preferably use a non-magnetic feeler gauge to check the gaps. If necessary, loosen the stator cross-head screws, reposition the stator, then tighten the screws (photo). Also check the condition of the rubber O-ring on the distributor body and if necessary renew it.

8 To refit the distributor, first align the rotor arm segment with the two lines on the rim. The marks on the body and gear as shown in Fig. 4.1 should also be in alignment.

9 Check that the engine is still on TDC, No. 1 cylinder firing, then hold the distributor over the location hole with the marks on the retaining plate and cylinder head aligned. Insert the distributor into the cylinder head. As the drivegear engages the camshaft gear, the rotor arm will turn anti-clockwise and align with the mark on the rim.

10 Insert and tighten the distributor retaining bolt, then reconnect the radio suppressor earth wire, the pulse generator plug and the vacuum advance pipe.

11 Refit the distributor cap and tighten the screws. Reconnect the battery negative lead.

12 Check and if necessary adjust the ignition timing as described in Section 4.

1.0a Electronic module location

1.0b Ignition condenser

2.6a Unscrew the retaining bolt ...

2.6b ... and remove the distributor

2.7 Checking the distributor air gaps

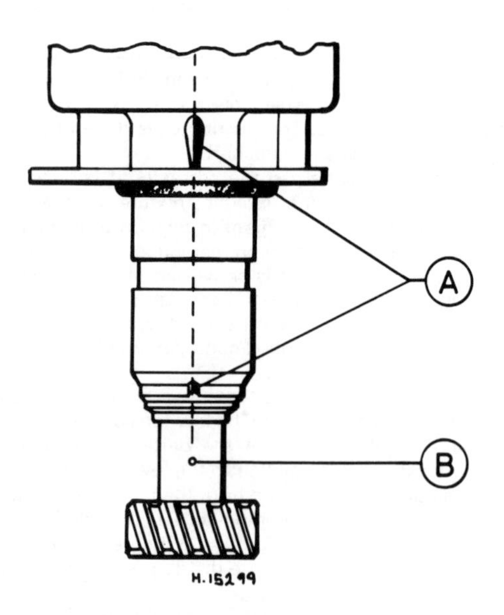

Fig. 4.1 Distributor shaft alignment marks (A) on the body and drivegear (B) (Sec 2)

3 Distributor – dismantling, overhaul and reassembly

Note: *The distributor is designed to operate over very high mileages, and when wear eventually takes place, particularly between the shaft and body, the complete distributor should be renewed. However, if wear between these components is not excessive, the distributor can be overhauled provided that spares are available.*

1 With the distributor removed, pull the rotor arm from the upper shaft (photo).

2 Using two screwdrivers, prise off the reluctor together with the roll pin (photo). Use rag beneath the screwdrivers to prevent damage to the distributor body.

3 Remove the screw securing the wiring clip to the side of the distributor (photo).

4 Remove the cross-head screws from the stator and withdraw the stator, spacer and sleeves, retainer, and pulse generator coil (photos).

5 Remove the vacuum advance unit retaining screws and washers, unhook the operating arm from the pick-up base, and withdraw the unit and gasket (photo).

6 Withdraw the pick-up base (1 screw) (photos).

7 Prise the cap from the rotor shaft, then remove the screw and washers while holding the drivegear shoulder with grips.

8 Unhook the centrifugal weight springs and lift off the rotor shaft (photo).

9 Hold the distributor body shoulder in a soft-jawed vice. Use a pin punch to drive out the drivegear roll pin.

10 Remove the drivegear and withdraw the shaft.

11 Extract the circlips and remove the centrifugal weights from the lower shaft.

12 Clean all components with paraffin and wipe dry. Examine each part for damage and deterioration. If the shaft-to-body wear is excessive, renew the complete distributor. Clean any carbon from the rotor arm and distributor cap and check them for tracking. Check that the carbon brush moves freely in the distributor cap against the spring tension. Using an ohmmeter, check that the resistance of the pulse generator is as given in the Specifications.

13 Reassembly is a reversal of dismantling, but lubricate all bearing surfaces with a molybdenum-based grease. When installing the rotor shaft, first align the marks on the drivegear and body, then fit the rotor shaft with the flat facing away from the vacuum advance operating arm location (Fig. 4.3). Make sure that the pick-up base turns freely in the body, and when installing the reluctor, locate the split in the roll pin away from the flat on the rotor shaft (photo).

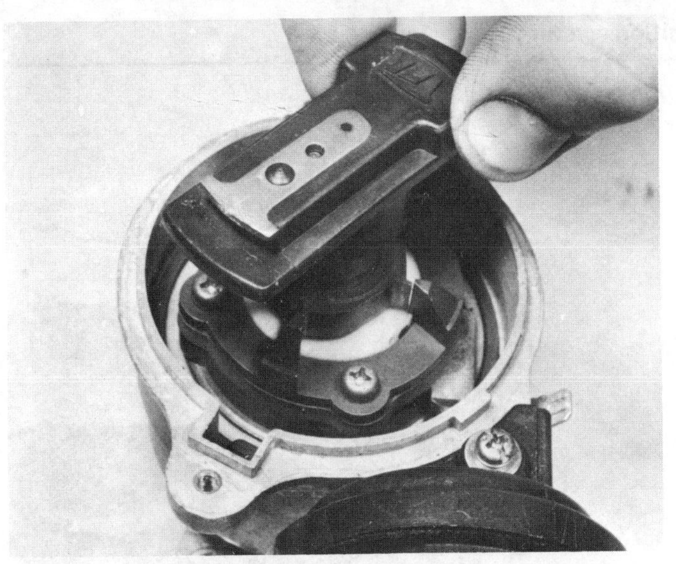
3.1 Removing the rotor arm

3.2 Removing the reluctor and roll pin

3.3 Removing the wiring clip

3.4a Removing the spacer and retainer

3.4b Removing the pulse generator coil

3.5a Disconnect the operating arm ...

3.5b ... and remove the vacuum advance unit

3.6a Remove the clamp ...

3.6b ... and lift out the pick-up base

3.8 The distributor centrifugal weight mechanism

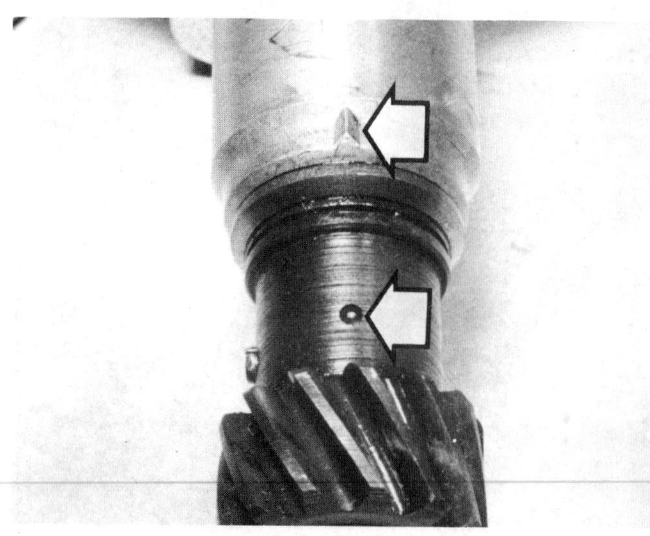
3.13 Drivegear and body alignment marks (arrowed)

4 Ignition timing – adjustment

1 There are three marks on the crankshaft pulley – the white groove indicates TDC, the red groove indicates 5° BTDC and the yellow groove indicates 11° BTDC. On Trio-matic models the ignition timing is 12° BTDC, therefore it will be necessary to make an additional mark in advance of the 11° mark. To do this, measure the distance between the TDC mark and the 5° mark and deduct the result from the distance between the 5° mark and the 11° mark. On a 160 mm (6.25 in) diameter crankshaft pulley the additional dimension will be 1.4 mm (0.055 in).

Initial setting

2 If it is necessary to make an initial setting in order to run the engine, remove No 1 spark plug (crankshaft pulley end), then turn the engine *anti-clockwise* until compression can be felt in No 1 cylinder using a finger or thumb over the spark plug hole. Continue turning the engine until the correct timing mark on the crankshaft pulley is aligned with the rib on the lower timing cover (photo).

3 Remove the distributor cap and check that the rotor arm segment is pointing toward the No 1 HT lead position – if not, the distributor must be removed.

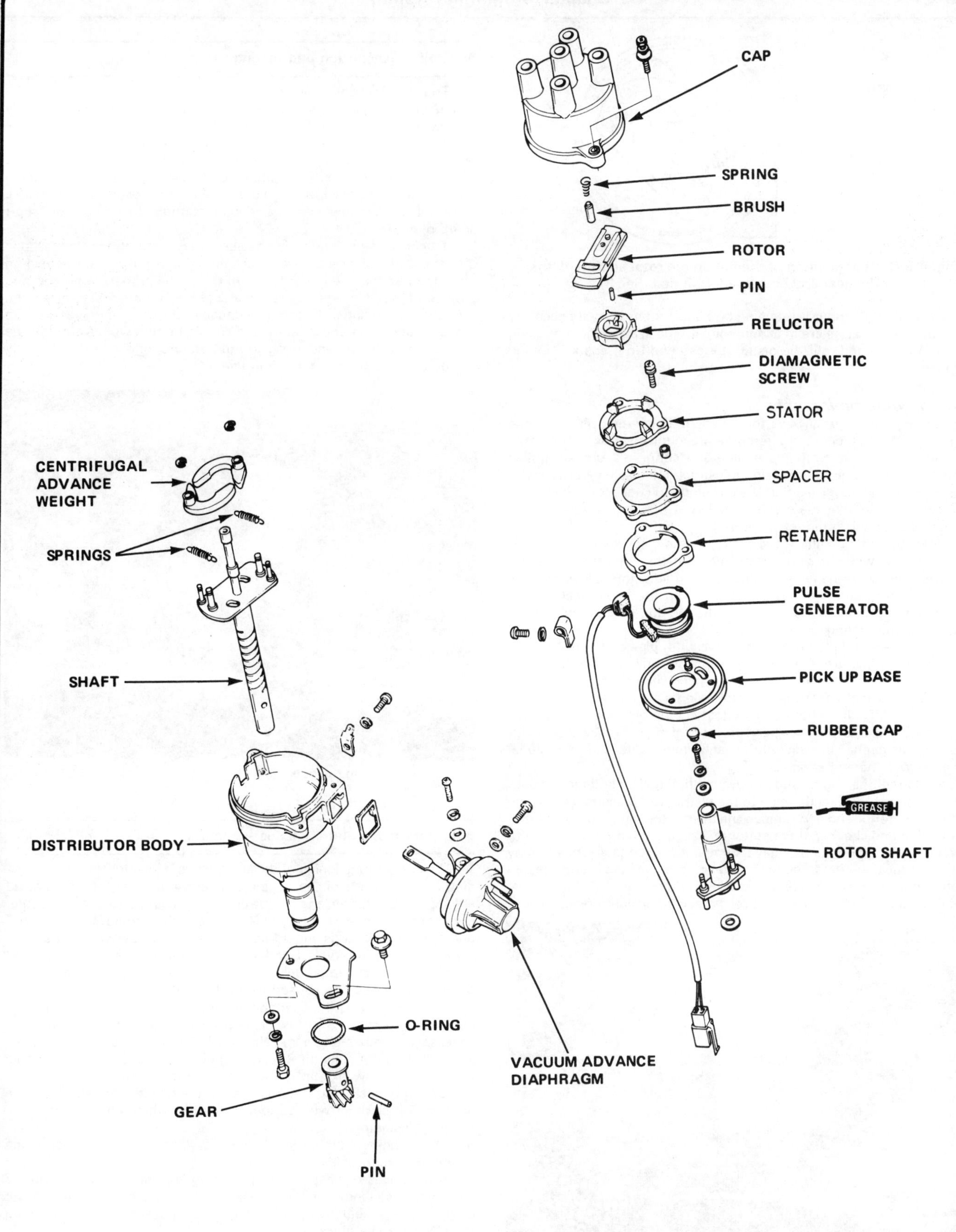

Fig. 4.2 Exploded view of the distributor (Sec 3)

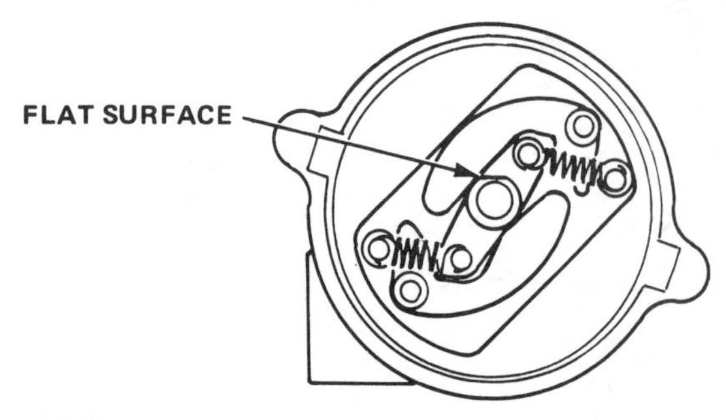

Fig. 4.3 Correct position of the flat on the rotor shaft with the drivegear and body marks aligned (Sec 3)

4 Loosen the distributor retaining bolt and turn its body if necessary until the reluctor arms are in alignment with the stator segments, then tighten the bolt and refit the distributor cap and No 1 spark plug and HT lead.

Stroboscopic timing light setting

5 This method must always follow any initial setting. First run the engine to normal operating temperature, indicated by the electric cooling fan starting. Stop the engine and connect a timing light in accordance with the manufacturer's instructions (usually between No 1 spark plug and its HT lead). It is also helpful to connect a tachometer in order to check that the engine is idling at the correct speed.
6 Start the engine and let it idle.
7 Point the timing light at the timing marks. They should appear to be stationary, with the appropriate mark on the crankshaft pulley in line with the rib on the lower timing cover. If adjustment is necessary, loosen the distributor retaining bolt and turn the body clockwise to advance and anti-clockwise to retard the ignition timing. Tighten the bolt when the setting is correct.
8 Disconnect and plug or clamp the vacuum pipe on the distributor, then gradually increase the engine speed while still pointing the timing light at the timing marks. The pulley mark should appear to move clockwise, proving that the centrifugal weights are operating. Accurate checking is difficult without special test equipment, but if the timing fails to advance as engine speed rises, or if the advance is jerky or uneven, dismantle the distributor and investigate the centrifugal advance weights and springs.
9 Switch off the engine and remove the timing light and tachometer.
10 Reconnect the vacuum pipe to the distributor. Disconnect the pipe at the carburettor end and remove the distributor cap. Suck on the end of the pipe and check that the stator and segments move clockwise to advance the ignition. If not, the vacuum unit may be faulty, or you may not be sucking hard enough. Have the vacuum unit tested professionally before deciding that it needs renewal.
11 Refit the distributor cap and reconnect the vacuum pipe.

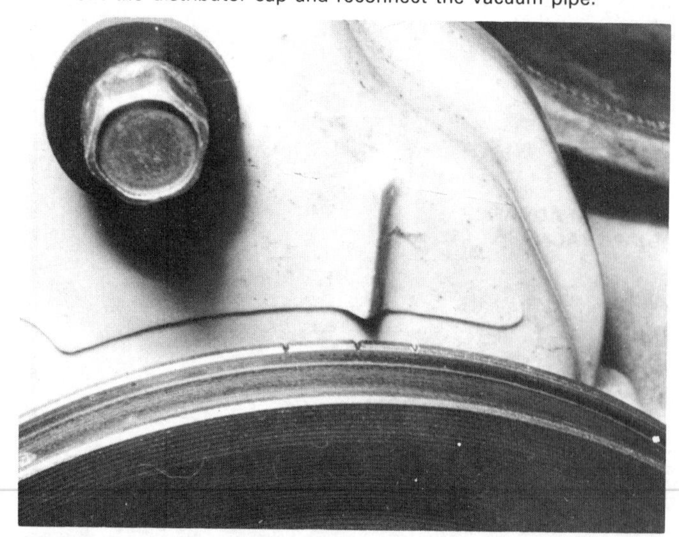

4.2 Crankshaft pulley set at 5° BTDC

5 Coil – description and testing

1 The coil is located on the left-hand side of the bulkhead in the engine compartment (photo), and it should be wiped down periodically to prevent high tension (HT) voltage loss through possible arcing.
2 To ensure the correct HT polarity at the spark plugs, the coil LT leads must always be connected correctly. The blue lead from the electronic module should be connected to the negative (-) terminal on the coil, and the black and yellow lead to the positive (+) terminal. Incorrect connections can cause bad starting, misfiring, and short spark plug life.
3 To check the coil primary and secondary winding resistances, pull off the plastic cover and disconnect the LT and HT wires. Connect an ohmmeter across the LT terminals to check the primary windings, and between the positive (+) LT terminal and the HT terminal to check the secondary windings. If the resistances are not as given in the Specifications, the coil is faulty and should be renewed. Note that the resistances will vary according to temperature, and that the coil may get quite hot after it has been in use.

5.1 Coil location on the bulkhead

6 Spark plugs and HT leads – general

1 The correct functioning of the spark plugs is vital for the correct running and efficiency of the engine. It is essential that the plugs fitted are appropriate for the engine (the correct type is specified at the beginning of this Chapter). If this type is used, and the engine is in good condition, the spark plugs should not need attention between scheduled service renewal intervals. Spark plug cleaning is rarely necessary, and should not be attempted unless specialised equipment is available, as damage can easily be caused to the firing ends.
2 When removing the spark plugs, first check that the HT leads are numbered so that they may be refitted to their correct positions. If necessary, number the leads. No 1 cylinder is nearest the drivebelt.
3 Pull the plug caps off the plugs. Pull on the cap, not on the lead. Clean any dirt away from the area around the plugs.
4 Unscrew each plug in turn. Use a proper spark plug spanner, or a deep socket spanner with a rubber insert. Anything else may damage the plug insulators.
5 The condition of the spark plugs will also tell much about the overall condition of the engine.
6 If the insulator nose of the spark plug is clean and white, with no deposits, this is indicative of a weak mixture, or too hot a plug. (A hot plug transfers heat away from the electrode slowly – a cold plug transfers it away quickly).
7 If the tip and insulator nose is covered with hard black-looking deposits, then this is indicative that the mixture is too rich. Should the plug be black and oily, then it is likely that the engine is fairly worn.
8 If the insulator nose is covered with light tan to greyish brown deposits, then the mixture is correct and it is likely that the engine is in good condition.

9 The spark plug gap is of considerable importance, as, if it is too large or too small, the size of the spark and its efficiency will be seriously impaired. The spark plug gap should be set to the figure given in the Specifications.
10 To set it, measure the gap with a feeler gauge, and then bend open or close the *outer* plug electrode until the correct gap is achieved. The centre electrode should *never* be bent as this may crack the insulation and cause plug failure, if nothing worse.
11 Note that, as the cylinder head is of aluminium alloy, it is recommended that a little anti-seize compound (such as Copaslip) is applied to the plug threads before they are fitted.
12 Refitting the spark plugs is a reversal of the removal procedure. Screw in the plugs by hand until the sealing washer just seats, then tighten by no more than a quarter-turn using a spark plug spanner. If a torque wrench is available, tighten the plugs to the specified torque.
13 Refit the HT leads to the spark plugs, making sure that each lead is in its correct position. Push the plug caps firmly onto the tops of the plugs.
14 Periodically the spark plug HT leads should be wiped clean and checked for security. At the same time their resistance may be checked with an ohmmeter and compared with the value given in the Specifications.

7 Fault diagnosis – ignition system

By far the majority of breakdown and running troubles are caused by faults in the ignition system, either in the low tension or high tension circuit. There are two main symptoms indicating ignition faults. Either the engine will not start or fire, or the engine is difficult to start and misfires. If it is a regular misfire, ie the engine is only running on two or three cylinders, the fault is almost sure to be in the secondary or high tension circuit. If the misfiring is intermittent, the fault could be in either the high or low tension circuits. If the car stops suddenly or will not start at all, it is likely that the fault is in the low tension circuit. Loss of power and overheating, apart from faulty carburation settings, can be due to faults in the pulse generator and electronic module or incorrect ignition timing.

Engine fails to start

1 If the engine fails to start and the car was running normally when it was last used, first check there is fuel in the petrol tank. If the engine turns over normally on the starter motor and the battery is evidently well charged, then the fault may be in either the high or low tension circuits. First check the HT circuit (if the battery is known to be fully charged, the ignition light comes on, and the starter motor fails to turn the engine, check the tightness of the leads on the battery terminals and the security of the earth lead to its connection to the body. It is quite common for the leads to have worked loose, even if they look and feel secure. If one of the battery terminal posts gets very hot when trying to work the starter motor, this is a sure indication of a faulty connection to that terminal.
2 One of the most common reasons for bad starting is wet or damp HT leads or distributor. Remove the distributor cap. If condensation is visible internally, dry the cap with a rag, then refit it and wipe over the leads. Alternatively, using a moisture dispersant such as Holts Wet Start can be very effective in starting the engine. To prevent the problem recurring, Holts Damp Start can be used to provide a sealing coat, so excluding any further moisture from the ignition system. In extreme difficulty, Holts Cold Start will help to start a car when only a very poor spark occurs.
3 If the engine still fails to start, check that current is reaching the plugs, by disconnecting each plug lead in turn at the spark plug end and holding the end of the cable about $\frac{3}{16}$ in (5 mm) away from the cylinder head. Spin the engine on the starter motor.
4 Sparking between the end of the cable and the head should be fairly strong with a regular blue spark. (Hold the lead with rubber to avoid electric shocks). If current is reaching the plugs, then remove them and regap them. The engine should now start.
5 If there is no spark at the plug leads, take off the HT lead from the centre of the distributor cap and hold it to the head as before. Spin the engine on the starter once more. A rapid succession of blue sparks between the end of the lead and the block indicates that the coil is in order and that the distributor cap is cracked, the rotor arm faulty or the carbon brush in the top of the distributor cap is not making good contact with the rotor arm.
6 If there are no sparks from the end of the lead from the coil, check the connections at the coil end of the lead. If it is in order, start checking the low tension circuit.
7 Use a 12V voltmeter or a 12V bulb and two lengths of wire. With the ignition switch on, test between the low tension wire to the coil (it is marked +) and ground. No reading indicates a break in the supply from the ignition switch. Check the connections at the switch to see if any are loose.
8 With a reading at the coil + terminal, measure the voltage (or connect the test lamp) between the coil – terminal and earth. With the ignition on and the engine stationary, 12V should be measured (or the test lamp should light). If not, check the wiring from the – terminal to the electronic module. If a multimeter is available, disconnect the coil and measure the primary (LT) winding resistance. The correct resistance is given in the Specifications.
9 With satisfactory readings at both + and – terminals, check the voltage across the + and – terminals with the engine cranking on the starter motor. A reading of 1 to 3 volts should be obtained. If so, check the coil secondary resistance against that specified, then check the resistance of the HT leads (see Section 6). If not, carry on with the checks below.
10 Disconnect the module connector. With the ignition on, measure the voltage on the coil side of the connector between the black and the blue wires, then between the black and the black/yellow wires. 12V should be obtained in each case. If not, check the wiring from the ignition coil to the module. If so, proceed as described below.
11 Disconnect the pulse generator connector. Check the continuity of the blue and the red wires which connect the pulse generator to the module. Both wires should show continuity.
12 If the wiring is satisfactory, connect ohmmeter probes across the pulse generator and measure its resistance. This should be within the limits given in the Specifications. If not, renew the pulse generator; if so, renew the module.

Engine misfires

13 If the engine misfires regularly, run it at a fast idling speed. Pull off each of the plug caps in turn and listen to the note of the engine. Hold the plug cap in a dry cloth or with a rubber glove as additional protection against a shock from the HT supply.
14 No difference in engine running will be noticed when the lead from the defective circuit is removed. Removing the lead from one of the good cylinders will accentuate the misfire.
15 Remove the plug lead from the end of the defective plug and hold it about $\frac{3}{16}$ (5 mm) away from the cylinder head. Restart the engine. If the sparking is fairly strong and regular the fault must lie in the spark plug.
16 The plug may be loose, the insulation may be cracked, or the points may have burnt away giving too wide a gap for the spark to jump. Worse still, one of the points may have broken off. Either renew the plug, or reset the gap, and then test it.
17 If there is no spark at the end of the plug lead, or if it is weak and intermittent, check the ignition lead from the distributor to the plug. If the insulation is cracked or perished, renew the lead. Check the connections at the distributor cap.
18 If there is still no spark, examine the distributor cap carefully for tracking. This can be recognised by a very thin black line running between two or more electrodes, or between an electrode and some other part of the distributor. These lines are paths which now conduct electricity across the cap thus letting it run to earth. The only answer is a new distributor cap.
19 Apart from the ignition timing being incorrect, other causes of misfiring have already been dealt with under the section dealing with the failure of the engine to start. To recap – these are that:

(a) The coil may be faulty giving an intermittent misfire
(b) There may be damaged wire or loose connection in the low tension circuit
(c) There may be a fault in the electronic module or pulse generator

20 If the ignition timing is too far retarded, it should be noted that the engine will tend to overheat, and there will be a quite noticeable drop in power. If the engine is overheating and the power is down, and the ignition timing is correct, then the carburettors should be checked, as it is likely that this is where the fault lies.

Chapter 5 Clutch

Contents

Specifications

Clutch type	Single dry plate with diaphragm spring type pressure plate, cable actuation
Pressure plate	
Maximum distortion	0.15 mm (0.006 in)
Driven plate	
Diameter	190 mm (7.48 in)
Minimum thickness	6.1 mm (0.24 in)
Minimum rivet depth	0.2 mm (0.008 in)
Maximum run-out	1.0 mm (0.040 in)
Clutch adjustment	
Pedal free play	23 to 30 mm (0.91 to 1.18 in)
Release arm free play	4.4 to 5.4 mm (0.17 to 0.21 in)

Torque wrench settings	**lbf ft**	**Nm**
Pressure plate bolts	9	12
Release fork lockbolt	18	24

1 General description

The clutch is of single dry plate type, with a diaphragm spring type pressure plate. Actuation is by cable from a pendant pedal.

The driven plate is free to slide along the splined mainshaft, and is held in position between the flywheel and the pressure plate by the pressure of the diaphragm spring. Friction lining material is riveted to the driven plate on each side, and the driven plate also incorporates radial rubber cushion dampers to absorb transmission shocks and ensure a smooth take-up of drive.

When the clutch pedal is depressed, the cable pulls the release arm, and the release fork presses the release bearing against the central fingers of the diaphragm spring. The diaphragm spring flexes and the pressure plate is released from the driven plate. Drive then ceases to be transmitted to the gearbox.

When the clutch pedal is released, the diaphragm spring forces the pressure plate into contact with the friction linings on the driven plate, which is also moved fractionally along the mainshaft and into contact with the flywheel. The driven plate is now firmly sandwiched between the pressure plate and flywheel, and the drive is taken up.

As the friction linings wear, the pressure plate moves closer to the flywheel and the cable free movement will decrease. Periodic adjustment of the clutch cable is therefore necessary.

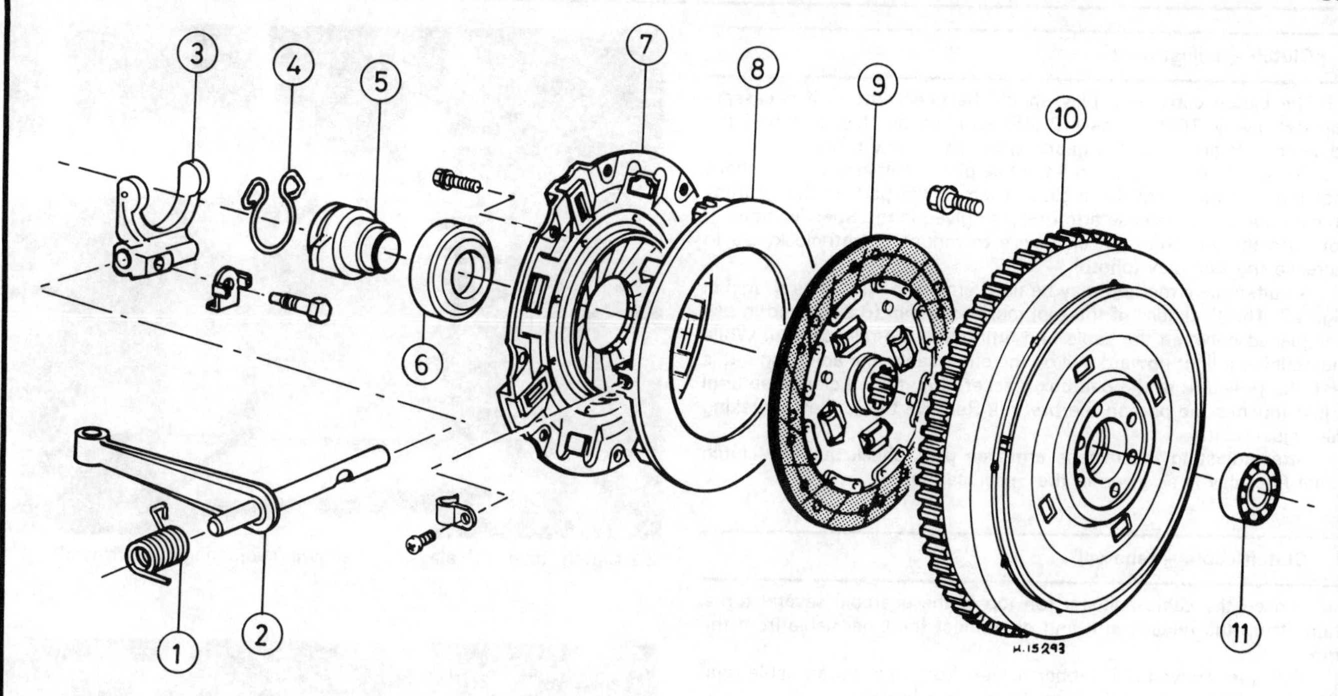

Fig. 5.1 Clutch components (Sec 1)

1 Return spring
2 Release arm and shaft
3 Release fork
4 Spring clip
5 Bearing holder
6 Release bearing
7 Clutch cover
8 Pressure plate
9 Driven plate
10 Flywheel
11 Spigot bearing

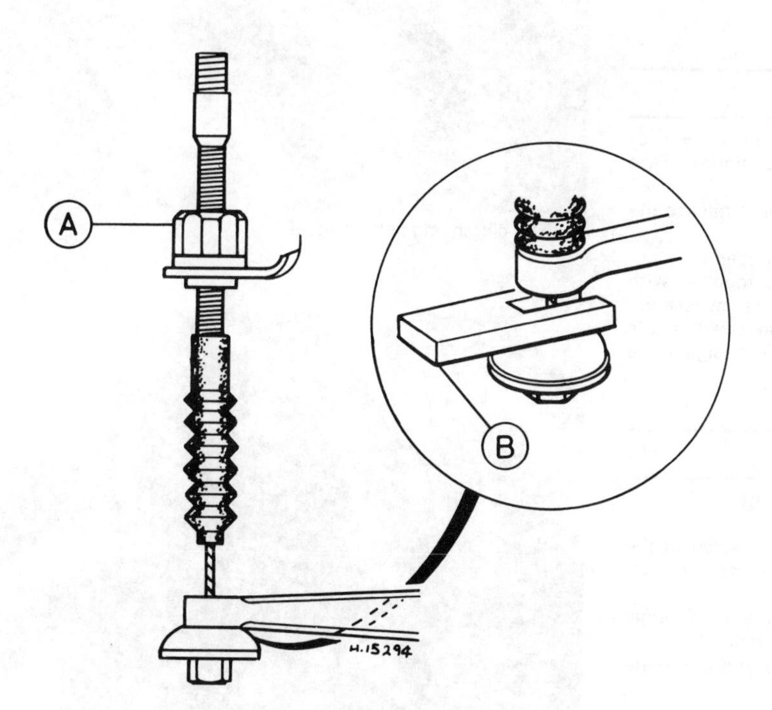

Fig. 5.2 Clutch cable adjusting nut (A) and special tool (B) (Sec 2)

Tool thickness = 5 mm (0.2 in)
Tool overall length = 40 mm (1.6 in)
Slot width = 10 mm (0.4 in)
Slot length = 20 mm (0.8 in)

2 Clutch – adjustment

1 The clutch cable free play should be checked and if necessary adjusted every 7500 miles (12 000 km). To do this, first find the adjuster. It is on top of the gearbox, by the battery tray.
2 Pull up the outer cable until the free play is eliminated, then check that the distance from the adjusting nut to the pad on the gearbox bracket equals the release arm free play given in the Specifications. If not, turn the adjusting nut clockwise to reduce or anti-clockwise to increase the free play (photo).
3 An alternative method may be used employing a tool as shown in Fig. 5.2. The thickness of the tool must be 5 mm (0.2 in), and in use it is placed between the cable end fitting and the release arm. While maintaining a light upward pull on the outer cable, the adjusting nut is first unscrewed from the gearbox bracket, then turned clockwise until it just touches the pad on the bracket. Remove the tool after making the adjustment.
4 After adjusting the release arm free play, check that the clutch pedal free play is as given in the Specifications.

2.2 Clutch cable and release arm showing adjusting nut (arrowed)

3 Clutch cable – renewal

1 Loosen the cable adjuster (on top of the gearbox) several turns, then lift up the release arm and disconnect the inner cable from the arm.
2 Pull the convoluted rubber cover from the outer cable and disconnect the outer cable from the gearbox bracket.
3 Working inside the car, unhook the inner cable from the top of the clutch pedal.
4 Prise the dust cover and fitting from the bulkhead then withdraw the complete clutch cable. Note that a rubber O-ring is located on the cable fitting.
5 Check the inner and outer cables for fraying, wear and deterioration. If necessary, renew the cable assembly.
6 Fit the new cable using a reversal of the removal procedure. However, first lubricate the inner cable with a little molybdenum disulphide-based grease. With the cable fitted, adjust it as described in Section 2.

4.1 The clutch and brake pedals

4 Clutch pedal – removal and refitting

1 The clutch and brake pedals are both mounted on the same pivot bolt located in the pedal bracket beneath the facia (photo). First unhook the clutch and brake pedal return springs.
2 Unscrew the pivot bolt and withdraw it far enough to release the clutch pedal.
3 Unhook the inner cable and withdraw the clutch pedal.
4 Extract the spacer and bushes and examine them, together with the footpad rubber, for wear. Renew the components as necessary.
5 Refitting is a reversal of removal. Lubricate the bushes with a little molybdenum disulphide-based grease. When completed, adjust the clutch cable as described in Section 2.

5 Clutch – removal

1 Remove the gearbox as described in Chapter 6.
2 Mark the clutch cover in relation to the flywheel.
3 Hold the flywheel stationary with a screwdriver inserted in the starter ring gear. Alternatively a tool similar to the BL tool No. 18G 1350 (Fig. 5.4) may be made.
4 Unscrew the clutch cover bolts a little at a time in diagonal sequence until the diaphragm spring pressure is released.
5 Remove the bolts and withdraw the clutch cover and driven plate (friction disc) from the face of the flywheel (photos).

5.5a Removing the clutch cover ...

6 Clutch – inspection

1 Examine the friction surfaces of the pressure plate and flywheel for scoring and cracking. If only light scoring is evident, the parts may be re-used, but if excessive, the pressure plate and cover must be renewed and the flywheel friction face ground flat. If the flywheel is

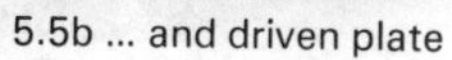

5.5b ... and driven plate

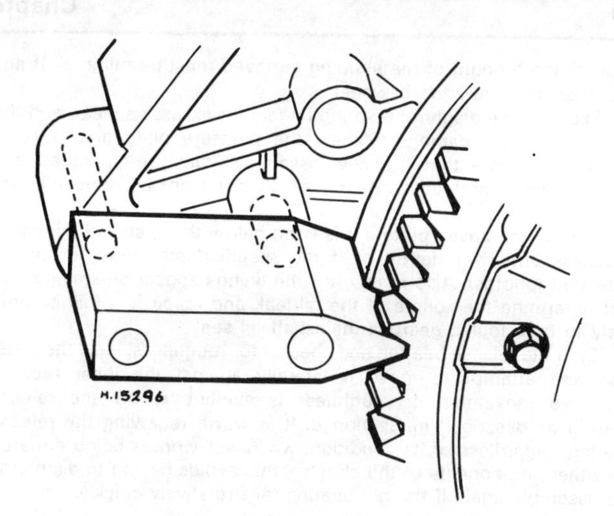

Fig. 5.4 BL tool No 18G 1350 for holding the flywheel stationary (Sec 5)

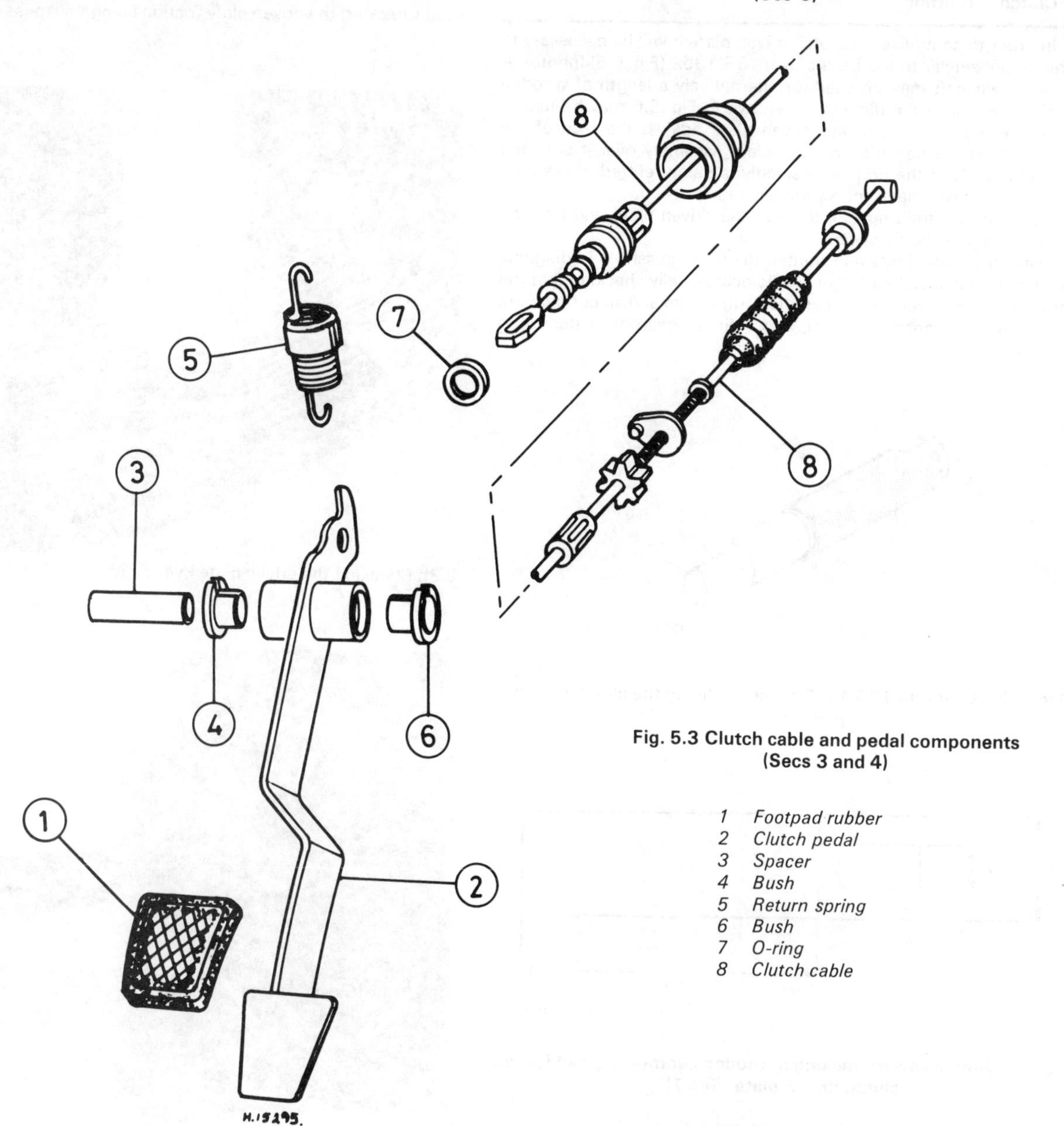

Fig. 5.3 Clutch cable and pedal components (Secs 3 and 4)

1 *Footpad rubber*
2 *Clutch pedal*
3 *Spacer*
4 *Bush*
5 *Return spring*
6 *Bush*
7 *O-ring*
8 *Clutch cable*

refaced, the amount of metal being removed must be minimal. If any doubt exists, renew the flywheel.

2 Examine the diaphragm spring fingers for excessive wear, and the clutch cover for damage. Renew the pressure plate and cover if necessary – note that the new assemblies are pre-lubricated and covered with a protective coating which **must not** be removed with solvent.

3 Renew the driven plate if it is worn below the specified minimum thickness and rivet depth, or if the specified maximum run-out is exceeded (photos). Also renew it if the linings appear oil-stained, but first determine the source of the oil leak and repair it – this is most likely to be a fouled gearbox mainshaft oil seal.

4 Spin the release bearing and check it for roughness. Hold the outer race and attempt to move it laterally against the inner race. If excessive movement or roughness is evident, renew the release bearing as described in Section 8. It is worth renewing the release bearing, regardless of its condition, whenever work is being done on the other components of the clutch – this avoids having to dismantle the assembly again if the old bearing fails relatively quickly.

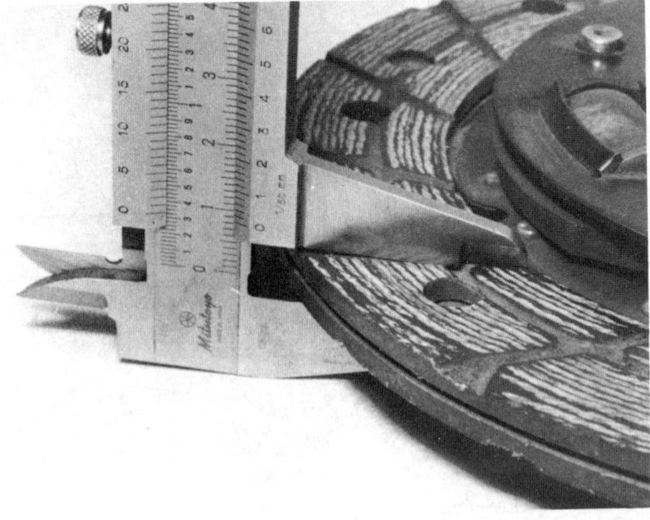

6.3a Checking the driven plate friction lining thickness

7 Clutch – refitting

1 In order to centralise the clutch driven plate it will be necessary to obtain a tool similar to the BL tool No. 18G 1352 (Fig. 5.5) (photo). A gearbox mainshaft may be used, or alternatively a length of wooden dowel rod made to the dimensions shown in Fig. 5.6 may be used.

2 Locate the flat side of the driven plate against the face of the flywheel, then position the pressure plate assembly over it onto the flywheel dowels. If the original assembly is being refitted, make sure that the previously made marks are aligned.

3 Insert the centralising tool through the driven plate and into the spigot bearing in the flywheel.

4 Insert the cover bolts and tighten them progressively in diagonal sequence to the specified torque, while occasionally checking that the centralising tool is free to move in the centre plate and spigot bearing.

5 Remove the centralising tool, then refit the gearbox as described in Chapter 6.

6.3b Checking the driven plate rivet depth

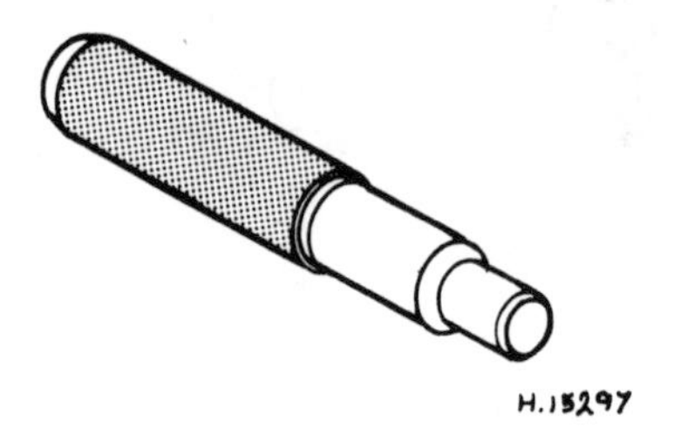

Fig. 5.5 BL tool No 18G 1352 for centralising the clutch driven plate (Sec 7)

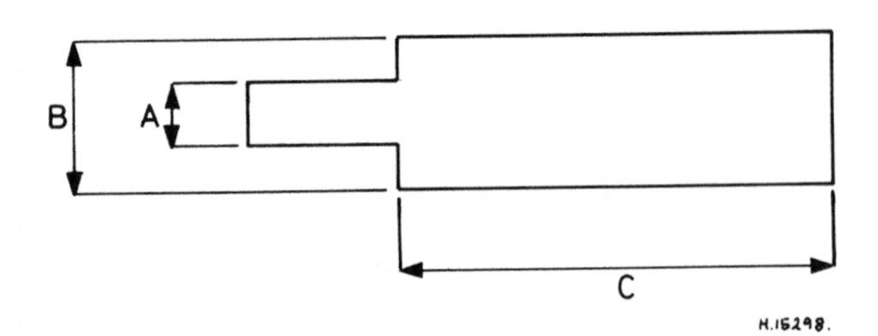

Fig. 5.6 Dimensions for making a wooden centralising tool for the clutch driven plate (Sec 7)

A 15.1 mm (0.593 in)
B 19.8 mm (0.780 in)
C 152.0 mm (6.0 in)

7.1 Using a universal clutch centralising tool

8.2 Release bearing location showing end of retaining clip

8.3 Clutch release bearing and holder

8.5 Clutch release fork location, showing retaining bolt

8.6 Clutch release arm and return spring

8 Clutch release bearing and arm – removal and refitting

1 Remove the gearbox as described in Chapter 6.
2 Using a screwdriver, prise the ends of the clip from the release fork taking care not to bend the clip out of shape (photo).
3 Slide the release bearing and holder from the sleeve inside the clutch housing (photo).
4 Spin the bearing and check it for roughness. Attempt to move the outer race laterally against the inner race. If excessive wear or any roughness is evident the bearing should be renewed. Check the inner bore of the holder and if this is worn excessively, renew the holder. To separate the bearing from the holder, support the bearing and drive out the holder using a suitable stepped mandrel – **do not** re-use a removed bearing. Drive the new bearing onto the holder using a suitable metal tube on the bearing inner race. Note that the bearing is pre-packed with grease and must not be washed in solvent.
5 If necessary, the release fork and arm can be removed from the clutch housing. Flatten the tab washer and unscrew the fork retaining bolt (photo).
6 Unhook the return spring, then withdraw the release arm and shaft and remove the fork (photo).
7 Check the dust seal in the clutch housing. If necessary, prise it out and press a new seal into position.
8 Refitting is a reversal of removal, but lubricate the clutch housing sleeve and release shaft with a molybdenum disulphide-based grease. Renew the release fork lockbolt tab washer and bend it onto the bolt head after tightening the bolt to the specified torque.

9 Fault diagnosis – clutch

Symptom	Reason(s)
Clutch slip	Insufficient cable free play Driven plate badly worn Oil or grease contamination of friction linings
Clutch judder	Worn or loose engine/gearbox mountings Oil or grease contamination of friction linings Excessive flywheel/pressure plate run-out Driven plate badly worn
Clutch drag (failure to disengage)	Incorrect adjustment Driven plate sticking on mainshaft splines Faulty pressure plate/cover assembly Oil or grease contamination of friction linings Flywheel spigot bearing seized
Noise evident on depressing clutch pedal	Dry or worn release bearing Worn or broken diaphragm fingers

Chapter 6 Manual gearbox

Contents

Specifications

Type

Five forward speeds and reverse; synchromesh on all forward speeds

Ratios

1st	2.916:1
2nd	1.764:1
3rd	1.181:1
4th	0.846:1
5th	0.714:1
Reverse	2.916:1
Final drive	4.642:1

Overhaul data

Mainshaft endfloat	0.09 to 0.30 mm (0.004 to 0.012 in)
Countershaft endfloat	0.09 to 0.30 mm (0.004 to 0.012 in)
5th gear endfloat	0.05 to 0.38 mm (0.002 to 0.015 in)
2nd, 3rd and 4th gear endfloat	0.05 to 0.18 mm (0.002 to 0.007 in)
Selective spacers available	28.10 to 28.13 mm (1.103 to 1.107 in) in four different thicknesses
1st gear endfloat	0.03 to 0.18 mm (0.001 to 0.007 in)
Selective thrust washers available	1.89 to 1.98 mm (0.074 to 0.078 in) in three different thicknesses
Minimum synchro ring-to-gear clearance	0.40 mm (0.016 in)
Maximum reverse idler gear-to-shaft clearance	0.14 mm (0.006 in)
Maximum selector fork-to-synchro sleeve clearance	1.0 mm (0.040 in)
Maximum selector guide-to-reverse gear clearance	0.7 mm (0.028 in)
Minimum diameter of end cover seal	50.1 mm (1.97 in)
Final drive gear backlash	0.14 to 0.25 mm (0.006 to 0.010 in)
Planet gear backlash	0.05 to 0.15 mm (0.002 to 0.006 in)
Selective washers available	0.7 to 1.0 mm (0.028 to 0.039 in) in increments of 0.1 mm (0.0039 in)
Differential endfloat	0.15 mm (0.006 in)
Selective circlips available	2.45 to 2.95 mm (0.096 to 0.116 in) in increments of 0.1 mm (0.0039 in)

Lubrication

Lubricant capacity – refill	2.5 litres (4.5 pints)
Lubricant capacity – from dry	2.7 litres (4.75 pints)
Lubricant type/specification*	Multigrade engine oil, viscosity SAE 10W/30 or 10W/40 (Duckhams QXR, Hypergrade or 10W/40 Motor Oil)

* **Note**: *The vehicle manufacturer specifies a 10W/40 oil to meet warranty requirements for models produced after August 1983. Duckhams QXR and 10W/40 Motor Oil are available to meet these requirements*

Torque wrench settings

	lbf ft	Nm
Drain plug	30	40
Filler plug	33	45
Selector fork bolts	9	12
Reverse selector arm nut	18	24
Selector rod bolts	13	17
Selector rod detent plugs	16	22
Transmission housing bolts	20	27
Countershaft locknut	66	90
5th gear housing bolts	9	12
Speedometer drivegear	7	10
Mainshaft locknut	44	60
End cover bolts	9	12
Clutch housing bolts	33	45
Selector torque rod to transmission	7	10
Selector torque rod to body	16	22
Selector rod bolt	16	22
Gear lever ball retainer nut	7	10
Gear lever knob locknut	5	7

1 General description

The manual gearbox incorporates five forward speeds and one reverse, with synchromesh engagement on all forward gears. Gearshift is by means of a floor-mounted lever and a single rod to the gearbox. A torsion rod from the gearbox ensures positive gearchanges during torque reaction movement of the engine.

The final drive gear and differential are integral components and are located at the rear of the gearbox. Gear selection is by means of a single selector shaft mounted across the gearbox, and three selector shafts mounted in-line with the mainshaft incorporating the selector forks.

Filler and drain plugs are located on the right-hand side of the gearbox housing.

When overhauling the gearbox, due consideration should be given to the costs involved, since it is often more economical to obtain a service exchange or good secondhand gearbox than to fit new parts to the existing gearbox.

When checking the gearbox oil level, always insert a finger through the level plug hole, as oil will collect around the plug even with a low oil level.

2 Gearbox – removal and refitting

1 Disconnect the battery negative lead and unbolt the cable from the gearbox, noting its location.
2 Pull the rubber boot from the gearbox end of the speedometer cable. Remove the clip and withdraw the cable from the gearbox and support spring.
3 Disconnect the reversing lamp switch wires.
4 Remove the starter motor as described in Chapter 10.
5 Loosen the clutch cable adjuster several turns, then lift up the release arm and disconnect the inner cable from the arm. Pull the convoluted rubber cover from the outer cable and disconnect the outer cable from the gearbox bracket.
6 Jack up the front of the car and support it on axle stands. Apply the handbrake and remove the right-hand front wheel.
7 Position a suitable container beneath the gearbox, then unscrew the drain plug with a $\frac{3}{8}$ in square drive and drain the oil. Also unscrew the filler plug with a 17 mm spanner. Refit the plugs when the oil has drained.
8 Remove the screws and withdraw the access plate from the right-hand inner wing valance (photo).
9 Unscrew the bolt from the engine rear steady bar at the clutch housing brackets, then unbolt the brackets (photo).
10 Unscrew the damper bracket bolts from the clutch housing (photo).
11 Prise off the clip, then, using a suitable drift, drive out the roll pin securing the gearchange rod to the gearbox selector shaft (photo). If the pin is seized in position it may be necessary to heat the rod in order to remove it. Pull the rod from the shaft.
12 Unscrew the mounting bolt and detach the gearchange torsion rod from the gearbox. Tie the rod to one side. Remove the large washer from the mounting pin (photos).
13 Unscrew and remove the two lower bolts from the engine rear mounting brackets, then loosen the top bolt.
14 Remove the anti-roll bar as described in Chapter 11.
15 Unscrew and remove the front suspension control arm inner pivot bolts.
16 Using a tyre lever or similar lever, force the inner ends of the driveshafts from the differential gears. Disengage the right-hand driveshaft completely and tie it to one side.
17 Unbolt the engine front steady bar bracket from the clutch housing (photo).
18 Support the gearbox with a trolley jack and unscrew the remaining gear-to-engine bolts.
19 Withdraw the gearbox from the engine, at the same time removing the left-hand driveshaft from the differential. Remove the engine damper bracket.
20 Lower the gearbox and remove it from under the car.
21 Refitting is a reversal of removal, but first apply a little grease to the splines on the mainshaft and lubricate the driveshaft oil seals with a little gearbox oil. Make sure that the clutch housing dowels are fitted correctly. Tighten all bolts to the specified torque, but delay tightening

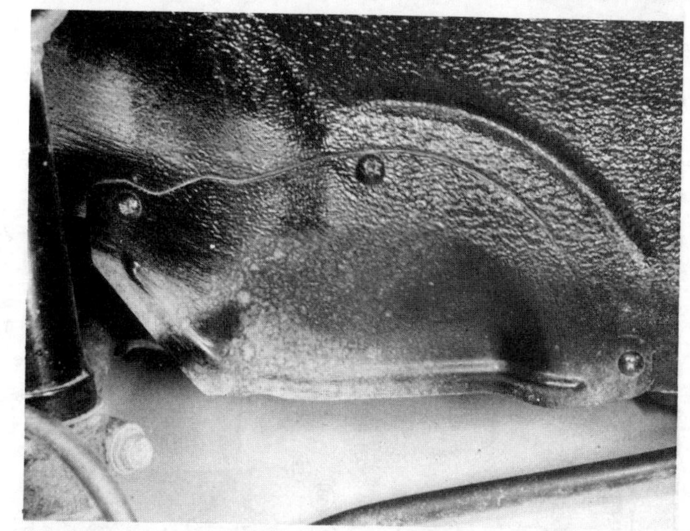

2.8 Gearbox access plate location under the right-hand inner wing valance

2.9 Rear steady bar mounting brackets

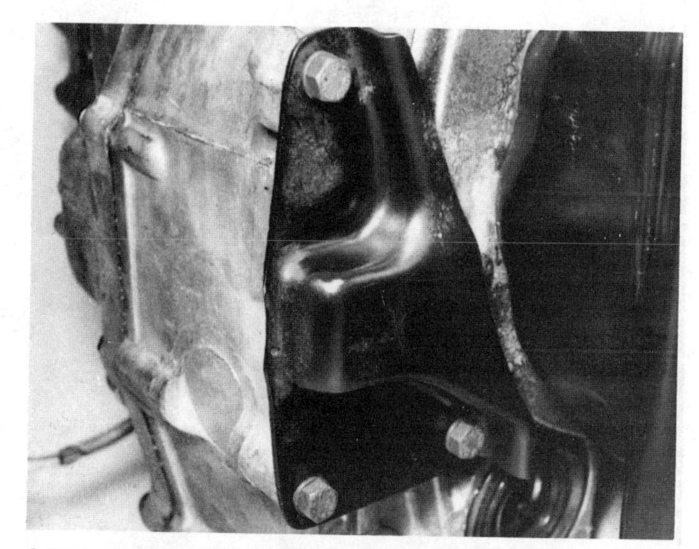

2.10 Engine damper bracket

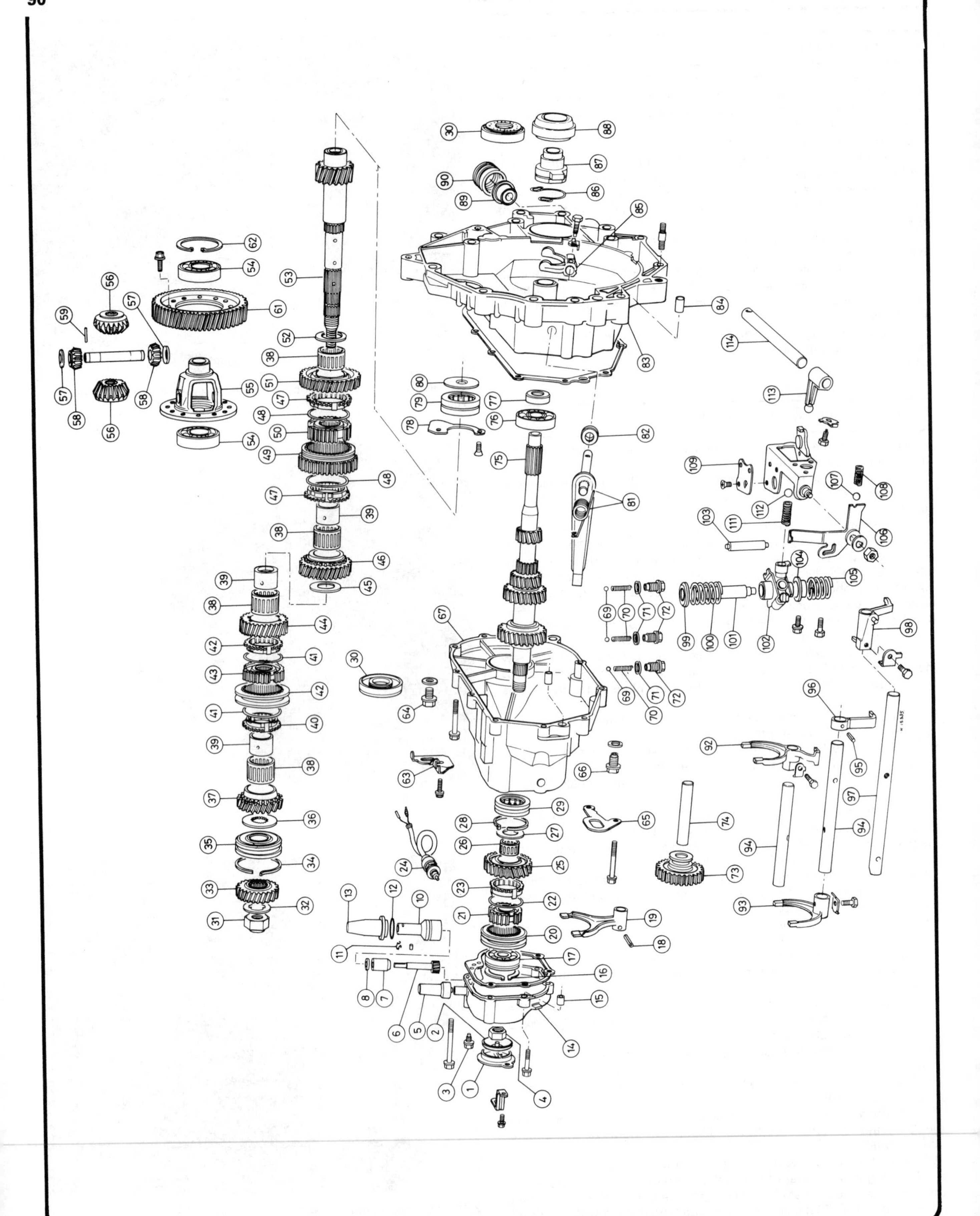

Fig. 6.1 Exploded view of the gearbox (Sec 3)

1 *End cover*
2 *Oil barrier plate*
3 *Speedometer pinion housing bolt*
4 *Mainshaft locknut*
5 *Breather cap*
6 *Speedometer drive gear pinion*
7 *Bush*
8 *Pinion seal*
9 *Dowel*
10 *Housing*
11 *Retaining clip*
12 *O-ring*
13 *Dust cover*
14 *5th gear housing*
15 *Dowel pin*
16 *Snap-ring*
17 *Bearing*
18 *Roll pin*
19 *5th gear selector fork*
20 *Synchro sleeve*
21 *Synchro hub*
22 *Synchro spring*
23 *Synchro ring*
24 *Reversing light switch*
25 *5th gear – mainshaft*
26 *Needle bearing*
27 *Thrust washer*
28 *Snap-ring*
29 *Bearing*
30 *Differential oil seal*
31 *Countershaft locknut*
32 *Dished washer*
33 *5th gear – countershaft*
34 *Snap-ring*
35 *Bearing*
36 *Thrust washer*
37 *4th gear*
38 *Bearing*
39 *Spacer collar*
40 *Synchro ring*
41 *Synchro spring*
42 *Synchro sleeve*
43 *Synchro hub*
44 *3rd gear*
45 *Spacer washer*
46 *2nd gear*
47 *Synchro ring*
48 *Synchro spring*
49 *Synchro sleeve*
50 *Synchro hub*
51 *1st gear*
52 *Selective thrust washer*
53 *Countershaft*
54 *Bearing*
55 *Differential carrier*
56 *Differential gear*
57 *Thrust washer*
58 *Differential pinion*
59 *Roll pin*
60 *Pinion shaft*
61 *Final drive gear*
62 *Circlip*
63 *Clutch cable bracket*
64 *Level plug*
65 *Lifting bracket*
66 *Drain plug*
67 *Housing*
68 *Dowel pin*
69 *Detent ball*
70 *Detent spring*
71 *Washer*
72 *Detent plug*
73 *Reverse idler gear*
74 *Reverse idler shaft*
75 *Mainshaft*
76 *Bearing*
77 *Oil seal*
78 *Bearing retainer plate*
79 *Bearing*
80 *Oil guide plate*
81 *Clutch release arm and spring*
82 *Dust seal*
83 *Clutch housing*
84 *Dowel pin*
85 *Clutch release fork*
86 *Release bearing clip*
87 *Release bearing holder*
88 *Release bearing*
89 *Selector shaft oil seal*
90 *Selector shaft gaiter*
91 *1st/2nd gear selector shaft*
92 *1st/2nd gear selector fork*
93 *3rd/4th gear selector fork*
94 *3rd/4th gear selector shaft*
95 *Roll pin*
96 *3rd/4th gear selector guide*
97 *5th/reverse selector shaft*
98 *Reverse gear selector guide*
99 *Spring retainer*
100 *Spring*
101 *Selector arm shaft*
102 *Selector arm*
103 *Interlock shaft*
104 *Spring retainer*
105 *Spring*
106 *Reverse gear selector arm*
107 *Detent ball*
108 *Detent spring*
109 *Retainer plate*
110 *Selector arm holder*
111 *Detent spring*
112 *Detent ball*
113 *Selector shaft arm*
114 *Selector shaft*

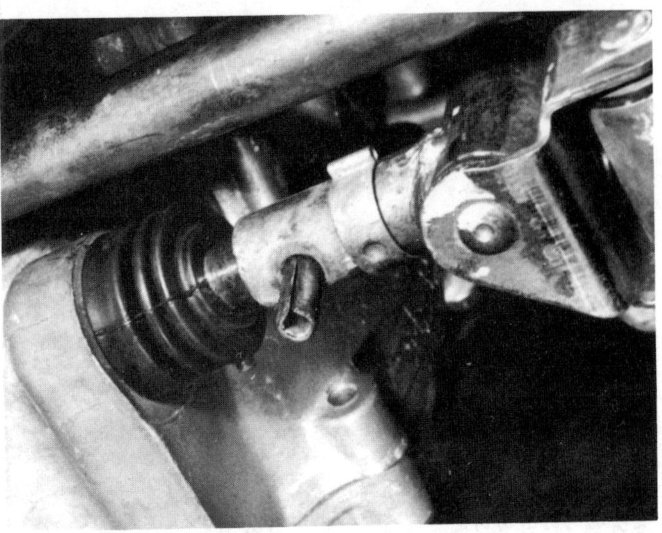
2.11 Gearchange rod roll pin location

2.12a Removing the gearchange torsion rod ...

2.12b ... and washer

2.17 Front steady bar bracket

the control arm inner pivot bolts to the specified torque (given in Chapter 11) until the weight of the car is on the front suspension.
22 Make sure that the driveshaft inner ends are fully entered in the differential gears.
23 Fill the gearbox with oil. Note the warning given in Section 1.
24 Adjust the clutch cable as described in Chapter 5.

3 Gearbox – overhaul

Dismantling

1 Remove the gearbox as described in Section 2 and clean the exterior with paraffin.
2 Unscrew the speedometer pinion housing retaining bolt and lift out the pinion and housing (photos).
3 Pull the breather cap from the 5th gear housing (photo).
4 Unbolt and remove the end cover, noting the location of the wiring clip. Remove the oil barrier plate (photos).
5 Lock the mainshaft using BL tool 18G1357, or a nut splitter and block of wood (see photo 3.80).
6 Bend up the collar from the mainshaft locknut and unscrew the locknut *(left-hand thread)* (photo).
7 Remove the nut splitter or BL tool.
8 Unbolt and remove the 5th gear housing. Remove the gasket. If necessary, unscrew and remove the reversing lamp switch (photos).
9 Temporarily insert a length of dowel rod in the selector rod. Select reverse by turning the rod clockwise against the spring, then pushing the rod inwards.
10 Using a suitable drift, drive out the roll pin securing the 5th gear selector fork to the shaft (photo).
11 Mark the 5th gear synchro sleeve and hub in relation to each other, then slide off the fork and synchro sleeve (photo).
12 Using two levers, remove the synchro hub, followed by the synchro ring and spring, 5th gear, needle bearing and thrust washer (photos).
13 Bend up the collar from the countershaft locknut and unscrew the locknut.
14 Remove the dished washer and 5th gear from the countershaft (photos).
15 Select neutral, then unscrew the three detent plugs from the bottom of the gearbox housing and remove the springs and balls (photos). Put them in a safe place.
16 Unbolt the clutch cable bracket and remove the gearbox housing-to-clutch housing bolts, noting the location of the lifting bracket (photo).
17 Using a mallet or block of wood, drive the gearbox housing from the clutch housing. At the same time move the clutch release arm to one side to clear the housing (photo). Remove the gasket.
18 Drive the differential oil seal from the gearbox housing. Expand the circlips and, using a suitable metal tube, drive out the mainshaft and

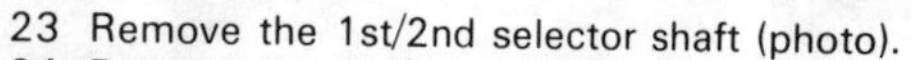

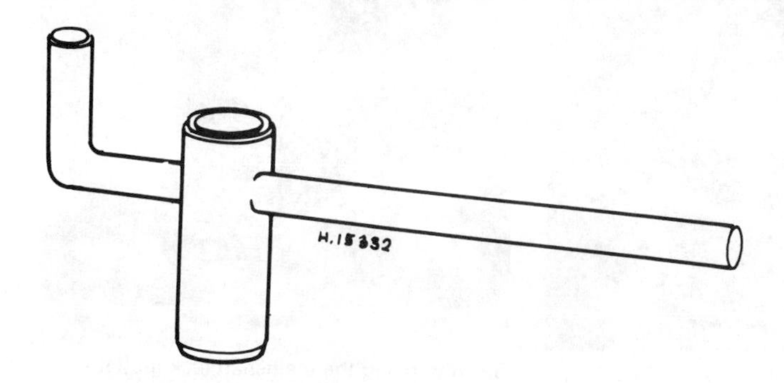

Fig. 6.2 BL tool 18G 1357 for locking the mainshaft (Sec 3)

countershaft bearings (photo). Take great care not to damage the oil seal in the countershaft bearing if the bearing is to be re-used.
19 Remove the reverse idler shaft and release the idler gear from the selector guide (photos).
21 Flatten the tab washers and unscrew the three selector fork bolts (photo).
22 Remove the 5th/reverse selector shaft and guide (photo).
23 Remove the 1st/2nd selector shaft (photo).
24 Remove the 3rd/4th selector shaft and fork (photo).
25 Move the 1st/2nd synchro sleeve to the 2nd gear position and remove the 1st/2nd selector fork (photo).
26 Lift the mainshaft and countershaft from the clutch housing together, then separate the two shafts (photo).
27 Unbolt the selector arm holder from the clutch housing moving the selector arm as necessary to gain access (photo). Note that the chromium-headed bolts are in the middie.
28 Lift the differential from the clutch housing (photo).
29 Extract the circlip and drive the differential oil seal from the clutch housing (photo).
30 Remove the selector shaft rubber gaiter (photo).
31 Bend up the locktab and unscrew the bolt securing the selector arm to the selector shaft. Remove the selector shaft and withdraw the arm. Prise the oil seal from the clutch housing (photos).
32 Unscrew the countershaft bearing retainer plate screws using an inpact screwdriver and remove the plate (photo).
33 Using BL tools 18G 284 (see Chapter 7) or similar, extract the countershaft bearing followed by the oil guide plate.
34 Drive the mainshaft bearing and oil seal from the clutch housing.
35 Remove the clutch release bearing and arm as described in Chapter 5.
36 Dismantle the countershaft by removing the thrust washer

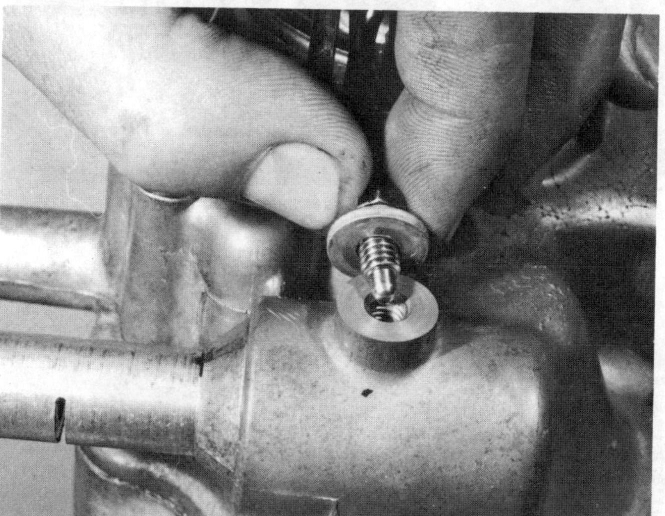

3.2a Remove the bolt ...

3.2b ... and withdraw the speedometer pinion housing

3.3 Removing the breather cap

3.4a Note the wiring clip location ...

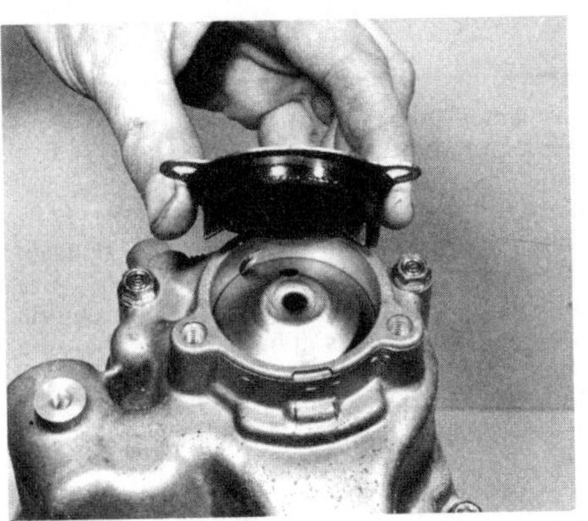
3.4b .. and then remove the end cover ...

3.4c ... and oil barrier plate

3.6 Removing the mainshaft locknut (left-hand thread)

3.8a Reversing lamp switch

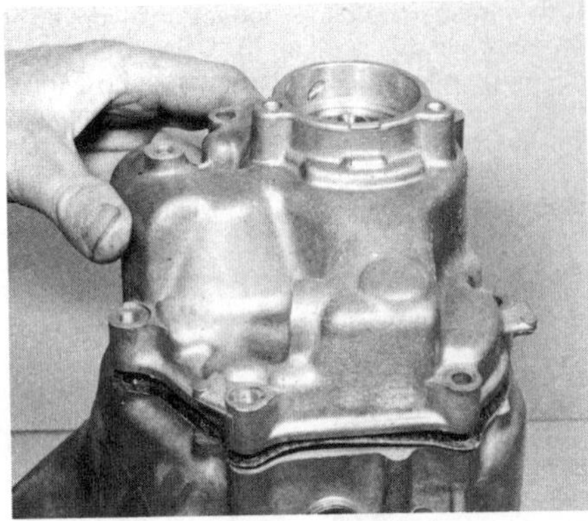
3.8b Removing the 5th gear housing

3.10 5th gear selector fork roll pin

3.11 Slide off the 5th gear selector fork and synchro sleeve

3.12a Remove the synchro hub and ring ...

3.12b ... 5th gear and needle bearing ...

3.12c ... and thrust washer from the mainshaft

3.14a Removing the dished washer ...

3.14b ... and 5th gear from the countershaft

3.15a Removing a detent plug

3.15b Detent plug showing ball and spring

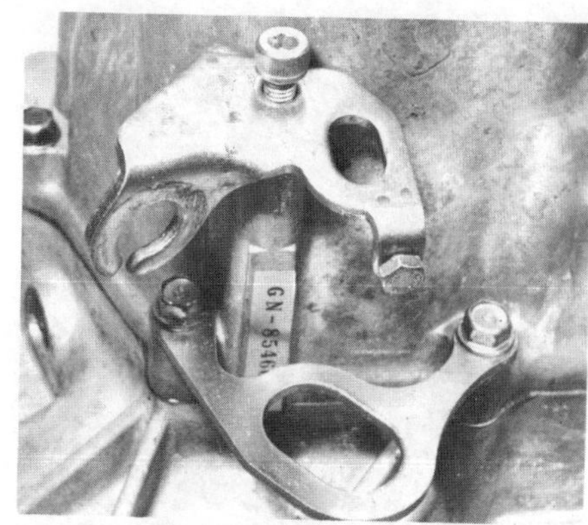
3.16 Removing the clutch cable bracket

3.17 Lifting off the gearbox housing

3.18 Mainshaft and countershaft bearing locations in the gearbox housing

3.19 Reverse idler gear and shaft

3.20a Reverse selector arm nut and special washer

3.20b Removing the reverse selector arm

3.20c Reverse selector arm detent ball location

3.21 The selector forks and bolts

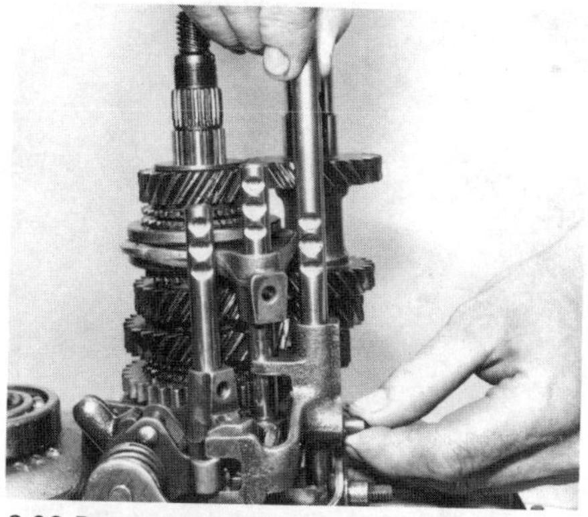
3.22 Removing the 5th/reverse selector shaft and guide

3.23 Removing the 1st/2nd selector shaft

3.24 Removing the 3rd/4th selector shaft and fork

3.25 Removing the 1st/2nd selector fork

3.26 Withdrawing the mainshaft and countershaft

3.27 Removing the selector arm holder

3.28 Differential located in the clutch housing

3.29 Inner view of differential oil seal and circlip

3.30 Selector shaft rubber gaiter

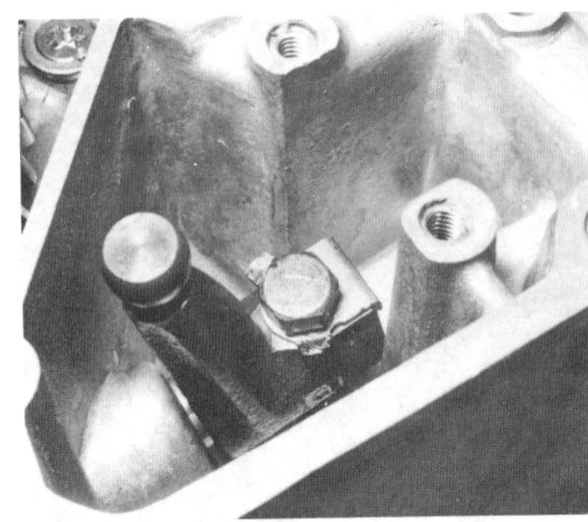
3.31a Unscrew the bolt ...

3.31b ... remove the selector arm ...

3.31c ... and withdraw the selector shaft

3.31d Selector shaft oil seal location

3.32 Countershaft and mainshaft bearing locations in the clutch housing

3.36a Remove the thrust washer ...

3.36b ... 4th gear and synchro ring

3.36c ... needle bearing and spacer collar

3.37 Removing the 3rd/4th synchro hub and synchro ring

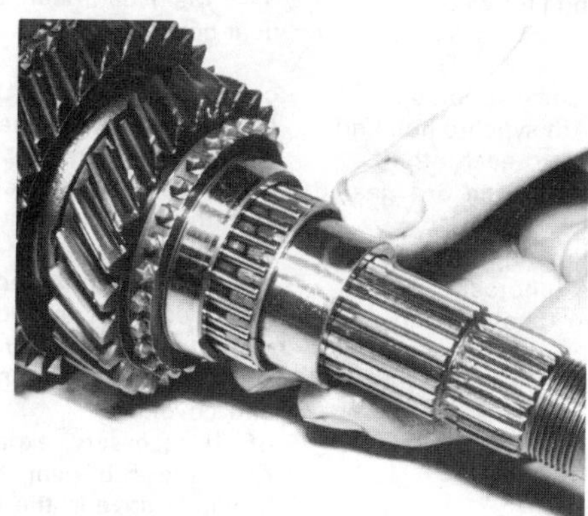

3.38 Removing the 3rd gear, needle bearing and spacer collar

3.39a Remove the spacer washer ...

3.39b ... 2nd gear and synchro ring ...

3.39c ... needle bearing and spacer collar

3.40 Removing the 1st/2nd synchro hub and synchro ring

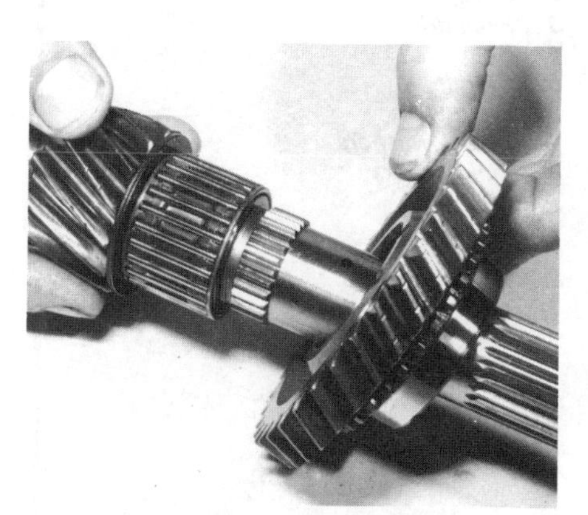

3.41a Removing the 1st gear and needle bearing ...

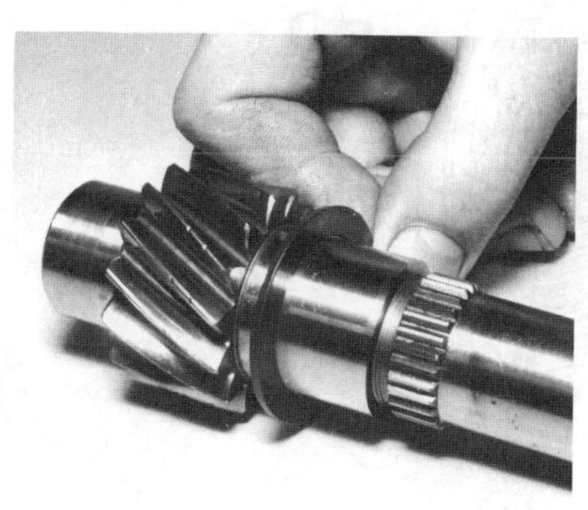

3.41b ... and thrust washer

3.41c The dismantled countershaft

3.43 Checking a synchro ring for wear

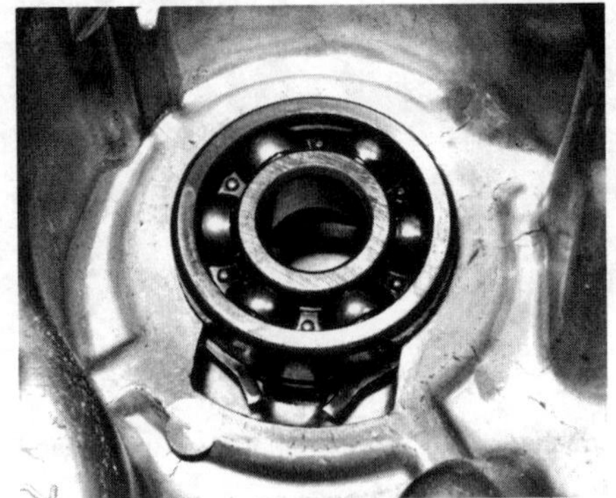
3.46 Mainshaft bearing location in the 5th gear housing

followed by 4th gear, needle bearing and spacer collar (photos).
37 Remove the synchro ring and spring, and 3rd/4th synchro hub and sleeve (photo). Mark the hub and sleeve in relation to each other.
38 Remove the synchro ring and spring followed by the 3rd gear, needle bearing and spacer collar (photo).
39 Remove the spacer washer, 2nd gear, synchro ring and spring, then remove the needle bearing and spacer collar (photos).
40 Remove the 1st/2nd synchro hub and sleeve (photo). Mark the hub and sleeve in relation to each other.
41 Remove the synchro ring and spring followed by the 1st gear, needle bearing and thrust washer (photo).

Examination

42 Clean all the components in paraffin and examine them for wear and damage. Check the gear teeth for excessive wear and pitting. Spin the bearings by hand and check them for roughness and excessive lateral movement.
43 Check each synchro ring in turn by locating the ring on its gear cone and rotating it until it grips. Using a feeler blade, measure the clearance between the synchro ring and gear faces (photo). If less than the minimum amount given in the Specifications, renew the ring.
44 Position each selector fork in its synchro ring in its synchro sleeve, and the selector guide on the reverse gear. Using a feeler blade, measure the clearances. If more that the maximum amounts given in the Specifications, renew them.
45 Check that the holes in the breather cap are clean. Measure the diameter of the end cover sealing lip in three places 120° apart – if less than the minimum amount given in the Specifications, renew the end cover.
46 If necessary, expand the circlip and drive the mainshaft bearing from the 5th gear housing using a suitable metal tube (photo). Similarly drive in the new bearing with the metal tube contacting the outer track only, and with the bearing part number facing outwards.
47 If required, the differential assembly may be dismantled, referring to Fig. 6.3. However, mark each component for position before removing it. Note that the final drive gear bolts have a *left-hand thread*. A puller will be necessary in order to remove the differential bearings. The chamfer on the final drive gear inside diameter must face the carrier.

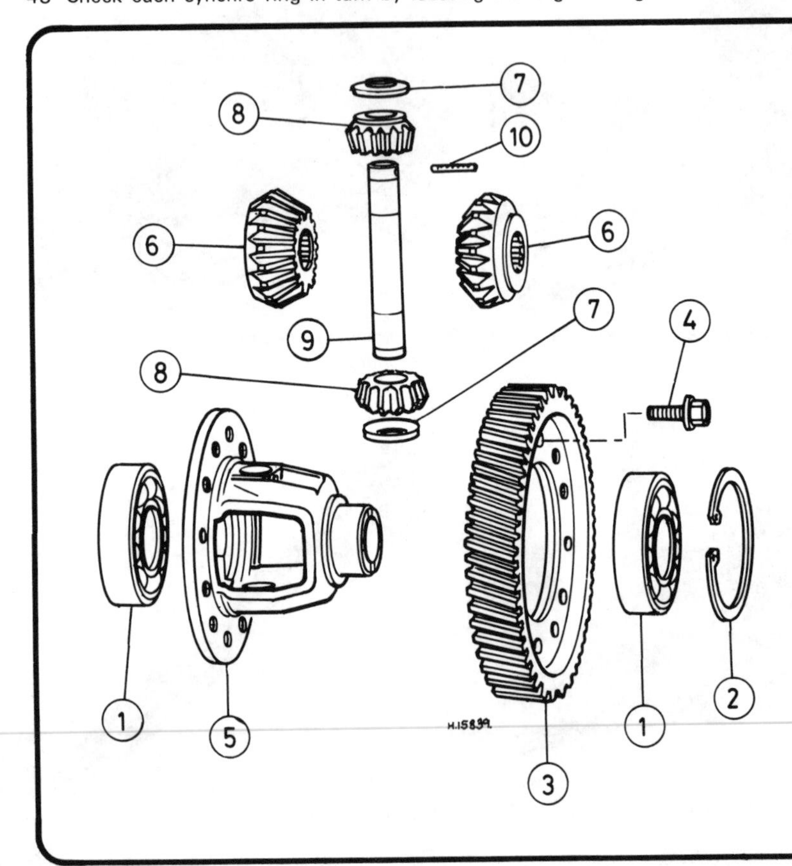

Fig. 6.3 Exploded view of the differential (Sec 3)

1 *Bearings*
2 *Circlip*
3 *Final drive gear*
4 *Bolt*
5 *Carrier*
6 *Side gears*
7 *Thrust washers*
8 *Pinion gears*
9 *Pin*
10 *Roll pin*

Reassembly

48 With all components renewed as necessary commence reassembly by fitting all the components to the countershaft up to and including the splined thrust washer. With the countershaft on end, press down on the thrust washer and use a feeler gauge to measure the endfloat of the gears. If more than that given in the Specifications, select and fit new spacer collars or a thrust washer as applicable.

49 Locate the 5th gear thrust washer on the mainshaft followed by the needle bearing, 5th gear, and the synchro hub. With the mainshaft on end, press down on the synchro hub and use a feeler gauge to measure the gear endfloat. If more than that given in the Specifications, renew the thrust washer. Remove the components from the mainshaft.

50 Using a suitable metal tube, drive the mainshaft oil seal and bearing squarely into the clutch housing, having first lubricated the oil seal with gearbox oil.

51 Insert the selector shaft in the clutch housing and locate it in the selector arm. Fit the bolt and locktab, tighten the bolt, and bend the locktab onto the bolt head to lock it.

52 Lubricate the oil seal with grease. Drive it into position over the selector shaft using a metal tube.

53 Refit the rubber gaiter with the small drain hole facing downwards.

54 Locate the countershaft bearing oil guide plate in the clutch housing, then drive in the bearing using a metal tube on the outer track.

55 Fit the bearing retainer plate, insert the screws and tighten them with an impact screwdriver. Stake the edge of each screw to the clutch housing with a centre-punch.

56 Fit the circlip in the groove in the clutch housing and lower the differential into position.

57 Fit the selector arm holder, making sure that the socket is located on the selector arm. Insert and tighten the bolts.

58 Mesh the mainshaft with the countershaft, then fit them simultaneously to the clutch housing.

59 Move the 1st/2nd synchro sleeve to the 2nd gear position and fit the 1st/2nd selector fork in the sleeve groove. Move the sleeve back to the neutral position.

60 Fit the 3rd/4th selector fork in the sleeve groove and insert the shaft.

61 Insert the 1st/2nd selector shaft.

62 Locate the 5th/reverse selector guide on the selector arm and insert the shaft.

63 Turn the selector shafts so that the detent grooves face away from the gears, then align the holes and insert the selector fork bolts and tab washers. Tighten the bolts and bend each tab washer onto one flat of the bolt head to lock it.

64 Insert the reverse detent spring and ball in the clutch housing, then fit the reverse selector arm, locating the slot over the guide pin. Fit the special washer and tighten the nut.

65 Engage the reverse idler gear with the selector guide and insert the shaft

66 Expand the circlip in the gearbox housing and drive the mainshaft bearing into position, until the circlip engages the groove, using a metal tube on the outer track. Similarly fit the countershaft bearing, making sure that the oil seal end faces into the gearbox.

67 Check that the housing dowel pins are in position, then locate a new gasket on the clutch housing (photos).

68 Lubricate the differential bearing outer track, the mainshaft, countershaft, and selector shafts with gearbox oil to help refitting of the gearbox housing. Align the gearbox housing with the 5th/reverse selector shaft, then lower it onto the clutch housing and lightly tap it into position.

69 Insert the housing bolts together with the lifting bracket and tighten them evenly to the specified torque in the sequence shown in Fig. 6.6 (photo).

70 Fit the clutch cable bracket and tighten the bolt.

71 Insert the three detent balls and springs in the holes in the bottom of the gearbox housing, then fit and tighten the plugs together with the washers.

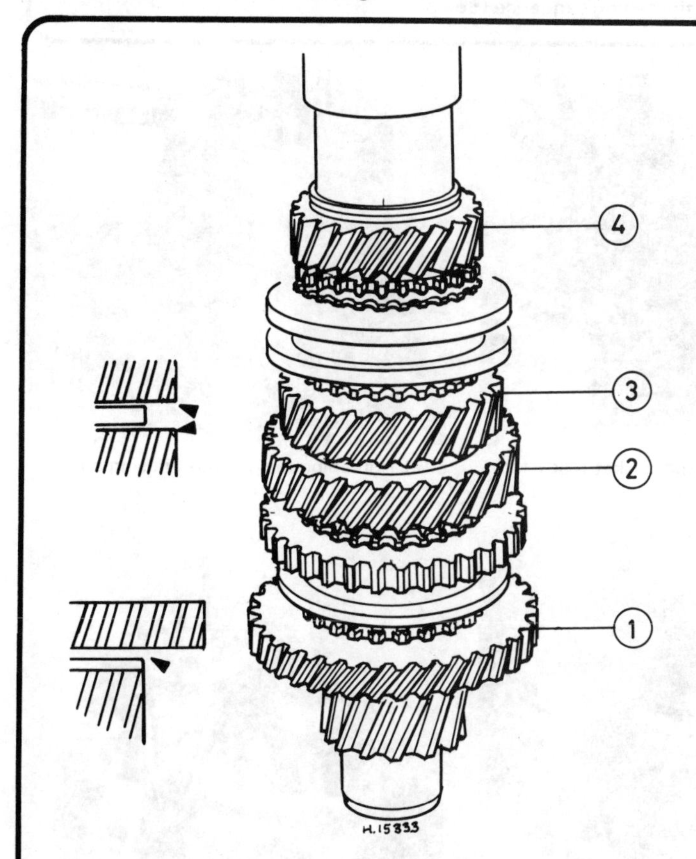

Fig. 6.4 Countershaft gear endfloat checking locations (Sec 3)

1 *1st gear*
2 *2nd gear*
3 *3rd gear*
4 *4th gear*

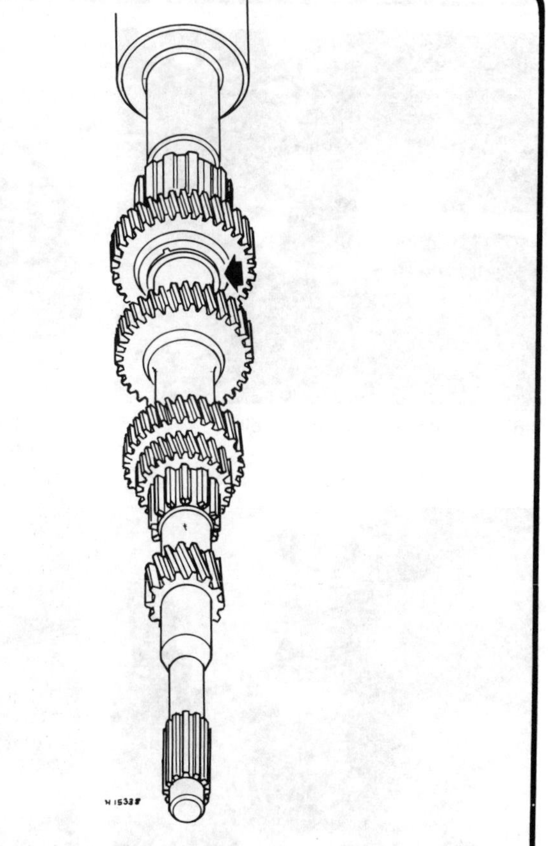

Fig. 6.5 Mainshaft 5th gear endfloat checking location – arrowed (Sec 3)

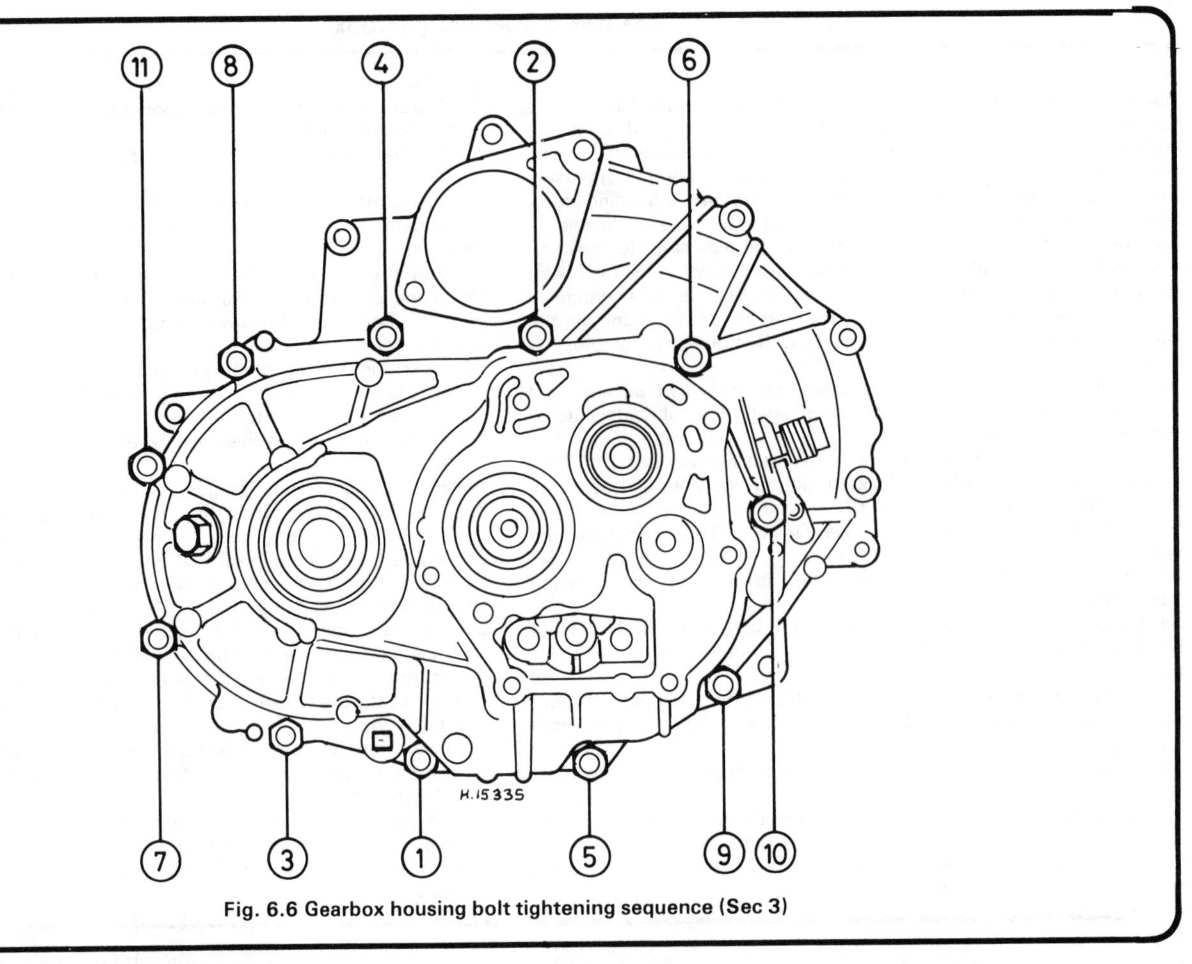

Fig. 6.6 Gearbox housing bolt tightening sequence (Sec 3)

3.67a A clutch housing dowel pin

3.67b Clutch housing and gasket ready for fitting of gearbox housing

3.69 Tightening the gearbox housing bolts

3.74a Tightening the countershaft locknut

3.74b Staking the countershaft locknut

3.79 Gearbox housing and gasket ready for fitting of 5th gear housing

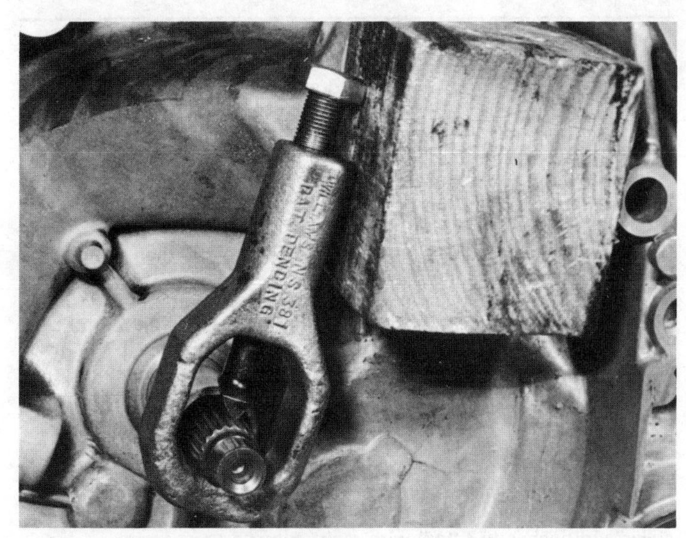
3.80a Using a nut splitter and a block of wood to hold the mainshaft stationary. Do not overtighten!

3.80b Tightening the mainshaft locknut

72 Fit the 5th gear (boss end first) onto the countershaft splines followed by the dished washer (concave side first).
73 Select reverse gear and lock the mainshaft using BL tool 18G 1357, or a nut splitter and block of wood.
74 Fit the countershaft locknut and tighten it to the specified torque. Lock the nut by staking the collar (photos).
75 Fit the 5th gear thrust washer to the mainshaft followed by the needle bearing, 5th gear, synchro ring and spring.
76 Fit the 5th gear synchro hub (recessed side first) onto the mainshaft splines using a metal tube if necessary.
77 Locate the selector fork in the synchro sleeve groove so that the chamfer on the sleeve will face away from the 5th gear. Slide both components simultaneously over the 5th/reverse selector shaft and synchro hub, making sure that the previously made marks are aligned.
78 Secure the 5th gear selector fork to the shaft by driving in the roll pin.
79 Locate a new gasket on the gearbox housing. Fit the 5th gear housing, insert the bolts, and tighten them evenly and in diagonal sequence to the specified torque (photo).
80 Fit the mainshaft locknut *(left-hand thread)* and tighten it to the specified torque (photo). Loosen the nut, then retighten it to the same torque. Lock the nut by staking the collar.
81 Select neutral and remove the nut splitter or BL tool.
82 Align and fit the oil barrier plate. Fit the end cover, bolts and wiring clip, and tighten the bolts.
83 Fit the breather cap.
84 Insert the speedometer pinion and housing in the 5th gear housing. Fit the bolt and washer, and tighten the bolt.
85 Insert and tighten the reversing lamp switch.
86 Temporarily extract the differential bearing circlip from the clutch housing and, using a suitable metal tube, lightly drive the bearing and differential into the gearbox housing. Refit the circlip, then measure the clearance between the circlip and bearing outer track using a feeler blade. If the clearance is not the specified differential endfloat, select a circlip of the appropriate thickness and fit it.
87 Lubricate the differential oil seals with gearbox oil, then drive them into the housings using a block of wood.
88 Fit the clutch release bearing and arm as described in Chapter 5.
89 The gearbox is now ready for refitting as described in Section 2.

4 Differential oil seals – renewal

Left-hand side oil seal

1 Remove the left-hand driveshaft as described in Chapter 8.
2 Lever the oil seal from the gearbox and wipe clean its location.
3 Dip the new oil seal in gearbox oil, then drive it squarely into the clutch housing using a block of wood. Wipe away any excess oil.
4 Refit the driveshaft as described in Chapter 8.

Right-hand side oil seal

5 Jack up the front of the car and support it on axle stands. Apply the handbrake and remove the roadwheel.
6 Disconnect the battery negative lead.
7 Place a suitable container beneath the gearbox. Unscrew the filler plug with a 17 mm spanner, and unscrew the drain plug with a $\frac{3}{8}$ in square drive. Drain the oil, then refit the plugs.
8 Extract the split pin and unscrew the nut from the front suspension lower balljoint.
9 Using a separator tool, release the lower control arms and balljoint from the steering knuckle/hub.
10 Using a tyre lever or similar lever, force the inner end of the driveshaft from the differential while pulling the front hub outwards. Take care (particularly on cars with a serial number from 117 813 on) not to extend the driveshaft inner joint, otherwise the ball-bearings may fall out. Tie the driveshaft to one side.
11 Lower the oil seal from the gearbox and wipe clean its location (photo).
12 Dip the new oil seal in the gearbox oil, then drive it squarely into the gearbox housing using a block of wood. Wipe away any excess oil.
13 Pull the front hub outwards, then insert the inner end of the driveshaft into the differential and push it in until the spring clip engages the groove.

4.11 Levering out the right-hand side differential oil seal

14 Fit the lower control arm balljoint to the steering knuckle/hub, tighten the nut to the specified torque (see Chapter 11) and install the split pin.
15 Fill the gearbox with the specified oil.
16 Reconnect the battery negative lead, then refit the roadwheel and lower the car to the ground.

5 Selector shaft oil seal – renewal

1 Jack up the front of the car and support it on axle stands. Apply the handbrake.
2 Prise the clip from the gearchange rod then, using a suitable drift, drive out the roll pin. If the pin is seized in position it may help to heat it first.
3 Detach the gearchange rod from the selector shaft.
4 Pull off the rubber gaiter and lever the oil seal from the clutch housing.
5 Wipe clean the seal location, then lubricate the new seal with grease and drive it into position using a metal tube.
6 Fit the rubber gaiter with the small drain hole facing downwards.
7 Locate the gearchange rod on the selector shaft and align the roll pin holes.
8 Drive in the roll pin and position the clip over it as shown in Fig. 6.7.
9 Check and top up the gearbox oil level as necessary, then lower the car to the ground.

6 Speedometer pinion and housing – removal, examination and refitting

1 The speedometer pinion and housing are located on the right-hand end of the gearbox. First pull up the cable dust cover, extract the spring clip and withdraw the cable from the housing.
2 Unscrew and remove the housing bolt and washer, and withdraw the pinion and housing.
3 Pull the pinion from the housing, extract the dowel pin, and remove the bush and seal. Remove the outer O-ring seal.
4 Clean the components in paraffin and wipe dry. Examine them for wear and damage and renew them as necessary. Obtain new seals.
5 Refitting is a reversal of removal, but lubricate the components with gearbox oil and make sure that the dowel pin hole is aligned with the bolt hole.

7 Gearchange lever – removal, examination and refitting

1 Jack up the front of the car and support it on axle stands. Apply the handbrake.
2 Unscrew and remove the pivot bolt and disconnect the gearchange rod from the bottom of the gear lever (photo).
3 Pull off the seals, extract the bushes (if fitted), and press out the spacer collar. Remove the O-rings from the spacer collar.
4 Unscrew the knob from the top of the gear lever.
5 Remove the headlamp adjuster knob and plate, then remove the screws and withdraw the console.
6 Unscrew the screws and withdraw the ring and gear lever gaiter.
7 Extract the circlip from the top of the torsion rod and lift out the gear lever.
8 Note the location of the gear lever seat and stopper ring, then remove them. Remove the O-rings from the seat and withdraw the dust cover from the lever.
9 Examine the gear lever nut, gear lever, bushes, spacer collar and pivot bolt for wear and damage and renew them as necessary. Renew the O-rings and seals as a matter of course.
10 Refitting is a reversal of removal, but lubricate the seat, spacer collar and bushes (if fitted) with multi-purpose grease.

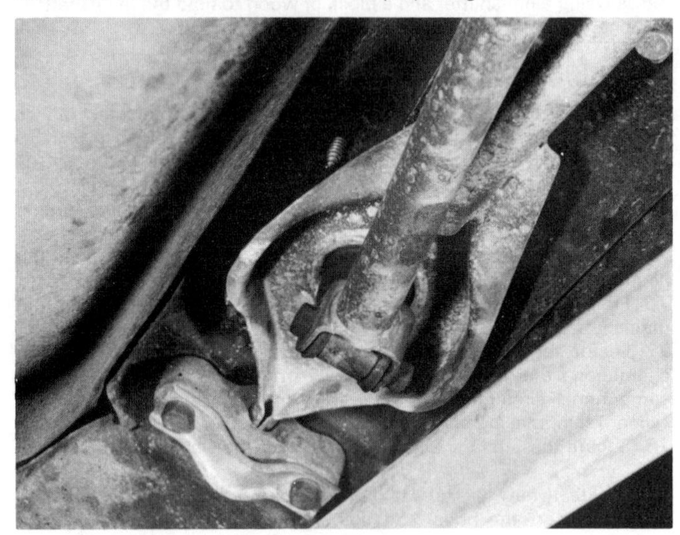

7.2 View of the gearchange rod from under the car

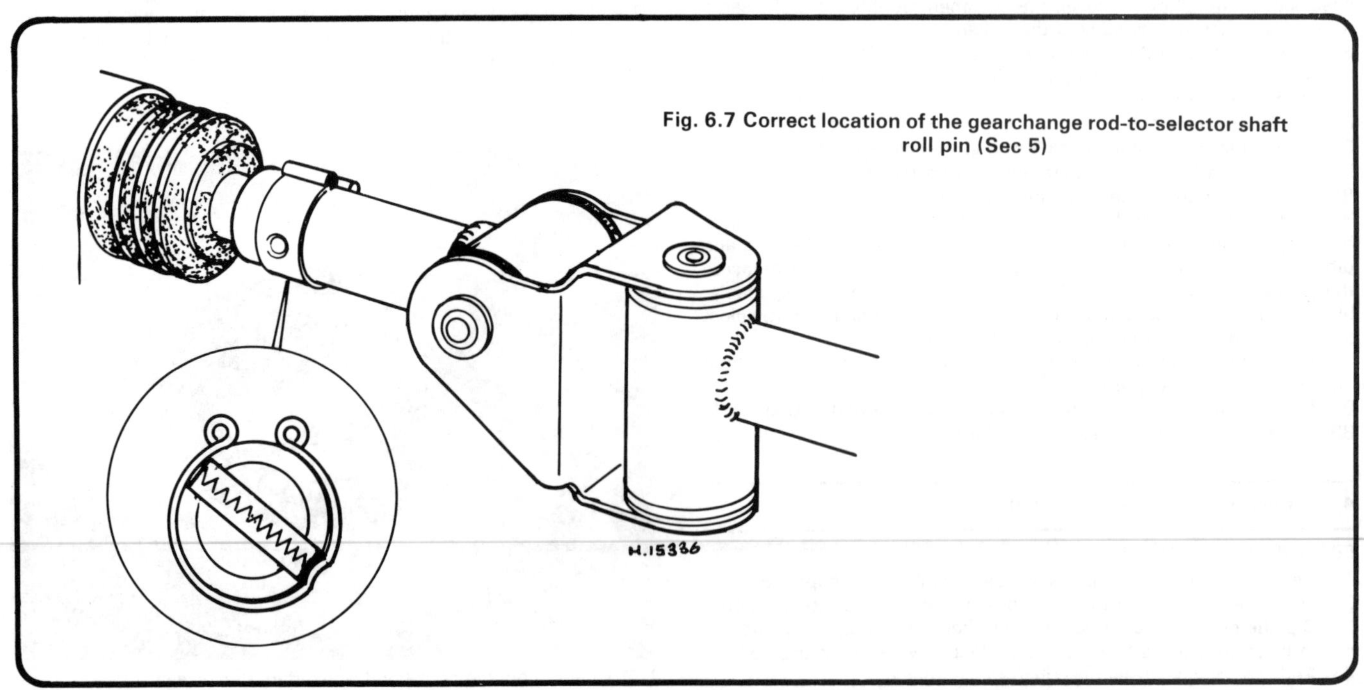

Fig. 6.7 Correct location of the gearchange rod-to-selector shaft roll pin (Sec 5)

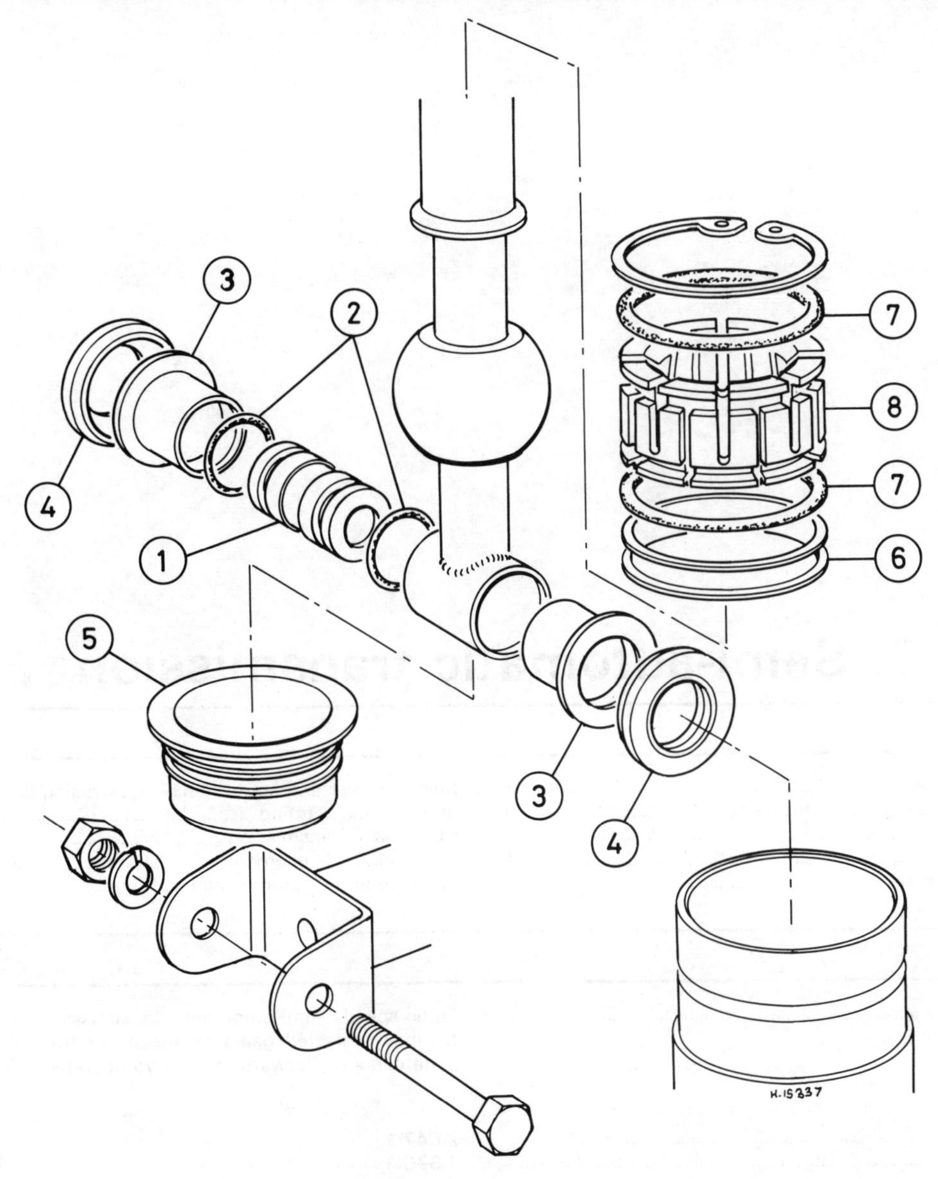

Fig. 6.8 Exploded view of the gearchange lever components (Sec 7)

1 *Spacer collar*
2 *O-rings*
3 *Bushes (if fitted)*
4 *Sealing washers*
5 *Dust cover*
6 *Stopper ring*
7 *O-rings*
8 *Gear lever seat*

8 Fault diagnosis – manual gearbox

Symptom	Reason(s)
Ineffective synchromesh	Worn synchro rings
Jumps out of gear	Worn synchro rings and sleeves Weak or broken detent springs Worn selector forks Worn gears and engagement dogs
Noisy operation	Worn bearings and gears Oil level low or incorrect grade
Difficult engagement of gears	Clutch cable out of adjustment Partially seized spigot bearing in flywheel Worn selector components Oil grade incorrect (too thick)

Chapter 7 Semi-automatic transmission

Contents

Specifications

Type	Three-speed semi-automatic transmission wih torque converter. Manually selected gears by means of hydraulically-operated multi-plate clutches (forward) and servo-operated selector fork (reverse)

Ratios

1st (L)	2.047:1
2nd (★)	1.370:1
3rd (OD)	1.032:1
Reverse (R)	1.954:1
Final drive	3.105:1

Test data

Stall speed	2300 to 2900 rpm
Hydraulic pressure at 1000 rpm:	
Line pressure	6.0 to 7.0 kgf/cm^2 (85 to 100 lbf/in^2)
Clutch pressure	5.5 to 7.0 kgf/cm^2 (78 to 100 lbf/in^2)

Overhaul data

Oil pump:	
Driven gear endfloat	0.03 to 0.08 mm (0.001 to 0.003 in)
Driven gear radial clearance	0.05 to 0.15 mm (0.002 to 0.006 in)
Drivegear radial clearance	0.21 to 0.39 mm (0.008 to 0.015 in)
Servo valve return spring free length (minimum)	28 mm (1.10 in)
Mainshaft Low gear endfloat	0.08 to 0.20 mm (0.003 to 0.008 in)
Mainshaft Drive gear endfloat	0.07 to 0.15 mm (0.003 to 0.006 in)
Countershaft 3rd gear endfloat	0.07 to 0.15 mm (0.003 to 0.006 in)
Selector splined washers available	2.97 to 3.40 mm (0.117 o 0.134 in) in nine different sizes
Countershaft Drive gear endfloat	0.07 to 0.15 mm (0.003 to 0.006 in)
Selective washers available	2.27 to 2.60 mm (0.089 to 0.102 in) in seven different sizes
Countershaft reverse gear endfloat	0.10 to 0.20 mm (0.004 to 0.008 in)
Clutch piston spring free length	27 to 29 mm (1.1 to 1.14 in)
Endplate to-top disc clearance	2.2 to 3.65 mm (0.087 to 0.144 in) in eleven different sizes
Final drivegear backlash	0.14 to 0.25 mm (0.006 to 0.010 in)
Planet gear backlash	0.05 to 0.15 mm (0.002 to 0.006 in)

Selective washers available	0.7 to 1.0 mm (0.028 to 0.039 in) in increments of 0.1 mm (0.0039 in)
Differential endfloat	0.15 mm (0.006 in)
Selective circlips available	2.45 to 2.95 mm (0.096 to 0.116 in) in increments of 0.10 mm (0.0039 in)

Transmission fluid

Fluid capacity – refill	2.5 litres (4.5 pints)
Fluid capacity – from dry	4.9 litres (8.75 pints)
Lubricant type/specification	Dexron II type automatic transmission fluid (Duckhams D-Matic)

Torque wrench settings

	lbf ft	Nm
Drain plug	30	40
Mainshaft locknut – endfloat check	22	30
Mainshaft locknut – final	70	95
Countershaft locknut – endfloat check	22	30
Countershaft locknut – final	70	95
Speedometer drivegear bolt	7	10
Selector cable bolt	20	27
Selector arm locking screw	9	12
Valve body bolt	9	12
Regulator bolt	9	12
Servo bolt	9	12
Reverse selector fork bolt	9	12
Transmission housing bolt	30	40
Parking pawl locking bolt	10	14
Idler shaft bolt	9	12
Transmission end cover	9	12
Torque converter housing	33	45
Torque converter to driveplate	9	12
Torque converter assembly bolts	9	12
Oil cooler banjo bolt	21	29
Oil cooler hose connector	21	29
Final drivegear	74	100

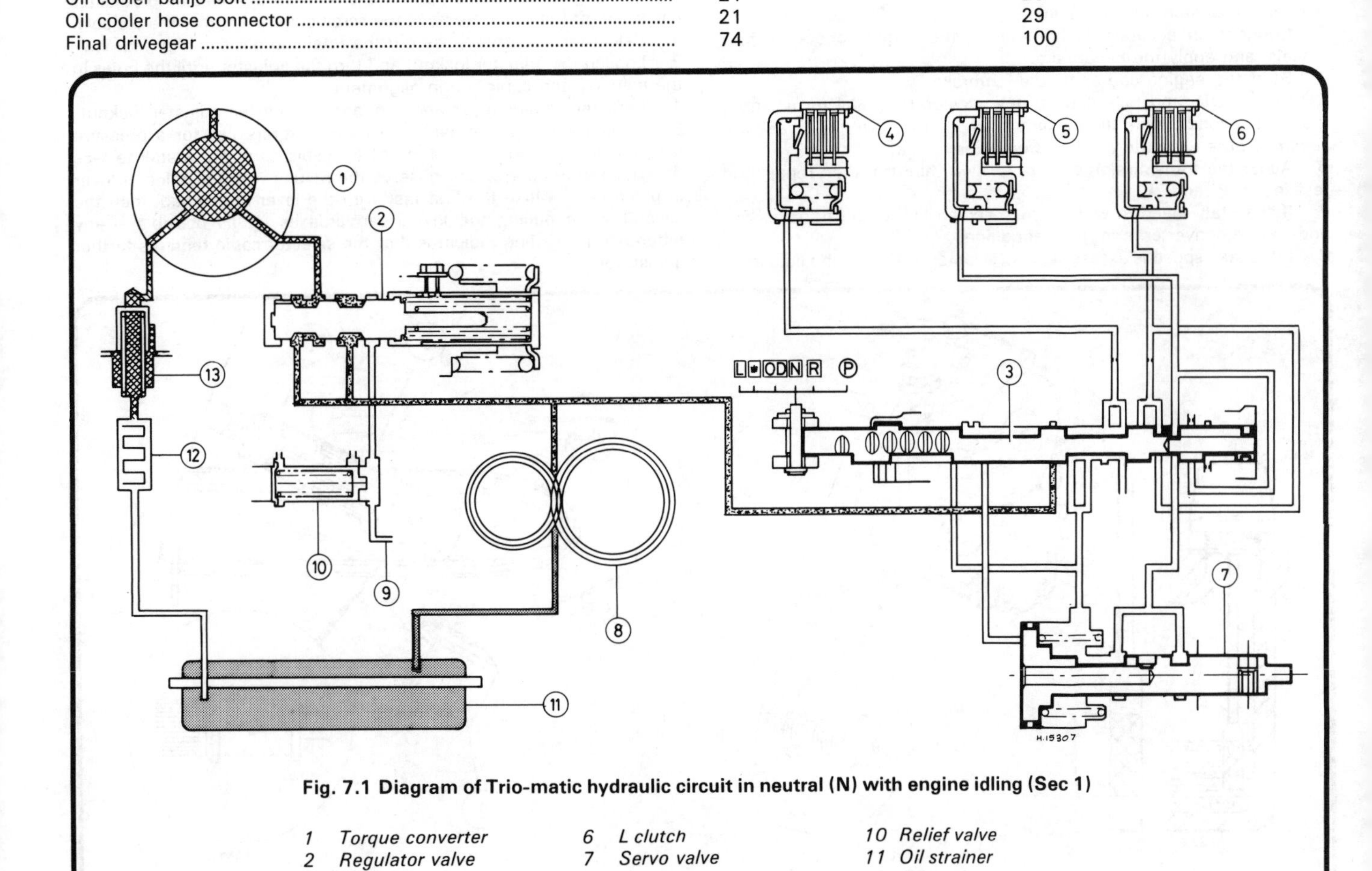

Fig. 7.1 Diagram of Trio-matic hydraulic circuit in neutral (N) with engine idling (Sec 1)

1 *Torque converter*
2 *Regulator valve*
3 *Manual valve*
4 *OD clutch*
5 *☆ clutch*
6 *L clutch*
7 *Servo valve*
8 *Oil pump gears*
9 *Fluid supply pipe*
10 *Relief valve*
11 *Oil strainer*
12 *Oil cooler*
13 *Converter check valve*

1 General description

The Trio-matic transmission incorporates three forward ratios and reverse. Drive from the engine is via a torque converter which provides torque multiplication when starting from rest or when accelerating.

All gears are selected manually by a selector lever, and engine braking access in each gear during overrun. Gears are engaged by three hydraulically-operated multi-plate clutches and a servo, which lock the appropriate gear to the mainshaft and countershaft.

The transmission fluid is pumped to the torque converter and to various lubrication points, and it is cooled by an oil cooler incorporated into the right-hand side of the radiator.

If the transmission develops a fault, it is advisable to take the car to a BL garage or transmission specialist for accurate diagnosis to be made before removing the unit. This is necessary because special equipment must be used to check the hydraulic pressure at each selector position.

When working on the transmission, cleanliness is most important to prevent damage to and malfunction of the hydraulic components. Only lint-free cloth should be used for cleaning. Do not use grease or any oil other than the specified transmission fluid, and clean the components with chlorinated industrial solvent only.

2 Stall test – transmission

1 The purpose of the stall test is to check the condition of the multi-plate clutches, torque converter and hydraulic circuit. For accurate testing the engine must be in good working order.

2 Run the engine to normal operating temperature, then check that the transmission fluid level is on the top mark on the dipstick (see Section 3). Switch off the engine.

3 Connect an accurate tachometer to the engine, check all four wheels, and apply the handbrake.

4 Start the engine and apply the footbrake.

5 Select 'OD' and fully depress the accelerator pedal for no more than ten seconds. Note the maximum engine rpm. *Do not exceed ten seconds, otherwise the transmission will overheat.*

6 Allow the transmission to cool for two minutes. then repeat the test in 'L', 'R' and '★'.

7 If the stall speed is within the specified limits, the transmission and torque converter is in good condition.

8 If the stall speed is excessive in all selector positions, the fluid level may be low, oil pump faulty, oil strainer clogged or the pressure regulator faulty.

9 If the stall speed is excessive in '★' and 'R', the 'D' clutch is slipping.

10 If the stall speed is excessive in 'L', the 'L' clutch is slipping.

11 If the stall speed is excessive in 'OD', the 'OD' clutch is slipping.

12 If the stall speed is low in all selector positions, either the engine output is low (check that the throttle opens fully) or the torque converter stator is slipping. The latter will also result in poor acceleration from rest and inability to pull away on steep gradients.

13 Disconnect the tachometer from the engine.

3 Fluid level – checking

1 Apply the handbrake and select 'P'. Run the engine for a few minutes, then switch off and complete the check immediately.

2 Remove the headlamp washer reservoir, then unscrew the dipstick from the transmission end housing and wipe the blade with lint-free cloth.

3 Insert the dipstick, but do not screw it in, then withdraw it and check that the level is on the high mark. If not, top it up through the dipstick hole using the specified fluid.

4 Insert and tighten the dipstick, and refit the headlamp washer reservoir.

5 Frequent need for topping up suggests a leak which must be investigated. Do not overlook the oil cooler and its connections.

4 Selector cable – adjustment

1 Working inside the car, pull the knob from the headlamp adjuster and prise off the plate. Remove the screws and withdraw the console.

2 Select reverse, then prise out the retaining pin and clip (Fig. 7.3).

3 Loosen the adjuster locknut and turn the adjuster until the holes in the adjuster and cable are in alignment.

4 Refit the retaining pin and clip, and tighten the adjuster locknut.

5 To check the adjustment, the manufacturers call for a pressure test, but if a pressure gauge is not available carry out a stall test as described in Section 2 and observe the results with the selector lever in position 'L'. Make the first test with the lever untouched, then the second while pulling the lever rearwards as far as possible – any difference in reading indicates that the selector cable requires further adjustment.

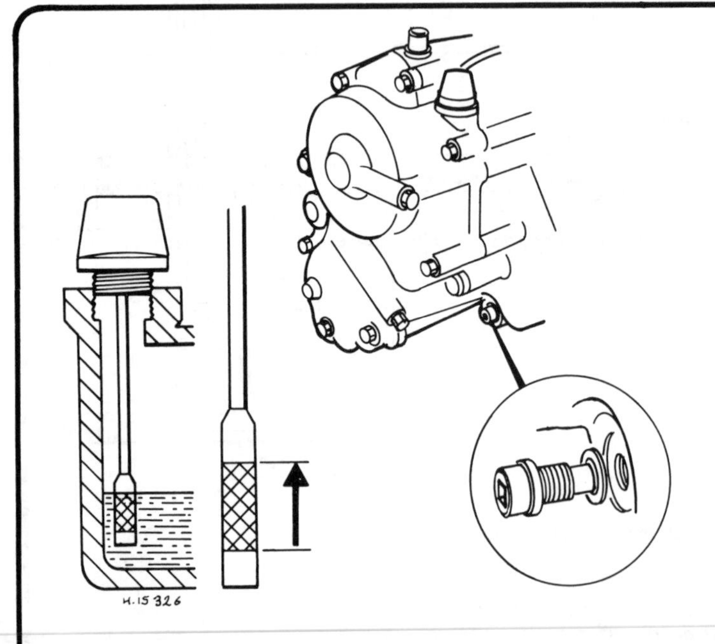

Fig. 7.2 Location of the fluid level dipstick and drain plug (Sec 3)

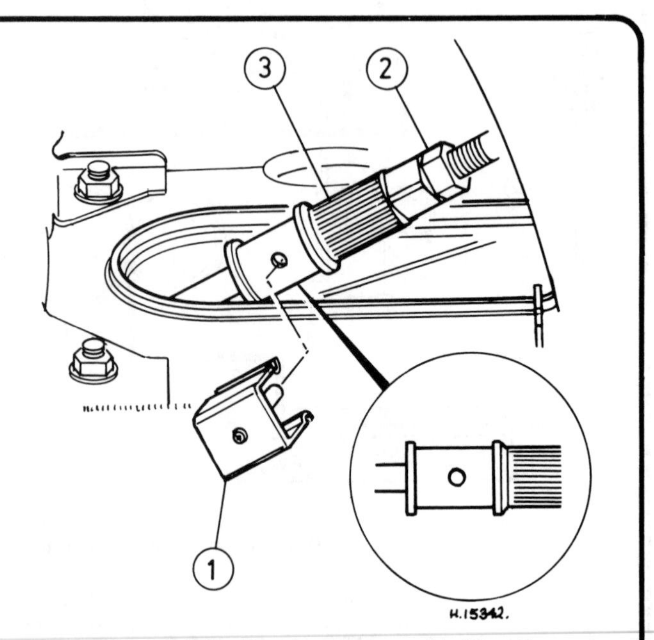

Fig. 7.3 Adjusting the selector cable (Sec 4)

1 *Retaining pin and clip*
2 *Locknut*
3 *Adjuster*

6 If a pressure gauge (to 100 lbf/in^2) and adaptor are available, connect them to the Low clutch test point (see Fig. 7.4). Run the engine to normal operating temperature, then with it idling, apply the handbrake and footbrake and select 'L'. Check the pressure first with the lever untouched, then while pulling the lever rearwards as far as possible – if the pressure drops when pulling the lever, the selector cable requires further adjustment.
7 Remove the pressure gauge (if applicable) and check that the engine can only be started with the selector lever in positions 'P' and 'N'. Check that the reversing lights operate only in position 'R', and also that the selector lever cannot be moved from 'N' to 'R' without depressing the lever button.
8 Refit the console and the headlamp adjuster knob and plate.

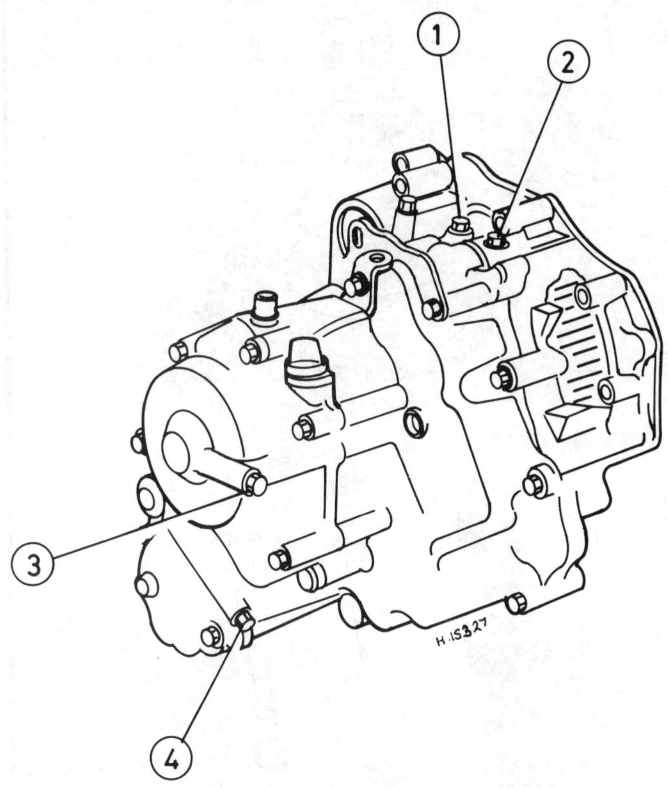

Fig. 7.4 Fluid pressure testing points (Sec 4)

1 Line pressure
2 Drive (☆) clutch
3 Low clutch
4 OD clutch

5 Transmission – removal and refitting

1 Disconnect the battery negative lead and the earth cable from the transmission. Remove the gear selector console and disconnect the selector cable (Section 4).
2 Remove the starter motor and disconnect the speedometer cable as described in Chapter 10.
3 Loosen the clips, then disconnect and plug the oil cooler hoses at the transmission.
4 Detach the steady bar from the rear of the engine and converter housing brackets, then unbolt the bracket.
5 Apply the handbrake, then jack up the front of the car and support it on axle stands.
6 Place a suitable container beneath the transmission. Unscrew and remove the dipstick, then unscrew the drain plug using a $\frac{3}{8}$ in square drive and drain the fluid. Temporarily refit the drain plug.
7 Connect a suitable hoist to the engine and support its weight.
8 Remove the anti-roll bar and disconnect the front suspension control arms from the body, referring to Chapter 11. Release the selector cable bracket from the transmission housing.
9 Unscrew the engine front and rear mounting nuts from the centre beam. Unbolt the centre beam from the body.
10 Unbolt and remove the engine rear mounting and bracket, and the front steady bar brackets.
11 Using a thin lever, release the inner ends of the driveshafts from the differential gears. Pull the right-hand driveshaft out completely, but leave the left-hand driveshaft half entered.
12 Unbolt the engine damper bracket and the converter housing lower cover.
13 Mark the driveplate and torque converter in relation to each other, then unscrew the bolts while holding the assembly stationary with a lever inserted in the starter ring gear. It will be necessary to turn the engine in order to reach all of the bolts.
14 Support the transmission with a trolley jack and remove the transmission-to-engine bolts.
15 Withdraw the transmission from the engine, making sure that the torque converter is held firmly engaged with the stator shaft and mainshaft. At the same time withdraw the left-hand driveshaft from the differential – take care (particularly on cars with a serial number from 117 813 on) not to extend the driveshaft inner joint, otherwise the ball-bearings may fall out.
16 Refitting is a reversal of removal, but refer to Chapter 8 for the driveshaft refitting procedure. Make sure that the converter housing dowels are correctly located. When bolting the torque converter to the driveplate, initially insert the bolts closely then turn the engine through two complete revolutions to centralize the torque converter before tightening the bolts in diagonal sequence to the specified torque.
17 Fit a new washer to the transmission drain plug and tighten the plug, then fill the transmission with the specified fluid and refit the dipstick. After running the engine and selecting all drive positions, recheck the fluid level.

6 Transmission – overhaul

1 Remove the transmission as described in Section 5 and clean the exterior with paraffin.
2 Slide the torque converter from the transmission.
3 Remove the breather cap and unscrew the dipstick.
4 Unbolt and remove the end housing. Extract the circlips and remove the oil pipes, flanges, and O-rings. Remove the end housing gasket.
5 Move the selector shaft to the 'P' position and lock the mainshaft using BL tool 18G 1361 or 1357, or a nut splitter and block of wood (see Chapter 6).
6 Bend up the staking from the mainshaft locknut and unscrew the locknut *(left-hand thread)*.
7 Slide off the Low clutch assembly.
8 Remove the nut splitter or BL tool.
9 Bend up the staking from the countershaft locknut and unscrew the locknut.
10 With neutral selected, slide off the parking gear and mainshaft Low gear together with the thrust washer and needle race.
11 Extract the mainshaft O-rings, together with the needle bearing, needle race, and inner race.
12 Note the location of the parking pawl and springs, then remove the mechanism.
13 Slide the Low gear from the countershaft.
14 Turn the selector shaft as necessary to align the roll pin with the slot in the transmission housing. Unbolt the transmission housing and remove the gasket.
15 Expand the circlips and drive the mainshaft and countershaft bearings from the transmission housing using a suitable metal tube.
16 Unbolt the reverse idler gear holder and shaft, and withdraw the idler gear and needle bearing from the housing.
17 Drive the differential oil seal from the housing.
18 Flatten the tab washer and unscrew the reverse selector fork bolt from the end of the servo valve.
19 Slide off the reverse selector fork together with the countershaft reverse gear, needle bearing, inner race and selector sleeve.
20 Pull out the two oil feed pipes.
21 Lift out the mainshaft and countershaft together.
22 Unbolt the servo valve housing and remove the return spring, shaft and O-ring.
23 Unbolt the regulator assembly. Unscrew the stop bolt and remove the cap, seat, springs and valve.
24 Withdraw the stator shaft and the stop pin.
25 Disconnect the manual valve from the selector shaft arm, then unbolt the valve block and remove the pump gears and shaft.
26 Remove the separator plate and oil strainer.
27 Lift out the differential assembly

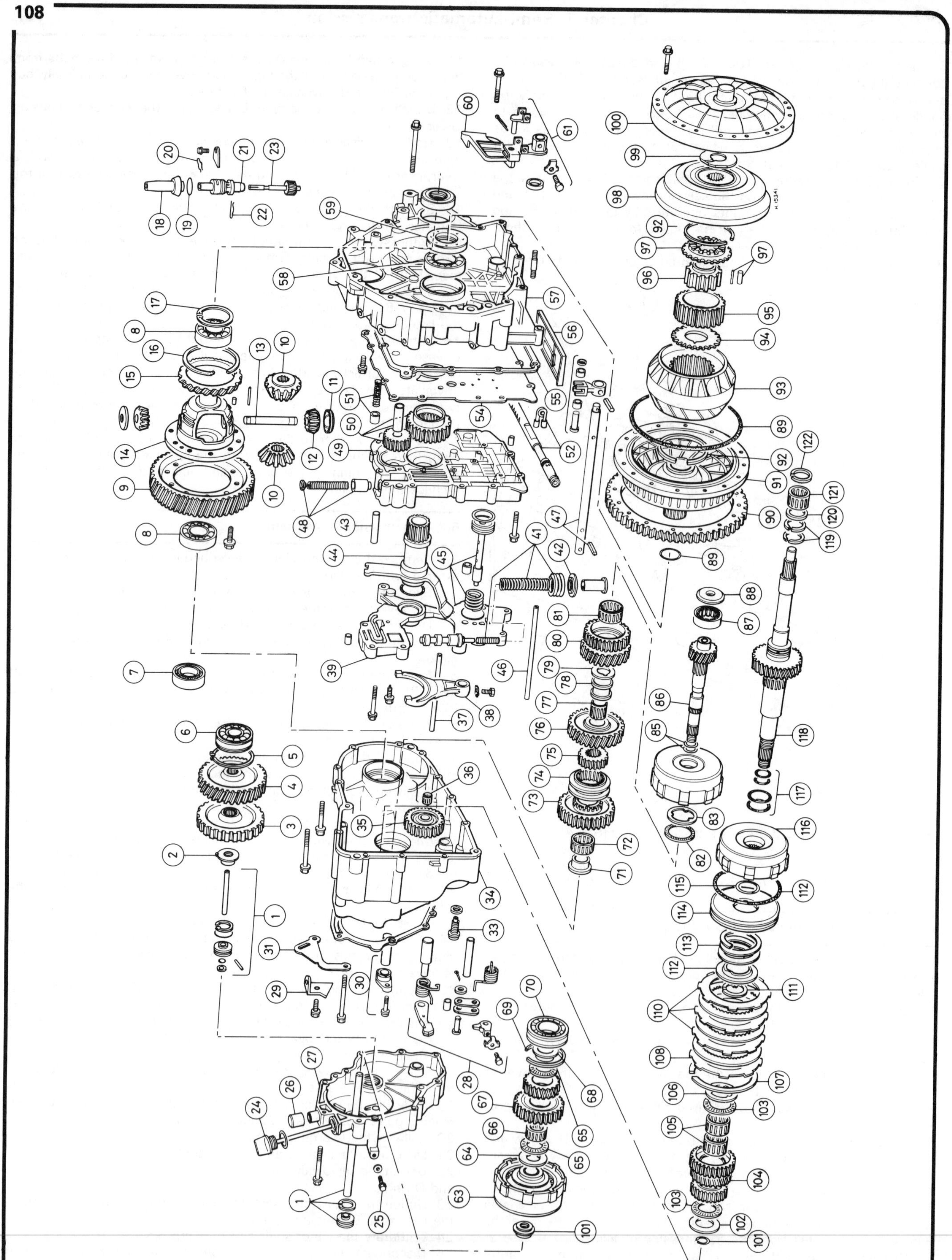

Fig. 7.5 Exploded view of the Trio-matic transmission (Sec 6)

1 *Oil feed pipe assembly*
2 *Countershaft locknut*
3 *Parking gear*
4 *Countershaft low gear*
5 *Snap-ring*
6 *Countershaft bearing*
7 *Differential oil seal*
8 *Differential bearing*
9 *Final drive gear*
10 *Differential gears*
11 *Thrust washers*
12 *Pinion gear*
13 *Pinion shaft*
14 *Differential carrier*
15 *Speedometer gear*
16 *Snap-ring*
17 *Differential circlip*
18 *Dust cover*
19 *O-ring*
20 *Speedometer cable clip*
21 *Pinion housing*
22 *Pinion clip*
23 *Speedometer drive pinion*
24 *Dipstick*
25 *Oil pressure point plug*
26 *Breather cap*
27 *End housing*
28 *Parking pawl and mechanism*
29 *Earth cable bracket*
30 *Reverse idler gear holder and shaft*
31 *Lifting bracket*
32 *End housing gasket*
33 *Drain plug*
34 *Gearbox housing*
35 *Reverse idler gear*
36 *Reverse idler gear bearing*
37 *Oil feed pipe*
38 *Reverse gear selector fork*
39 *Regulator valve housing*
40 *Regulator valve*
41 *Regulator valve springs*
42 *Regulator valve spring retainer*
43 *Stator shaft stop pin*
44 *Stator shaft*
45 *Servo valve, spring and housing*
46 *Oil feed pipe*
47 *Selector shaft and roll pin*
48 *Relief valve and spring*
49 *Valve block*
50 *Oil pump gears and shaft*
51 *Converter check valve and spring*
52 *Manual valve and detent*
53 *Selector shaft arm and clevis pin*
54 *Separator plate*
55 *Gearbox housing gasket*
56 *Oil strainer*
57 *Converter housing*
58 *Torque converter bearing*
59 *Torque converter oil seal*
60 *Selector cable retainer*
61 *Selector arm*
62 *Mainshaft locknut*
63 *Low clutch*
64 *Thrust washer*
65 *Thrust needle race*
66 *Needle bearing*
67 *Mainshaft low gear*
68 *Inner race*
69 *Snap-ring*
70 *Mainshaft bearing*
71 *Inner race*
72 *Needle bearing*
73 *Countershaft reverse gear*
74 *Reverse selector sleeve*
75 *Reverse hub gear*
76 *Countershaft drive gear*
77 *Needle bearing*
78 *Spacer collar*
79 *Thrust washer*
80 *Countershaft OD gear*
81 *Needle bearing*
82 *Thrust needle race*
83 *Splined washer*
84 *OD clutch*
85 *Countershaft O-rings*
86 *Countershaft*
87 *Countershaft bearing*
88 *Oil barrier plate*
89 *Converter O-rings*
90 *Starter ring gear*
91 *Impeller*
92 *Stator snap-ring*
93 *Stator*
94 *Stator side plate*
95 *One-way clutch outer race*
96 *One-way clutch cam*
97 *One-way clutch roller and spring*
98 *Turbine*
99 *Thrust washer*
100 *Torque converter cover*
101 *Snap-ring*
102 *Thrust washer*
103 *Thrust needle race*
104 *Mainshaft drive gear*
105 *Needle bearings*
106 *Splined washer*
107 *Snap-ring*
108 *Clutch end plate*
109 *Clutch drive plates*
110 *Clutch steel discs*
111 *Snap-ring*
112 *Spring retainer*
113 *Piston return spring*
114 *Clutch piston*
115 *Piston O-rings*
116 *Drive clutch drum*
117 *Mainshaft O-rings*
118 *Mainshaft*
119 *Mainshaft seals*
120 *Collar*
121 *Needle bearing*
122 *Snap-ring*

28 Unscrew the clamp bolt and withdraw the speedometer pinion.
29 Extract the differential bearing circlip, then drive the oil seal from the converter housing.
30 Using BL tools 18G 284, or similar, extract the countershaft bearing followed by the oil barrier plate.
31 Drive out the torque converter housing and oil seal.
32 Drive out the roll pin and remove the selector arm from the selector shaft, then withdraw the selector shaft and seal.
33 Extract the housing dowel pins.
34 Dismantle the Low clutch by extracting the circlip and removing the endplate, clutch plates and steel discs. Using BL tool 18G 1016 or similar, compress the piston return spring, extract the spring clip, then remove the retainer, return spring, piston and O-rings from the clutch drum.
35 Examine the check valve on the piston for damage, then dip the O-rings in transmission fluid and fit them to the clutch drum and piston groove.
36 Insert the piston in the drum squarely to avoid damage to the O-rings, then use the special tool to fit the return spring, retainer and spring clip.
37 Invert the steel discs and clutch plates alternately, and retain with the endplate and circlip.
38 Using a feeler blade, check that the endplate-to-stop disc clearance is as given in the Specifications. If not, select an endplate of different thickness to correct the clearance.
39 Check the operation of the Low clutch by directing air pressure from an air line in the oil hole on the clutch drum hub.
40 Slide the reverse hub from the countershaft, followed by the Drive gear, needle bearing, spacer collar and thrust washer.
41 Remove the 'OD' gear, needle bearing, thrust race and splined washer, then slide off the 'OD' clutch.
42 Overhaul the 'OD' clutch using the procedure described in paragraphs 34 to 39 inclusive.
43 Assemble all the components to the countershaft, including a new bearing if required, then tighten the locknut to the specified torque. Using a feeler blade, measure the 'OD' (3rd) gear endfloat and Drive (★) gear endfloat. If not as given in the Specifications, select washers of different thicknesses to correct the endfloat.
44 Fit the components to the countershaft, up to and including the reverse hub.
45 Extract the circlip from the end of the mainshaft and remove the needle bearing and collar, followed by the O-rings.
46 From the opposite end of the mainshaft extract the circlip and remove the thrust washer, race, Drive gear, needle bearings, race and splined washer. Slide off the Drive clutch.
47 Overhaul the Drive (★) clutch using the procedure described in paragraphs 34 to 39 inclusive.
48 Assemble all the components to the mainshaft, including a new bearing if required, then tighten the locknut to the specified torque. Using a feeler blade, measure the Low gear endfloat and Drive gear endfloat. If not as given in the Specifications, select washers of different thicknesses to correct the endfloat.
49 Fit the components to the mainshaft up to and including the circlip.
50 Clean the converter housing, then drive in the torque converter bearing with a suitable metal tube.
51 Fit the oil seal, with its lip facing inwards, using a block of wood.
52 Support the converter housing with blocks of wood below the countershaft bearing position.
53 Drive the oil barrier plate into the converter housing, followed by the countershaft bearing, using a suitable metal tube.
54 Fit the housing dowel pin.
55 Fit the seal and selector shaft, then locate the arm on the shaft and drive in the roll pin.
56 If required, the differential assembly may be dismantled, referring to Fig. 7.10. However, mark each component for position before removing it. Note that the final drivegear bolts have a *left-hand thread.* A puller will be necessary in order to remove the differential bearings. The chamfer on the final drivegear inside diameter must face the carrier, and similarly the chamfer on the speedometer drivegear inside diameter must face the carrier.
57 Fit the differential bearing circlip to the converter housing and lower the differential assembly into position.
58 Fit the speedometer pinion assembly and secure with the clamp and bolt.
59 Slide the manual valve from the valve block.
60 Remove the relief valve, check valve and springs from the valve block.
61 Locate the oil pump gears in the valve block. Use feeler blades and a straight-edge to check the endfloat and radial clearances as given in the Specifications. If worn excessively, new components will be required.
62 Fit the relief valve, check valve and springs to the valve block. Insert the manual valve and check that the detent spring and rollers are correctly engaged.
63 Fit the oil strainer, dowel pin and separator plate.
64 Fit the oil pump gears and shaft.
65 Fit the valve block and tighten the bolts evenly to the specified torque in diagonal sequence, working outwards from the oil pump. Check that the pump gears turn freely and that the shaft is correctly engaged.
66 Connect the manual valve to the selector shaft arm with the clevis pin and secure with the split pin.
67 Insert the stator shaft and stop pin.
68 Insert the valve, springs, seat and cap in the regulator assembly and tighten the stop bolt.
69 Check that the dowel pins are located correctly, then fit the regulator assembly to the valve block and tighten the bolts to the specified torque. Ensure that the stator shaft turns freely.
70 Fit the servo valve assembly complete with O-ring, shaft and return spring. Check that the dowel pins are correctly located and tighten the bolts in diagonal sequence to the specified torque.
71 Mesh the countershaft with the mainshaft and lower them into position in the converter housing assembly.
72 Fit the reverse selector fork and sleeve, with the sleeve groove facing the countershaft Drive gear.
73 Turn the servo valve so that the flat faces the hole in the selector fork, align the holes, and insert the bolt. Tighten the bolt to the specified torque and lock it by bending the tab washer.
74 Fit the countershaft reverse gear, together with the inner race and needle bearing.
75 Insert the short oil feed pipe in the servo valve housing, and the long oil feed pipe in the valve block.
76 Expand the circlips in the transmission housing and fit the mainshaft and countershaft bearings, making sure that the circlips engage the grooves in the outer races.
77 Locate the reverse idler gear in the transmission housing, with the chamfered teeth facing the torque converter housing, then fit the reverse idler gear holder and shaft and tighten the bolts. Fit the needle bearing on the shaft.
78 Turn the selector shaft as necessary to align the roll pin with the slot in the transmission housing, then fit the transmission housing to the converter housing together with a new gasket. If necessary, rotate the reverse idler gear in order to align the gears.
79 Insert and tighten the bolts to the specified torque in diagonal sequence.
80 Slide the Low gear into the countershaft with the radius hub towards the bearing.
81 Fit the parking pawl mechanism in its previously noted position, making sure that the spring coil is not trapped.
82 Fit the Low gear inner race to the mainshaft, followed by the needle race and needle bearing.
83 Locate the countershaft parking gear in the central recessed area of the mainshaft Low gear, then slide both gears simultaneously onto their respective shafts.
84 Fit the needle race and thrust washer to the mainshaft, followed by the O-rings.
85 Move the selector shaft to the 'P' position, then fit the countershaft locknut and tighten it to the specified torque. Lock the nut by staking the collar to the parking gear.
86 Fit the Low clutch to the mainshaft, rotating it until all clutch plates are engaged.
87 Lock the mainshaft using BL tool 18G 1361, or a nut splitter and block of wood. Fit the mainshaft locknut (*left-hand thread)* and tighten it to the specified torque. Lock the nut by staking the collar to the Low clutch.
88 Remove the nut splitter or BL tool.
89 Fit the oil feed pipes, O-rings, and flanges to the end housing together with the circlips.
90 Fit the end housing to the transmission housing with a new gasket. Insert the bolts and tighten them to the specified torque in diagonal sequence.

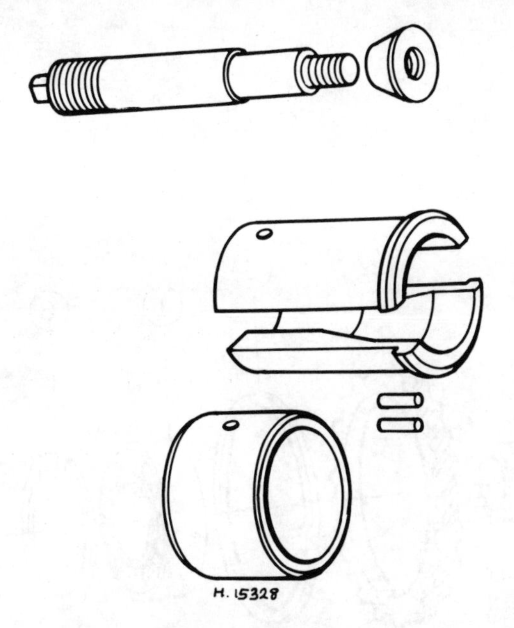

Fig. 7.6 BL tools 18G 284 for use with a slide hammer when removing the countershaft bearing (Sec 6)

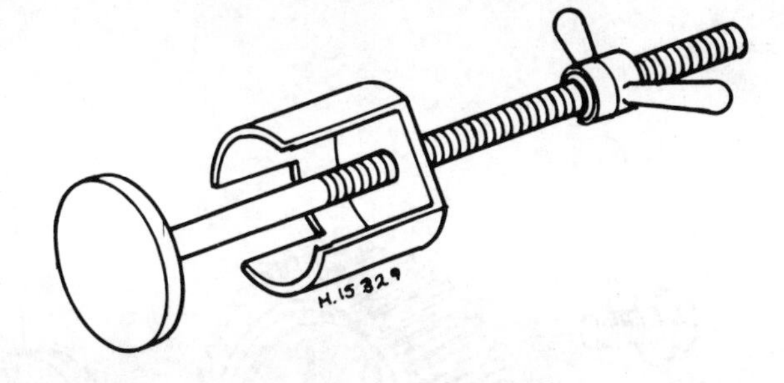

Fig. 7.7 Clutch return spring compressor (Sec 6)

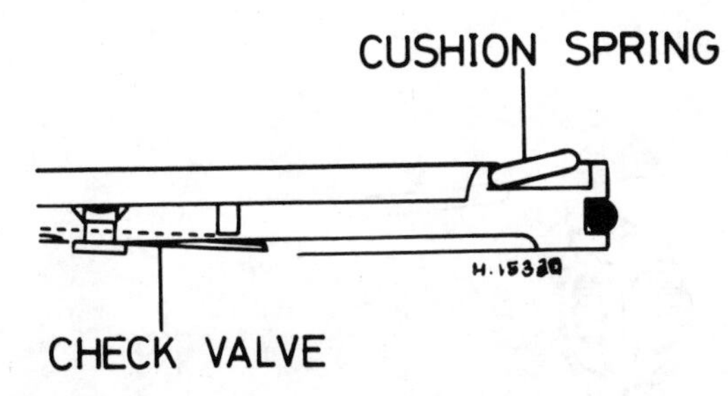

Fig. 7.8 Cross-section of a clutch piston (Sec 6)

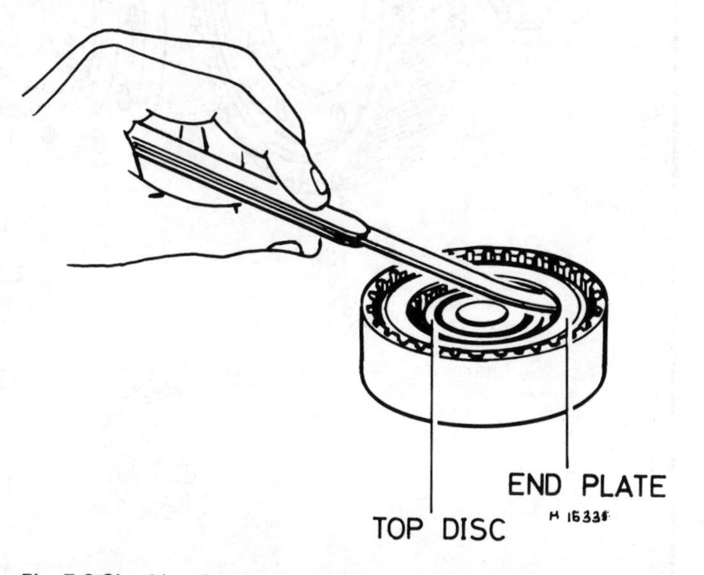

Fig. 7.9 Checking the clutch endplate-to-top disc clearance (Sec 6)

91 Fit the dipstick and breather cap.
92 Temporarily extract the differential bearing circlip from the converter housing and, using a suitable metal tube, lightly drive the bearing and differential into the transmission housing. Refit the circlip, then measure the clearance between the circlip and bearing outer track using a feeler blade. If the clearance is not the specified differential endfloat, select a circlip of a different thickness and fit it.
93 Lubricate the differential oil seals with transmission fluid, then drive them into the housings using a block of wood.
94 If required the torque converter may be dismantled, referring to Fig. 7.12. However, mark each component for position before removing it. Renew the two O-rings. Tighten the torque converter bolts to the specified torque in the sequence shown in Fig. 7.14.
95 Lubricate the oil seal in the converter housing with transmission fluid, then slide the torque converter into position. The transmission is now ready for refitting as described in Section 5.

7 Differential oil seals – renewal

Left-hand side oil seal

1 Remove the left-hand driveshaft as described in Chapter 8.
2 Lever the oil seal from the transmission and wipe clean its location using lint-free cloth.
3 Dip the new oil seal in transmission fluid, then drive it squarely into the converter housing using a block of wood. Wipe away any excess fluid.
4 Refit the driveshaft as described in Chapter 8.

Right-hand side oil seal

5 Jack up the front of the car and support it on axle stands. Apply the handbrake and remove the roadwheel.
6 Disconnect the battery negative lead.
7 Place a suitable container beneath the transmission. Unscrew and remove the dipstick, then unscrew the drain plug using a $\frac{3}{8}$ in square drive and drain the fluid. Refit and tighten the drain plug.
8 Extract the split pin and unscrew the nut from the front suspension lower balljoint.
9 Using a separator tool, release the lower control arm and balljoint from the steering knuckle/hub.
10 Using a tyre lever or similar lever, force the inner end of the driveshaft from the differential while pulling the front hub outwards. Take care (particularly on cars with a serial number from 117 813 on) not to extend the driveshaft inner joint, otherwise the ball-bearings may fall out. Tie the driveshaft to one side.
11 Lower the oil seal from the transmission and wipe clean its location using lint-free cloth.
12 Dip the new oil seal in transmission fluid, then drive it squarely into the transmission housing using a block of wood. Wipe away any excess fluid.
13 Pull the front hub outwards, then insert the inner end of the driveshaft into the differential and push it in until the spring clip engages the groove.
14 Fit the lower control arm balljoint to the steering knuckle/hub. Tighten the nut to the specified torque (see Chapter 11) and install the split pin.
15 Fill the transmission with the specified fluid.
16 Reconnect the battery negative lead, then refit the roadwheel and lower the car to the ground.

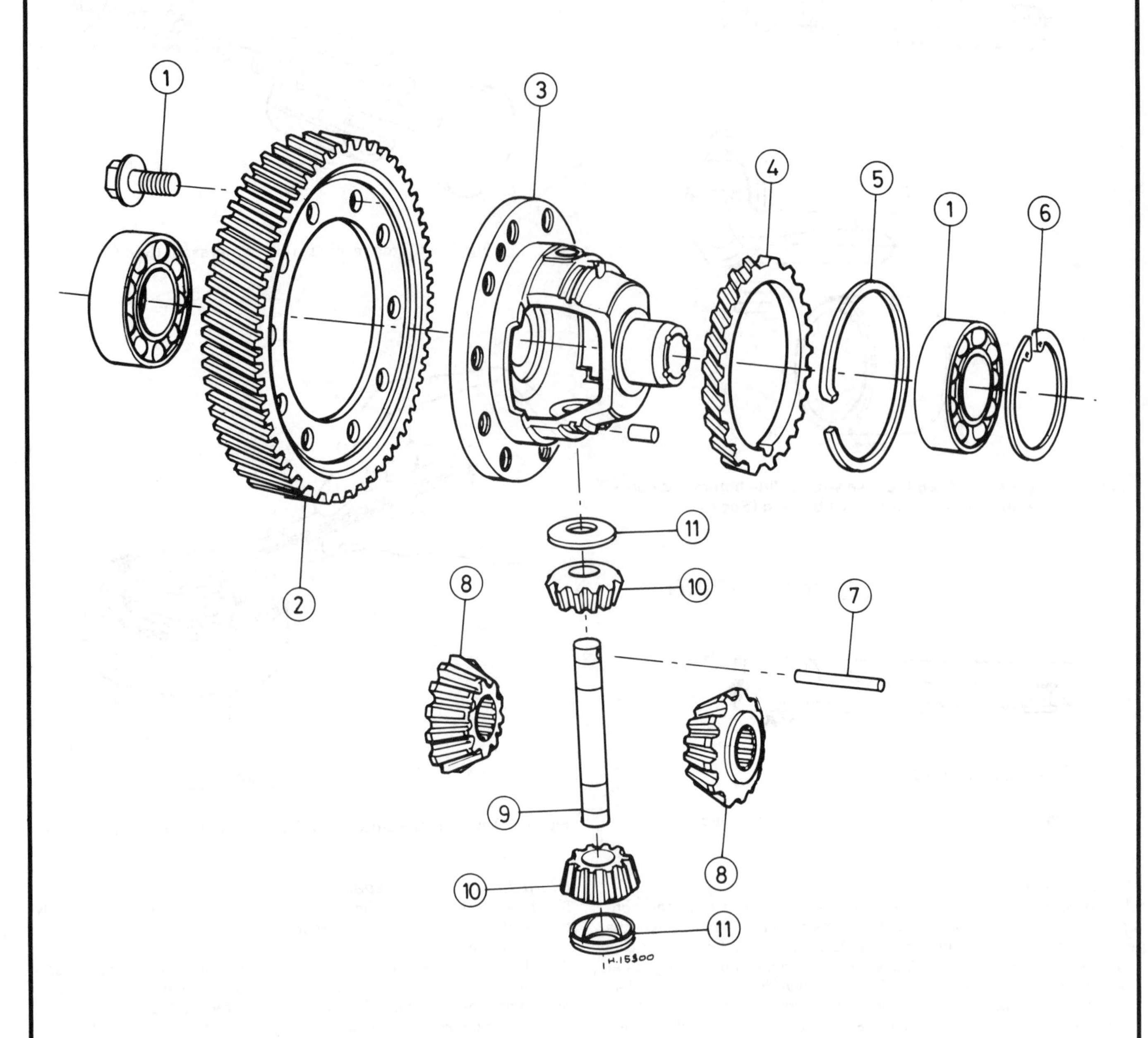

Fig. 7.10 Exploded view of the differential (Sec 6)

1 *Differential carrier bearings*
2 *Final drive gear*
3 *Differential carrier*
4 *Speedometer gear*
5 *Snap ring*
6 *Differential bearing circlip*
7 *Roll pin*
8 *Differential gears*
9 *Pinion shaft*
10 *Pinion gears*
11 *Thrust washers*

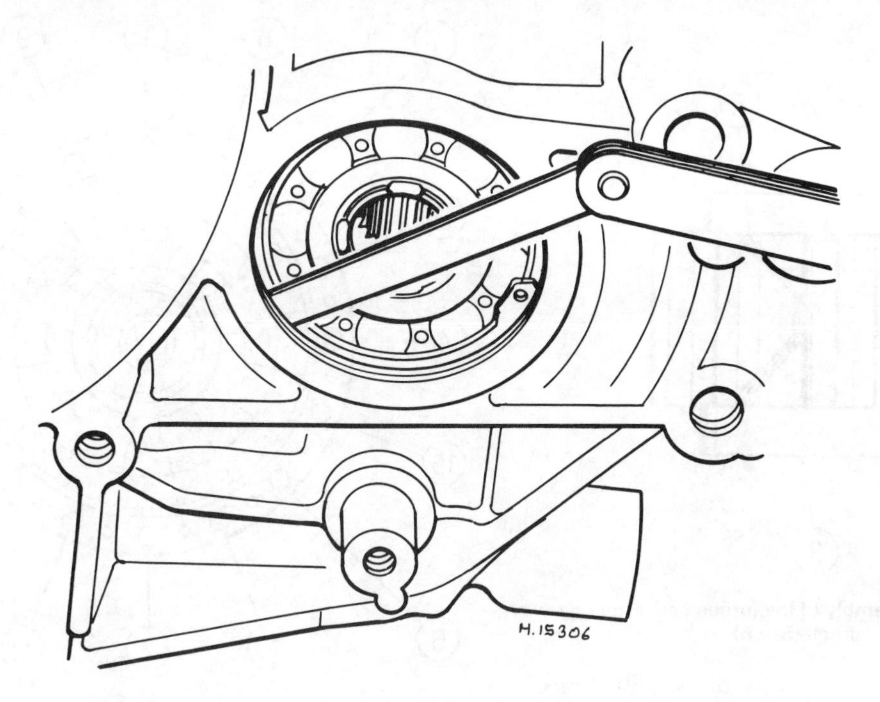

Fig. 7.11 Checking the differential endfloat with a feeler blade (Sec 6)

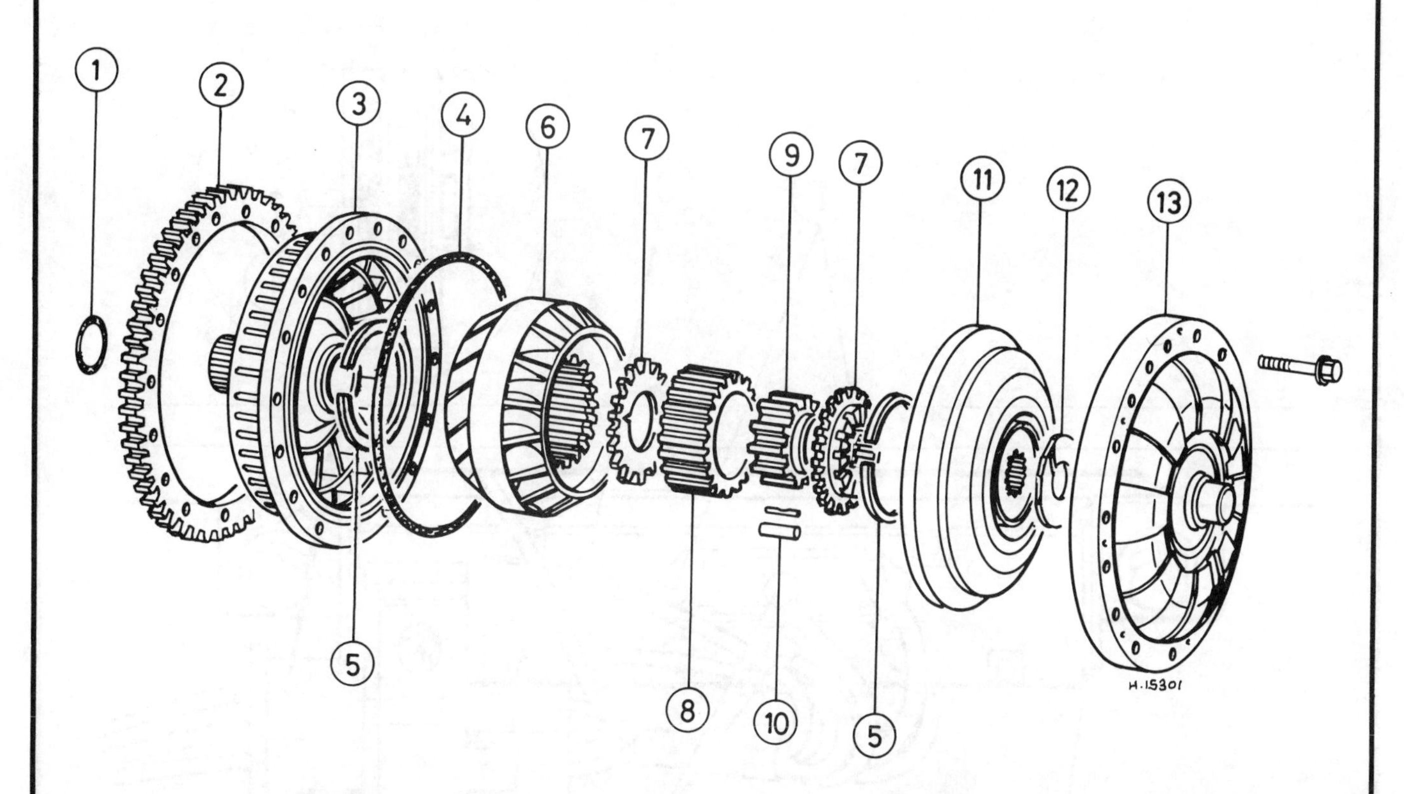

Fig. 7.12 Exploded view of the torque converter (Sec 6)

1 O-ring
2 Starter ring gear
3 Impeller
4 O-ring
5 Circlips
6 Stator
7 Side plates
8 One-way clutch outer race
9 One-way clutch cam
10 Roller and spring
11 Turbine
12 Thrust washer
13 Cover

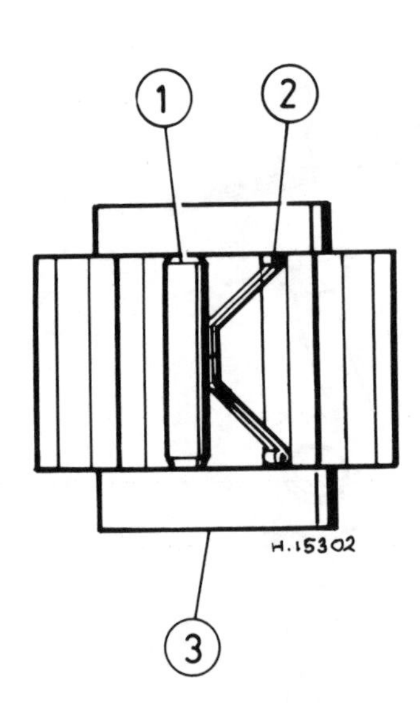

Fig. 7.13 Correct assembly of the torque converter one-way clutch (Sec 6)

1 Roller
2 Spring
3 One-way clutch cam

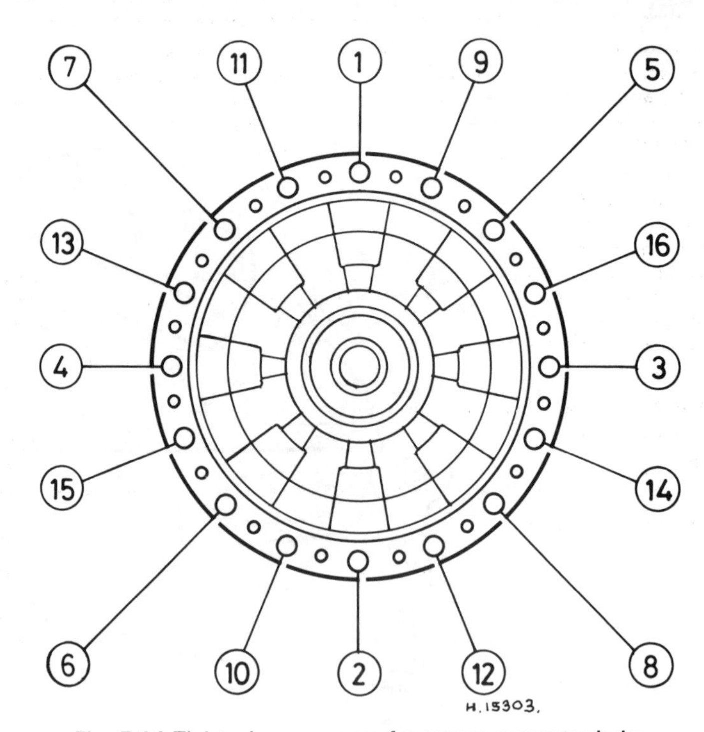

Fig. 7.14 Tightening sequence for torque converter bolts (Sec 6)

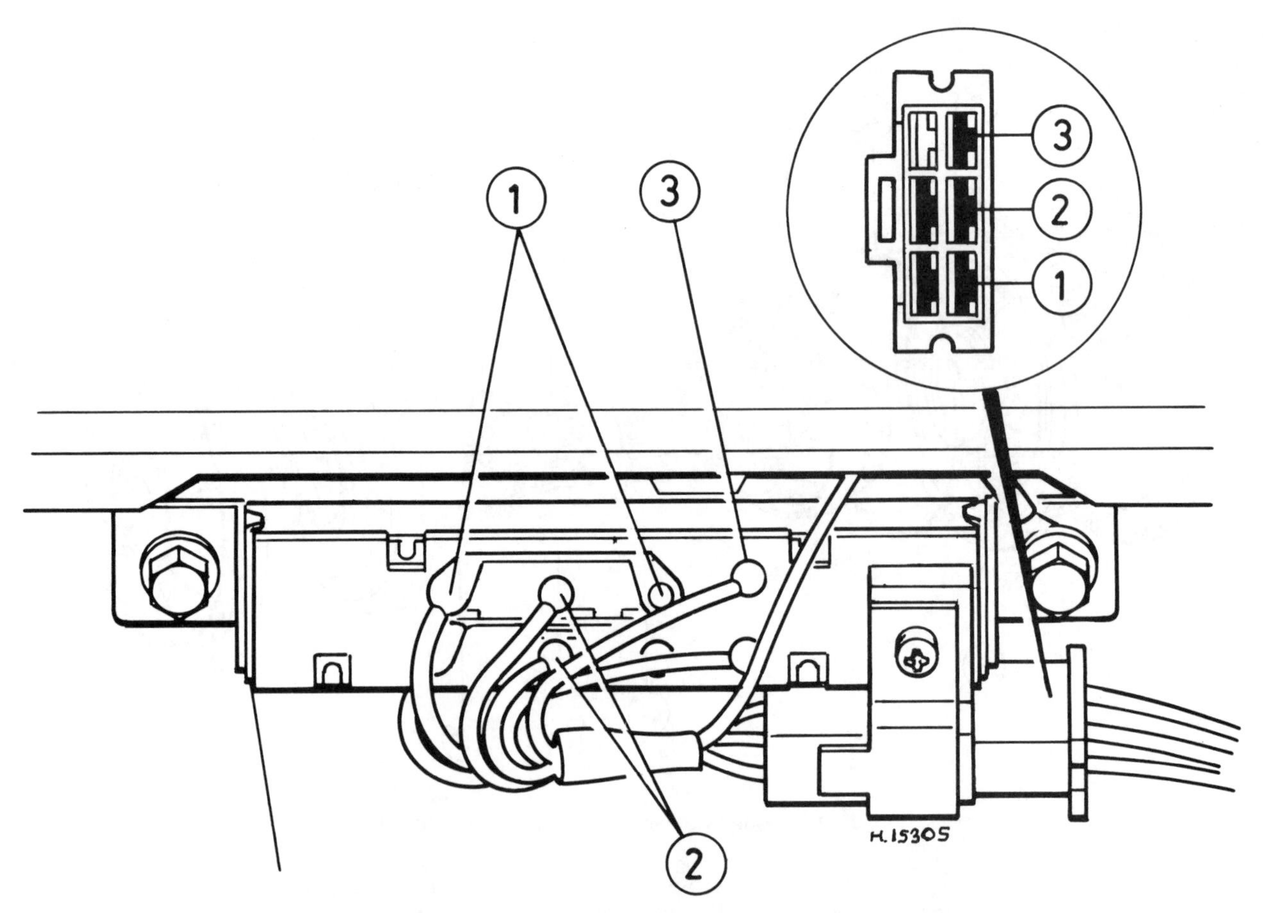

Fig. 7.15 Starter inhibitor/light switch connections (Sec 8)

1 Inhibitor switch
2 Reversing light switch
3 'OD' light switch

8 Selector lever and starter inhibitor/reversing light switch – removal and refitting

1 Remove the control console (Section 4, paragraph 1).

Selector lever

2 Disconnect the selector lamp cable and the starter inhibitor/reversing lamp switch wires.
3 Select reverse, then prise out the retaining pin and clip.
4 Individual components may now be renewed as necessary. To renew the selector lamp, remove the panel and turn the bulb holder 90° clockwise to extract it.
5 Refitting is a reversal of removal. Lightly grease all moving parts, and make sure that the selector slide cover passes under the mounting bracket.
6 Adjust the selector cable as described in Section 4.

Inhibitor switch

7 Disconnect the wiring plug and remove the switch unit complete.
8 A defective switch must be renewed, no repairs being possible.
9 Refitting is a reversal of removal. Align the switch slider with the selector pin, and make sure the earth wire is above the switch.
10 Check for correct operation of the switch on completion. The starter should operate only in positions 'N' or 'P', the reversing light in position 'R' and the overdrive warning light in position 'OD'.

9 Fault diagnosis – semi-automatic transmission

Symptom	Reason(s)
Loss of drive in all gears	Faulty oil pump Low fluid level Clogged oil strainer Sticking regulator valve or servo valve Broken mainshaft Broken selector cable
Drive only in ★ and OD	Faulty Low clutch Broken Low clutch oil feed pipe
Drive only in L and OD	Faulty Drive (★) clutch Broken Drive (★) clutch oil feed pipe
Drive only in L and ★	Faulty OD clutch Broken OD clutch oil feed pipe
Drive only in L, ★ and OD	Sticking servo valve or reverse selector sleeve
Increase in engine speed when changing from L to ★	Worn Drive (★) clutch Partially blocked Drive (★) clutch oil supply
Increase in engine speed when changing from ★ to OD	Worn OD clutch Partially blocked OD clutch oil supply
Transmission overheats	Torque converter stator one-way clutch seized

Chapter 8 Driveshafts

Contents

Specifications

Type	Solid shafts, splined to inner and outer constant velocity joints	
Length (between shoulders)		
Right-hand driveshaft	462 mm (18.2 in)	
Left-hand driveshaft	755.5 mm (29.7 in)	
Torque wrench settings	**lbf ft**	**Nm**
Driveshaft-to-hub nut	111	150
Lower control arm balljoint nut	26	35

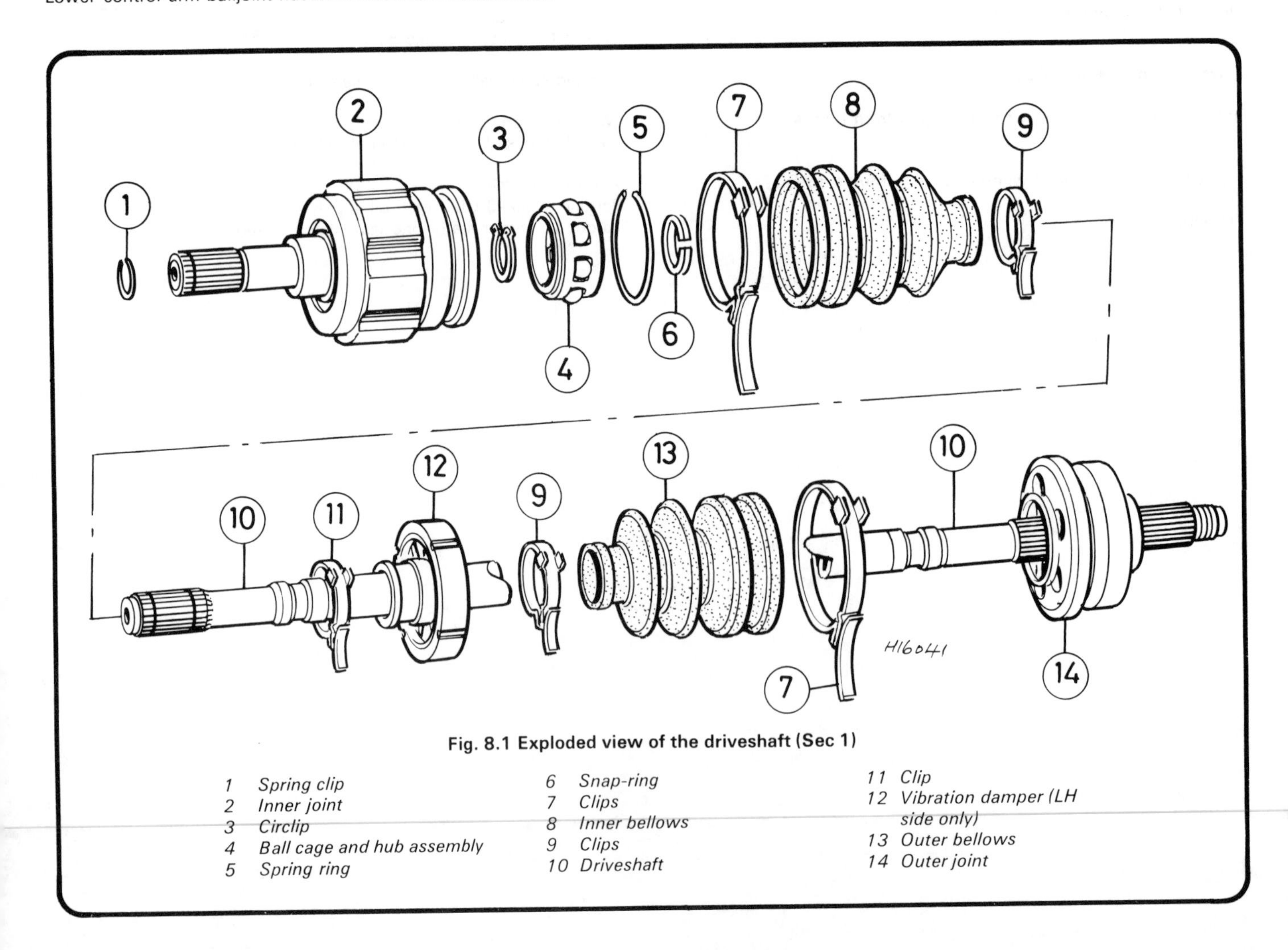

Fig. 8.1 Exploded view of the driveshaft (Sec 1)

1 Spring clip
2 Inner joint
3 Circlip
4 Ball cage and hub assembly
5 Spring ring
6 Snap-ring
7 Clips
8 Inner bellows
9 Clips
10 Driveshaft
11 Clip
12 Vibration damper (LH side only)
13 Outer bellows
14 Outer joint

1 General description

Drive is transmitted from the splined final drive differential gears to the inner constant velocity joints. Splined solid driveshafts are connected to the inner and outer constant velocity joints. Drive is transmitted through the splined driving flange to the front wheels. A vibration damper is fitted to the outer end of the left-hand side driveshaft.

Excessive wear in the driveshaft outer constant velocity joints will result in loud 'clicks' on full left or right turns under load.

2 Drive – removal and refitting

1 Remove the trim cap from the centre of the front roadwheel. Relieve the staking on the hub nut.
2 Using a socket or box spanner, loosen the hub nut – an extension bar may be required as the nut is very tight.
3 Jack up the front of the car and support it on axle stands. Apply the handbrake and remove the roadwheel.
4 Place a suitable container beneath the gearbox and drain the oil or transmission fluid, referring if necessary to Chapter 6 or 7.
5 Unscrew and remove the hub nut. Note that the nut must not be re-used, as once removed its self-locking function is reduced.
6 Extract the split pin and unscrew the nut from the front suspension lower balljoint.
7 Using a separator tool, release the lower control arm and balljoint from the steering knuckle/hub.
8 With a mallet and a block of wood, tap the outer end of the driveshaft through the hub while pulling the hub outwards. However, take care (particularly on cars with a serial number from 117 813 on) not to extend the driveshaft inner joint, otherwise the ball-bearings may fall out. If any doubt exists as to whether this has occurred, the rubber gaiter must be removed and the inner joint examined.
9 Using a tyre lever or similar lever, force the inner end of the driveshaft from the differential gear and withdraw the driveshaft from the car. The driveshaft is located by a spring clip which engages a groove in the differential side gear; after the driveshaft has been moved approximately 12 mm (0.5 in) the clip will be free of the groove and the driveshaft will move more easily (photos).
10 To refit the driveshaft, first lubricate the differential oil seal with a little gearbox oil or transmission fluid (as applicable).
11 Insert the inner end of the driveshaft into the differential gear, pushing it in until the spring clip engages the groove (photo). Do not extend the inner joint.
12 Locate the steering knuckle/hub over the outer end of the driveshaft and tap the hub drive flange until the driveshaft is fully entered.
13 Screw the new hub nut finger tight onto the end of the driveshaft.
14 Fit the lower control arm balljoint to the steering knuckle/hub, tighten the nut to the specified torque, and install the split pin.
15 Check that the drain plug is tight, then refill the gearbox with oil or transmission fluid as applicable.
16 Tighten the hub nut to half the specified torque, then refit the roadwheel and lower the car to the ground.
17 Tighten the hub nut to the final specified torque and lock it by tapping the collar into the groove in the driveshaft.
18 Refit the trim cap to the centre of the roadwheel.

3 Driveshaft – overhaul

1 With the driveshaft removed, release the clips from the inner bellows and slide the bellows from the inner joint.
2 Extract the spring ring from inside the inner joint housing and slide the housing from the ball cage.
3 Extract the circlip from the inner end of the driveshaft.
4 Note the fitted position of the ball cage and hub assembly, then pull the assembly from the driveshaft. Remove the snap-ring.
5 With the inner face of the hub uppermost, use a screwdriver to lever the balls from the cage.
6 Slide the inner bellows from the driveshaft.
7 On the left-hand side driveshaft, release the clip and slide off the vibration damper.

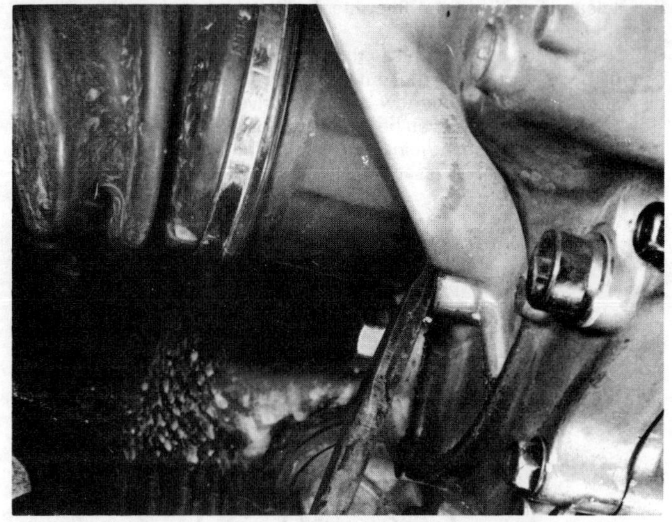

2.9a Using a lever to remove the driveshaft from the differential gear

2.9b Driveshaft inner joint

2.11 Inserting the driveshaft

8 Release the clips from the outer bellows and remove the bellows from the driveshaft.
9 Clean all the components with paraffin and examine them for wear and damage. Note that the outer constant velocity joint cannot be dismantled, and if worn a new complete driveshaft must be obtained. However, the inner joint can be renewed separately. Check the bellows for splitting and the inner joint components for excessive wear. Renew the bellows clips if necessary.

10 Reassembly is a reversal of dismantling, but pack the constant velocity joints with molybdenum disulphide grease – the inner joint housing and hub should be packed with 100 grams ($3\frac{1}{2}$ oz) of grease.
11 On the left-hand side driveshaft, position the vibration damper as shown in Fig. 8.3, next to the outer joint.
12 Make sure that the bellows are free of distortion, and secure the clips by closing the levers and bending the locktabs.

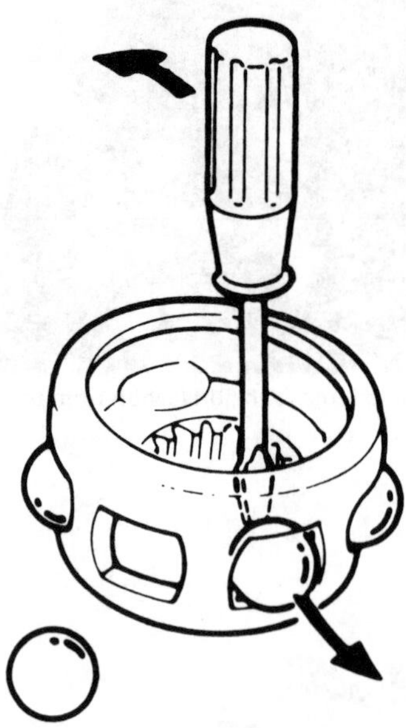

Fig. 8.2 Removing the balls from the inner joint hub and cage (Sec 3)

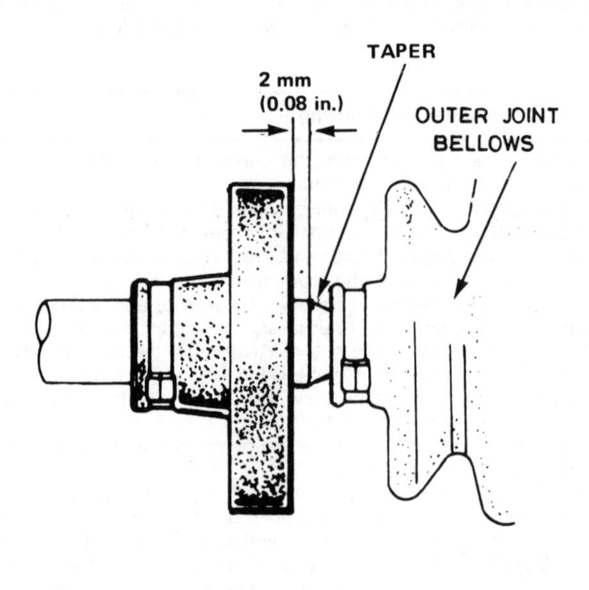

Fig. 8.3 Correct position of the vibration damper on the left-hand side driveshaft (Sec 3)

4 Fault diagnosis – driveshafts

Symptom	Reason(s)
Vibration and noise on lock	Worn driveshaft joints
Noise on taking up drive	Worn drive flange and driveshaft splines Loose driveshaft-to-hub nut Worn driveshaft joints Loose roadwheel nuts

Chapter 9 Braking system

Contents

Specifications

System type

Four-wheel hydraulic, with discs front and self-adjusting drums rear. Dual diagonal type hydraulic circuit with rear brake proportioning valve and servo assistance. Cable-operated handbrake on rear wheels

Front brakes

Disc diameter	215 mm (8.465 in)
Disc thickness (minimum)	9.0 mm (0.354 in)
Disc run-out (maximum)	0.15 mm (0.006 in)
Pad lining thickness (minimum)	1.5 mm (0.060 in)

Rear brakes

Drum internal diameter (maximum)	181 mm (7.126 in)
Lining thickness (minimum)	2.0 mm (0.080 in)

Hydraulic fluid

Hydraulic fluid to SAE J1703 or FMVSS 116 DOT 3 (Duckhams Universal Brake and Clutch Fluid)

Torque wrench settings

	lbf ft	Nm
Caliper mounting bolt	58	78
Caliper union bolt	26	35
Caliper guide pin bolt	20	27
Front brake bleed screw	7	9
Rear brake bleed screw	5	7
Master cylinder to servo	11	15
Master cylinder stop bolt	7	9
Servo mounting	9	12
Servo pushrod locknut	8	11
Brake pipe union nuts	11	15
Rear brake backplate and stub axle bolt	41	55

1 General description

The braking system is of four-wheel hydraulic type, with discs at the front and self-adjusting drum brakes at the rear. The brake lines are Teflon coated and routed inside the right-hand side sill for added protection. Dual hydraulic circuits ensure that in the event of hydraulic failure in one circuit, the car can be safely stopped using the remaining circuit.

A direct-acting brake servo unit is fitted, and a proportioning valve in the hydraulic circuits limits the pressure to the rear brakes under heavy braking in order to prevent the rear wheels locking in advance of the front wheels.

The cable-operated handbrake operates on the rear wheels, and when applied the 'P' warning light on the instrument panel is illuminated with the ignition on. The '!' warning light on the instrument panel is illuminated with the ignition on only if the hydraulic fluid level in the master cylinder reservoir drops to a dangerous level (photo).

2 Routine maintenance

1 The brake fluid level should be checked every week and, if necessary, topped up with the specified brake fluid to the maximum level mark on the fluid reservoir. However, it should be noted that as the front disc pads wear, the level will drop approximately 6.0 mm (0.25 in), and when the pads are renewed the level will rise the same amount. Therefore, provided the level remains near the maximum mark, it is not essential to top it up. Should there be an appreciable drop in the fluid level or if it requires constant topping up, the system is leaking and should be repaired without delay.
2 Every 7500 miles (12 000 km) the hydraulic pipes and unions should be checked for chafing, leakage, cracks and corrosion. At the same time the handbrake cables and linkage should be lubricated.
3 Every 15 000 miles (24 000 km) the front disc pads and discs should be checked for wear and condition, and at the same time the servo vacuum hose should be checked for security and condition.
4 Every 30 000 miles (48 000 km) the rear brake shoe linings and drums should be checked for wear and condition. At the same time the brake hydraulic fluid should be renewed, and if the car is operated under constant heavy braking, it is also recommended that the system internal seals and flexible hoses are renewed.

3 Disc pads – inspection and renewal

1 Apply the handbrake, then jack up the front of the car and support it on axle stands. Remove the roadwheels.
2 The pad wear can be checked through the hole in the front of the caliper, although it is preferable to check the full area of the pads for uneven wear (photo).
3 Unscrew and remove the caliper lever guide pin bolt, then swing the caliper upwards to reveal the pads.
4 Check the pad lining thickness. If any one is worn below the specified minimum amount, renew the pads on *both* front brakes. If the pads do not require renewal but are worn unequally, they may be changed to the opposite side of the disc.
5 To remove the pads, withdraw the shim from the outer pad, then withdraw the disc pads from the caliper bracket (photos).
6 Unclip and remove the anti-rattle springs (photos).
7 Brush the dust and dirt from the caliper, piston recess, disc, pads, and shim, but *do not inhale it as it is injurious to health.* Scrape any scale or rust from the disc and also clean the splash guard.
8 Refit the anti-rattle springs to the caliper bracket. Apply a little silicone grease to the backing plate shoulders and to both sides of the shim.
9 Using a piece of wood, press the piston back into the caliper. At the same time check the level of brake fluid in the reservoir; if this is near the top of the reservoir, loosen the caliper bleed screw to release the fluid while the piston is being depressed. Tighten it immediately afterwards.
10 Locate the disc pads in the caliper bracket with the linings facing the disc, then fit the shim to the outer pad.
11 Swing the caliper down over the pads, insert the lower guide pin bolt and tighten it to the specified torque.
12 Repeat the procedure on the remaining front brake, then refit the roadwheels and lower the car to the ground.
13 Depress the footbrake pedal several times to set the pads, then check and if necessary top up the level of brake fluid in the master cylinder reservoir.

4 Rear brake shoes – inspection and renewal

1 The brake drum is integral with the rear hub – first remove the brake drum/hub as described in Chapter 11. If difficulty is experienced due to the drum being worn excessively and fouling the brake shoes, prise the handbrake lever stop plate from the backplate in order to allow the brake shoes to retract further.
2 Brush the dust from the brake drum, brake shoes and backplate, but *do not inhale it as it is injurious to health.* Scrape any scale or rust from the drum (photo).
3 Measure the brake shoe lining thickness. If any one is worn down

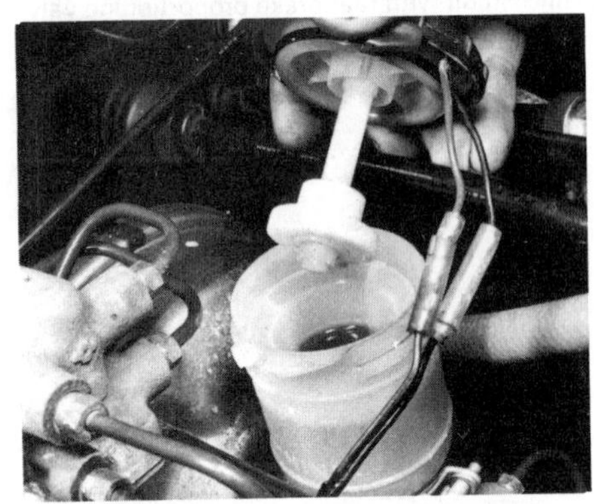

1.0 Hydraulic fluid level warning switch in the master cylinder reservoir cap

3.2 Disc caliper showing inspection hole (arrowed)

3.5a Removing the disc pads

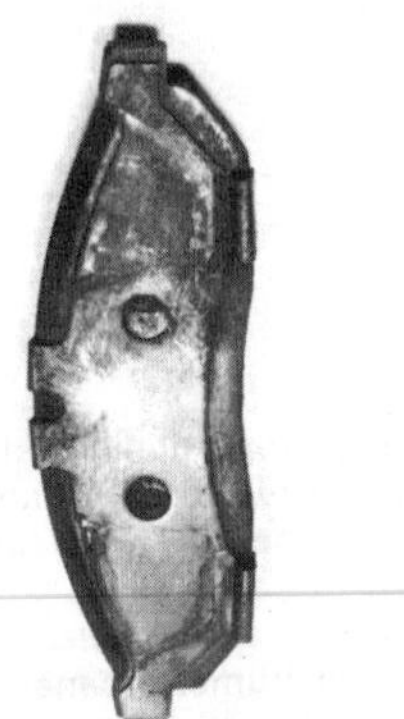

3.5b The disc pads showing (left) shim attached to outer pad

3.6a Anti-rattle spring location

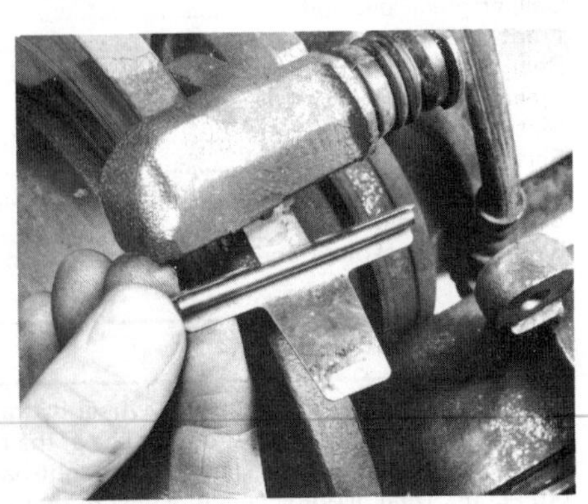

3.6b Removing an anti-rattle spring

to the specified minimum amount, or if it is nearly worn down to the rivets (where applicable), renew *all four* rear brake shoes. If the linings are in good condition, refit the brake drum/hub as described in Chapter 11.

4 To remove the brake shoes, first note the location of the return springs, and to which holes they are fitted. It is important not to interchange the top and bottom return springs.

5 Remove the anti-rattle springs by depressing them with a pair of pliers and turning them through 90° (photo).

6 Disconnect the small spring from the self-adjusting link and trailing shoe (photo).

7 Using a screwdriver or adjustable spanner, lever the shoes from the wheel cylinder, then similarly lever the shoes from the anchor plate (photo). Withdraw the shoes and remove the return springs.

8 If necessary the self-adjusting link can be removed from the backplate by disconnecting the handbrake cable at the clevis pin, unhooking the return spring, and withdrawing the link through the rubber boot.

9 Clean the backplate. If there are any signs of loss of grease from the rear hub bearings, the oil seal should be renewed as described in Chapter 11. If hydraulic fluid is leaking from the wheel cylinder, it must be repaired or renewed as described in Section 7. **Do not** touch the footbrake pedal while the shoes are removed. Position an elastic band over the wheel cylinder pistons to retain them.

10 Refit the self-adjusting link to the backplate and reconnect the handbrake cable and return spring. Return the self-adjusting quadrant to shorten the link length.

11 Apply a little silicone grease to the shaded areas shown in Fig. 9.2 on the backplate, wheel cylinder pistons and anchor plate. Remove the elastic band from the wheel cylinder.

12 Place the new shoes on a flat surface in their approximate fitted attitude (refer to Fig. 9.2 if necessary). The marks on the edges of the linings must face outwards. Hook the upper return spring to the outer facing sides of the shoes, and the lower return spring to the inner facing sides of the shoes.

13 Hold the shoes over the backplate, then lever them first onto the wheel cylinder and adjusting link, then onto the anchor plate.

14 Hook the small spring to the link and trailing shoe.

15 Apply a little sealant to the heads of the anti-rattle spring pins where they contact the backplate, then insert them through the brake shoe webs and fit the anti-rattle springs.

16 Make sure that the brake shoes are positioned centrally on the backplate, then refit the brake drum/hub as described in Chapter 11.

17 Depress the footbrake pedal several times to operate the self-adjusting mechanism.

18 Repeat the procedure on the remaining rear brake.

4.2 Rear brake shoe components

4.5 Rear brake shoe anti-rattle spring location

4.6 Rear brake self-adjusting link

4.7 Rear brake anchor plate and lower return spring

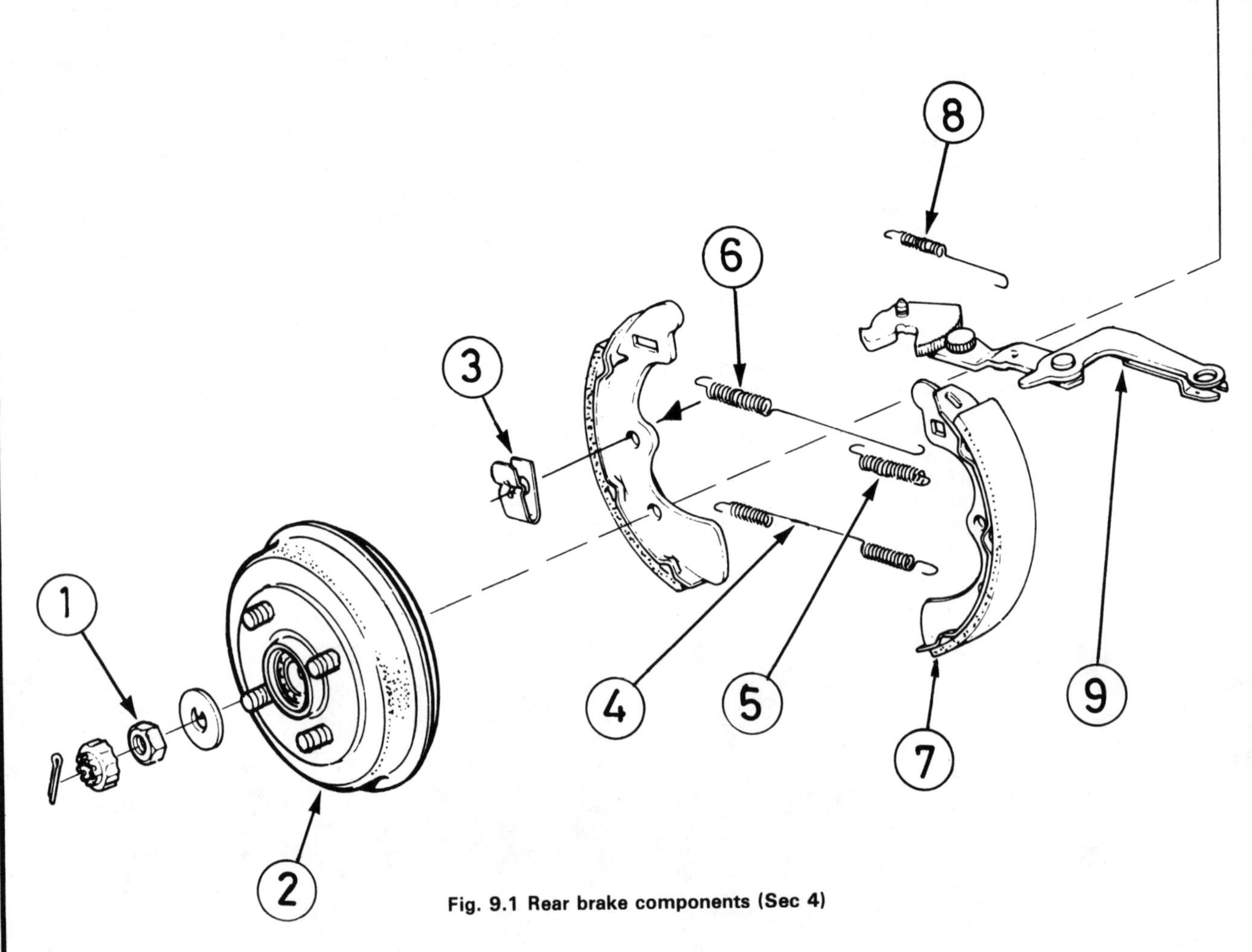

Fig. 9.1 Rear brake components (Sec 4)

1 *Nut*
2 *Drum*
3 *Anti-rattle spring*
4 *Lower return spring*
5 *Link spring*
6 *Upper return spring*
7 *Brake shoe*
8 *Ratchet spring*
9 *Self-adjusting link*

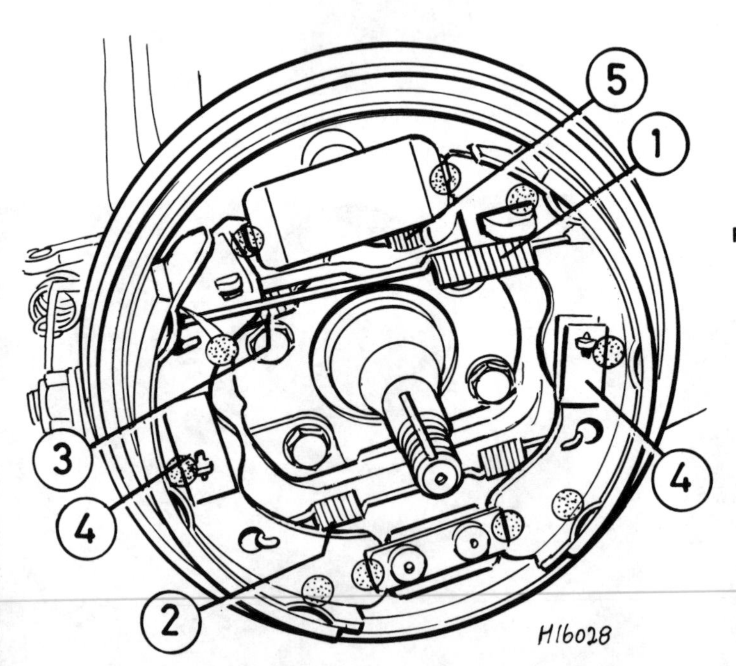

Fig. 9.2 Fitted location of rear brake components. Shaded circles show lubrication areas (Sec 4)

1 *Upper return spring*
2 *Lower return spring*
3 *Link spring*
4 *Anti-rattle springs*
5 *Self-adjusting link ratchet*

5 Disc caliper – removal, overhaul and refitting

1 Remove the disc pads as described in Section 3.
2 Swing the caliper down and either pinch the hydraulic hose with a brake hose clamp, or alternatively tighten the fluid reservoir cap onto a piece of plastic sheeting. The latter may not prove very effective as the cap incorporates a level sensor, but it will prevent some loss of fluid in the subsequent procedure.
3 Unscrew the union bolt and disconnect the hose from the caliper. Recover the two washers. Cover the end of the hose with a small polythene bag and an elastic band.
4 Unscrew the upper guide pin bolt and withdraw the caliper from the car (photo).
5 Unbolt the caliper bracket from the steering knuckle and if necessary remove the guide pins and dust seals.
6 Wash clean the exterior of the caliper and wipe dry.
7 Prise the dust seal from the piston and housing. Using low air pressure (eg from a tyre foot pump) through the hydraulic fluid supply hole, force the piston from the caliper bore.
8 Using a non-metallic instrument (eg a plastic knitting needle) prise the piston seal from the caliper bore.
9 Clean the piston and caliper with methylated spirit, then inspect their surfaces for damage, wear and corrosion. Check the caliper and mounting bracket for cracks and the guide pin rubber boots for splits.

5.4 Removing the disc caliper upper guide pin bolt

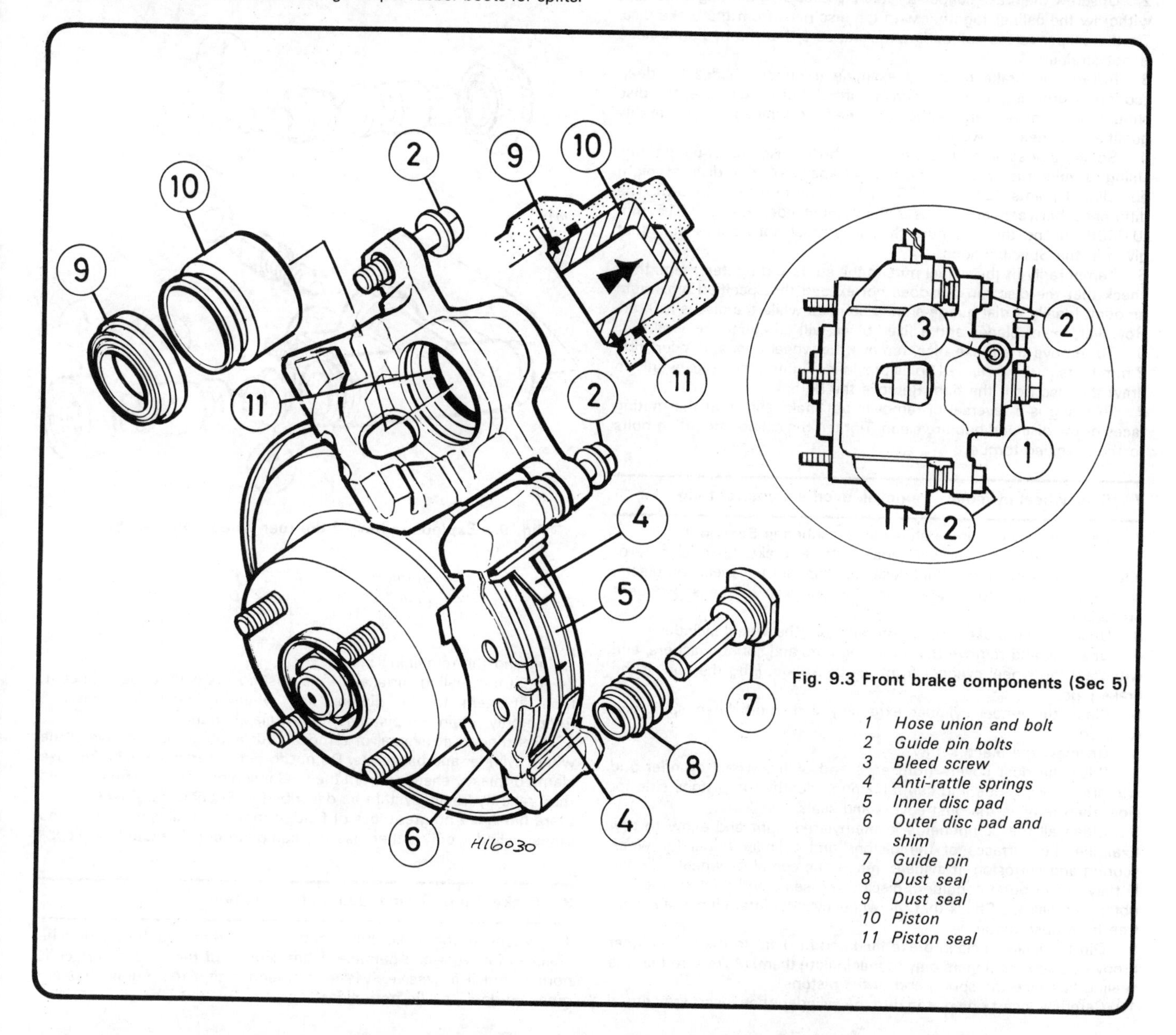

Fig. 9.3 Front brake components (Sec 5)

1 Hose union and bolt
2 Guide pin bolts
3 Bleed screw
4 Anti-rattle springs
5 Inner disc pad
6 Outer disc pad and shim
7 Guide pin
8 Dust seal
9 Dust seal
10 Piston
11 Piston seal

If the caliper and piston are in good condition, discard the old seals and obtain a repair kit of new seals; otherwise, renew the unit complete.
10 Dip the new piston seal in clean brake fluid and manipulate it into the caliper bore groove using the fingers only.
11 Fit the dust seal to the piston and insert the piston in the caliper. Locate the dust seal outer lip in the caliper groove.
12 Fit the caliper bracket complete with guide pins and seals to the steering knuckle and tighten the bolts to the specified torque.
13 Locate the caliper on the bracket and insert the upper guide pin bolt. Tighten the bolt to the specified torque.
14 With the caliper over the disc reconnect the hydraulic hose, union bolt and washers. Tighten the bolt to the specified torque. Remove the brake hose clamp or plastic sheeting from the reservoir (as applicable).
15 Refit the disc pads as described in Section 3.
16 Bleed the brake hydraulic system as described in Section 12. Provided that there has been no great loss of fluid, it may be sufficient to bleed the caliper only, or the caliper and its diagonally opposite rear wheel cylinder.

6 Brake disc – examination, removal and refitting

1 Jack up the front of the car and support it on axle stands. Apply the handbrake and remove the roadwheel.
2 Unscrew the brake caliper-to-steering knuckle mounting bolts, and withdraw the caliper together with the disc pads from the brake disc. Tie the caliper to the coil spring, making sure that the hydraulic hose is not strained.
3 Rotate the brake disc and examine it on both sides for deep scoring or grooving. Light scoring is normal, but if excessive, the disc should be removed and either renewed or refaced by a suitably qualified engineering works.
4 Scrape any scale and rust from the brake disc and wipe it clean. Using a micrometer measure the thickness of the disc at eight equidistant points 19 mm (0.75 in) from the outer rim (photo). The difference between any measurement must not exceed 0.015 mm (0.0006 in) and the minimum thickness must not be less than that given in the Specifications.
5 Temporarily fit the wheel nuts to the studs and tighten them, then check that the disc run-out does not exceed the specified maximum amount. Ideally a dial guage should be used while the disc is rotated. However, feeler blades and a fixed block will do equally as well.
6 To remove the brake disc, remove the wheel nuts and insert two 8 mm bolts in the threaded holes provided. Tighten the bolts evenly to draw the disc from the hub. Remove the bolts.
7 Refitting is a reversal of removal, but make sure that the mating faces of the disc and hub are clean. Tighten the caliper mounting bolts to the specified torque.

6.4 Checking the brake disc thickness

7 Rear wheel cylinder – removal, overhaul and refitting

1 Remove the rear brake shoes as described in Section 4.
2 Pinch the rear hydraulic hose with a brake hose clamp, or alternatively tighten the fluid reservoir cap onto a piece of plastic sheeting, in order to minimise the loss of fluid in the subsequent procedure.
3 Unscrew the brake pipe union nut from the wheel cylinder.
4 Unscrew and remove the mounting nuts and spring washers, and withdraw the wheel cylinder from the backplate. Plug the end of the brake pipe.
5 Clean the wheel cylinder externally with methylated spirit and wipe dry.
6 Unscrew the bleed screw.
7 Prise the dust covers from each end of the wheel cylinder and withdraw the pistons and central spring. Identify the pistons side for side, then remove the dust covers and seals.
8 Clean all the components in methylated spirit and allow to dry. Examine the surfaces of the pistons and cylinder bores for wear, scoring and corrosion. If evident, renew the complete wheel cylinder. If they are in good condition, discard the seals and dust covers and obtain a repair kit. Check that the wheel cylinder internal passages are free from obstruction.
9 Dip the seals in clean brake fluid and fit them to the piston inner grooves, using the fingers only to manipulate them. Make sure that the sealing lips face the spring end of the pistons.
10 Carefully insert one piston into the cylinder, then insert the central spring and the remaining piston.
11 Coat the sealing surfaces of the dust covers with rubber lubricant, then fit them to the pistons and wheel cylinder. If necessary, temporarily retain the pistons with an elastic band.
12 Refitting is a reversal of removal, but apply sealant between the wheel cylinder and backplate. Do not forget to remove the brake hose clamp or plastic sheeting from the fluid reservoir cap, then finally bleed the brake hydraulic system as described in Section 12. Provided that there has been no great loss of fluid, it may be sufficient to bleed the wheel cylinder only, otherwise the complete circuit should be bled.

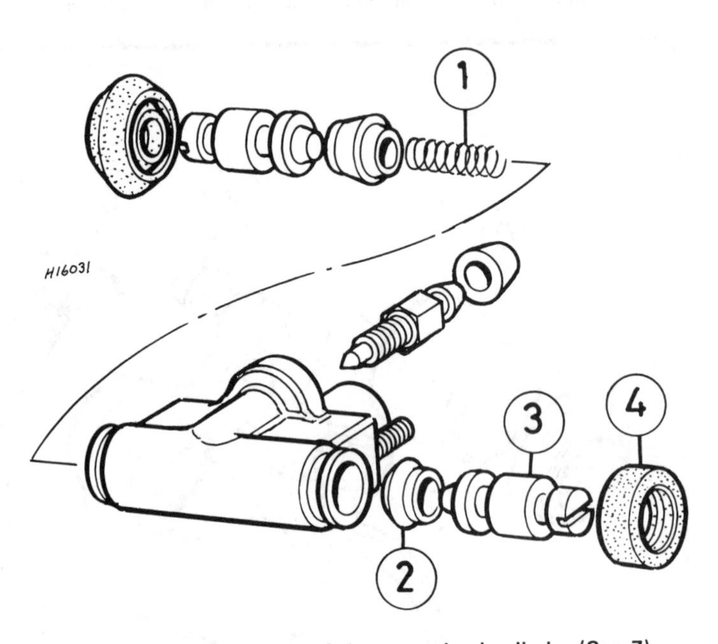

Fig. 9.4 Exploded view of the rear wheel cylinder (Sec 7)

1 Spring
2 Seal
3 Piston
4 Dust cover

8 Brake drum – inspection and renovation

1 Whenever the brake drums and hubs are removed, they should be checked for wear and damage. Light scoring of the friction surface is normal, but if excessive, it is recommended that the drums/hubs are renewed as a pair (ie both sides).

2 After a high mileage, the friction surface may become oval. Where this has occurred, it may be possible to grind the surface true, but this should only be carried out by a qualified engineering works. The internal diameter of the drum after refinishing must not exceed the maximum specified (photo).

9 Master cylinder – removal, overhaul and refitting

1 Depress the footbrake pedal several times to dissipate the vacuum in the servo unit.
2 Attach a bleed tube to the bleed screw on one of the front brake calipers and insert its free end in a small container. Loosen the bleed screw, then pump the footbrake pedal until no more fluid emerges. Tighten the bleed screw and repeat the procedure on the remaining front brake caliper.
3 Disconnect the fluid level sensor wiring from the reservoir filler cap (photo).
4 Protect the paintwork beneath the master cylinder with rags, then unscrew the brake pipe union nuts and remove the pipes from the master cylinder.
5 Unscrew and remove the nuts and spring washers and withdraw the master cylinder from the front of the servo unit. Take care not to spill any brake fluid on the paintwork, otherwise repainting may be necessary. If accidentally spilt, swill off immediately with copious amounts of cold water.
6 Clean the exterior of the master cylinder with methylated spirit and wipe dry.
7 Unscrew the reservoir filler cap and remove the filter and the cap seal.
8 Loosen the clip and remove the reservoir from the master cylinder.
9 Slightly depress the primary piston, then extract the circlip from the mouth of the master cylinder using circlip pliers. Extract the primary piston and spring assembly.
10 Slightly depress the secondary piston, then unscrew and remove the stop bolt and washer from the side of the master cylinder. Tap the cylinder on a block of wood to remove the secondary piston and spring assembly.
11 Clean all the components in methylated spirit and examine them for wear and damage. In particular, check the surfaces of the pistons and cylinder bore for scoring and corrosion. If evident, renew the complete master cylinder, but if the cylinder bore is in good condition the primary and secondary piston assemblies can be renewed. Seal repair kits do not appear to be available, at least from BL sources.
12 Check that the inlet and outlet ports are free and unobstructed. Dip the pistons and seals in clean brake fluid.
13 Grip the master cylinder vertically in a soft-jawed vice.
14 Insert the secondary piston and spring assembly into the cylinder – rotate the piston as each seal enters the bore. Similarly insert the primary piston assembly.
15 Depress the pistons with a screwdriver and refit the stop bolt and washer and the retaining circlip. Tighten the stop bolt to the specified torque.
16 Remove the cylinder from the vice, refit the reservoir with the level marks facing forwards, and tighten the clip.
17 Refit the filter, seal and cap to the reservoir.
18 Refitting is a reversal of removal, but if either piston assembly has been renewed or if the complete master cylinder has been renewed, it will be necessary to adjust the vacuum servo pushrod as described in Section 17. Tighten the mounting nuts to the specified torque and finally bleed the complete hydraulic system as described in Section 12.

10 Proportioning valve – removal and refitting

1 The brake proportioning valve is located in the engine compartment on the right-hand side of the bulkhead, just above the master cylinder (photo). A faulty valve will cause either rear wheel to lock during normal braking, and if this occurs the valve should be renewed.
2 Protect the surrounding paintwork with rags. If brake fluid is accidentally spilled, wash it off immediately with cold water.
3 Identify each brake pipe for position, then unscrew the union nuts, withdraw the pipes, and seal the pipe ends with masking tape to prevent the entry of dust and dirt.

8.2 Rear brake drum grinding limit

9.3 Master cylinder showing fluid level sensor wiring

10.1 Brake proportioning valve

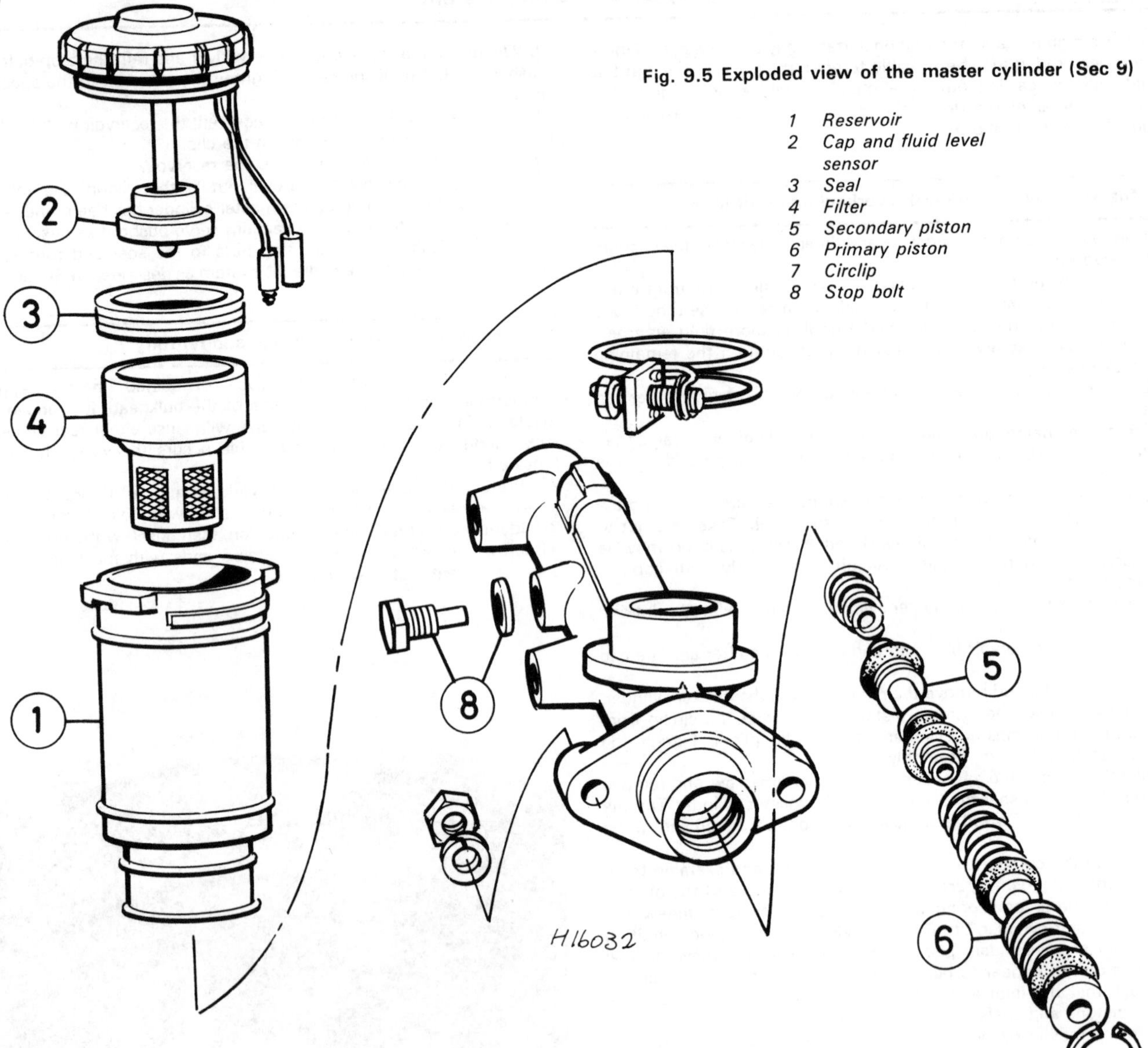

Fig. 9.5 Exploded view of the master cylinder (Sec 9)

1 Reservoir
2 Cap and fluid level sensor
3 Seal
4 Filter
5 Secondary piston
6 Primary piston
7 Circlip
8 Stop bolt

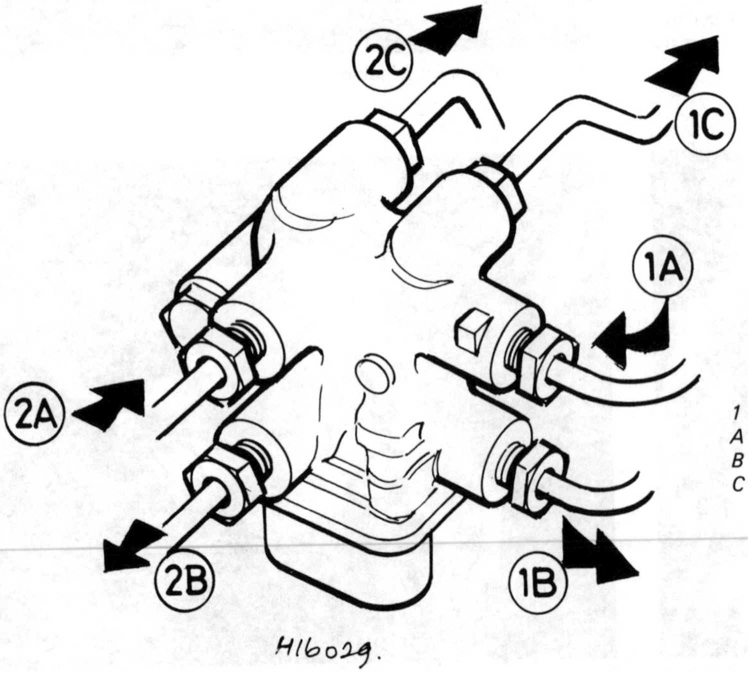

Fig. 9.6 Proportioning valve and pipe locations (Sec 10)

1	*Primary circuit*	*2*	*Secondary circuit*
A	*From master cylinder*	*A*	*From master cylinder*
B	*To front brake LH*	*B*	*To front brake RH*
C	*To rear brake RH*	*C*	*To rear brake LH*

4 Unscrew the mounting bolt and withdraw the valve, taking care not to spill any brake fluid on the paintwork.
5 Refitting is a reversal of removal, but tighten the union nuts to the specified torque and make sure that the unit is vertical before tightening the mounting bolt. Finally bleed the complete hydraulic system as described in Section 12.

11 Hydraulic brake lines and hoses – inspection, removal and refitting

1 At the interval given in Section 2 clean the rigid brake lines and flexible hoses and check them for damage, leakage, chafing and cracks (photo). If the rigid pipes are corroded excessively, they must be renewed. Check the retaining clips for security, and clean away any accumulations of dirt and debris.
2 To remove a rigid brake line in front of the proportioning valve is straightforward. Attach a bleed tube to the bleed screw on the appropriate front brake caliper and insert its free end in a small container. Loosen the bleed screw and pump the footbrake pedal until no more fluid emerges. Tighten the bleed screw, then unscrew the union nuts at each end of the pipe and withdraw the pipe, at the same time prising out the rubber grommet where necessary.
3 To remove a rear rigid brake line, first remove the rear seat cushion and backrest as described in Chapter 12. Remove the right-hand side sill mouldings. Jack up the rear of the car and support it on axle stands. Chock the front wheels and remove the appropriate rear roadwheel. Attach a bleed tube to the bleed screw on the appropriate rear wheel cylinder, and with the tube in a small container and the bleed screw loose, pump the footbrake pedal until no more fluid emerges. Tighten the bleed screw, then unscrew the union nuts at each end of the pipe and withdraw the pipe from the clips and grommets.
4 Refitting of a rigid brake line is a reversal of removal.
5 To remove a flexible brake hose, first pump the hydraulic fluid from the appropriate brake line as described in paragraph 2 or 3. Unscrew the rigid brake line union nut(s) while holding the end of the flexible hose with a spanner. Extract the retaining clip(s) from the mounting bracket(s) and, on the front flexible hoses, unscrew the caliper union bolt and hose clip bolt.
6 Refitting of a flexible brake hose is a reversal of removal, but make sure that it is not kinked or twisted. The front hoses, however, should be biased away from the roadwheel in the following manner. First attach the hose to the caliper with the union bolt and washers, then fit the clip to the strut and tighten the bolt. Turn the upper end of the hose 90° clockwise (as viewed from above) for the right-hand hose, or anti-clockwise for the left-hand hose, then locate it in the bracket and insert the retaining clip.
7 Bleed the complete hydraulic system as described in Section 12 after fitting a rigid brake line or flexible brake hose.

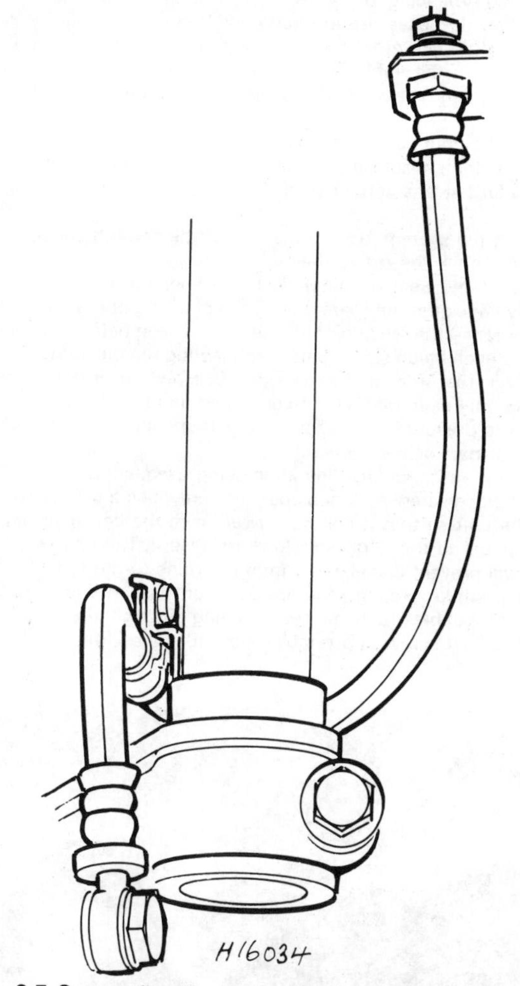

Fig. 9.7 Correct fitted position of a front brake flexible hose (Sec 11)

12 Hydraulic system – bleeding

1 If any of the hydraulic components in the braking system have been removed or disconnected, or if the fluid level in the master cylinder has been allowed to fall appreciably, it is inevitable that air will have been introduced into the system. The removal of all this air from the hydraulic system is essential if the brakes are to function correctly, and the process of removing it is known as bleeding.
2 There are a number of one-man, do-it-yourself, brake bleeding kits currently available from motor accessory shops. It is recommended that one of these kits should be used wherever possible as they greatly simplify the bleeding operation and also reduce the risk of expelled air and fluid being drawn back into the system.
3 If one of these kits is not available then it will be necessary to gather together a clean jar and a suitable length of clear plastic tubing which is a tight fit over the bleed screw, and also to engage the help of an assistant (photo).

11.1a Hydraulic hose fixing on the front suspension strut

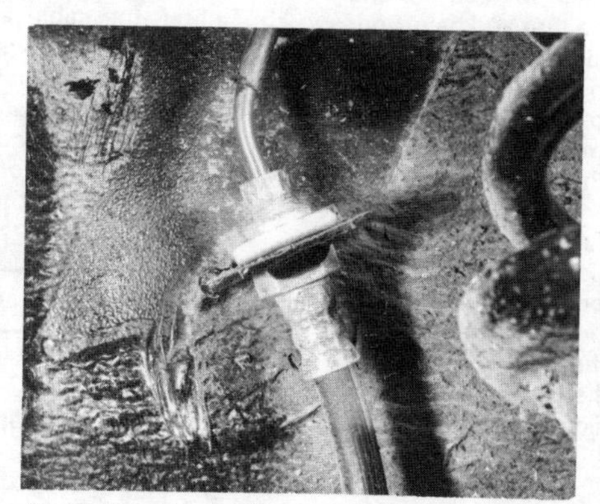
11.1b Front hydraulic hose bracket

11.1c Rear hydraulic hose bracket

4 Before commencing the bleeding operation, check that all rigid pipes and flexible hoses are in good condition and that all hydraulic unions are tight. Take great care not to allow hydrualic fluid to come into contact with the vehicle paintwork, otherwise the finish will be seriously damaged. Wash off any spilled fluid immediately with cold water.
5 If hydraulic fluid has been lost from the master cylinder, due to a leak in the system, ensure that the cause is traced and rectified before proceeding further or a serious malfunction of the braking system may occur.
6 To bleed the system jack up the rear of the car and support it on axle stands. Chock the front wheels.
7 Remove the master cylinder filler cap and top up the reservoir. Periodically check the fluid level during the bleeding operation and top up as necessary – the reservoir must be kept at least half full. Clean the area around each bleed screw before connecting the bleed tube. Bleed the system in the order shown in Fig. 9.8. However, if the hydraulic system has only been partially disconnected and suitable precautions were taken to prevent further loss of fluid, it should only be necessary to bleed that part of the system.
8 If a one-man brake bleeding kit is being used, connect the outlet tube to the bleed screw and then open the screw half a turn. If possible position the unit so that it can be viewed from the car, then depress the brake pedal to the floor and slowly release it. The one-way valve in the kit will prevent dispelled air from returning to the system at the end of each stroke. Repeat this operation until clean hydraulic fluid, free from air bubbles, can be seen coming through the tube. Now tighten the bleed screw and remove the outlet tube (photo).

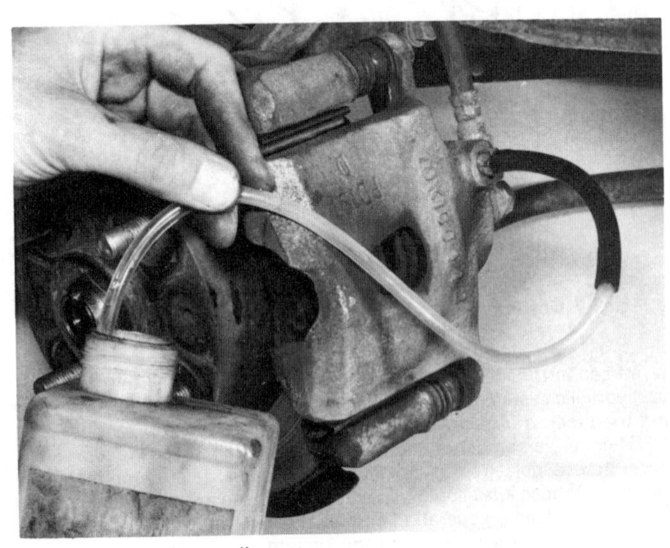

12.8 Bleeding a front caliper

9 If a one-man brake bleeding kit is not available, connect one end of the plastic tubing to the bleed screw and immerse the other end in the jam jar containing sufficient clean hydraulic fluid to keep the end of the tube submerged. Open the bleed screw half a turn and have your assistant depress the brake pedal to the floor and then slowly release it. Tighten the bleed screw at the end of each downstroke to prevent expelled air and fluid from being drawn back into the system. Repeat this operation until clean hydraulic fluid, free from air bubbles, can be seen coming through the tube. Now tighten the bleed screw and remove the plastic tube.
10 If the entire system is being bled, the procedures described above should now be repeated at each wheel. Do not forget to recheck the fluid level in the master cylinder at regular intervals and top up as necessary.
11 When completed, recheck the fluid level in the reservoir, top up if necessary and refit the cap. Check the 'feel' of the brake pedal which should be firm and free from any 'sponginess' which would indicate air still present in the system.
12 Discard any expelled hydraulic fluid as it is likely to be contaminated with moisture, air and dirt which makes it unsuitable for further use.

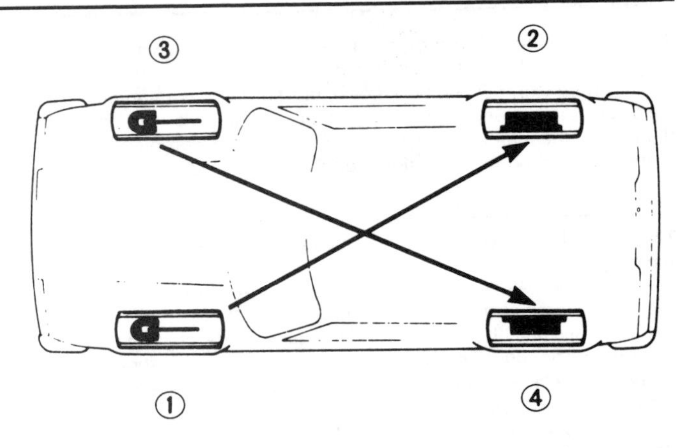

Fig. 9.8 Sequence for bleeding the hydraulic system (Sec 12)

13 Handbrake cables – removal, refitting and adjustment

Removal and refitting

1 Adjust the driver's seat to the fully forward position and tilt the backrest forwards.
2 Extract the rear ashtray and remove the rear cover from the handbrake lever (photo).
3 Chock the front wheels and release the handbrake. Extract the split pin and remove the clevis pin securing the cable to the lever. Unbolt the guide plate (photo).
4 Jack up the rear of the car and support it on axle stands.
5 Working beneath the rear of the car, unscrew the cable adjusting nut and slide the cable end from the trunnion pin (photo). Remove the pin from the equaliser and the spring from the cable end.
6 Release the rear cable guides from their clips, then unhook both rear cables from the equaliser and brake shoe operating levers (photo).
7 Detach the rear floor heat shield.
8 Support the fuel tank with a trolley jack and a block of wood, then unscrew and remove the mounting bolts and slightly lower the tank to gain access to the handbrake cable.
9 Release the cable guide from the clip and the cable from the guide channels.
10 Prise out the front rubber dust seal and withdraw the front cable from under the car.
11 Refitting is a reversal of removal, but lubricate the guides, cable ends and equaliser with multi-purpose grease. Adjust the cable as follows.

Adjustment

12 Depress the footbrake pedal several times to make sure that the rear brakes are adjusted by the self-adjusting mechanism.
13 Chock the front wheels, then jack up the rear of the car and support it on axle stands.
14 Fully release the handbrake lever, then pull it onto the first notch.
15 Tighten the cable adjusting nut on the equaliser until both rear wheels drag slightly when rotated by hand.
16 Fully release the handbrake and check that both rear wheels can be freely rotated by hand.
17 Fully apply the handbrake lever by 4 to 8 notches and check that both rear wheels are locked.
18 Lower the car to the ground.

14 Handbrake lever and switch – removal and refitting

1 Adjust the driver's seat to the fully forward position and tilt the backrest forwards.
2 Extract the rear ashtray and remove the rear cover from the handbrake lever.
3 Chock the front wheels and release the handbrake. Extract the split pin and remove the clevis pin securing the cable to the lever.
4 Disconnect the switch wiring at the connector.

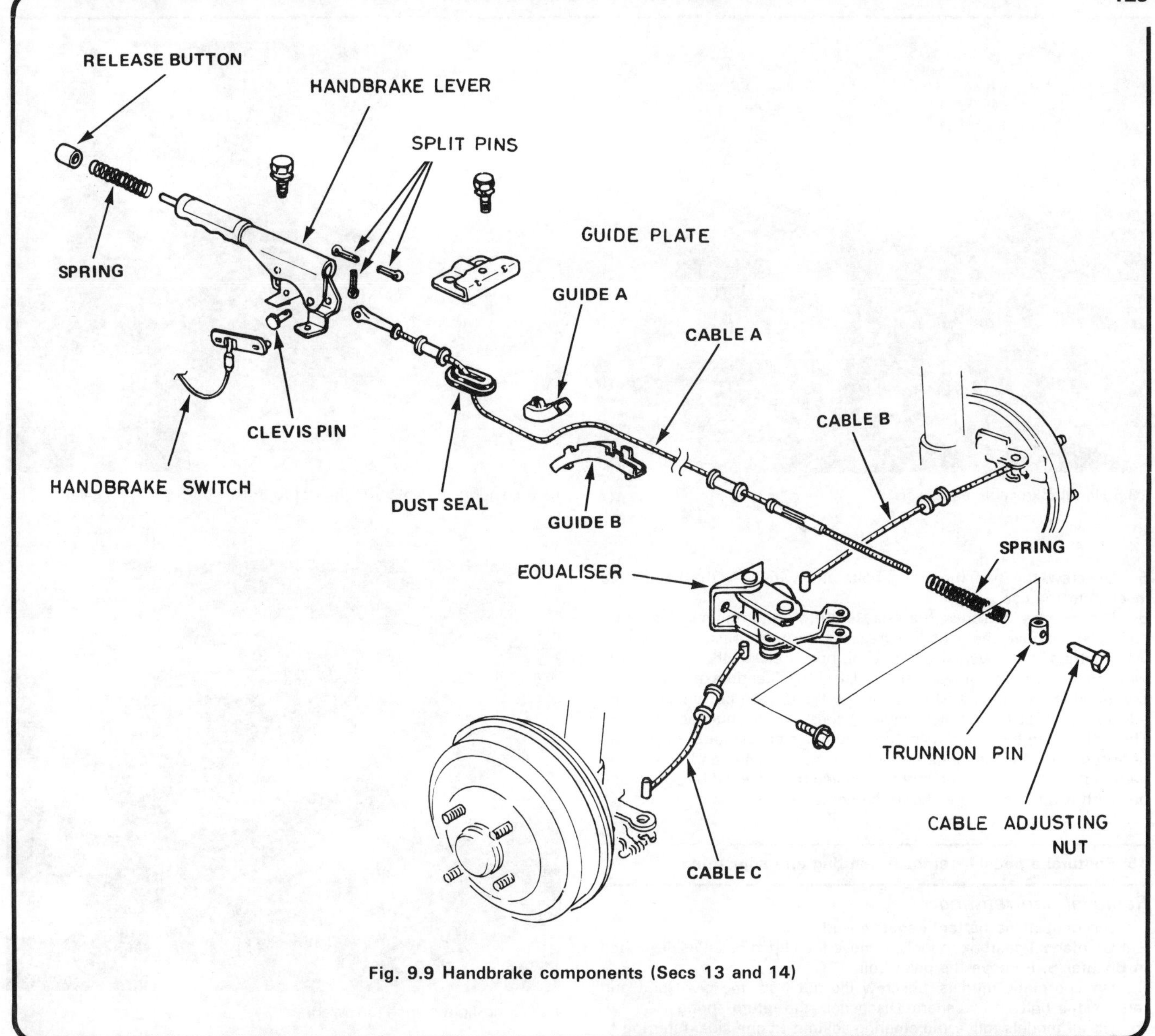

Fig. 9.9 Handbrake components (Secs 13 and 14)

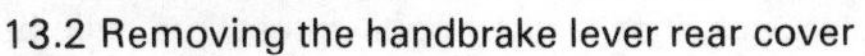

13.2 Removing the handbrake lever rear cover

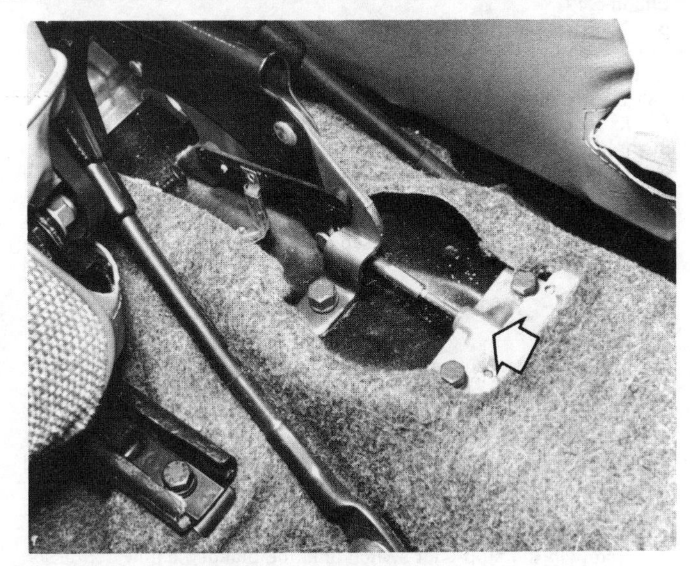

13.3 Handbrake lever and (arrowed) guide plate

13.5 Handbrake cable equaliser

13.6 Handbrake cable attachment to brake shoe operating lever

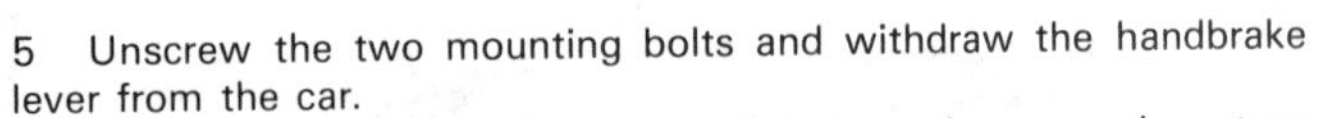

5 Unscrew the two mounting bolts and withdraw the handbrake lever from the car.

6 If necessary, unscrew the release button and remove the return spring. To remove the switch extract the two split pins.

7 Refitting is a reversal of removal, but lubricate the pivot points with multi-purpose grease and adjust the handbrake cables as described in Section 13. The position of the release button should be adjusted so that the ratchet pawl engages and disengages correctly. The switch can be tested using an ohmmeter or test lamp connected between the disconnected end of the switch wire and a suitable earthing point. With the handbrake applied there should be continuity, but with it released there should be no continuity.

15 Footbrake pedal – removal, refitting and adjustment

Removal and refitting

1 Disconnect the battery negative lead.

2 On manual gearbox models, remove the clutch pedal as described in Chapter 5. Remove the pivot bolt.

3 On Trio-matic models, unscrew the nut from the pivot bolt and remove the bolt and washers. Disconnect the return spring.

4 On all models move the steering column to one side, referring to Chapter 11.

5 Connect bleed tubes between both front brake caliper bleed screws and suitable containers. Have an assistant depress the footbrake pedal and hold it down after loosening both bleed screws half a turn, then tighten the bleed screws.

6 Extract the split pin and clevis pin, detach the pedal from the servo pushrod, and withdraw the pedal.

7 Extract the spacer and bushes and examine them together with the pad rubber for wear. Renew the components as necessary.

8 Refitting is a reversal of removal, but lubricate the bushes with a little molybdenum disulphide-based grease and top up the fluid level in the master cylinder. When complete, adjust the pedal height as follows.

Adjustment

9 Prise the pad rubber from the pedal and pull back the floor covering below the pedal. With the pedal fully released, measure the distance from the floor to the underside of the pedal (Fig. 9.11). If the distance is not as given in Fig. 9.11, first loosen the locknut on the stop-light switch and unscrew the switch until it is clear of the pedal (photo). Disconnect the wires from the switch if necessary.

10 Loosen the locknut on the servo pushrod and, using pliers, turn the pushrod in or out until the pedal height is correct. Tighten the locknut.

11 Screw in the stop-light switch until the plunger is fully depressed with the threaded end just touching the pedal, then unscrew it half a turn and tighten the locknut.

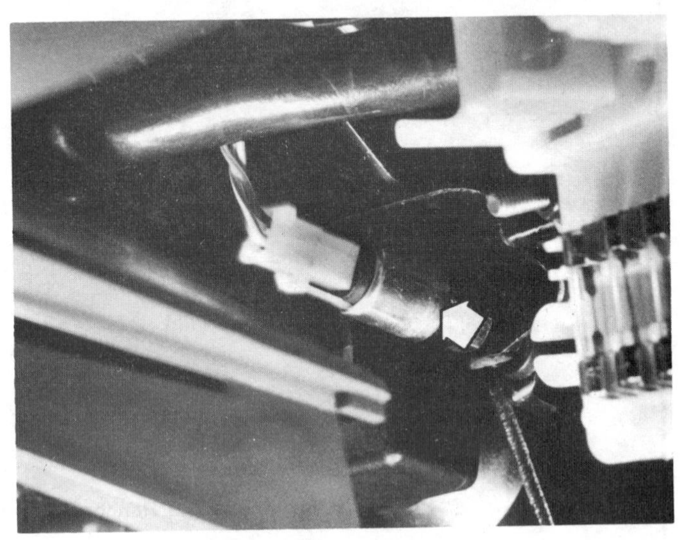

15.9 Stop-light switch (arrowed)

12 Refit the pad rubber, then check that the stop-lights go on and off as the pedal is depressed and released. Note that the stop-lights will operate without the ignition being switched on.

16 Vacuum servo unit – description and testing

1 The direct-acting vacuum servo unit is located between the footbrake pedal and the master cylinder, and provides assistance to the driver when the pedal is depressed.

2 The unit operates by vacuum derived from the inlet manifold (photo), and it basically comprises a booster diaphragm and a non-return valve.

3 With the footbrake pedal released, vacuum is channelled to both sides of the diaphragm. When the pedal is depressed, one side of the diaphragm is opened to the atmosphere. The resultant pressure difference is harnessed to assist in depressing the master cylinder pistons.

4 Under normal operating conditions the vacuum servo unit is very reliable. If a fault occurs, the unit can be overhauled using a repair kit of seals and a diaphragm. In the event of a failure the hydraulic system is in no way affected, except that higher pedal pressures will be necessary.

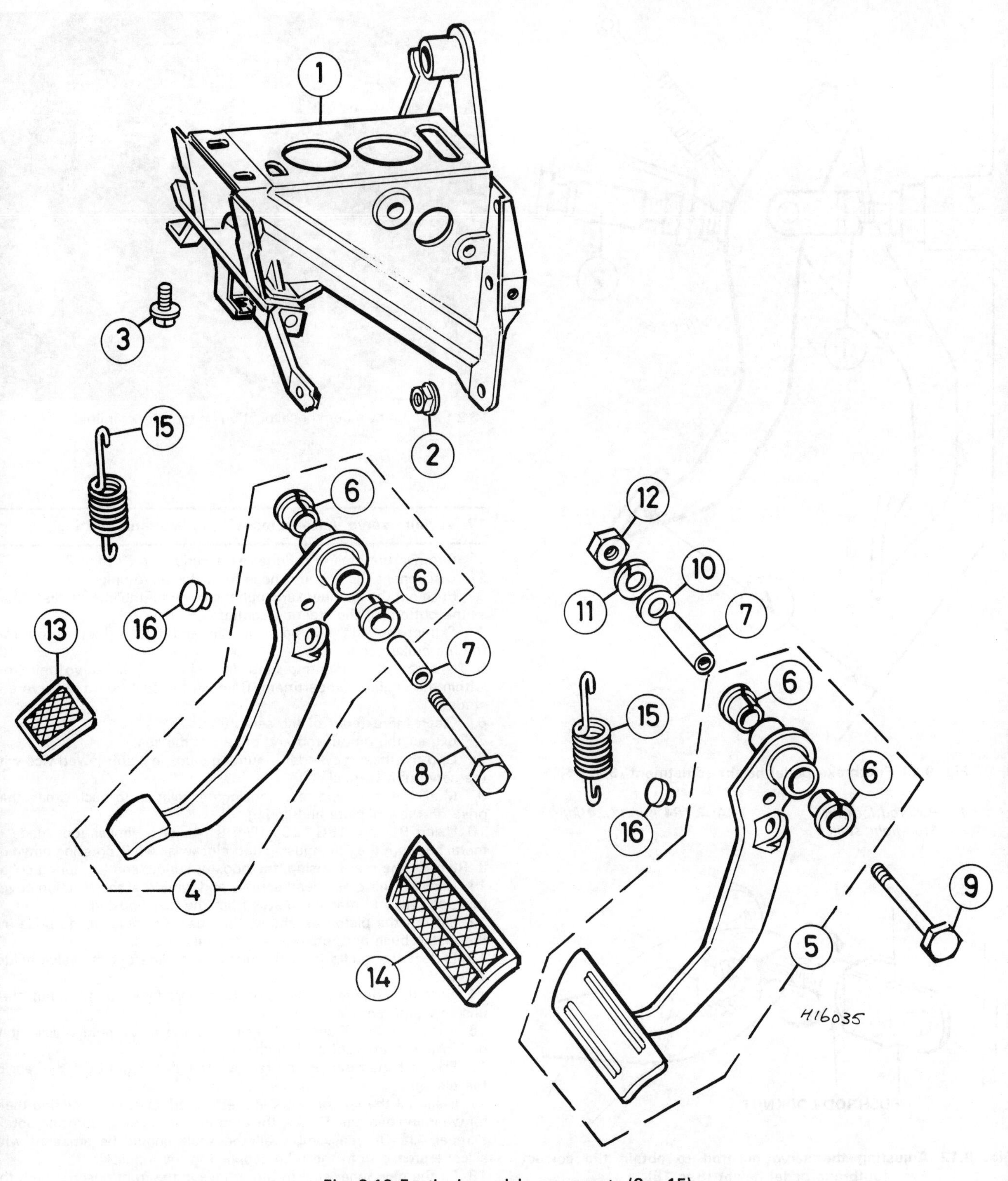

Fig. 9.10 Footbrake pedal components (Sec 15)

1 *Pedal bracket*
2 *Nut*
3 *Bolt*
4 *Pedal assembly (manual gearbox models)*
5 *Pedal assembly (Triomatic models)*
6 *Bush*
7 *Spacer*
8 *Pivot bolt*
9 *Pivot bolt*
10 *Plain washer*
11 *Spring washer*
12 *Nut*
13 *Pad*
14 *Pad*
15 *Return spring*
16 *Stop pad*

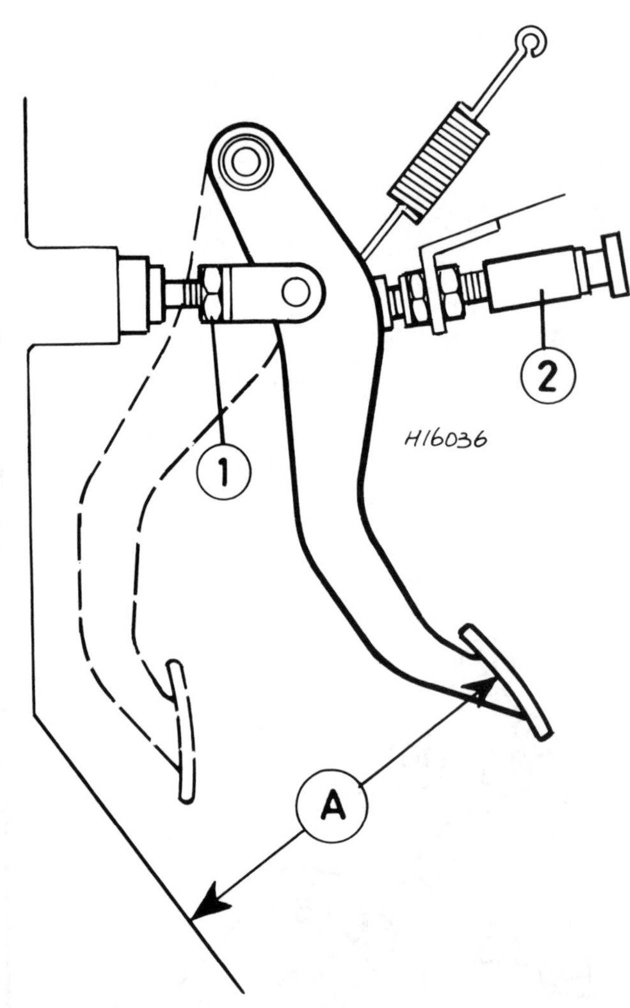

Fig. 9.11 Footbrake pedal height adjustment (Sec 15)

1 *Pushrod locknut*
2 *Stop-light switch*

A = 184 mm (7.24 in)

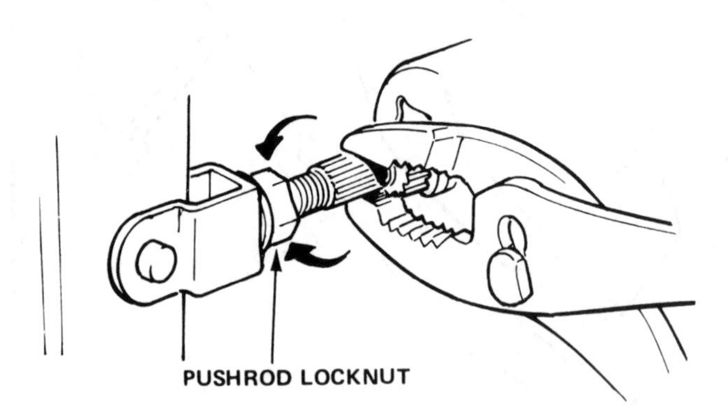

Fig. 9.12 Adjusting the servo pushrod to obtain the correct footbrake pedal height (Sec 15)

5 To test the servo unit, depress the footbrake pedal several times with the engine stopped in order to dissipate the vacuum. Depress the pedal hard and hold it down; the pedal should remain stationary, but if it drops, the hydraulic circuit is faulty and possibly leaking.
6 With the pedal still depressed, start the engine. If the pedal drops slightly, the servo unit is functioning correctly. If the pedal remains stationary, the unit is not working and is either faulty or has a faulty vacuum supply.

16.2 Servo unit vacuum hose location on the inlet manifold

17 Vacuum servo unit – removal, overhaul and refitting

1 Remove the master cylinder as described in Section 9.
2 Disconnect the vacuum hose from the servo unit.
3 Prise out the fasteners and pull the cover off the intermediate shaft at the bottom of the steering column.
4 Extract the split pin and clevis pin, and detach the pushrod from the footbrake pedal.
5 Unscrew the mounting nuts and withdraw the servo unit from within the engine compartment. Remove the seal from the servo unit studs.
6 Clean the exterior of the servo unit.
7 Extract the output rod and prise out the seal.
8 Grip the master cylinder mounting studs in a soft-jawed vice with the servo unit vertical.
9 Mark the front and rear housings in relation to each other, then prise off the lockplate and spring.
10 Using BL tool 18G 1205 (Fig. 9.14), or a similar tool made of metal bar, turn the rear housing anti-clockwise while pressing down on it. Remove the rear housing, the booster spring, and the spring collar.
11 Remove the cross-head screws and withdraw the reaction cover, reaction ring and reaction plates from the rear housing.
12 Lift out the piston assembly, then use a screwdriver to prise out the piston bush and retainer, and the piston seal.
13 Extract the circlip from the piston and slide out the valve holder assembly.
14 Note the relative positions of the pushrod yoke and locknut, then unscrew and remove them.
15 Prise out the E-clip and dismantle the valve holder assembly, noting the location of each item.
16 Prise off the retainer and remove the diaphragm from the rear of the piston.
17 Clean all the components in methylated spirit and examine them for wear and damage. Renew the components as necessary and obtain a repair kit. On reassembly all the seals should be smeared with silicone grease from the tube supplied in the repair kit.
18 Fit the new inner seal to the groove in the front pushrod with the sealing lip facing rearwards.
19 Fit the outer seal to the groove in the valve holder.
20 Insert the rear pushrod through the valve holder into the front pushrod, and fit the outer seal metal end to the inner seal lip.
21 Slide the inner and outer valve springs over the rear pushrod, followed by the spring seat, felt silencer and E-clip.
22 Slide the foam filter over the rear pushrod and screw on the adjuster and locknut, but do not tighten them at this stage.
23 Locate the new diaphragm on the rear of the piston. Secure it by pressing on the new lockwasher with a suitable metal tube.
24 Smear the piston tube with silicone grease, then press in the valve

holder assembly and fit the circlip to the front pushrod.
25 Smear the rear housing bore with silicone grease, then press in the new piston seal, bush, and retainer. Press the retainer in until the seal contacts the housing shoulder.
26 Locate the piston and diaphragm assembly in the rear housing.
27 With the front of the piston uppermost, insert the reaction plates with their rounded edges outward.
28 Smear the reaction ring rubber with silicone grease, then locate it on the reaction plates, fit the cover, and tighten the screws.
29 With the front housing mounting studs in a soft-jawed vice, fit the collar and spring.
30 Lower the piston and rear housing onto the front housing, and locate the diaphragm outer lip in the recess. Using the special tool, press down the rear housing and turn it clockwise, making sure that the previously made marks are aligned. Secure the housings by pressing on the lockplate and spring.
31 Remove the servo unit from the vice.
32 Insert the output rod in its seal, then insert them both into the front housing and press the seal fully into position.
33 Fit the locknut and yoke to their previously noted positions on the rear of the pushrod.
34 The pushrod must now be adjusted, and BL tool 18G 1362 will be required, together with a vacuum pump and gauge. If these items are unavailable, the adjustment must be entrusted to a suitably equipped garage.
35 Place the adjustment tool over the mouth of the master cylinder (Fig. 9.17) and adjust the centre screw to just contact the primary piston.
36 Without altering the adjustment tool, place the other end over the mouth of the servo unit while applying 20 in Hg (500 mm Hg) of vacuum. The clearance between the output rod and the tool centre screw should be 0.4 mm (0.016 in) measured with a feeler blade. If not, turn the pushrod adjuster until the clearance is correct, then tighten the locknut.
37 Refitting is a reversal of removal. Refer to Section 9 when refitting the master cylinder.

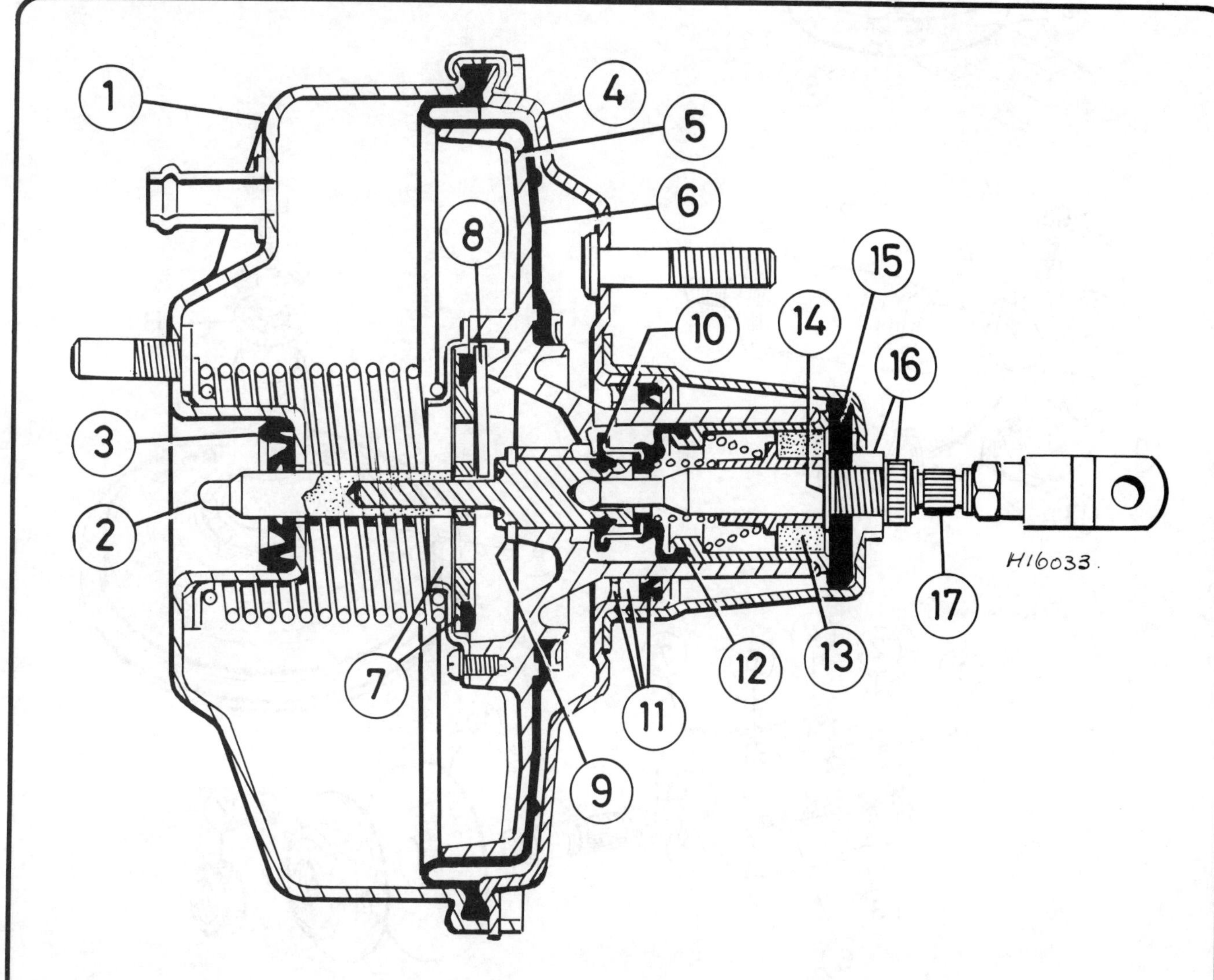

Fig. 9.13 Cross-section of the vacuum servo unit (Sec 17)

1 *Front housing*
2 *Output rod*
3 *Seal*
4 *Rear housing*
5 *Piston*
6 *Diaphragm*
7 *Reaction ring and cover*
8 *Reaction plates*
9 *Circlip*
10 *Seal*
11 *Piston seal, bush, and retainer*
12 *Outer seal*
13 *Felt silencer*
14 *E-clip*
15 *Foam filter*
16 *Adjuster and locknut*
17 *Pushrod*

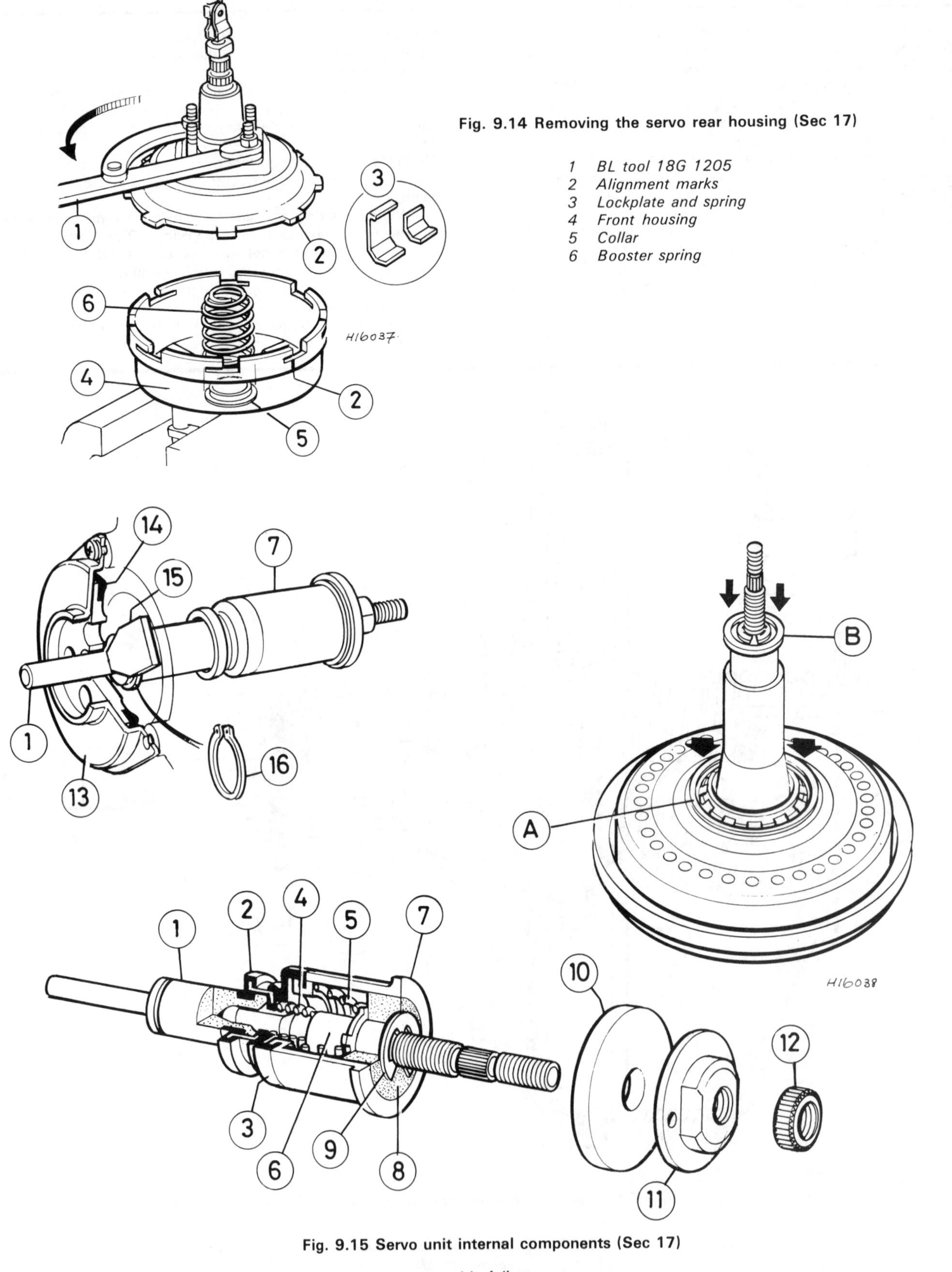

Fig. 9.14 Removing the servo rear housing (Sec 17)

1 *BL tool 18G 1205*
2 *Alignment marks*
3 *Lockplate and spring*
4 *Front housing*
5 *Collar*
6 *Booster spring*

Fig. 9.15 Servo unit internal components (Sec 17)

1 *Pushrod*
2 *Inner seal*
3 *Outer seal*
4 *Inner spring*
5 *Outer spring*
6 *Spring seat*
7 *Valve holder*
8 *Felt silencer*
9 *E-clip*
10 *Foam filter*
11 *Adjuster*
12 *Locknut*
13 *Reaction cover*
14 *Reaction ring*
15 *Reaction plates*
16 *Circlip*
A *Installing the diaphragm retainer*
B *Installing the valve holder*

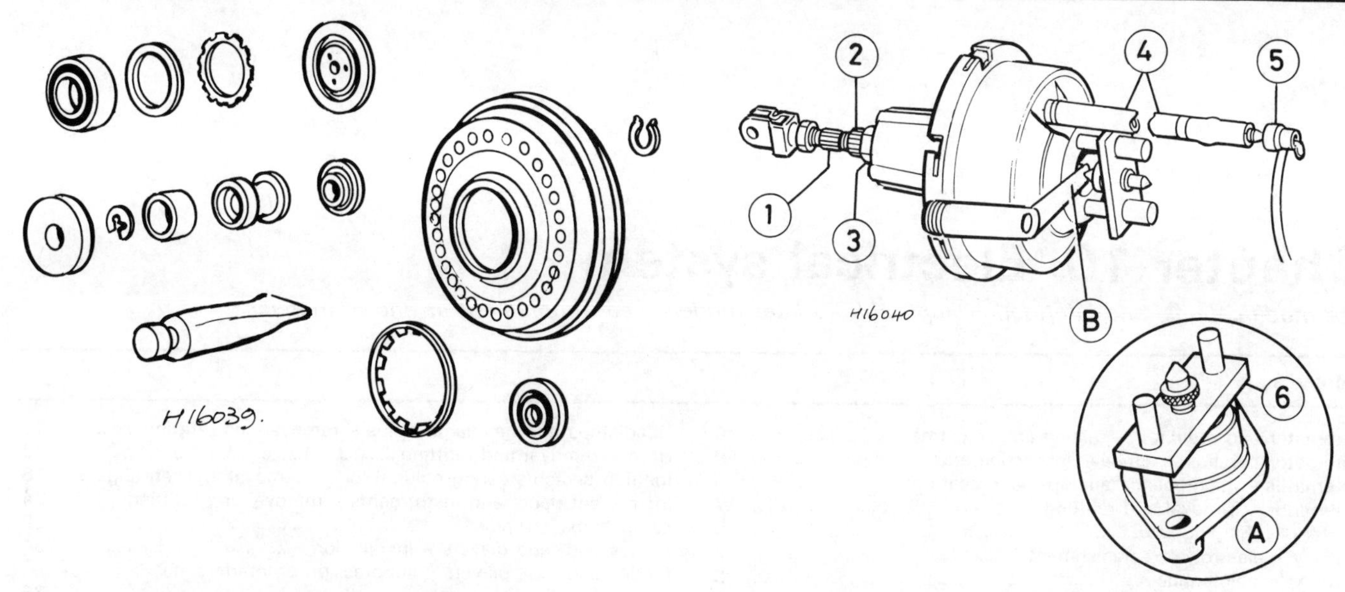

Fig. 9.16 Servo unit repair kit components (Sec 17)

Fig. 9.17 Adjusting the servo pushrod (Sec 17)

1 Pushrod
2 Locknut
3 Adjuster
4 Vacuum hose
5 Vacuum pump adaptor
6 BL tool 18G 1362
A Setting the tool on the master cylinder
B Checking the pushrod clearance

18 Fault diagnosis – braking system

Symptom	Reason(s)
Excessive pedal travel	Brake fluid leak Rear brake self-adjusting mechanism seized Air in hydraulic system
Uneven braking and pulling to one side	Contaminated linings Seized wheel cylinder or caliper Unequal tyre pressures Different lining material at each wheel
Brake judder	Worn drums and/or discs Loose suspension anchor point Loose caliper mounting bolts
Brake pedal feels 'spongy'	Air in hydraulic system Faulty master cylinder seals
Excessive effort required to stop car	Servo unit faulty Seized wheel cylinder or caliper Incorrect or 'cheap' lining material Contaminated linings New linings not yet bedded-in Failure of one hydraulic circuit
Brakes overheat	Master cylinder faulty Seized calipers or wheel cylinders

Chapter 10 Electrical system

For modifications, and information applicable to later models, see Supplement at end of manual

Contents

Specifications

General

System type	12 volt, negative earth
Battery capacity	47 amp hr at 20 hr rate

Alternator

Output at 14 volts and 3000 engine rpm (4500 alternator rpm)	45 amps
Rotor winding resistance	3.9 to 4.1 ohms
Maximum permissible rotor speed	13 000 rpm
Minimum brush protrusion	5.5 mm (0.217 in)

Voltage regulator

Control voltage	13.5 to 14.5 volts
Minimum armature gap	0.5 mm (0.020 in)
Minimum angle gap	0.5 mm (0.020 in)
Points gap	0.4 to 1.2 mm (0.016 to 0.047 in)
Contact spring deflection	0.2 to 0.6 mm (0.008 to 0.024 in)

Starter motor

No-load running current	50 amps at 11 volts and 3000 starter rpm
Loaded running current	200 amps at 8 volts and 1200 starter rpm
Commutator minimum diameter	27.0 mm (1.06 in)
Brush spring tension	1.02 to 1.38 kgf (2.2 to 3.0 lbf)
Minimum brush length	10.0 mm (0.39 in)
Pinion clearance	0.1 to 4.0 mm (0.004 to 0.157 in)

Wiper blades ... Champion X-4103

Fuses

Yellow	10 amp
Blue	15 amp
Red	20 amp
Black on white	1 amp
Black on red	2.5 amp
Main fusible link	55 amp

For fuse application see text

Bulbs (typical)

	Wattage
Headlamps – halogen	60/55
Headlamps – tungsten	45/40
Sidelamps	5
Side repeater lamps	5
Stop/tail lamps	21/5
Direction indicator lamps	21
Reversing lamps	21
Number plate lamps	5
Luggage compartment lamp	5
Switch illumination lamps	2
Cigar lighter lamp	2.2
Trio-matic quadrant and switches	1.2
Panel, warning, gauge and ashtray lamps	1.2
Instrument lamps	3
Switch warning lamps	1.4
Heater controls	1.2

Torque wrench settings

	lbf ft	Nm
Battery base bracket	16	22
Alternator pulley nut	43	58
Alternator adjustment	19	26
Alternator mounting	33	45
Starter motor mounting	33	45
Reversing lamp switch	18	25
Windscreen wiper wheel box	10	14
Windscreen wiper arm	7	10

1 General description

The electrical system is of 12 volt negative earth type. The battery is charged by a belt-driven alternator. The starter motor is of pre-engaged type, incorporating a solenoid which moves the drive pinion into engagement with the ring gear before the motor is energised.

Although repair procedures are given in this Chapter, it may well be more economical to renew worn components as complete units.

2 Battery – removal and refitting

1 The battery is located on the right-hand side of the engine compartment (photo).

2 Loosen the nut and remove the clamp from the negative terminal.

3 Lift the plastic cover from the positive terminal, loosen the nut and remove the clamp.

4 Loosen the battery retaining bar nuts and move the bar to one side.

5 Lift the battery from the platform, taking care not to spill any electrolyte on the bodywork.

6 Remove the plastic tray and wash it clean in water. Also clean the battery platform and surrounding bodywork.

7 Refitting is a reversal of removal, but make sure that the polarity is correct before connecting the leads, and do not overtighten the terminal nuts (photo). Smear the terminal clamps with petroleum jelly.

3 Battery – maintenance

1 Normal weekly battery maintenance consists of checking the electrolyte level of each cell to ensure that the separators are covered with electrolyte. On some batteries the check can be made without removing the battery covers, since the case is translucent.

2.1 Battery location

2.7 Battery negative lead and earthing point

2 If the electrolyte level has dropped, remove the covers and add distilled or de-ionized water to each cell until the separators are just covered.
3 At the same time, the top of the battery should be wiped clean with a dry cloth, to prevent the accumulation of dust and dampness which may cause the battery to become partially discharged over a period.
4 Every 15 000 miles (24 000 km) or 12 months, whichever occurs first, disconnect and clean the battery terminals and leads. After refitting them and before fitting the plastic cover, smear the exposed metal with petroleum jelly.
5 At the same time, inspect the battery bar and platform for corrosion. If evident, remove the battery and clean the deposits away, then treat the affected metal with a proprietary anti-rust liquid and paint the original colour.
6 When the battery is removed for whatever reason, it is worthwhile checking it for cracks and leakage. Cracks can be caused by topping up the cells with distilled water in winter *after* instead of *before* a run. This gives the water no chance to mix with the electrolyte, so the former freezes and splits the battery case. If the battery case is fractured, it may be possible to repair it with a proprietary compound but this depends on the material used for the case. If electrolyte has been lost from a cell, refer to Section 4 for details of adding a fresh solution.
7 If topping up the battery becomes excessive and the case is not fractured the battery is being over-charged and the voltage regulator will have to be checked.
8 If the car covers a very small annual mileage it is worthwhile checking the specific gravity of the electrolyte every three months to determine the state of charge of the battery. Use a hydrometer to make the check, and compare the results with the following table.

	Ambient temperature above 25°C (77°F)	**Ambient temperature below 25°C (77°F)**
Fully charged	*1.210 to 1.230*	*1.270 to 1.290*
70% charged	*1.170 to 1.190*	*1.230 to 1.250*
Fully discharged	*1.050 to 1.070*	*1.110 to 1.130*

Note that the specific gravity readings assume an electrolyte temperature of 15°C (60°F); for every 10°C (18°F) below 15°C (60°F) subtract 0.007, or above, add 0.007.
9 If the battery condition is suspect first check the specific gravity of electrolyte in each cell. A variation of 0.040 or more between any cells indicates loss of electrolyte or deterioration of the internal plates.
10 A further test can be made using a battery heavy discharge meter. The battery should be discharged for a maximum of 15 seconds at a loss of three times the ampere-hour capacity (at the 20-hour discharge rate). Alternatively, connect a voltmeter across the battery terminals and spin the engine on the starter with the coil low tension negative lead disconnected and the headlamps, heated rear window and heater blower switched on.
11 If the voltmeter reading remains above 9.6 volts, the battery condition is satisfactory. If the voltmeter reading drops below 9.6 volts and the battery has already been changed as described in Section 5, it is faulty and should be renewed.

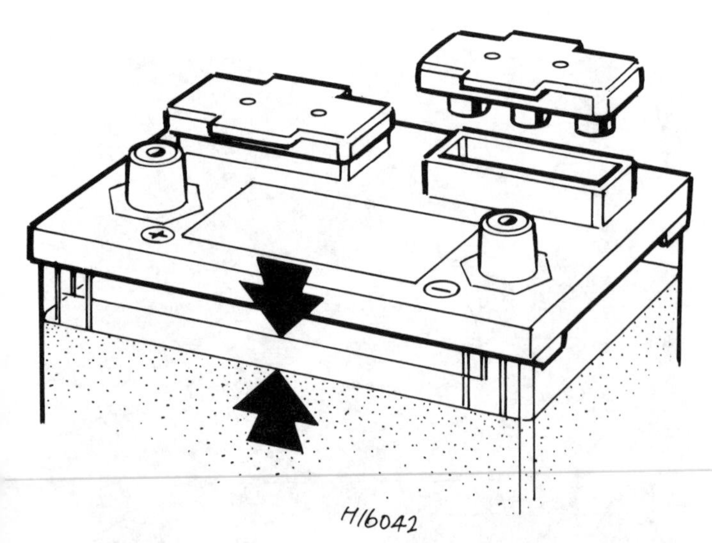

Fig. 10.1 Battery electrolyte minimum and maximum level marks (Sec 3)

4 Battery – electrolyte replenishment

1 If after fully charging the battery, one of the cells maintains a specific gravity which is 0.040 or more lower than the others, but the battery also maintains 9.6 volts during the heavy discharge test (Section 3), it is likely that electrolyte has been lost.
2 If a significant quantity of electrolyte has been lost through spillage it will not suffice merely to refill with distilled water. Top up the cell with a mixture of 2 parts sulphuric acid to 5 parts distilled water.
3 When mixing the electrolyte *never* add water to sulphuric acid – *always* pour the acid slowly onto the water in a glass container. *If water is added to sulphuric acid, it will explode!*
4 After topping up the cell with fresh electrolyte, recharge the battery, and check the hydrometer readings again.

5 Battery – charging

1 With normal motoring, the battery should be kept in a good state of charge by the alternator and never need charging from a mains charger.
2 However, as the battery ages, it may not be able to hold its charge and some supplementary charging may be needed. Before connecting the charger, disconnect the battery terminals or better still, remove the battery from the vehicle.
3 A trickle charger, charging at a rate of 1.5 amps, can safely be used overnight.
4 Special rapid 'boost' charges, which are claimed to restore the power of the battery in 1 to 2 hours, can be dangerous unless they are thermostatically controlled, as they can cause serious damage to the battery plates through overheating.
5 While charging the battery, ensure that the temperature of the electrolyte never exceeds 37.8°C (100°F).

6 Alternator – maintenance and special precautions

1 Periodically wipe away any dirt which has accumulated on the outside of the unit, and check that the wiring is firmly connected to the terminals. At the same time, check the tension of the drivebelt and adjust it if necessary as described in Chapter 2.
2 Take extreme care when making electrical circuit connections on the car, otherwise damage may occur to the alternator or other electrical components employing semi-conductors. Always make sure that the battery leads are connected to the correct terminals. Before using electric-arc welding equipment to repair any part of the car, disconnect the battery leads and alternator multi-plug. Disconnect the battery leads before using a mains charger. Never run the alternator with the multi-plug or a battery lead disconnected.

7 Alternator – removal and refitting

1 Disconnect the battery negative lead.
2 Pull the multi-plug from the rear of the alternator and disconnect the single wire.
3 Loosen the adjustment link bolt and the mounting pivot bolt (photo).
4 Swivel the alternator in towards the engine, and slip the drivebelt from the pulley.
5 Support the alternator, then remove the adjustment link bolt and the mounting pivot bolt.
6 Withdraw the alternator from the top of the engine on models with air conditioning, or from beneath the engine on models with air conditioning (photo).
7 Refitting is a reversal of removal, but before fully tightening the adjustment and pivot bolts, tension the drivebelt as described in Chapter 2.

7.3 Alternator drivebelt adjustment link bolt

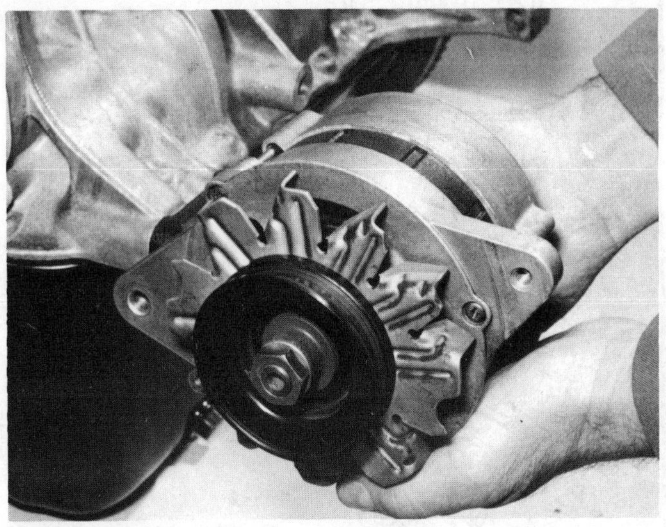

7.6 Removing the alternator

8 Alternator and regulator – testing and adjustment

Note: *A 0 to 60 amp ammeter, 0 to 20 volt voltmeter, and (ideally) a tachometer are required to carry out the following procedure.*

Alternator output

1 With the ignition switched off, disconnect the regulator multi-plug, then connect the ammeter and voltmeter as shown in Fig. 10.2 (photo).

2 Connect an additional wire between the white/red wire in the multi-plug to the battery positive terminal.

3 Run the engine at 3000 rpm with the headlamps and heated rear window heater switched on, and check that the alternator output is as given in the Specifications.

4 If the output is not as specified, stop the engine and reconnect the regulator multi-plug. Pull off the alternator multi-plug and connect a wire from the white/red wire pin on the alternator to the battery positive terminal.

5 Run the engine again as described in paragraph 3 – if the output is now as specified, there is an open-circuit in the white/red wire between the alternator and regulator.

6 If the output is still poor, check the white output wire between the alternator and fusible link for continuity. If the wire is good, the alternator is proved faulty and should be overhauled or renewed.

Voltage regulator

7 Check that all lights and accessories are switched off and that all fuses are intact.

8 Connect the ammeter and voltmeter as shown in Fig. 10.3, but leave the negative lead on the battery.

9 Start the engine and allow it to idle, then remove the negative lead from the battery.

10 *If the engine stops immediately,* reconnect the lead and start the engine again. Check the voltage at the black/yellow wire at the regulator multi-plug – if there is no voltage, check for continuity between the 10 amp regulator fuse and the multi-plug and rectify as necessary. If there is voltage, check the white/red wire between the regulator and alternator. If the alternator output is good but there is no voltage at the regulator white/red wire, the regulator is faulty.

11 *If the engine continues to run,* increase its speed progressively to between 2000 and 4000 rpm and check that the voltmeter reads the control voltage given in the Specifications. If the voltage is incorrect, check the relay adjustment as given in the following paragraphs.

Relay adjustment

12 Remove the regulator cover, making sure that it does not touch the internal components.

13 Connect the regulator multi-plug, start the engine and let it idle.

14 Disconnect the battery negative lead and connect the voltmeter between it and the battery positive terminal.

8.1 Regulator location – multi-plug is just below

15 Adjust the voltage to the specified amount using long-nosed pliers on the adjusting tab. Bend the tab up to increase the voltage or down to decrease it, but take care not to short the pliers to the body or exposed wiring.

16 Refit the cover and check the voltage again. Note that slightly different readings will be obtained with the cover on and off.

Points gap and armature gap

17 Disconnect the battery negative lead.

18 Remove the regulator cover and check the points gap and armature gap with reference to Fig. 10.5. If necessary bend the point posts.

Angle gap

19 Depress the armature plate and check that the angle gap and contact spring deflection are as given in the Specifications. If not, renew the regulator.

20 Refit the cover and disconnect the voltmeter, ammeter and tachometer. Reconnect the battery negative lead.

9 Alternator brushes – removal, inspection and refitting

1 Remove the alternator as described in Section 7.

2 Mark the end housings and stator in relation to each other, then unscrew and remove the three through-bolts (photo).

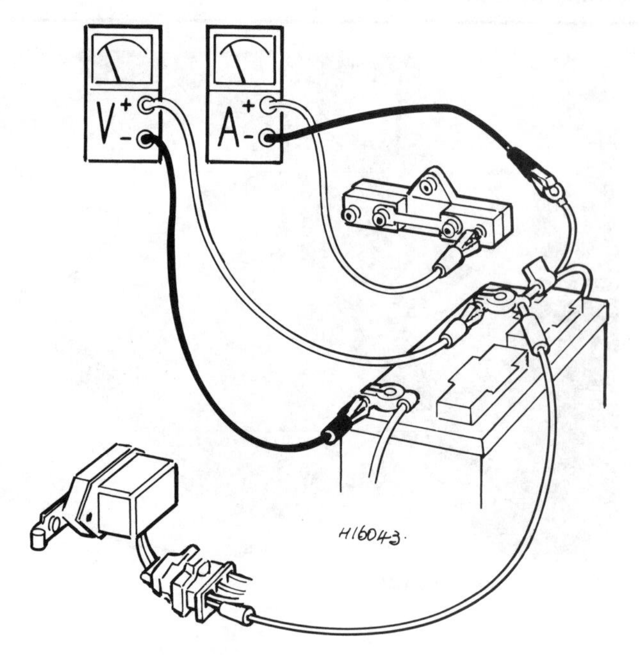

Fig. 10.2 Checking the alternator output (Sec 8)

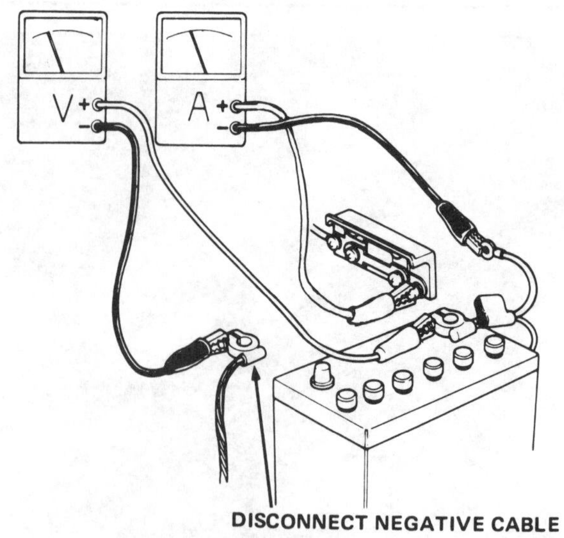

Fig. 10.3 Checking the voltage regulator (Sec 8)

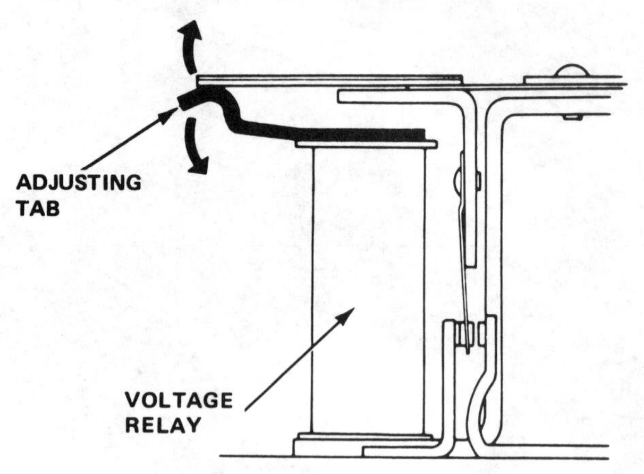

Fig. 10.4 Regulator voltage adjustment (Sec 8)

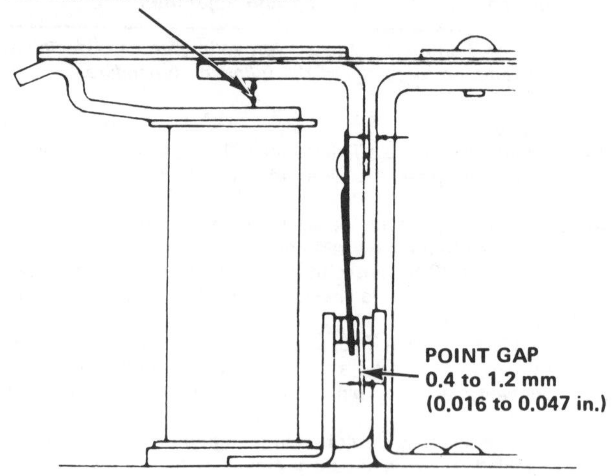

Fig. 10.5 Regulator points gap and armature gap adjustment (Sec 8)

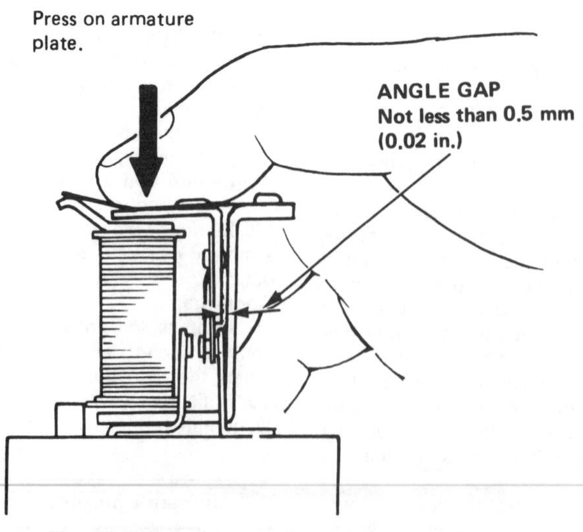

Fig. 10.6 Regulator angle gap checking (Sec 8)

3 Using a wooden mallet tap the front housing and rotor from the rear housing and stator (photo). Turn the rotor as the brushes move over the slip rings and rear bearing.
4 Unscrew the end cover nuts, noting the location of the suppressor, clip and insulation bushes.
5 Remove the end cover and withdraw the stator and diode plate, together with the bushes, from the end housing (photo).
6 Using vernier calipers, measure the protruding length of the brushes. If less than the minimum amount given in the Specifications, renew them as follows.
7 Using a soldering iron, unsolder the leads and withdraw the brushes and springs from the brush holder. Clean all traces of carbon from the brush holder.
8 Insert the new brushes and springs, and solder the leads in position using electrical (resin-cored) solder. Check that the brushes move easily in the holder.
9 Clean the rotor slip rings with a fuel-moistened cloth.
10 Reassembly of the alternator is a reversal of dismantling, but before inserting the rotor and end housing, depress the brushes into the holder and insert a small pin or stiff wire to keep them free of the slip rings (photos). Remove the pin when assembly is complete and seal the hole with a small amount of sealant.

9.2 Removing an alternator through-bolt

9.3 Withdrawing the alternator front housing and rotor

9.5 Alternator brush holder location

9.10a Brushes held depressed before assembling the alternator housings

9.10b Using welding wire to retain the alternator brushes

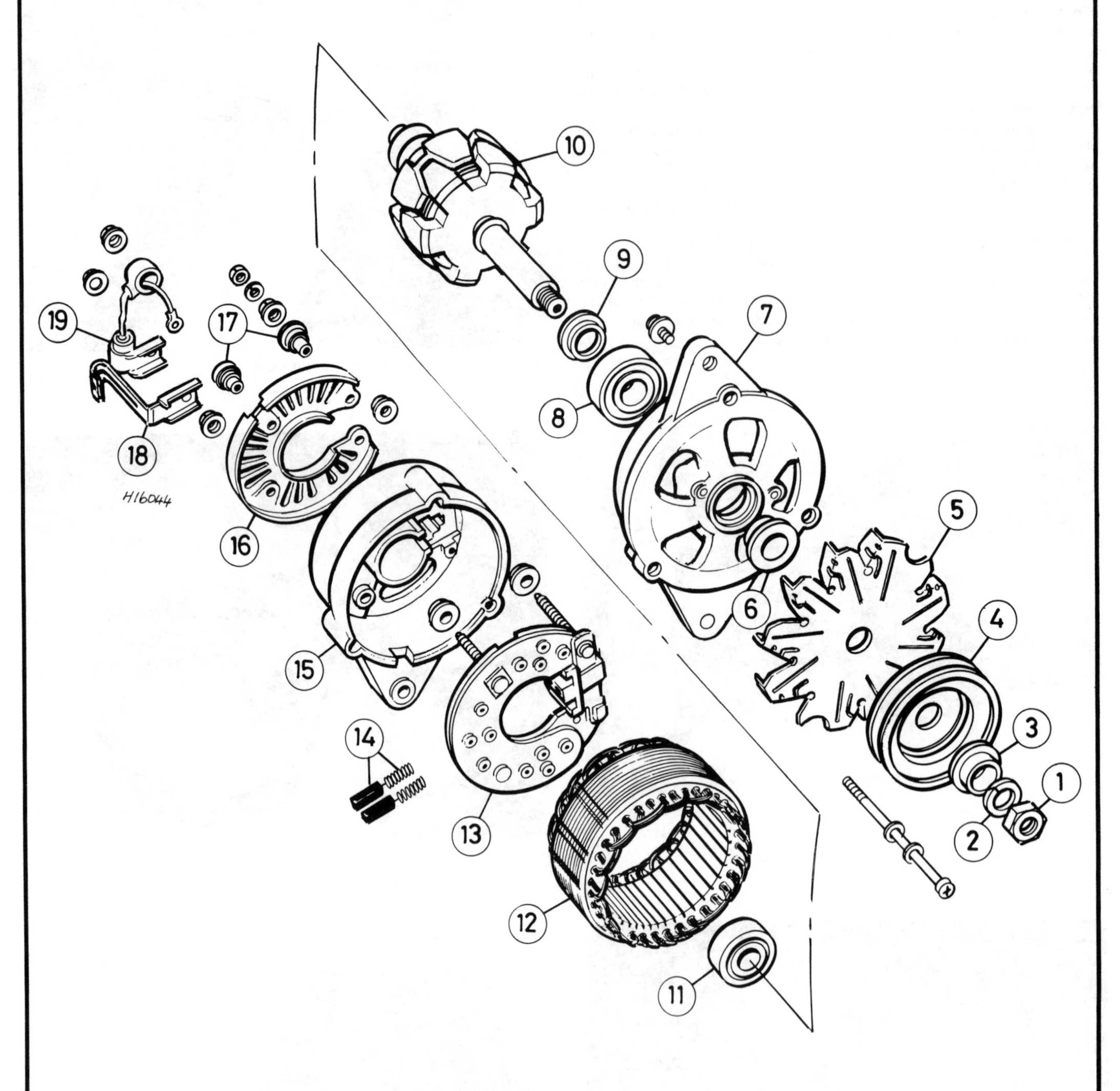

Fig. 10.7 Exploded view of the alternator (Sec 9)

1 *Pulley nut*
2 *Spring washer*
3 *Collar*
4 *Pulley*
5 *Fan*
6 *Collar*
7 *Drive end housing*
8 *Front bearing*
9 *Spacer*
10 *Rotor*
11 *Rear bearing*
12 *Stator*
13 *Rectifier*
14 *Brushes and springs*
15 *Slip ring end housing*
16 *End cover*
17 *Insulation bushes*
18 *Clip*
19 *Condenser*

10 Starter motor – testing in the car

1 If the starter motor fails to operate, first check the condition of the battery by switching on the headlamps. If they glow brightly, then gradually dim after a few seconds, the battery is in a discharged condition.
2 If the battery is in good condition, check the main supply cable and terminal on the starter motor and the engine earth cable for security. Also check the solenoid connection.
3 If the starter still fails to turn, use a voltmeter or 12 volt test lamp and leads to check that current is reaching the main supply cable terminal. Connect one lead to earth and the other to the terminal, when a reading should be obtained or the test lamp should glow.
4 With the ignition switched on and the ignition key held in position 'III' (start), check that current is reaching the solenoid control terminal and the solenoid-to-rotor terminal. If a voltmeter is being used there should not be any significant voltage drop across the solenoid, otherwise the solenoid contacts are worn or the solenoid operation is faulty.
5 If the correct voltage is available at the solenoid-to-motor terminal, yet it does not operate, the starter motor is faulty.

11 Starter motor – removal and refitting

1 Disconnect the battery negative lead.
2 Unscrew the terminal nut and disconnect the main supply cable, then pull off the solenoid supply cable. Remove the cables from the clip (photos).
3 Unscrew the mounting bolts (one with a nut) and withdraw the starter motor from the engine (photo). Note that the mounting bolts are of different lengths and that alternative holes are provided in the starter housing for manual gearbox and Trio-matic models.
4 Refitting is a reversal of removal. Tighten the mounting bolts to the specified torque.

12 Starter motor (direct type) – overhaul

1 It will be necessary to dismantle the starter motor in order to complete the following tasks:

(a) Brush removal and renewal
(b) Armature and commutator inspection
(c) Pinion gear and overspeed clutch inspection
(d) Pinion gearshift mechanism inspection

2 Begin the starter motor dismantling by removing the solenoid. Unscrew the nut and disconnect the motor cable from the solenoid, then unscrew the mounting nuts, withdraw the solenoid and unhook it from the lever.
3 Undo and remove the two screws securing the end cover, then prise off the cover with a screwdriver.
4 Pull out the locking plate and slide off the spring and rubber seal from the shaft.
5 Undo and extract the long through-bolts and remove the brush cover plate from the shaft, which will expose the brushplate assembly.
6 Carefully remove the brushes from their holders and slide the brushplate off the commutator.
7 Tap the starter pinion housing with a soft-faced mallet and detach the housing from the motor assembly complete with the armature.
8 To remove the pinion gear from the armature, hold the armature shaft in a vice fitted with soft jaws. Near the end of the shaft there is the travel stop ring which limits pinion movement. Drive back the collar to expose the ring.
9 Pull the ring out of its groove in the shaft with pliers, and then lift the gear and clutch off the shaft.
10 The motor is now dismantled and the parts should be laid out on a clean bench for inspection.
11 Measure the length of the brushes which should not be less than the minimum specified.
12 If possible check the brush spring tension when deflected to an equivalent position to when the brush is installed.
13 Use a multimeter set to read electrical resistance, to check the insulation between the positive and negative brush holders. Renew the holder if there is a low resistance recorded.
14 If the brushes have worn too short, they are renewed as follows. Unsolder the brushes from the connecting wires; take care when soldering new wires not to allow the solder to flow up the wires and bind the individual strands.
15 Fitting new brushes is simply the reversal of removal.
16 Clean the commutator with solvent and a non-fluffy cloth, scrape away any metal deposits from between the copper segments of the commutator. The commutator surface must be smooth, clean and free from scores and scratches.
17 The armature should then be checked for electrical insulation. Again use a multimeter to measure the electrical resistance between each segment of the commutator and the motor shaft. The resistance should be infinity. If a low resistance is measured the armature is faulty and should be renewed.
18 Examine the pinion gear teeth; if any are damaged the pinion/clutch assembly should be renewed.
19 Check the freedom of movement of the gear and clutch assembly along the spiral spline of the motor shaft.
20 If any binding is felt, renew the pinion clutch unit, it is improbable that the fault lies with the spiral spline.
21 Check the operation of the one-way clutch. Hold the pinion gear and turn the motor shaft clockwise when viewed from the pinion end. The clutch should not slip and the turning effort exerted on the shaft should be felt at the pinion. However, it should be possible to turn the pinion clockwise relative to the motor shaft. Renew the pinion/clutch assembly if it does not operate as required.
22 The solenoid is not repairable, and no attempt should be made to dismantle it. If it has been proven faulty, it should be renewed. If the solenoid only is suspected, the coil resistance may be checked by connecting a multimeter between the solenoid operating terminal and earth. If an open-circuit is found (infinite resistance) the solenoid is definitely faulty.
23 Reassembly is a reversal of dismantling.

11.2a Cable clip location on the starter motor

11.2b Solenoid main feed terminal on the starter motor

11.3 Removing the starter motor

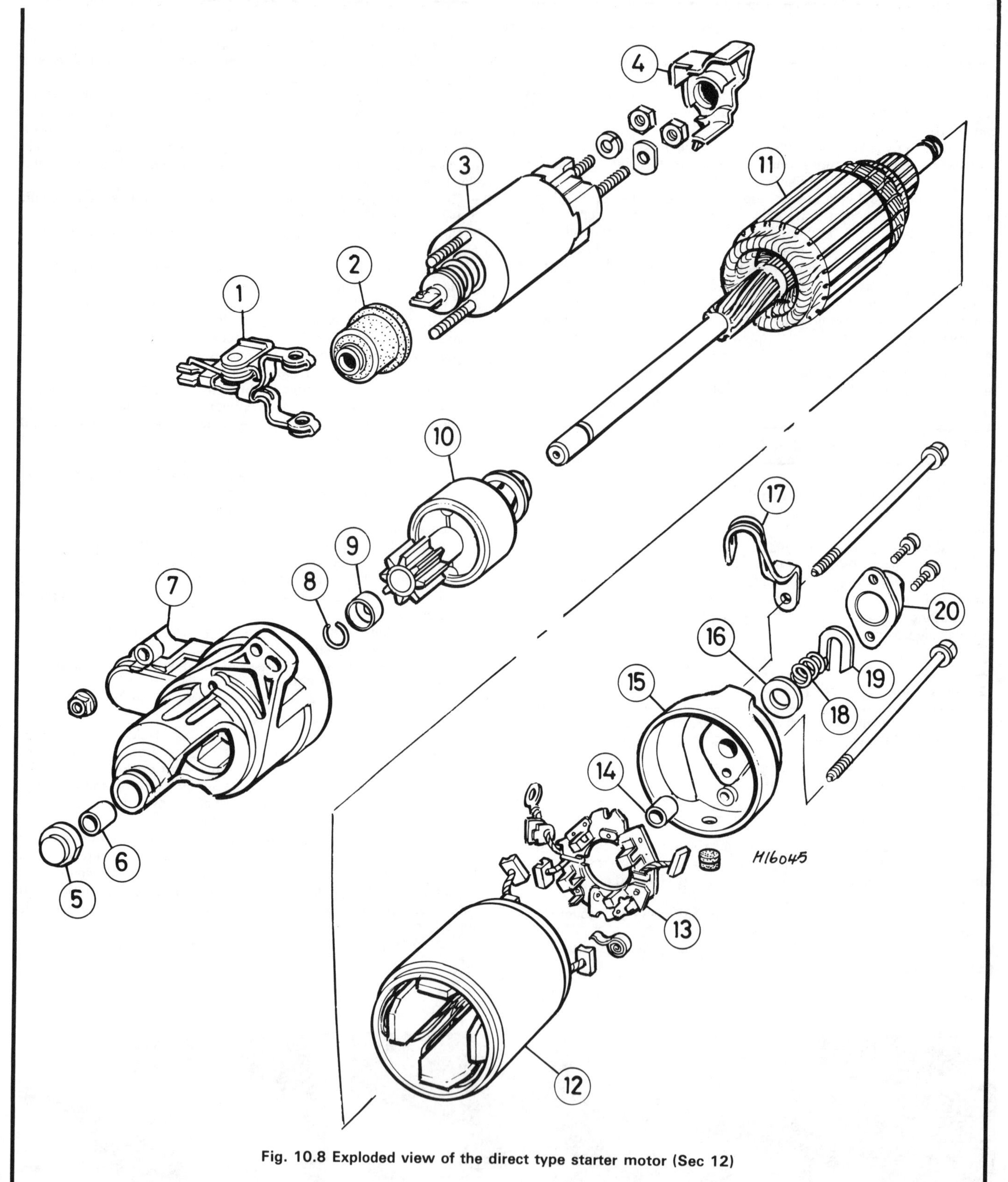

Fig. 10.8 Exploded view of the direct type starter motor (Sec 12)

1 Solenoid lever
2 Seal
3 Solenoid
4 Cover
5 Shaft end cover
6 Bearing
7 Gear cover
8 Stop ring
9 Collar
10 Overrun clutch
11 Armature
12 Field winding housing
13 Brush holder
14 Bearing
15 End cover
16 Rubber seal
17 Clip
18 Spring
19 Lockplate
20 End cap

13 Starter motor (reduction gear type) – overhaul

1 The reduction gear type starter motor differs from the direct type in that the solenoid is mounted in line with the starter drive pinion and the field frame assembly is located at the side and bolted to the common starter housing. Drive to the pinion clutch assembly is via an idler gear which runs in roller bearings on a shaft incorporated in the front of the starter solenoid housing.

2 To withdraw the field frame unit, disconnect the cable, then unscrew the retaining bolts from the starter housing and pull the unit clear.

3 To remove the solenoid, undo the retaining screws and remove them with lockwashers, noting to which screw the wire clip is fitted. Withdraw the solenoid cover and solenoid, taking care not to lose the solenoid spring and ball.

4 The starter pinion and clutch assembly, also the idler gear, are accessible on removal of the reduction gear housing from the starter solenoid housing.

5 Further dismantling is dependent on the nature of the fault, but in any case, all parts so far dismantled should be cleaned and examined for excessive wear or damage.

6 Examine the brushes and armature as described in Section 12. The minimum brush length allowable is given in Specifications. If the brushes have worn down to this length or less they must be renewed. Do not interchange the respective brushes.

7 Check that the overrun clutch operates correctly, moving freely in one direction and locked in the other direction.

8 Check the solenoid contact points and contacting face on the plunger. If they are pitted or burnt they can be refaced using 500 or 600 grade glasspaper. If they are severely damaged or marked, renew the solenoid housing assembly.

9 Reassembly is a reversal of dismantling, but lubricate the bearings and solenoid sleeve with multi-purpose grease.

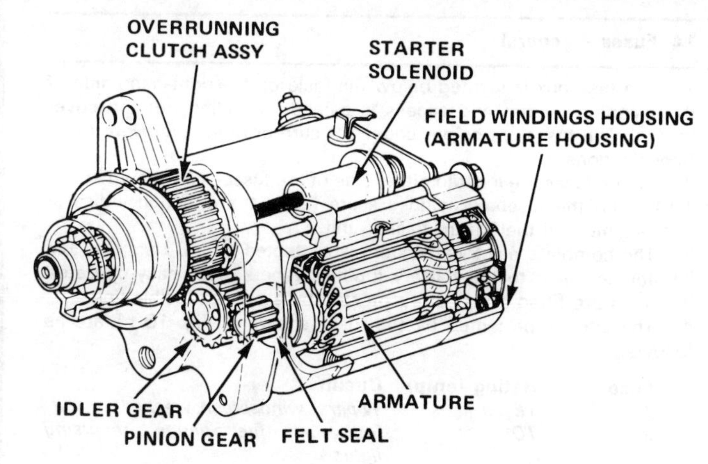

Fig. 10.9 Cutaway view of the reduction gear type starter motor (Sec 13)

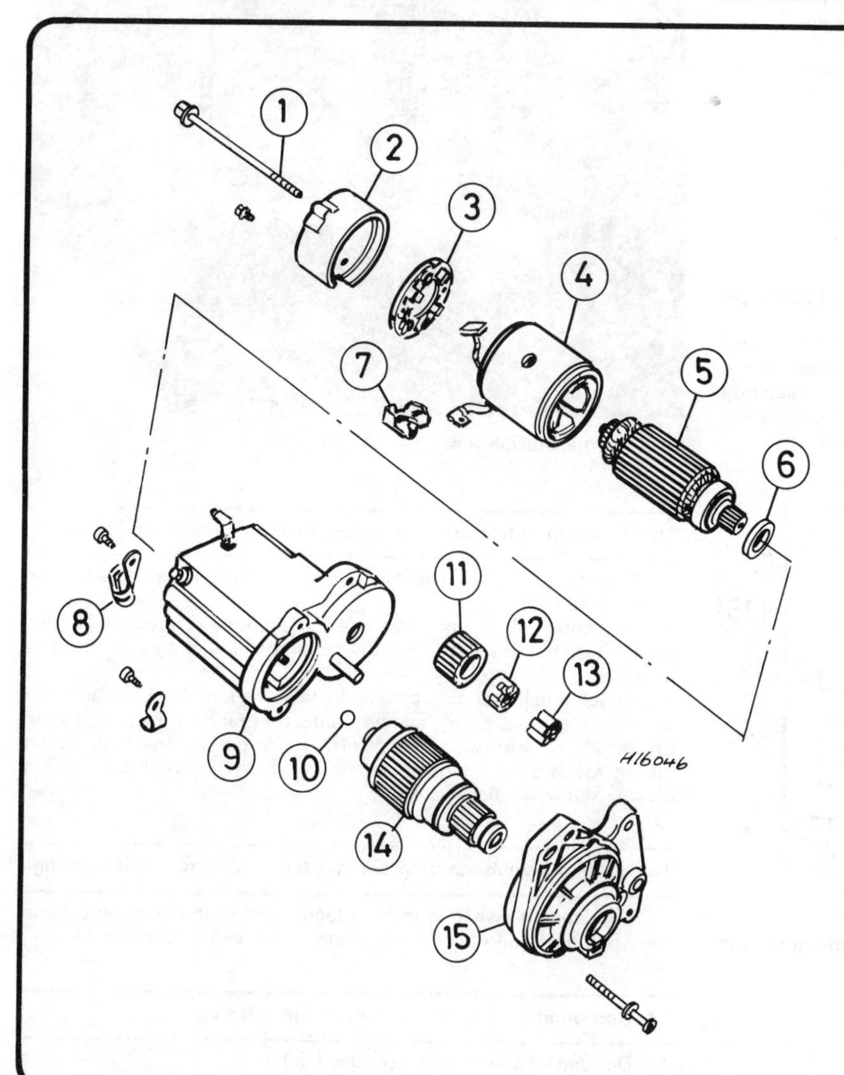

Fig. 10.10 Exploded view of the reduction gear type starter motor (Sec 13)

1 *Bolt*
2 *Frame*
3 *Brush holder plate*
4 *Yoke*
5 *Armature*
6 *Felt seal*
7 *Cover*
8 *Clip*
9 *Solenoid and housing*
10 *Steel ball*
11 *Idler gear*
12 *Bearing retainer*
13 *Roller bearing*
14 *Overrun clutch*
15 *Drive end housing*

14 Fuses – general

1 The fuse box is located below the facia on the right-hand side of the steering column and access is gained by sliding out the cover (photo). The fuses are colour coded for current rating as given in the Specifications.
2 In-line fuses are located either side of the fusebox as shown in Fig. 10.11 and the fusebox includes spare fuses, the direction indicator flasher unit, and the hazard flasher unit.
3 The complete electrical system is protected by a 55 amp fusible link located next to the battery (photo). Where electrically-operated windows are fitted, these are protected by a second fusible link.
4 The circuits protected by the fuses shown in Fig. 10.11 are as follows:

Fuse	Rating (amp)	Circuit
1	*15*	*Wipers, windscreen washer*
2	*10*	*Indicators, fuel gauge, reversing lights*
3	*10*	*Regulator, carburettor cut-off valve*
4	*15*	*Radiator fan, air conditioning condenser fan*
5	*15*	*Heater fan, air conditioning condenser clutch*
6	*15*	*Heated rear window*
7	*15*	*Horn, hazard lights, brake lights*
8	*10*	*Interior light, clock, lighter*
9	*15*	*Tail, number plate and instrument lights*
10	*10*	*Left headlamp main beam*
11	*10*	*Right headlamp main beam*
12	*10*	*Left headlamp low beam*
13	*10*	*Right headlamp low beam, rear foglamps*
14	*10*	*Radio*
15	*20*	*Headlamp washer*
16	*15*	*Front right electric window*
17	*15*	*Front left electric window*
18	*15*	*Rear right electric window*
19	*15*	*Rear left electric window*
20	*Various*	*Spare fuses*

Additionally there is either a 1 amp (radio) or a 2.5 amp (radio/tape unit) in-line fuse.
5 Always renew a fuse with one of identical rating and colour, and never renew it more than once without finding the source of the trouble (usually a short-circuit). Do not attempt to bypass persistently blowing fuses with silver foil or wire, not fit a fuse of a higher rating than that specified – component damage or fire may result.

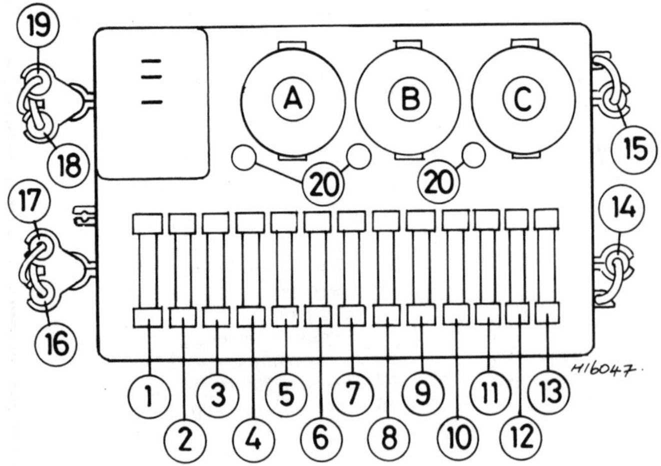

Fig. 10.11 Diagram of the fuse box. See text for fuse identification (Sec 14)

A *Hazard indicator flasher unit*
B *Hazard flasher unit*
C *Intermittent wipe unit (where fitted)*

14.1 Fuse box and flasher units

14.3 The main fusible link

15 Direction indicators and hazard flasher system – general

1 Both the direction indicators and hazard flasher units are located on the fuse board.
2 To remove either unit, disconnect the battery negative lead, slide out the fuse box cover, and pull the required unit directly from the fuse board.
3 Should the flashers become faulty in operation, check the bulbs for security and make sure that the contact surfaces are not corroded. Check all the wiring and terminals, not forgetting the bulb holder mountings. If the flashers are still faulty and the relevant fuse has not blown, renew the flasher unit.

16 Ignition switch/steering column lock – removal and refitting

The ignition switch is in an integral part of the steering column lock. Removal and refitting procedures are given in Chapter 11.

17 Combination switch – removal and refitting

1 Disconnect the battery negative lead.
2 Remove the steering wheel as described in Chapter 11.

3 Extract the turn signal cancelling cam from the combination switch.
4 Unscrew the cross-head screws and withdraw the lower shroud from the steering column (photo).
5 Loosen the column mounting nuts and bolts and withdraw the upper shroud (photo).
6 Disconnect the combination switch multi-plug and single wire after releasing the fuse-board (refer to Section 14).
7 Unscrew the cross-head screws and remove the combination switch from the outer steering column (photo).
8 Refitting is a reversal of removal. Refer to Chapter 11 for the correct tightening torques for the steering wheel and column mountings.

18 Facia switches – removal and refitting

1 Disconnect the battery negative lead.
2 Slide off the fuse box cover.
3 Reach up behind the switch, depress the plastic lugs, and push the switch from the facia.
4 Disconnect the wiring and withdraw the switch.
5 Refitting is a reversal of removal. Make sure that the switch is pressed fully into the facia.

19 Courtesy light switch – removal and refitting

1 Disconnect the battery negative lead.
2 Open the door and locate the courtesy light switch on the hinge pillar.
3 Remove the single screw and withdraw the switch.
4 Disconnect the supply wire and tie a loose knot in it to prevent it dropping into the pillar. Remove the switch.
5 Refitting is a reversal of removal.

20 Cigar lighter – removal and refitting

1 Disconnect the battery negative lead.
2 Remove the ashtray from the facia and remove the cigar lighter knob and element. Remove the lower panel.
3 Unscrew the retaining ring and withdraw the cigar lighter from the rear of the facia.
4 Disconnect the supply wire and the illumination bulb wire, and withdraw the cigar lighter.
5 Refitting is a reversal of removal.

21 Clock – removal and refitting

1 Disconnect the battery negative lead.
2 Remove the ashtray from the facia.
3 Remove the screw under the clock and ease the clock from the facia.
4 Disconnect the multi-plug and withdraw the clock and bracket.
5 Refitting is a reversal of removal.

22 Speedometer cable – removal and refitting

1 Disconnect the battery negative lead.
2 Reach up under the facia and disconnect the speedometer cable from the speedometer head by depressing the plastic clips.
3 Prise the cable grommet from the bulkhead in the engine compartment, and pull the cable through.
4 Pull the rubber boot from the gearbox end of the cable. Remove the clip and withdraw the cable from the gearbox and support spring (if fitted) (photo).
5 Refitting is a reversal of removal but make sure that the cable is routed to avoid any sharp curves.

23 Tachometer cable – removal and refitting

1 Disconnect the battery negative lead.
2 Reach up under the facia and disconnect the tachometer cable from the tachometer head by depressing the plastic clips.
3 Prise the cable grommet from the bulkhead in the engine compartment and disconnect the cable from the brake servo hose and fuel pipe clips.
4 Unscrew the cable nut from the drivegear housing on the right-hand end of the camshaft cover (photo).
5 Withdraw the tachometer cable from the car.
6 The cable is in two sections and if necessary may be supported by unscrewing the centre knurled nut (photos).
7 Refitting is a reversal of removal.

24 Instrument panel and instruments – removal and refitting

1 Disconnect the battery negative lead.
2 Pull off the heater/air conditioning control knobs and extract the control panel far enough to disconnect the wiring. Withdraw the panel.
3 Remove the heater/air conditioning quadrant screws.
4 Lift the coin tray lid, remove the screw, and withdraw the coin box and ventilator (photos).
5 Pull the plastic cover from the steering column upper mounting, then loosen the column mountings and lower the column. If necessary the steering wheel may be removed (see Chapter 11) for better access.
6 Remove the illumination bulb and holder from the instrument panel surround, then remove the screws and withdraw the surround (photos).
7 Reach up behind the instrument panel and disconnect the speedometer and tachometer cables by depressing the plastic clips.
8 Remove the screw and bolt, and withdraw the instrument panel far enough to disconnect the multi-plug. Remove the panel (photos).
9 To remove either the speedometer or tachometer head, first pull off the speedometer trip reset knob and remove the transparent cover (2 screws). Remove the cross-head screws from the rear of the tachometer head. Note that rubber washers are fitted to the tachometer head screws.
10 To remove the printed circuit, first remove all the warning light bulbs and holders. Note the location of the wires, then remove the wire terminal screws. Remove the temperature and fuel gauge nuts and

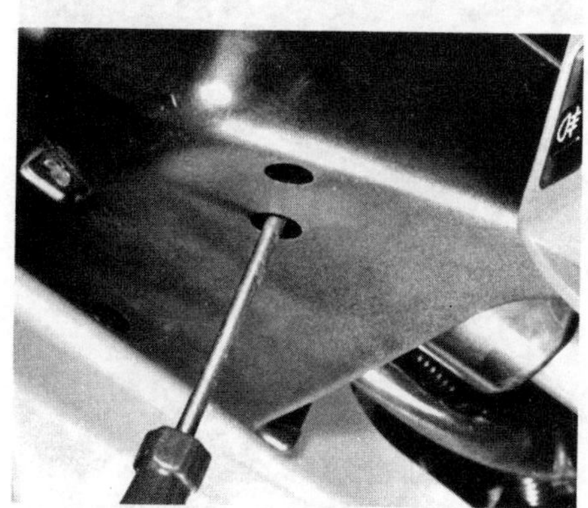

17.4 Removing the steering column lower shroud

17.5 Removing the steering column upper shroud

17.7 Combination switch location on the steering column

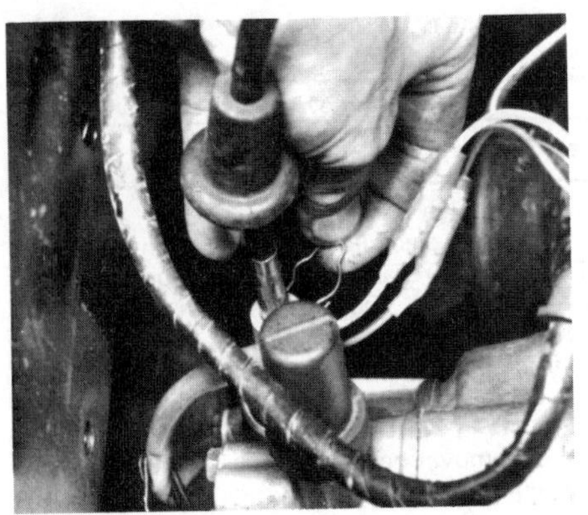

22.4 Removing the speedometer cable

23.4 Disconnecting the tachometer cable from the engine

23.6a Unscrew the knurled nut ...

23.6b ... and disconnect the tachometer cable sections

24.4a Remove the screw ...

24.4b ... and withdraw the coin box and ventilator

24.6a Removing the bulb and holder from the instrument panel surround

24.6b Remove the screw ...

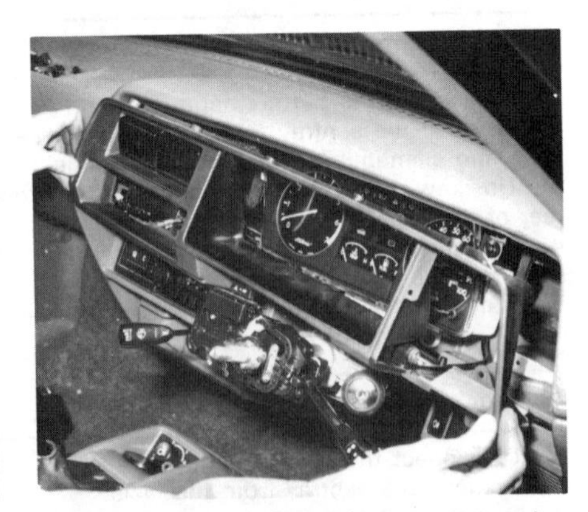

24.6c ... and withdraw the instrument panel surround

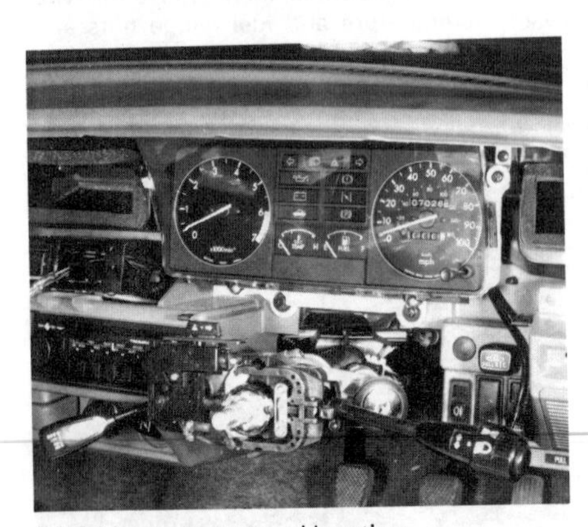

24.6d Instrument panel location

24.8a Removing the instrument panel

24.8b Instrument panel recess showing multi-plug and speedometer/tachometer cables

24.8c Front view of instrument panel

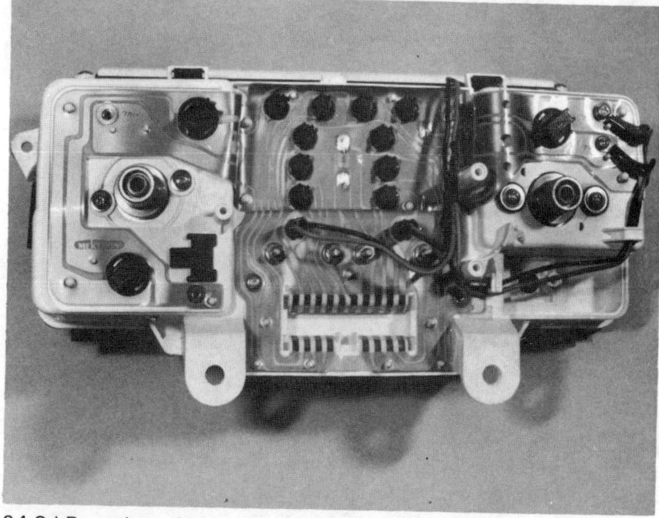

24.8d Rear view of instrument panel

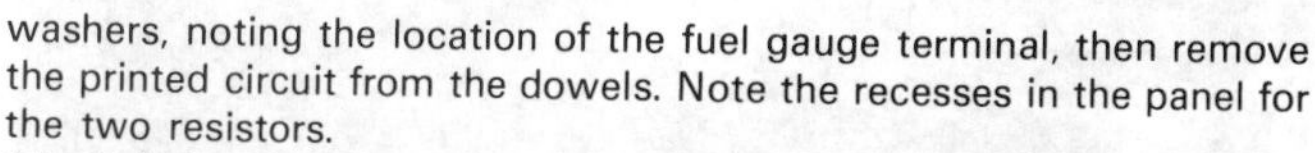

washers, noting the location of the fuel gauge terminal, then remove the printed circuit from the dowels. Note the recesses in the panel for the two resistors.

11 Refitting is a reversal of removal. Refer to Chapter 11 for the correct tightening torques for the steering column mountings and steering wheel (if removed).

25 Temperature and fuel gauges – removal and refitting

1 Remove the instrument panel as described in Section 24.

2 Pull off the speedometer trip reset knob, remove the two screws, and withdraw the transparent cover.

3 Note the location of the wire terminal on the rear of the panel, then remove the nuts and washers and withdraw the gauges.

4 Refitting is a reversal of removal.

26 Headlamps and headlamp bulbs – removal and refitting

Headlamp unit

1 Remove the radiator grille and headlamp surrounds as described in Chapter 12, Section 8.

2 Push the headlamp unit inwards and upwards to disengage it from the adjuster screws.

3 Pull the socket from the rear of the unit and remove the unit.

4 Remove the screw and separate the unit from the retaining rings. Remove the bulb.

5 Refitting is a reversal of removal.

Headlamp bulb

6 Open the bonnet and pull the socket from the rear of the headlamp unit (photo).

7 Pull off the rubber seal.

8 Push and twist the retaining ring, or release the clip(s), as applicable, then extract the bulb (photo). Do not touch the glass with the fingers as this can reduce the life of the bulb – clean the bulb with methylated spirit if necessary.

9 Refitting is a reversal of removal. Make sure that the rubber seal is positioned with the 'TOP' mark uppermost (photo).

27 Headlamps – alignment

1 The headlamp alignment should be checked every 15 000 miles (24 000 km). It is recommended that the alignment is carried out by a BL garage using modern beam setting equipment. However, in an emergency, the following procedure will provide an acceptable light pattern.

26.6 Disconnecting the socket from the headlamp unit

26.8a Release the clips ...

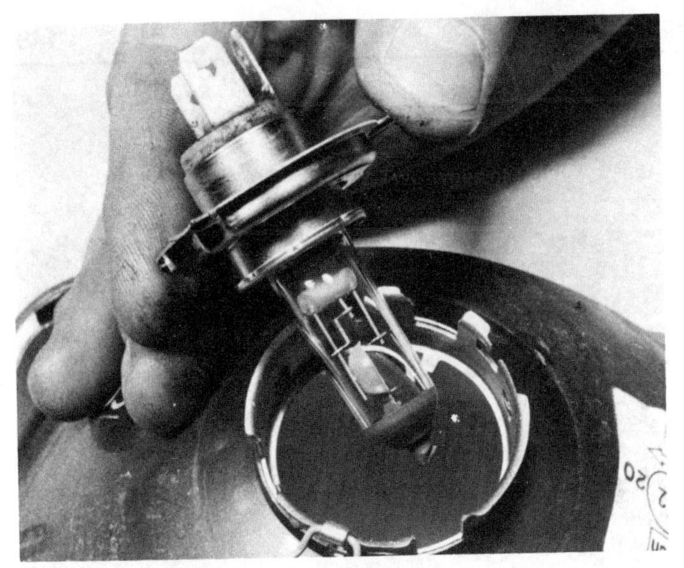

26.8b ... and extract the headlamp bulb

26.9 Headlamp bulb rubber seal

27.4a Headlamp horizontal adjustment

27.4b Headlamp vertical adjustment

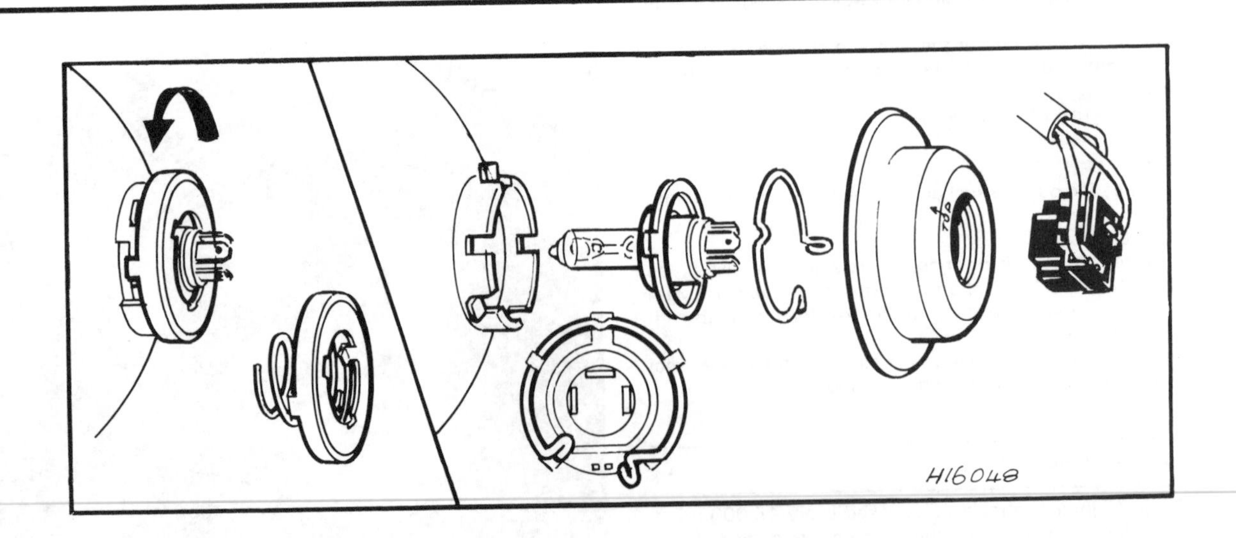

Fig. 10.12 Two types of headlamp bulb fitment. Photos show a third type (Sec 26)

2 Position the car on a level surface with tyres correctly inflated, approximately 10 metres (33 feet) in front of and at right-angles to a wall or garage door. Have two people sit in the front seats, or load the car with equivalent ballast.

3 Draw a horizontal line on the wall or door at headlamp centre height. Draw a vertical line corresponding to the centre-line of the car, then measure off a point either side of this, on the horizontal line corresponding with the headlamp centres.

4 Set the headlamp adjuster control to '0', then switch on the main beam and check that the areas of maximum illumination coincide with the headlamp centre marks. If not, turn the adjusting screws below and on either side of the headlamps as necessary (photos).

5 Holts Amber Lamp is useful for temporarily changing the headlight colour to conform with the normal usage on Continental Europe.

28 Headlamp adjuster – removal and refitting

1 The headlamp levelling adjuster is controlled hydraulically using ethylene glycol as a medium. A common cause of non-function is jamming of the piston through incomplete insertion of the headlamp retaining ring in the lower adjusting screw.

2 To remove the adjuster, disconnect the battery negative lead and remove the headlamp units as described in Section 26.

3 Unbolt the actuator brackets and disengage them from the actuators (photos).

4 Remove the plastic liners from under each wheel arch.

5 Slide out the fusebox cover and remove the fuse box from the bracket.

6 Pull back the carpet and disconnect the air conditioning drain tube (where applicable).

7 Open the glovebox and twist out the stops. Pull back the carpet.

8 Remove the adjuster knob and plate. Unscrew the screws and remove the console.

9 Unscrew the nut and remove the adjuster transmitter.

10 Unclip the tubes and pull them into the car together with the actuators.

11 Refitting is a reversal of removal.

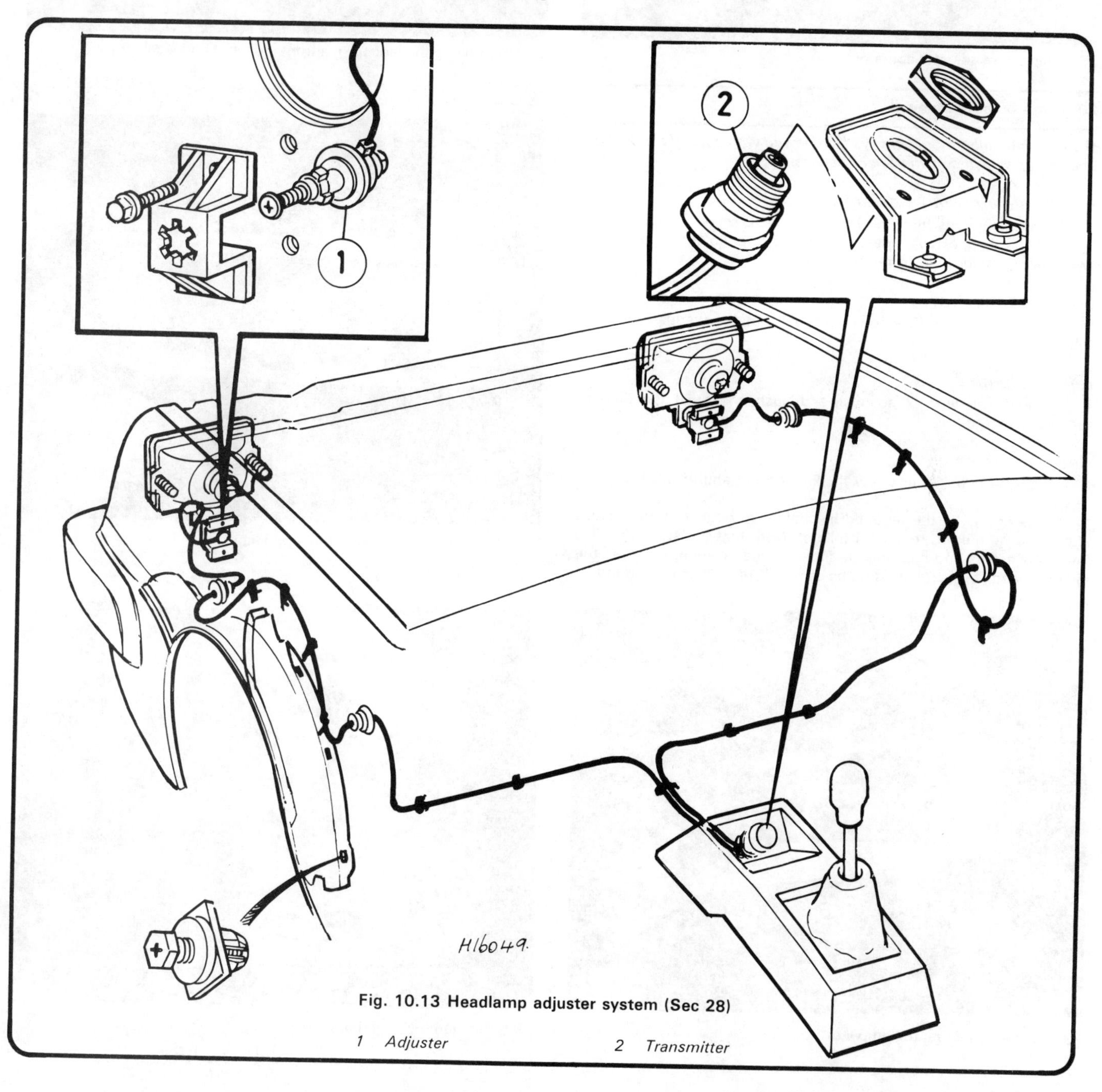

Fig. 10.13 Headlamp adjuster system (Sec 28)

1 Adjuster
2 Transmitter

28.3 Headlamp adjuster actuator

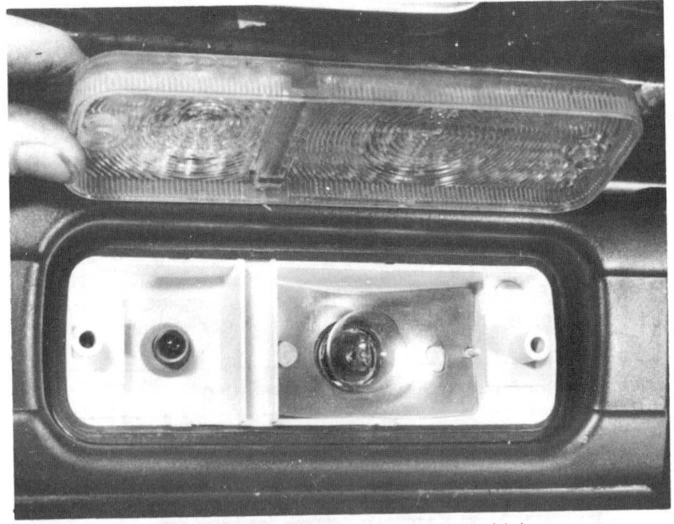
29.1 Removing the lens from a front indicator and sidelamp

29 Lamp bulbs – renewal

Note: *Lamp bulbs should always be renewed with ones of similar type and rating as listed in the Specifications.*

Front indicator and sidelamps

1 Remove the lens from the front bumper (2 screws) (photo).
2 Pull the wedge type sidelamp bulb from its holder, or push and twist the indicator bulb to remove it.

Side repeater lamp

3 Remove the lens (2 screws) and pull out the wedge type bulb (photo).

Rear foglamp

4 Remove the lens (2 screws), and push and twist the bulb to remove it (photo).

Rear lamp cluster

5 Open the boot lid, unscrew the knurled nut and lift off the cover (photo).
6 Press and twist the required bulbholder to remove it, then press and twist the bulb to remove it (photo). Note that the stop/tail bulbs have offset pins and can only be fitted in one position, whereas the indicator and reversing lamp bulbs can be fitted either way round.

29.3 Removing a side repeater lamp lens

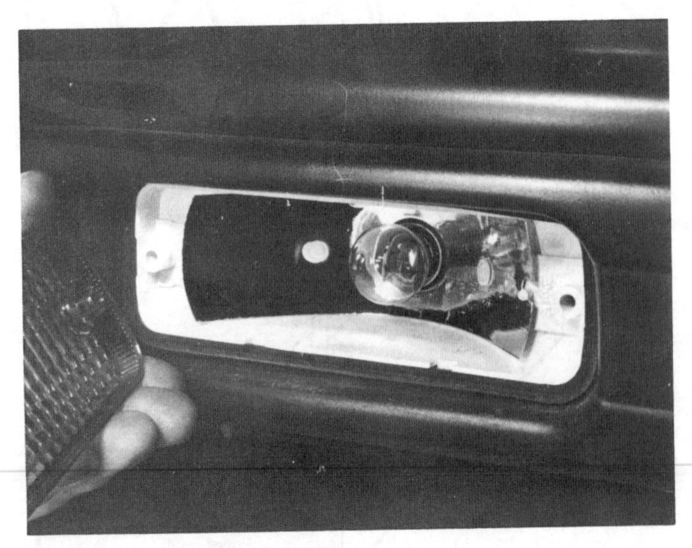
29.4 Removing a rear foglamp lens

29.5 Rear lamp cluster inner cover

Rear number plate lamps

7 Open the boot lid for better access.
8 Remove the two screws to release the lens, withdraw the lamp body, then press and twist the bulb to remove it (photo).

Luggage compartment lamp and interior lamp

9 Prise off the lens with a screwdriver and remove the festoon type bulb from the spring contacts (photos).
10 When fitting a new bulb, make sure that the contacts are tensioned sufficiently to grip the bulb.

Facia switch warning lamps

11 Remove the facia switch as described in Section 18.
12 Turn the bulbholder anti-clockwise, remove it, and pull out the bulb.

Ashtray lamp

13 Remove the ashtray and lower panel.
14 Remove the clock retaining screw and the ashtray carrier screws. Lower the carrier.
15 Twist the bulbholder anti-clockwise to remove it, then pull out the wedge type bulb and remove the green cover from the bulb.

Cigar lighter lamp

16 Remove the cigar lighter as described in Section 20.
17 Squeeze the bulbholder hood and remove it from the lighter.
18 Remove the bulbholder and press and twist the bulb to remove it. Remove the bulb cover.

Clock lamp

19 Remove the clock as described in Section 21.
20 Twist the bulbholder anti-clockwise to remove it, then pull out the wedge type bulb.

Trio-matic selector lamp

21 Pull the knob from the headlamp adjuster and prise out the plate.
22 Remove the screws and withdraw the console.
23 Remove the screws and lift the selector quadrant.
24 Twist the bulbholder a quarter turn anti-clockwise, remove it, and pull out the wedge type bulb.

Facia lamp

25 Lift the coin tray lid, remove the screw, and withdraw the coin box and ventilator.
26 Pull out the bulbholder, then push and twist the bulb to remove it.

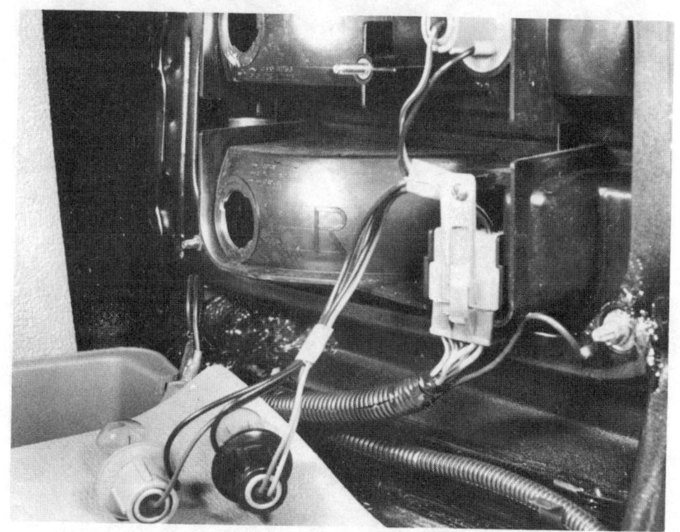

29.6 Removing the rear lamp cluster bulbs

29.8 Rear number plate lamp bulb

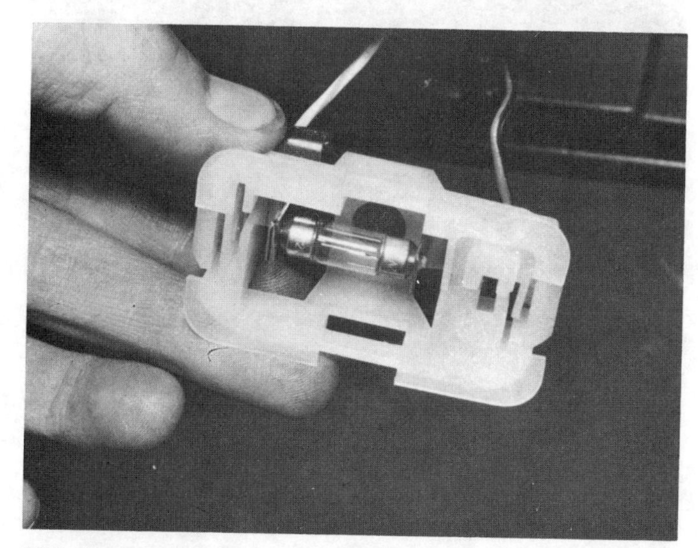

29.9a Luggage compartment lamp body and bulb

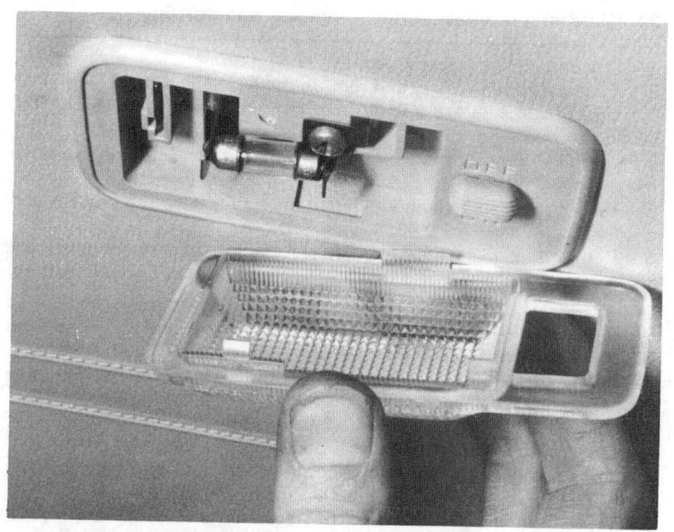

29.9b Removing the interior lamp lens

29.28 Removing an instrument panel bulb in its holder

29.31 Removing a heater control lamp bulb

Instrument panel lamps

27 Remove the instrument panel as described in Section 24.
28 Twist the bulbholder anti-clockwise to remove it, and pull out the wedge type bulb (photo).

Heater control lamps

29 Disconnect the battery negative lead.
30 Pull off the heater control knobs and extract the control panel far enough to disconnect the wiring. Withdraw the panel.
31 Unclip the endplate and pull the bulb from the connector pins (photo).
32 Remove the screws from the other end (if necessary), lift the lamp housing and pull the other bulb from the connector pins.

30 Wiper blades – renewal

1 The wiper blades should be renewed when they no longer clean the windscreen effectively.
2 Lift the wiper arm away from the windscreen.
3 Lift the spring retainer and separate the blade from the arm (photo).
4 Insert the new blade into the arm and make sure that the spring retainer is engaged correctly.

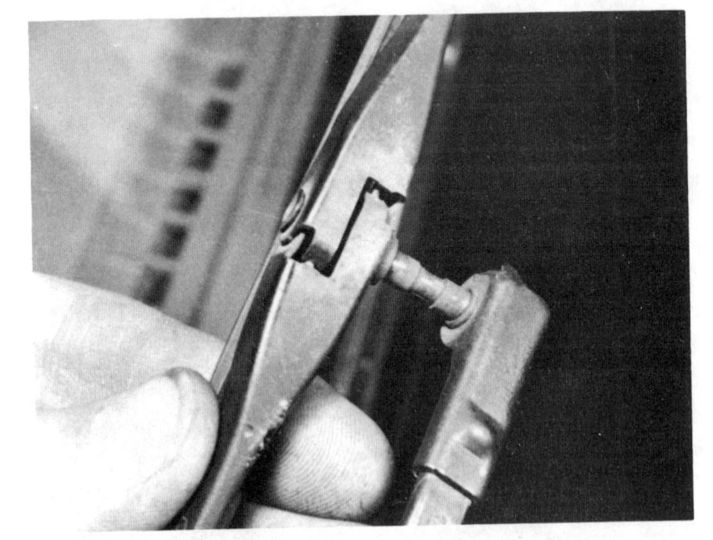

30.3 Removing a wiper blade

31 Windscreen wiper motor – removal and refitting

1 Disconnect the battery negative lead.
2 Prise out the fasteners and remove the heater intake grille (photo).
3 Unscrew the motor spindle nut, remove the link and move the linkage to one side.
4 Unbolt the motor bracket and disconnect the multi-plug. Remove the motor.
5 Remove the screws and separate the motor from the bracket and grommet.
6 Refitting is a reversal of removal, but before connecting the linkage, switch the motor on and off so that it is in its parked position.

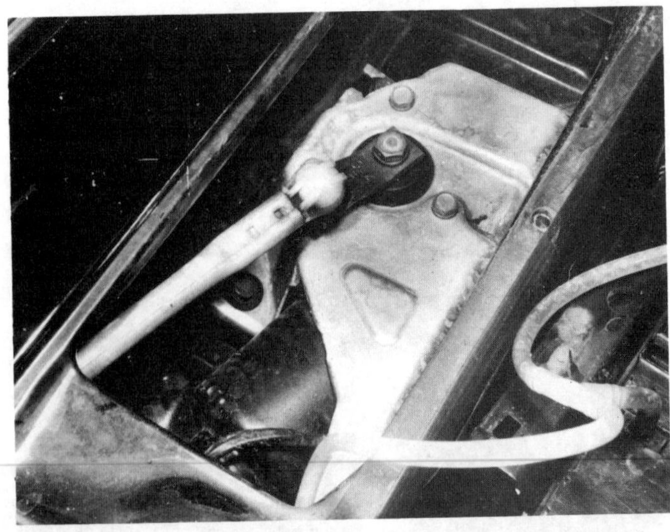

31.2 Windscreen wiper motor location (heater intake grille removed)

32 Windscreen wiper linkage – removal, overhaul and refitting

1 Disconnect the battery negative lead.
2 Prise out the fasteners and remove the heater intake grille.
3 Unscrew the motor spindle nut and remove the link.
4 Lift up the wiper arm caps, unscrew the nuts and lever off the arms, taking care not to damage the paintwork (photo).
5 Remove the pivot caps and unscrew the nuts. Remove the plain and rubber washers.

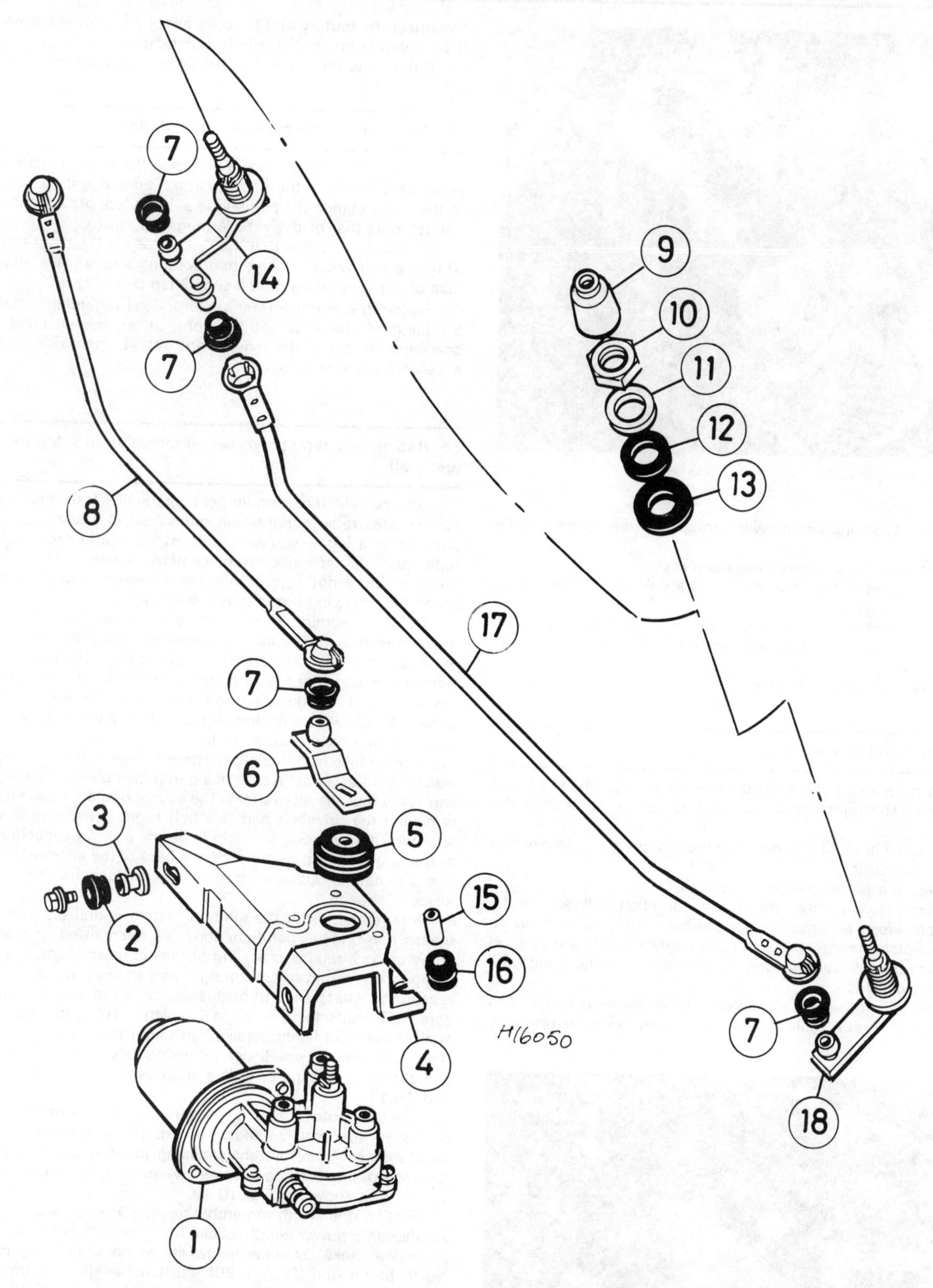

Fig. 10.14 Exploded view of the windscreen wiper motor and linkage (Secs 31 and 32)

1 *Wiper motor*
2 *Rubber*
3 *Special nut*
4 *Mounting bracket*
5 *Grommet*
6 *Link*
7 *Dust seal*
8 *Rod*
9 *Pivot cap*
10 *Arm pivot nut*
11 *Plain washer*
12 *Cushion rubber*
13 *Cushion rubber*
14 *Link*
15 *Motor mounting collar*
16 *Motor mounting rubber*
17 *Rod*
18 *Link*

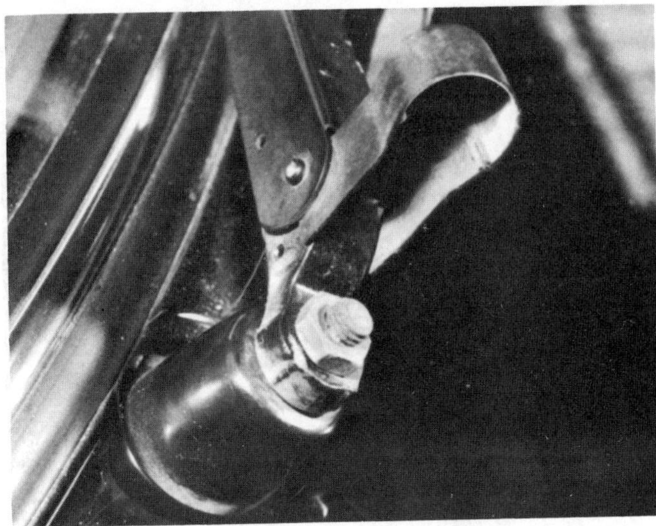

32.4 Windscreen wiper arm retaining nut location

6 Lower the linkage and withdraw it through the heater intake grille aperture.
7 Remove the rubber washers from the pivots.
8 Note the location of each rod, then separate them from the pivots together with the dust seals.
9 Examine the components for wear and renew them as necessary.
10 Lubricate the linkage joints with multi-purpose grease and re-assemble the linkage.
11 Refitting is a reversal of removal.

33 Horn – removal and refitting

1 The horn is located behind the bumper on the right-hand side of the car (photo). The horn circuit incorporates a relay located by the fuse box.
2 To remove the horn, first remove the radiator grille as described in Chapter 12, Section 8.
3 Disconnect the battery negative lead.
4 Disconnect the wires from the horn, then unbolt and remove it.
5 If the horn emits an unsatisfactory sound, it may be possible to adjust it, assuming the internal circuit and contact points are in good condition. Turn the adjustment screw on the rear of the horn until the best sound is achieved.
6 If the horn fails to work at all, remember that the relay could be at fault. Connect a 12 volt bulb to the horn supply wires, temporarily reconnect the battery and have an assistant operate the horn control. If the lamp lights, the supply is satisfactory.
7 Refitting is the reverse of the removal procedure.

33.1 Horn and mounting bracket

34 Radios and tape players – installation

A radio (or a combined radio/tape player) is standard equipment on all UK versions of the Acclaim at the time of writing. Any other unit of the same standard size may be substituted, provided its polarity is the same as that of the vehicle (negative earth).

Remember to check that the in-line fuse in the radio supply lead is of the correct value – a unit incorporating a tape player may require a fuse of a higher rating than a simple radio.

Follow the manufacturer's instructions regarding installation and trimming of the new set. If problems are experienced, consult a specialist in car audio equipment rather than risk damaging an expensive piece of gear.

35 Radios and tape players – suppression of interference (general)

All the electrical equipment originally fitted to the Acclaim incorporates radio suppression measures; in many cases, such suppression is a legal requirement to avoid interference with domestic radio and TV reception. Replacement components or accessories, however, may not incorporate the necessary suppressors. In such cases the following notes may prove useful.

Before assuming that interference levels are abnormally high, make sure that the radio and aerial are correctly installed and well earthed, and that the radio is correctly trimmed to the aerial. Remember also that the strength of reception will vary according to the waveband, the distance from the transmitter and the surrounding terrain. A radio which is straining to pick up a weak signal will be more sensitive to interference as well.

Interference from the alternator will appear as a whining noise, not dissimilar to a dentist's drill, rising and falling with engine speed. You can verify that the alternator is the source of the trouble by temporarily removing the drivebelt and (briefly!) running the engine without the alternator turning. Suppression is by means of a capacitor connected to the large (output) terminal on the back of the alternator (Fig. 10.15). The alternator originally fitted to the Acclaim has such a capacitor inside it already.

Interference from the ignition system is unlikely to be a problem unless non-original components have been fitted. If present, it will show up as a regular crackling or ticking noise at low engine speeds, rising to a whirring or chattering 'hash' at high speed. The most likely reason for interference from this source is the substitution of copper-cored HT leads for the original resistive HT leads. Some prejudice against resistive leads persists, although they are now more reliable than formerly. If you insist on using copper-cored HT leads, use suppressed plug caps or in-line suppressors as shown in Figs. 10.16 and 10.17.

Electric motors may be suppressed by connecting a capacitor across the terminals as shown in Fig. 10.18. Gauges can sometimes be a source of intermittent crackling interference, or a route for re-radiation of interference from elsewhere. In either case, suppression is achieved as shown in Fig. 10.19.

Finally, it is worth remembering that interference can be received via the radio power supply cable. Most modern sets will already have an in-line choke, as close to the set as possible, but if not, it is well worth fitting one (Fig. 10.20). Further benefit may be obtained by connecting a 'decoupling capacitor' of up to 1000 microfarads between the radio supply lead and earth. Such a capacitor must be of adequate working voltage – not less than 16 volts – and must be connected the right way round.

Other sources of interference may be boot and bonnet lids, which should be earthed using flexible metal straps. Brake static presents as a rushing or roaring noise when braking, and is often worst in dry weather. Kits to cure the problem may be available or you may not consider the annoyance enough to justify the cost.

If attention to the simple points above fails to cure your interference problem, consult your local car audio specialist. At least one major manufacturer produces a simple booklet on the subject.

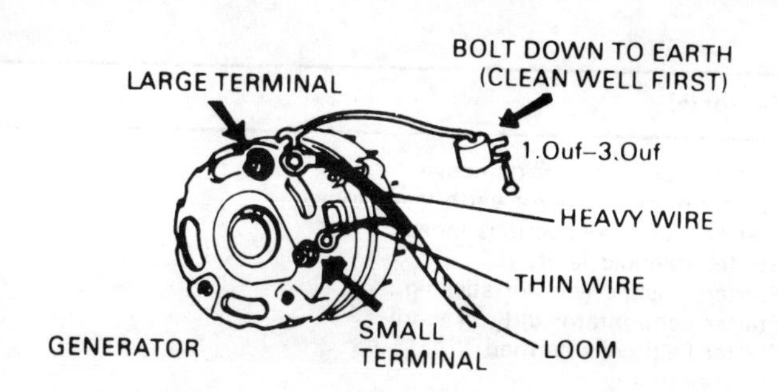

Fig. 10.15 The correct way to connect a capacitor to the alternator (Sec 35)

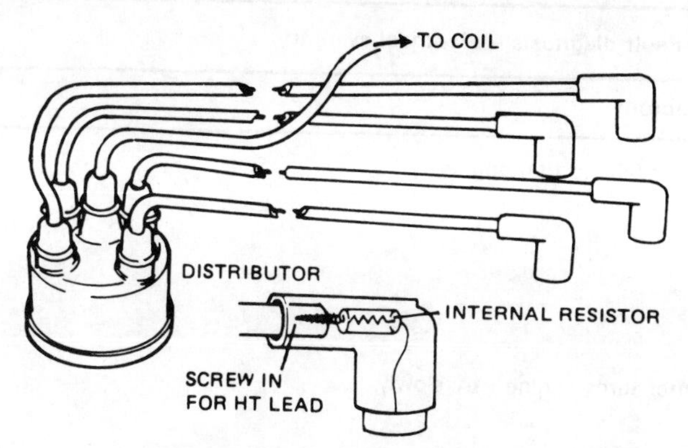

Fig. 10.16 Resistive spark plug caps (Sec 35)

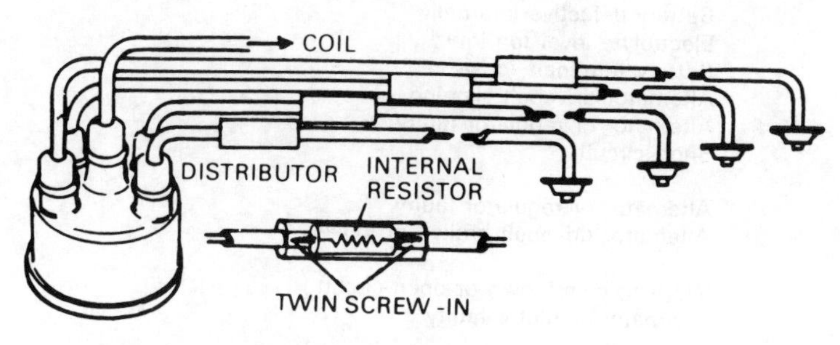

Fig. 10.17 Ignition HT lead suppressors (Sec 35)

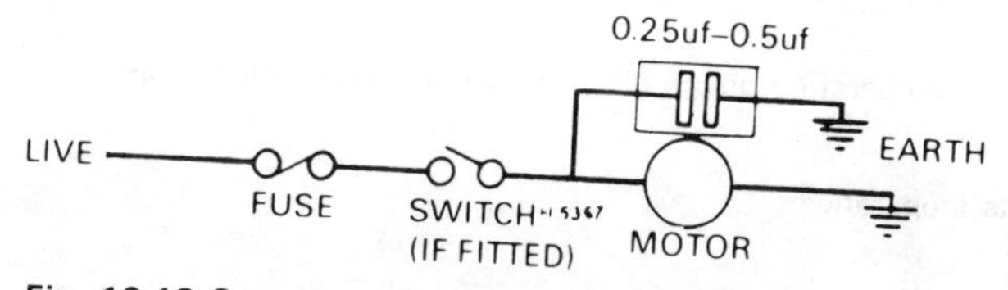

Fig. 10.18 Correct method of suppressing electric motors (Sec 35)

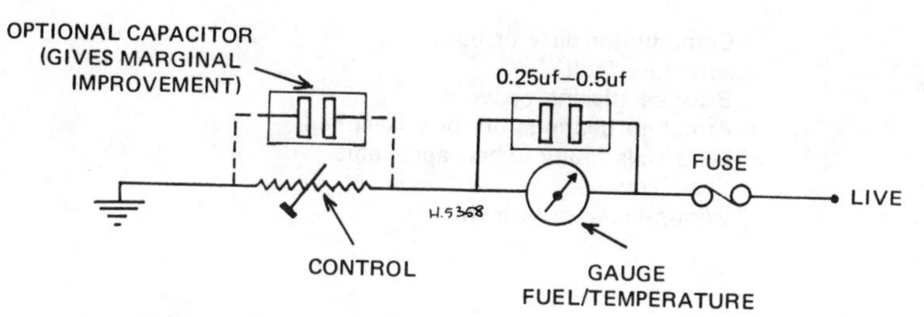

Fig. 10.19 Method of suppressing gauges and their control units (Sec 35)

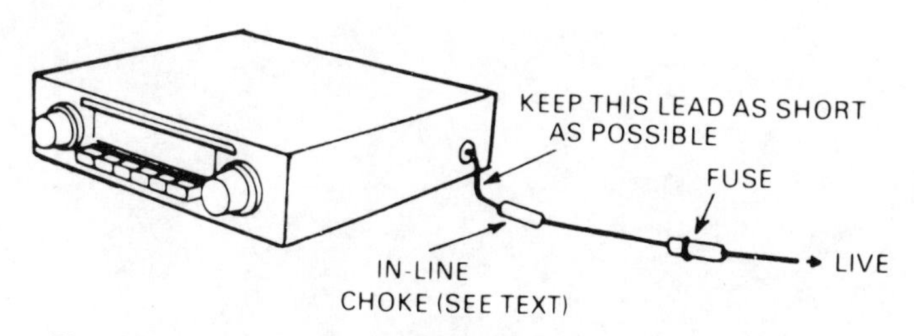

Fig. 10.20 An 'in-line' choke should be fitted into the live supply lead as close to the unit as possible (Sec 35)

36 Fault diagnosis – electrical system

Symptom	Reason(s)
Starter fails to turn engine	Battery discharged or defective Battery terminal and/or earth leads loose Starter motor connections loose Starter solenoid faulty Starter brushes worn or sticking Starter commutator dirty or worn Starter field coils earthed
Starter turns engine very slowly	Battery discharged Starter motor connections loose Starter brushes worn or sticking
Starter noisy	Pinion or ring gear teeth badly worn Mounting bolts loose
Battery will not hold charge for more than a few days	Battery defective internally Electrolyte level too low Battery terminals loose Alternator drivebelt slipping Alternator or regulator faulty Short-circuit
Ignition light stays on	Alternator or regulator faulty Alternator drivebelt broken or loose
Ignition light fails to come on	Warning bulb blown or open-circuit Alternator/regulator faulty
Fuel or temperature gauge gives no reading	Wiring open-circuit Sender unit faulty
Fuel or temperature gauge gives maximum reading all the time	Wiring short-circuit Gauge faulty
Lights inoperative	Bulb blown Fuse blown Battery discharged Switch faulty Wiring open-circuit Bad connection due to corrosion
Failure of component motor	Commutator dirty or burnt Armature faulty Brushes sticking or worn Armature bearings dry or misaligned Field coils faulty (when applicable) Fuse blown Wiring loose or broken

Key to Fig. 10.21

1 *Battery*
2 *Starter motor*
3 *Starter solenoid*
4 *Main fuses*
5 *Inhibitor switch – Trio-matic*
6 *Starter/ignition switch*
7 *Alternator*
8 *Regulator*
9 *No charge warning light*
10 *Ignition coil*
11 *Distributor and spark plugs*
12 *Ignition unit*
13 *Radiator cooling fan motor*
14 *Radiator fan thermostat*
15 *Carburettor solenoid – cut-off valve*
16 *Headlamp washer relay*
17 *Headlamp washer motor*
18 *Headlamp washer switch*
19 *Windscreen wiper motor*
20 *Windscreen wiper switch*
21 *Intermittent wiper relay*
22 *Screen washer switch*
23 *Screen washer motor*
24 *Rear window demister unit light*
25 *Radio/combination unit*
26 *Heater motor*
27 *Heater motor switch*
28 *Lighter*
29 *Luggage compartment switch*
30 *Luggage compartment lamp*
31 *Interior light*
32 *Front RH door switch*
33 *Front LH door switch*
34 *Rear RH door switch*
35 *Rear LH door switch*
36 *Luggage compartment warning light*
37 *Clock and lamp*
38 *Choke warning lamp and switch*
39 *Oil pressure warning lamp and switch*
40 *Handbrake warning lamp and switch*
41 *Brake fluid warning light and switch*
42 *Relay – brake check*
43 *Trio-matic 'OD' indicator lamp and switch*
44 *Temperature gauge and transmitter*
45 *Fuel gauge and transmitter*
46 *Reversing lamps and switch*
47 *Relay – direction indicators*
48 *Relay – hazard indicators*
49 *Hazard warning switch*
50 *Direction indicator switch*
51 *Front LH indicator*
52 *Side LH indicator*
53 *Rear LH indicator*
54 *LH indicator warning*
55 *RH indicator warning*
56 *Rear RH indicator*
57 *Side RH indicator*
58 *Front RH indicator*
59 *Hazard warning lamp*
60 *Stop-lamps and switch*
61 *Relay – horn*
62 *Horn and switch*
63 *Rear fog guard switch and warning lamp*
64 *Rear fog guard lamp*
65 *Trio-matic selector lamp*
66 *Front side lamp*
67 *Tail lamps*
68 *Number-plate lamps*
69 *Illumination lamp – instruments*
70 *Lighting switch*
71 *Dipswitch*
72 *Flasher switch*
73 *Low beam LH headlamp*
74 *Low beam RH headlamp*
75 *High beam LH headlamp*
76 *High beam RH headlamp*
77 *High beam warning lamp*

Colour code

BK	*Black*
GR	*Green*
BR	*Brown*
RD	*Red*
YW	*Yellow*
BL	*Blue*
WH	*White*

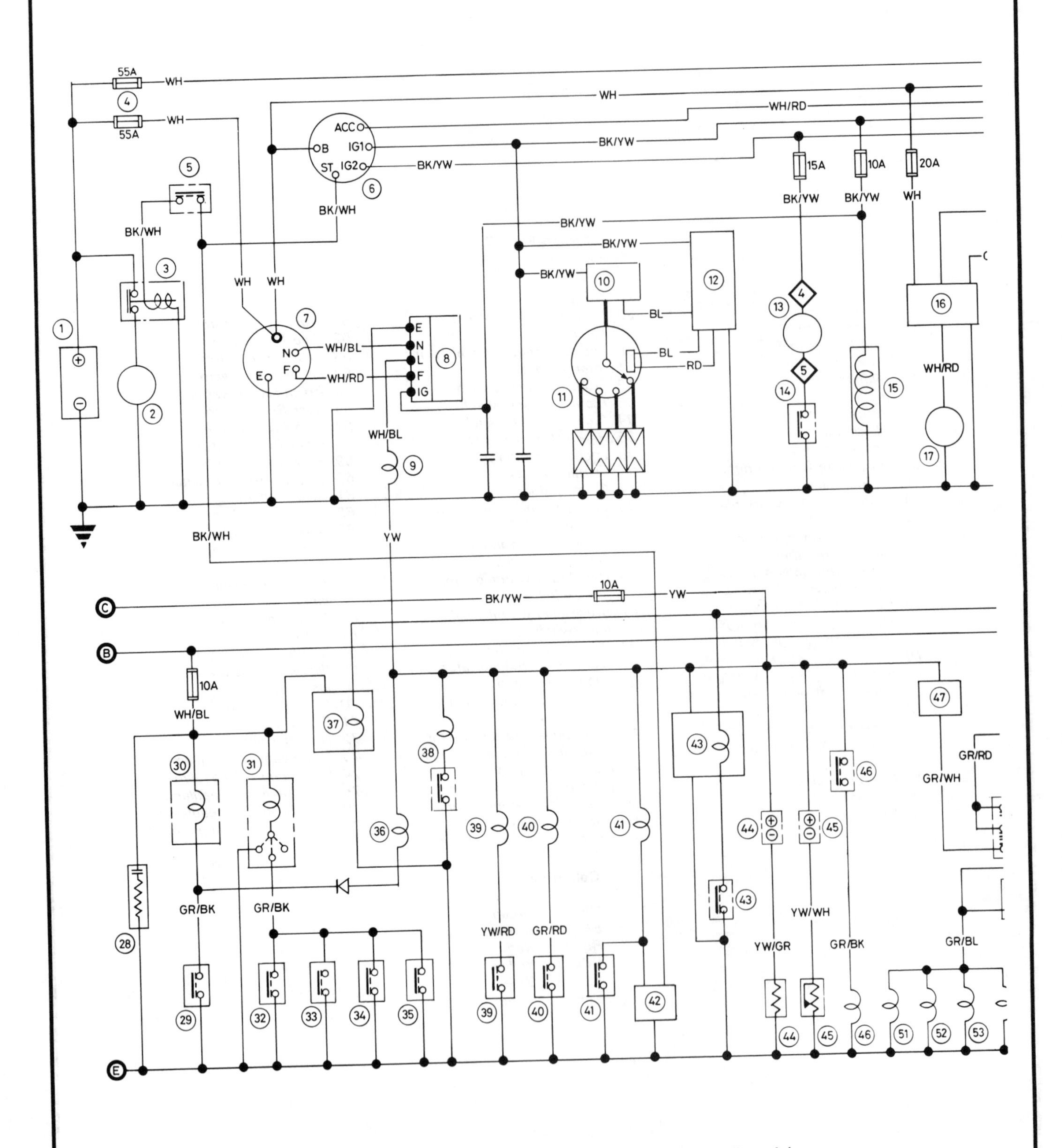

Fig. 10.21 Main wiring diagram. Not all items are fitted to all models

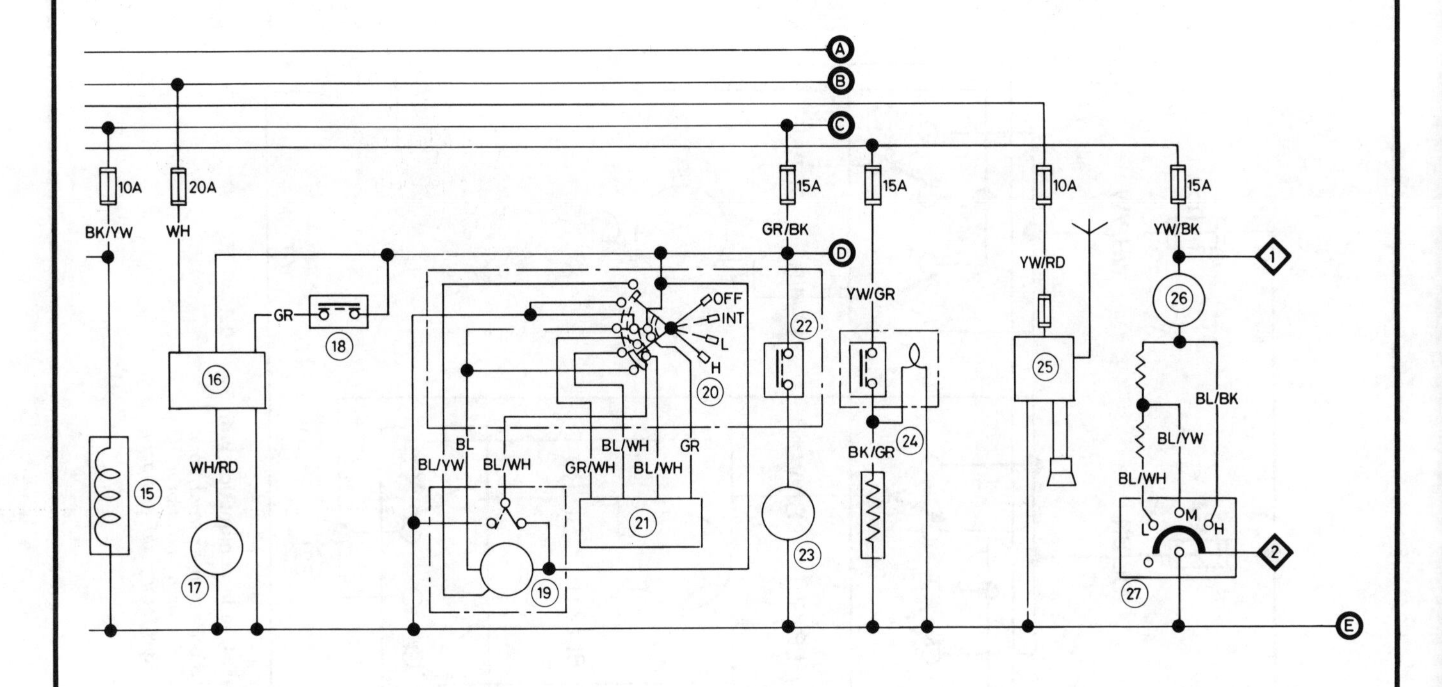

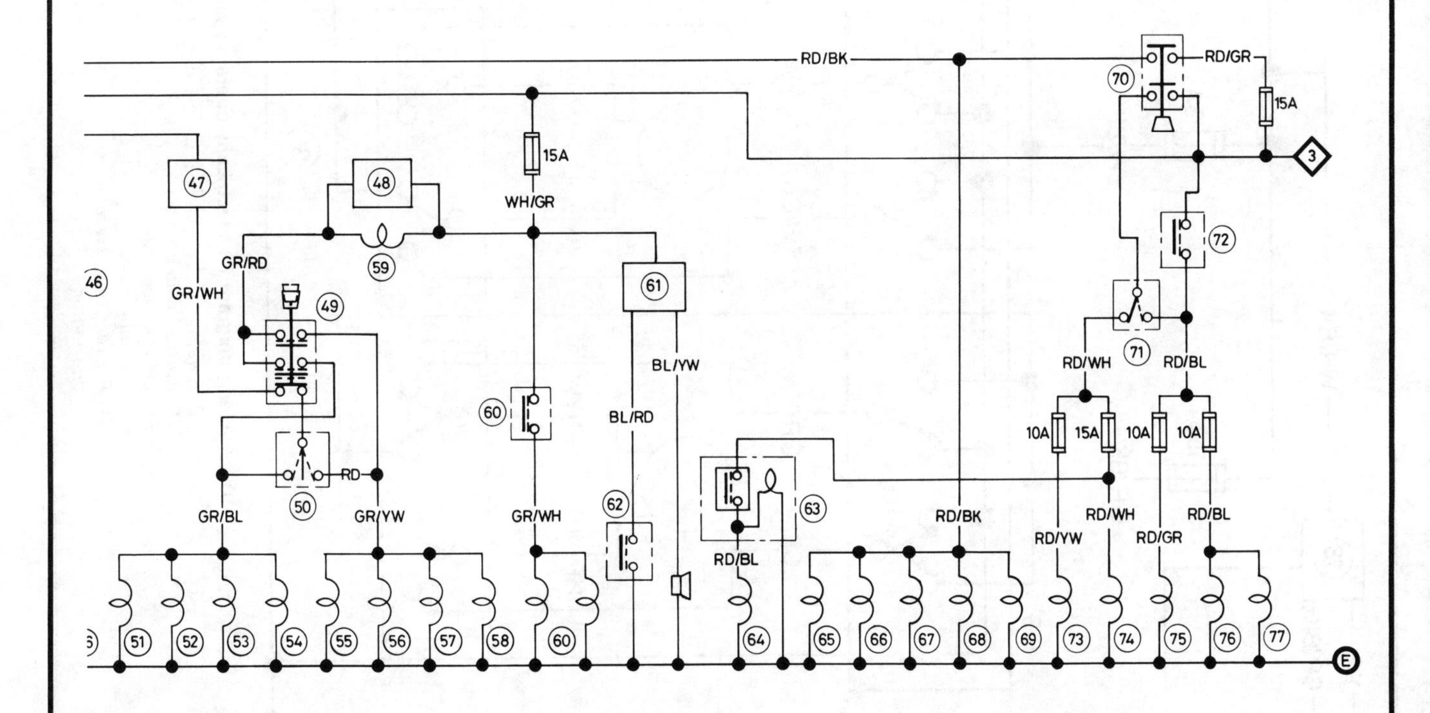

Fig. 10.21 (cont'd) Main wiring diagram. Not all items are fitted to all models

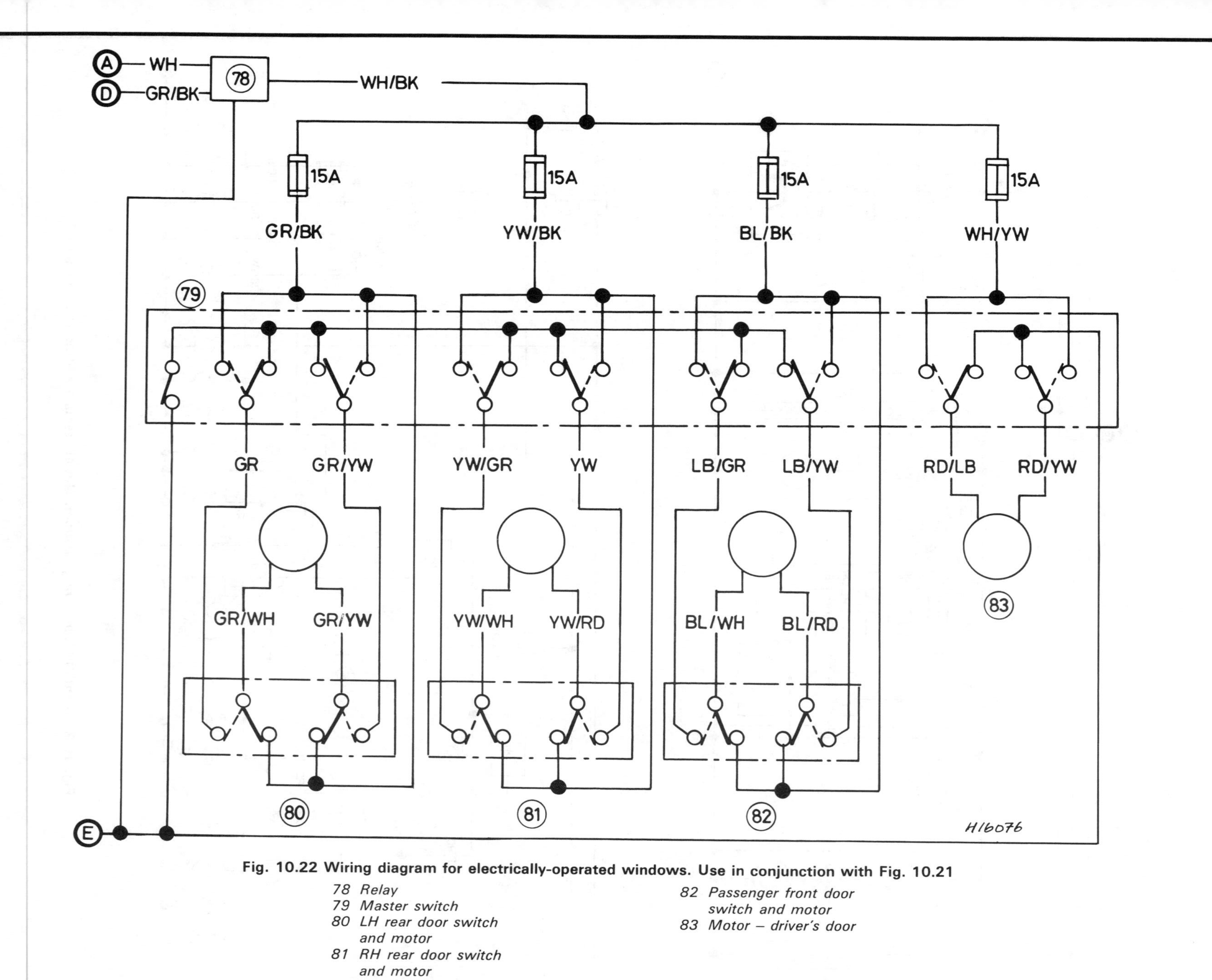

Fig. 10.22 Wiring diagram for electrically-operated windows. Use in conjunction with Fig. 10.21

78 Relay
79 Master switch
80 LH rear door switch and motor
81 RH rear door switch and motor
82 Passenger front door switch and motor
83 Motor – driver's door

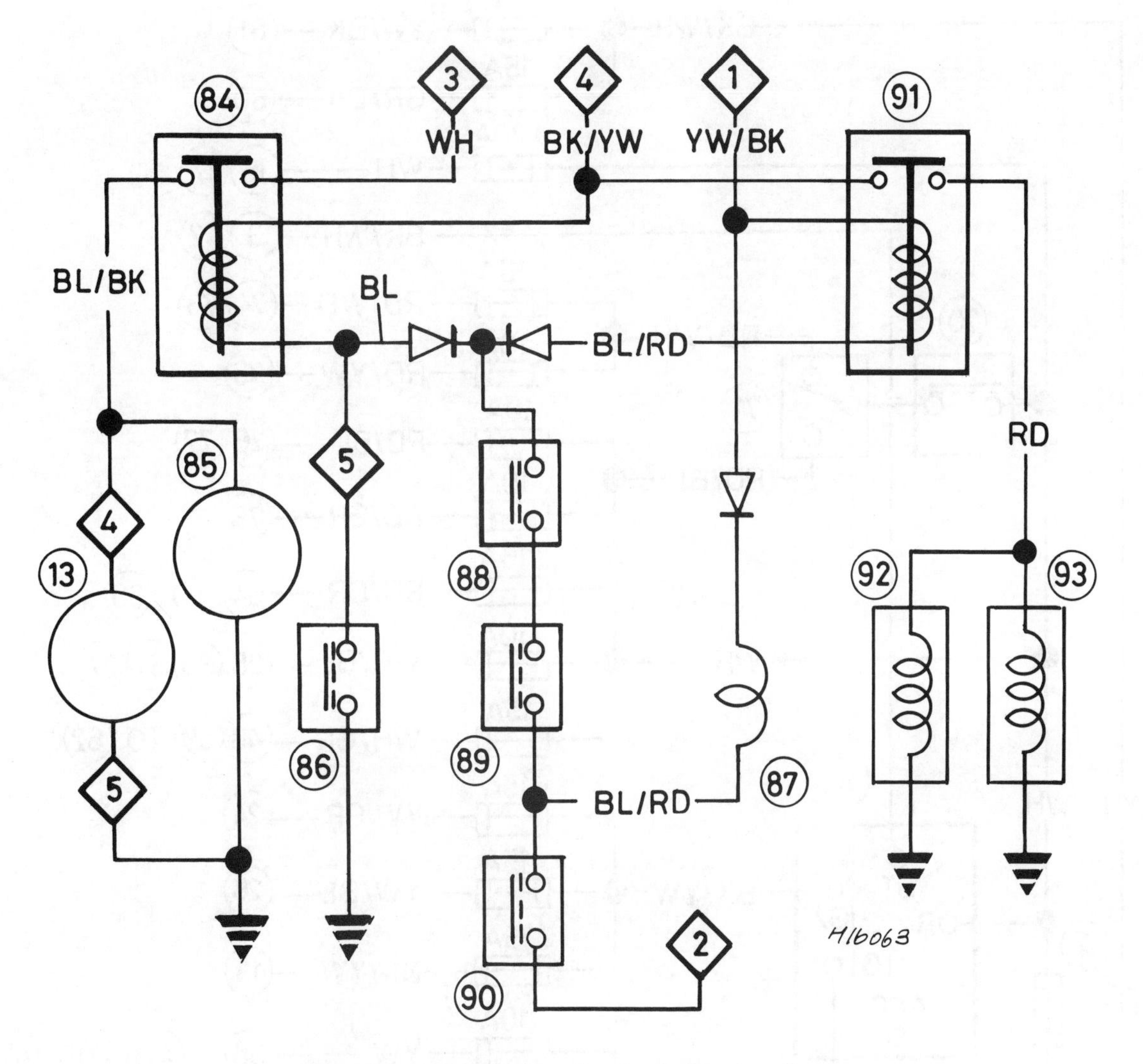

Fig. 10.23 Wiring diagram for air conditioning. Use in conjunction with Fig. 10.21

84 Relay – fan motors
85 Condenser fan motor
86 Condenser fan switch
87 Warning light
88 Pressure switch
89 Thermostat switch – radiator
90 Cooler switch
91 Relay – compressor clutch
92 Solenoid valve – idle speed boost
93 Magnetic clutch – compressor

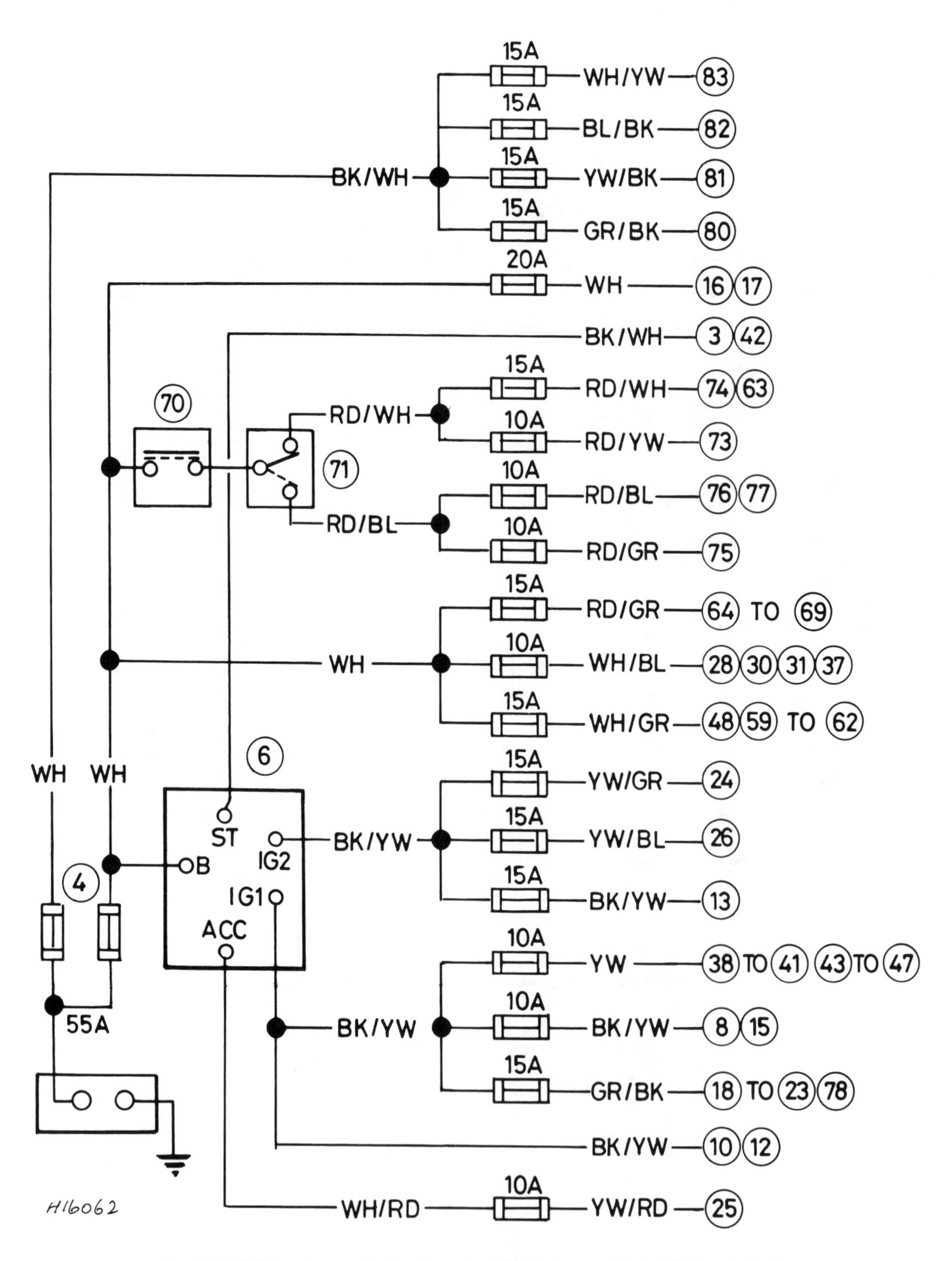

Fig. 10.24 Wiring diagram for the fuse circuits. For key see Figs. 10.21 and 10.22

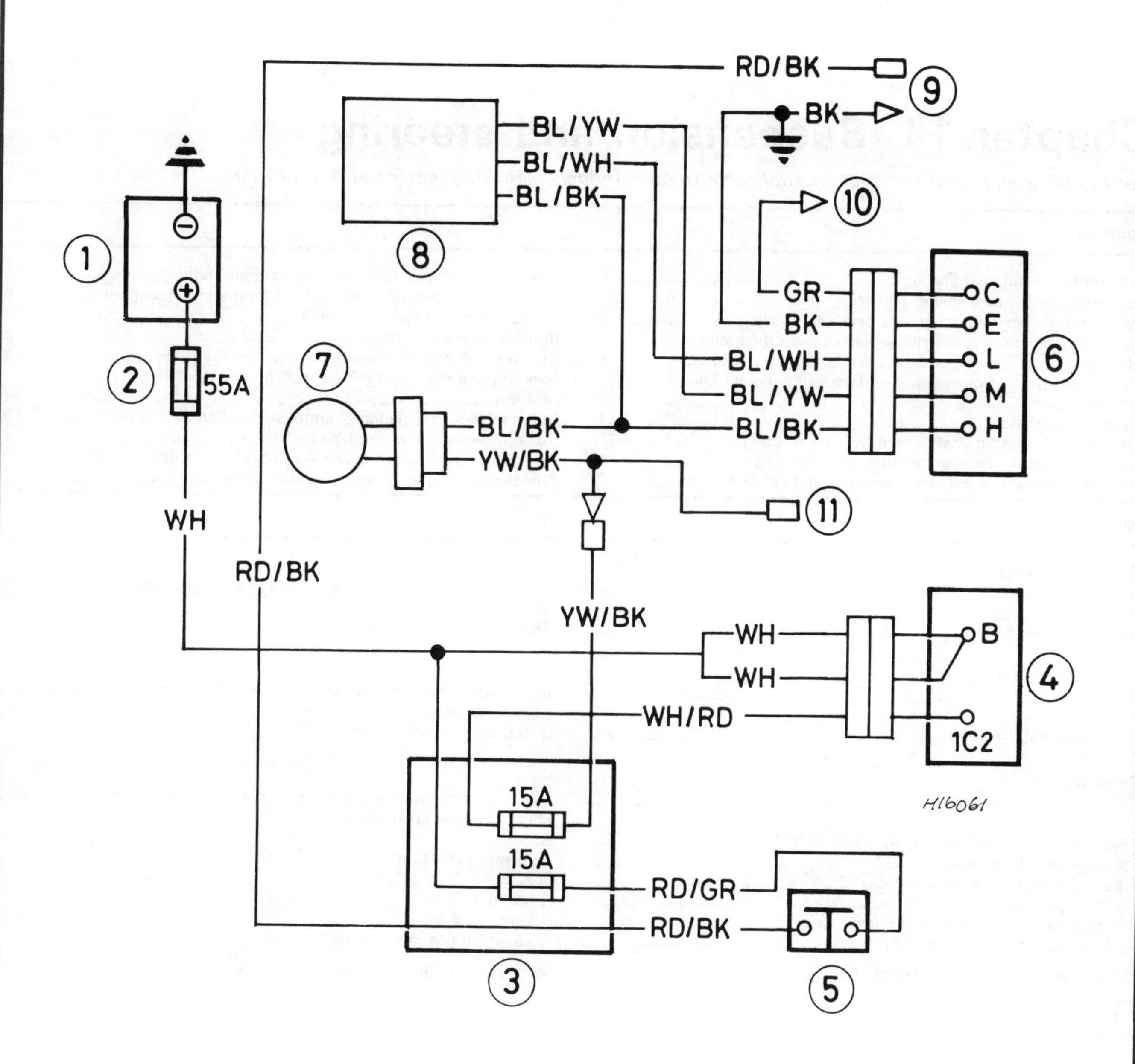

Fig. 10.25 Wiring diagram for the heater. For colour code see Fig. 10.21

1 *Battery*
2 *Main fuse*
3 *Fuse box*
4 *Ignition switch*
5 *Direction indicator switch*
6 *Blower switch*
7 *Blower motor*
8 *Blower resistor*
9 *To heater panel illumination*
10 *To air conditioner switch (if fitted)*
11 *To air conditioner harness (if fitted)*

Chapter 11 Suspension and steering

For modifications, and information applicable to later models, see Supplement at end of manual

Contents

Specifications

Front suspension

Type	Independent MacPherson strut and offset coil spring, control arm and anti-roll bar
Coil spring free length	294.5 mm (11.594 in)

Rear suspension

Type	Independent MacPherson strut and offset coil spring, trailing arm and transverse lower arm
Coil spring free length	316.5 mm (12.461 in)

Steering

Type	Rack-and-pinion, safety type energy-absorbing column, intermediate shaft with universal joints
Angle of inner wheel with outer wheel at 31°	37°
Steering wheel diameter	385 mm (15.15 in)
Steering wheel turns (lock-to-lock)	3.3
Steering gear ratio	17.8 to 1
Steering wheel free play (maximum)	10 mm (0.4 in)
Rack damper spring free length	26.3 to 28.6 mm (1.04 to 1.13 in)

Lubricant type/specification

Multi-purpose lithium-based grease (Duckhams LB10)

Wheel alignment

Front:	
Camber	0° ± 1°
Castor	1° 40′ ± 1° (early models), 2° 5′ ± 1° (later models)
King-pin inclination	12° 20′ ± 1° 30′
Toe-in/toe-out	Parallel, ± 2 mm (0.079 in) or ± 0° 12′
Rear:	
Camber	0° 15′ negative
Toe-in (each wheel)	1 mm ± 1 mm (0.04 ± 0.04 in) or 0° 6′ ± 0° 6′

Wheels

Type	Pressed steel disc, with vented centre
Size	4½J x 13
Rim run-out (maximum)	3 mm (0.12 in)

Tyres

Size:		
L	145SR x 13	
HL/HLS	155SR x 13	
CD	165/70SR x 13	
Pressures (cold) – lbf/in² (kgf/cm²):	Front	Rear
Up to 4 passengers	24 (1.7)	24 (1.7)
Fully laden, or towing	24 (1.7)	30 (2.1)

Torque wrench settings

	lbf ft	Nm
Front suspension		
Driveshaft/hub nut	111	150
Balljoint nut	26	35
Control arm inner pivot bolt	27	36
Anti-roll bar mounting bolts	29	39
Anti-roll bar LH bracket bolts	38	51
Anti-roll bar to control arm	32	44
Strut pinch-bolt	37	50
Strut upper mounting	33	45
Coil spring seat nut	17	23
Splash guard	4	5
Rear suspension		
Trailing arm front pivot bolt	63	85
Trailing arm rear bolt (outer)	74	100
Trailing arm track adjusting bolt (inner)	41	55
Lower control arm bolts	41	55
Strut pinch-bolt	37	50
Shock absorber top nut	33	45
Strut upper mounting	16	22
Stub axle	41	55
Steering		
Steering wheel nut	37	50
Steering column upper mounting	9	13
Steering column lower mounting	16	22
Intermediate shaft pinch-bolts:		
Forged coupling	22	30
Pressed steel coupling	17	23
Rack mounting	16	22
Rack adjustment locknut	18	25
Tie-rod to rack	55	75
Tie-rod end to steering knuckle	32	44
Tie-rod end locknut	32	44
Wheels		
Wheel nuts	59	80

1 General description

The front suspension is of independent MacPherson strut type incorporating offset coil springs, lower control arms, and an anti-roll bar.

The rear suspension is also of independent MacPherson strut type, incorporating offset coil spring, trailing arms, and transverse lower arms.

The steering is of rack-and-pinion type, incorporating a safety column and an intermediate shaft with universal joints.

All suspension and steering components are rubber-mounted to the body, and the suspension pivot bushes also incorporate rubber cushioning.

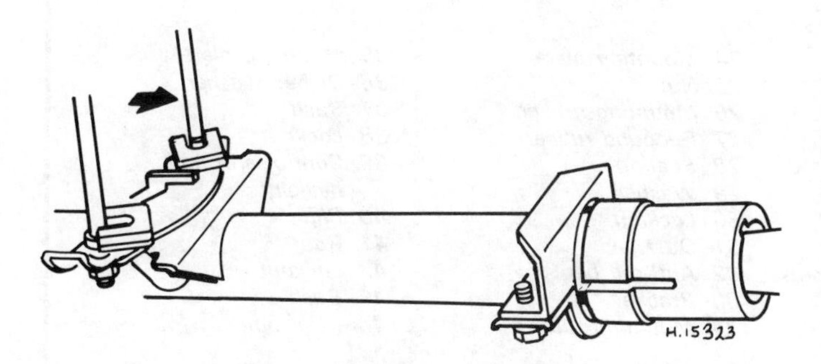

Fig. 11.1 Energy-absorbing column movement during impact (Sec 1)

2 Routine maintenance

1 Every 7500 miles (12 000 km) check the steering gear and balljoints for security, wear and damage. Also check the rack bellows for splitting.

2 Every 15 000 miles (24 000 km) check the suspension components and joints for security, wear, and damage. Also have the front and rear wheel alignment checked.

3 Every 60 000 miles (96 000 km) renew the grease in the rear wheel bearings.

3 Front suspension strut assembly – removal, overhaul and refitting

1 Jack up the front of the car and support it on axle stands. Apply the handbrake and remove the roadwheel.

2 Unbolt the hydraulic hose clip from the strut, then unscrew the brake caliper-to-steering knuckle mounting bolts and withdraw the caliper together with the disc pads from the brake disc. Tie the caliper to the brake pipe bracket, making sure that the hydraulic hose is not strained.

3 Support the lower control arm with a trolley jack. Unscrew and remove the pinch-bolt from the steering knuckle, then lower the jack and at the same time tap the knuckle from the bottom of the strut with a wooden mallet (photo).

4 Working in the engine compartment, prise off the strut dust cap. While supporting the strut, unscrew the self-locking nut (photo). If the spindle rotates, hold it stationary with an Allen key. Remove the washer.

5 Lower the strut assembly and withdraw it from the car (photo).

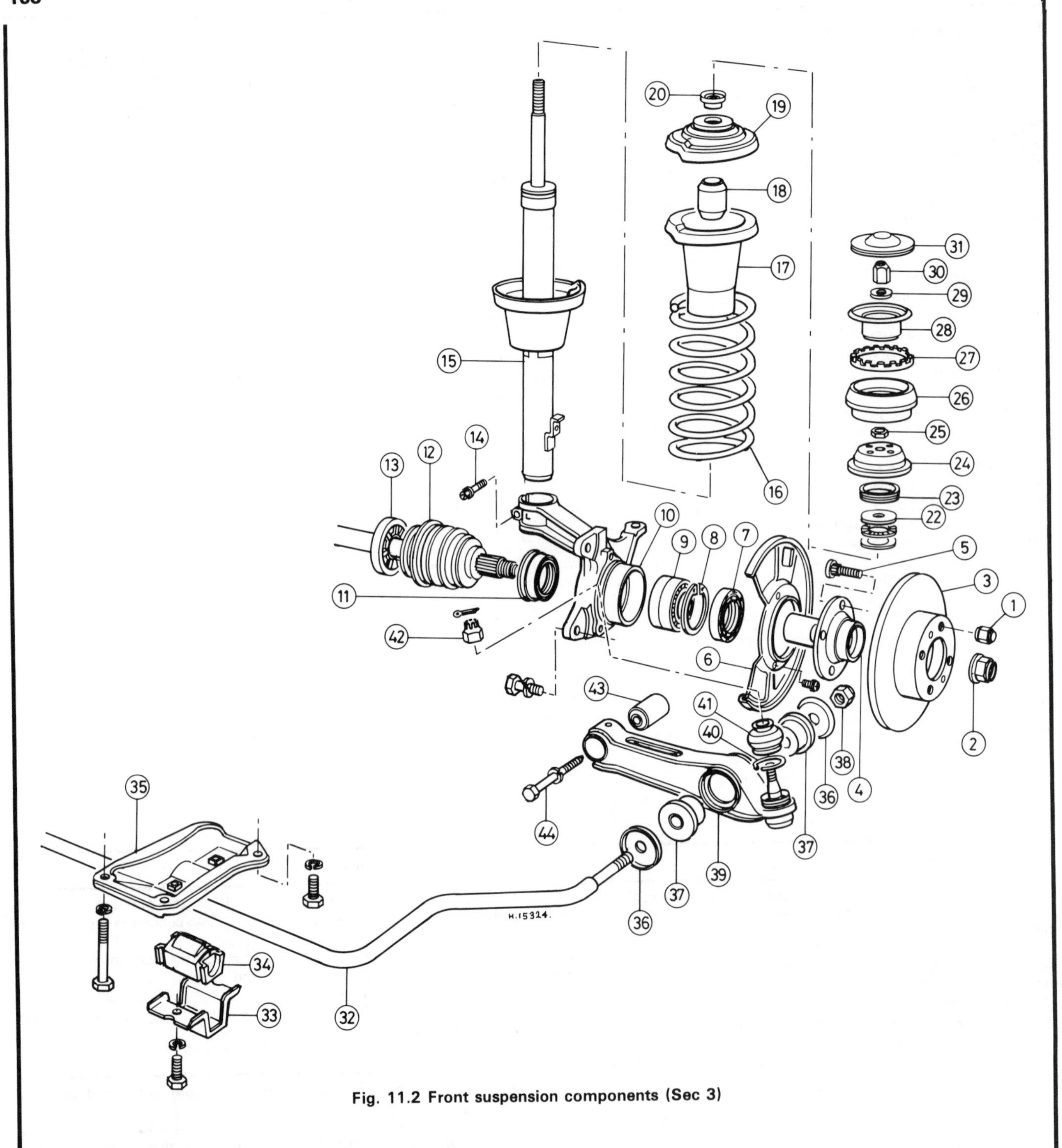

Fig. 11.2 Front suspension components (Sec 3)

1 *Roadwheel nut*
2 *Hub nut*
3 *Brake disc*
4 *Drive flange*
5 *Wheel stud*
6 *Splash guard*
7 *Oil seal*
8 *Circlip*
9 *Bearing*
10 *Steering knuckle*
11 *Oil seal*
12 *Driveshaft*
13 *Vibration damper*
14 *Pinch-bolt*
15 *Strut/shock absorber*
16 *Coil spring*
17 *Dust cover*
18 *Bump stop*
19 *Spring seat*
20 *Seal bush*
21 *Needle bearing and thrust race*
22 *Spacer*
23 *Dust seal*
24 *Mounting plate*
25 *Nut*
26 *Mounting rubber*
27 *Rebound rubber*
28 *Seating*
29 *Washer*
30 *Locknut*
31 *Dust cap*
32 *Anti-roll bar*
33 *Bracket*
34 *Mounting rubber*
35 *Mounting plate*
36 *Dished washer*
37 *Bush*
38 *Locknut*
39 *Control arm and balljoint*
40 *Clip*
41 *Boot*
42 *Locknut*
43 *Bush*
44 *Pivot bolt*

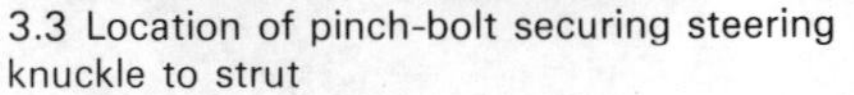

3.3 Location of pinch-bolt securing steering knuckle to strut

3.4 Front suspension strut cap

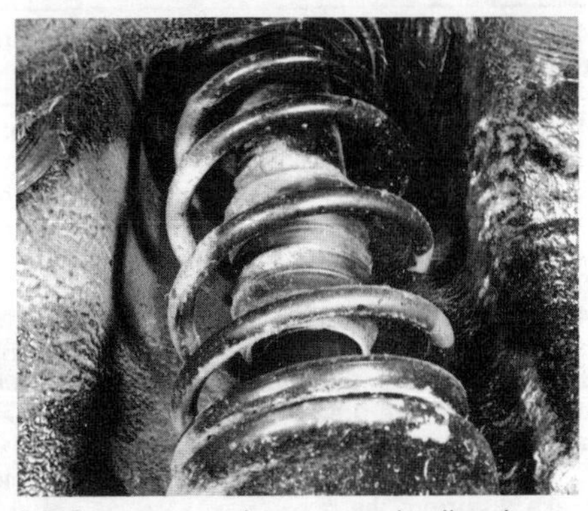

3.5 Front suspension strut and coil spring location

6 Using a spring compressor tool, compress the coil spring evenly until it is free of the upper spring seat. Use a proper spring compressor – **do not** improvise.

7 Unscrew the nut and remove the spring seat together with the mounting rubber and bearing from the shock absorber spindle. Carefully release the spring compressor (unless you are simply renewing the shock absorber).

8 Withdraw the coil spring, dust cover, and bump stop.

9 Clean all the components with paraffin and wipe dry, then examine them for wear, damage and deterioration. Check the operation of the shock absorber spindle through its full stroke, and renew it if there is any indication of leakage seizure or uneven movement. Check that the coil spring free length is as given in the Specifications.

10 Reassembly and refitting are reversals of dismantling and removal, but check that the coil spring is correctly located in the steps provided in the strut and upper seat. Lubricate the needle roller bearing with a molybdenum disulphide based grease before fitting it to the baseplate together with the bush, spacer, thrust washer, and seal. Tighten all nuts and bolts to the specified torque. When assembling the bottom of the strut to the steering knuckle, align the tab with the split in the knuckle as shown in Fig. 11.4. Always renew the top mounting self-locking nut.

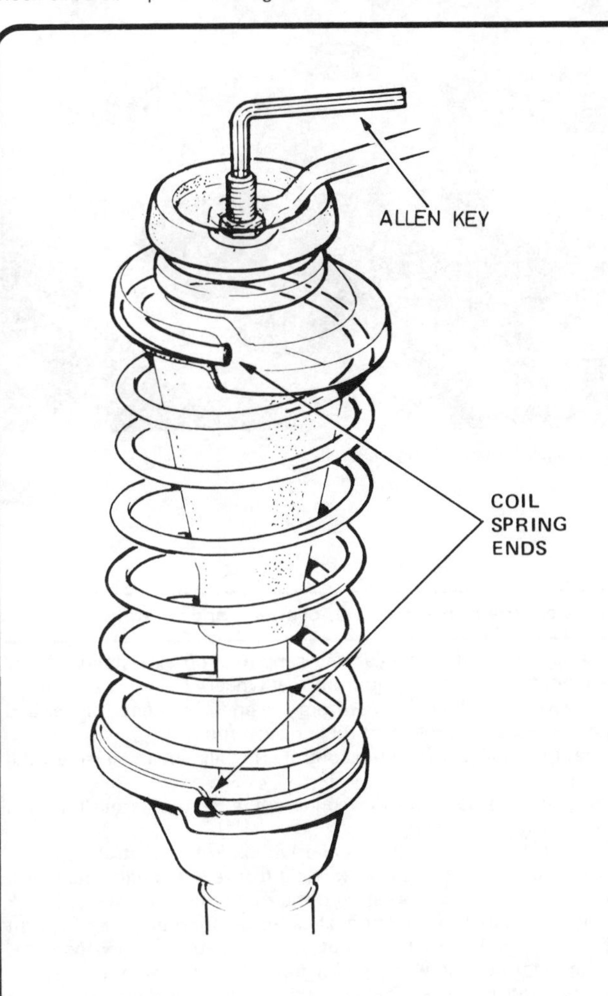

Fig. 11.3 Removing the suspension strut assembly (Sec 3)

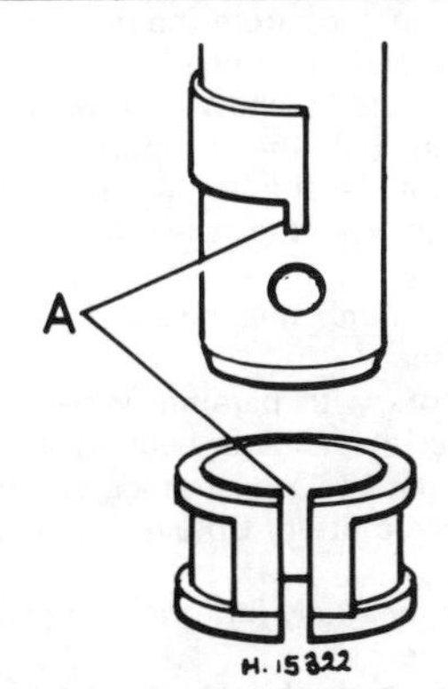

Fig. 11.4 Front suspension strut alignment tab and slot (A) (Sec 3)

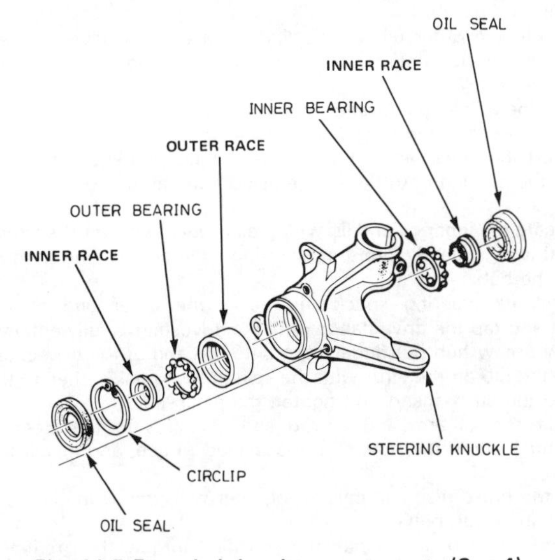

Fig. 11.5 Front hub bearing components (Sec 4)

4 Front hub and steering knuckle – removal, overhaul and refitting

1 Remove the trim cap from the centre of the front roadwheel (photo). Relieve the staking on the hub nut.
2 Using a socket or box spanner, loosen the hub nut – an extension bar may be required as the nut is very tight (photo).
3 Jack up the front of the car and support it on axle stands. Apply the handbrake and remove the roadwheel.
4 Unbolt the hydraulic hose clip from the strut, then unscrew the brake caliper-to-steering knuckle mounting bolts and withdraw the caliper together with the disc pads from the brake disc. Tie the caliper to the brake pipe bracket, making sure that the hydraulic hose is not strained.
5 Using two 8 mm bolts in the threaded holes provided, draw the brake disc from the hub.
6 Extract the split pin from the tie-rod end nut, and unscrew the nut. Similarly remove the split pin and nut from the control arm balljoint.
7 Using a separator tool, disconnect the tie-rod end and control arm from the steering knuckle.
8 Unscrew and remove the pinch-bolt, then tap the knuckle from the bottom of the strut with a wooden mallet.
9 Again using the wooden mallet, tap the outer end of the driveshaft through the hub. Withdraw the front hub and steering knuckle.
10 Mark the exterior of the knuckle with paraffin and wipe it dry.
11 Prise out the inner oil seal.
12 Mount the steering knuckle in a vice and drive the drive flange from the bearing using a metal tube. Take care not to damage the splash guard. The outer bearing inner race will probably come away with the flange, taking with it the outer oil seal.
13 Remove the outer bearing cage from the outer race, then remove the inner bearing inner race and inner bearing cage.
14 Remove the cross-head screws and withdraw the splash guard.
15 Extract the circlip from the hub, then support the hub and drive out the bearing outer race using a metal tube from the rear of the knuckle located on the central shoulder of the race. *Once removed, it is not possible to re-use the bearing.*
16 Using a puller, draw the outer bearing inner race from the drive flange and remove the oil seal.
17 Clean all the components with paraffin, wipe dry, and examine them for wear and damage. Inspect the bearing balls and races for wear and pitting. If necessary, the wheel studs can be pressed from the drive flange and new studs fitted. Obtain a new bearing and two new oil seals.
18 Drive the bearing outer race fully into the hub using a metal tube or mandrel on the outer edge.
19 Pack both bearing cages and lubricate the inner and outer races with a multi-purpose lithium-based grease.
20 Fit the outer bearing cage and its inner race, and insert the outer race circlip in the hub.
21 Lubricate the outer oil seal lip with grease, then drive the seal squarely into the hub until flush using a block of wood. The lip must face into the hub.
22 Install the splash guard and tighten the screws.
23 Fit the inner bearing cage and its inner race.
24 Support the drive flange, then locate the steering knuckle over it and drive the bearing onto the flange using a metal tube on the inner race.
25 Lubricate the inner oil and lip with grease, locate it over the flange hub, and drive it squarely into the hub using a metal tube. The lip must face into the hub.
26 Locate the steering knuckle/hub over the outer end of the driveshaft and tap the drive flange until the driveshaft is fully entered.
27 Screw a new hub nut finger tight onto the end of the driveshaft.
28 Align the tab on the strut with the split in the knuckle, then fit the knuckle to the strut. Insert and tighten the pinch-bolt.
29 Fit the control arm and tie-rod end balljoints to the steering knuckle/hub, tighten the nuts to the specified torque, and install the split pins.
30 Refit the brake disc and caliper together with the hydraulic hose clip, and tighten the bolts.
31 Tighten the hub nut to half the specified torque, then refit the roadwheel and lower the car to the ground.
32 Tighten the hub nut to the final specified torque and lock it by tapping the collar into the groove in the driveshaft.
33 Refit the trim cap to the centre of the roadwheel.

4.1 Removing the front wheel trim cap

4.2 Unscrewing the front hub nut

5 Front control arm – removal, overhaul and refitting

1 Jack up the front of the car and support it on axle stands. Apply the handbrake and remove the front roadwheel.
2 Unscrew the self-locking nut from the end of the anti-roll bar and remove the dished washer and rubber bush (photo).
3 Extract the split pin from the control arm balljoint and unscrew the nut (photo).
4 Using a separator tool, disconnect the control arm from the steering knuckle.
5 Unscrew the inner pivot bolt and withdraw the control arm.
6 Clean the control arm and examine it for wear and damage. Check the balljoint for excessive wear, and the rubber boot for splits. Check the pivot bush and anti-roll bar bushes for deterioration. The balljoint is integral with the control arm, but it is possible to renew the boot.
7 If the pivot bush is worn, pull it from the arm using a long bolt, metal tube, and washers. The new bush can be installed using the same method.
8 Refitting is a reversal of removal. Lightly lubricate the pivot bolt shank with molybdenum disulphide grease. Tighten the anti-roll bar nut and the pivot bolt to their specified torques with the weight of the car on the suspension.

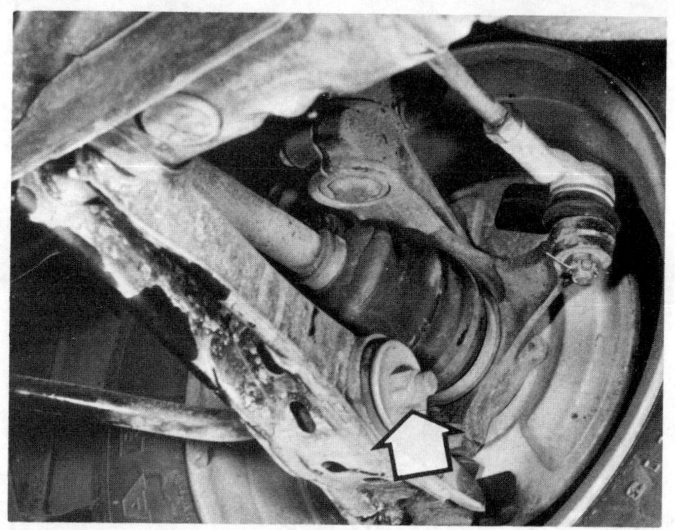
5.2 Front suspension control arm showing anti-roll bar securing nut (arrowed)

5.3 Front suspension control arm balljoint

6 Anti-roll bar – removal and refitting

1 Jack up the front of the car and support it on axle stands. Apply the handbrake and remove the front roadwheels.
2 Unscrew the front mounting clamp bolts and remove the clamps (photo).
3 Mark the anti-roll bar for position – new bars have a paint mark adjacent to the left-hand side clamp.
4 Unscrew both self-locking nuts from the ends of the anti-roll bar and remove the dished washers and rubber bushes.
5 Pull one end of the anti-roll bar from the control arm, then withdraw the bar. Remove the remaining rubber bushes and dished washers.
6 Examine all the bushes for wear and deterioration and if necessary renew them.
7 Refitting is a reversal of removal, but tighten the nuts and bolts to the specified torque with the weight of the car on the suspension.

6.2 Anti-roll bar front mounting clamp

7 Rear suspension strut assembly – removal, overhaul and refitting

1 Chock the front wheels, then jack up the rear of the car and support it on axle stands. Remove the roadwheel.
2 Pinch the rear hydraulic hose with a brake hose clamp, or alternatively tighten the fluid reservoir cap onto a piece of plastic sheeting, in order to minimise the loss of fluid in the subsequent procedure.
3 Unscrew the rigid brake pipe union nut from the strut bracket, then extract the spring clip and remove the flexible hose. Plug the open ends of the rigid pipe and flexible hose.
4 With the handbrake lever released, unhook the cable from the brake shoe operating lever.
5 Loosen the pivot bolts attaching the lower arm and trailing arm to the body.
6 Unscrew and remove the pinch-bolt from the hub carrier.
7 Working inside the boot compartment, unscrew and remove the strut upper mounting nuts and washers (photo). **Do not** unscrew the centre nut.
8 Tap the hub carrier from the bottom of the strut with a wooden mallet. Lower the strut assembly and withdraw it from the car.
9 Using a suitable spring compressor tool, compress the coil spring evenly until it is free of the upper mounting plate and rubber. Use a proper spring compressor – **do not** improvise. Remove the top dust cap.
10 Unscrew the nut from the shock absorber spindle while holding the spindle stationary with an Allen key. Remove the dished washer, mounting rubber and spacer.

7.7 Rear suspension strut upper mounting nuts (arrowed)

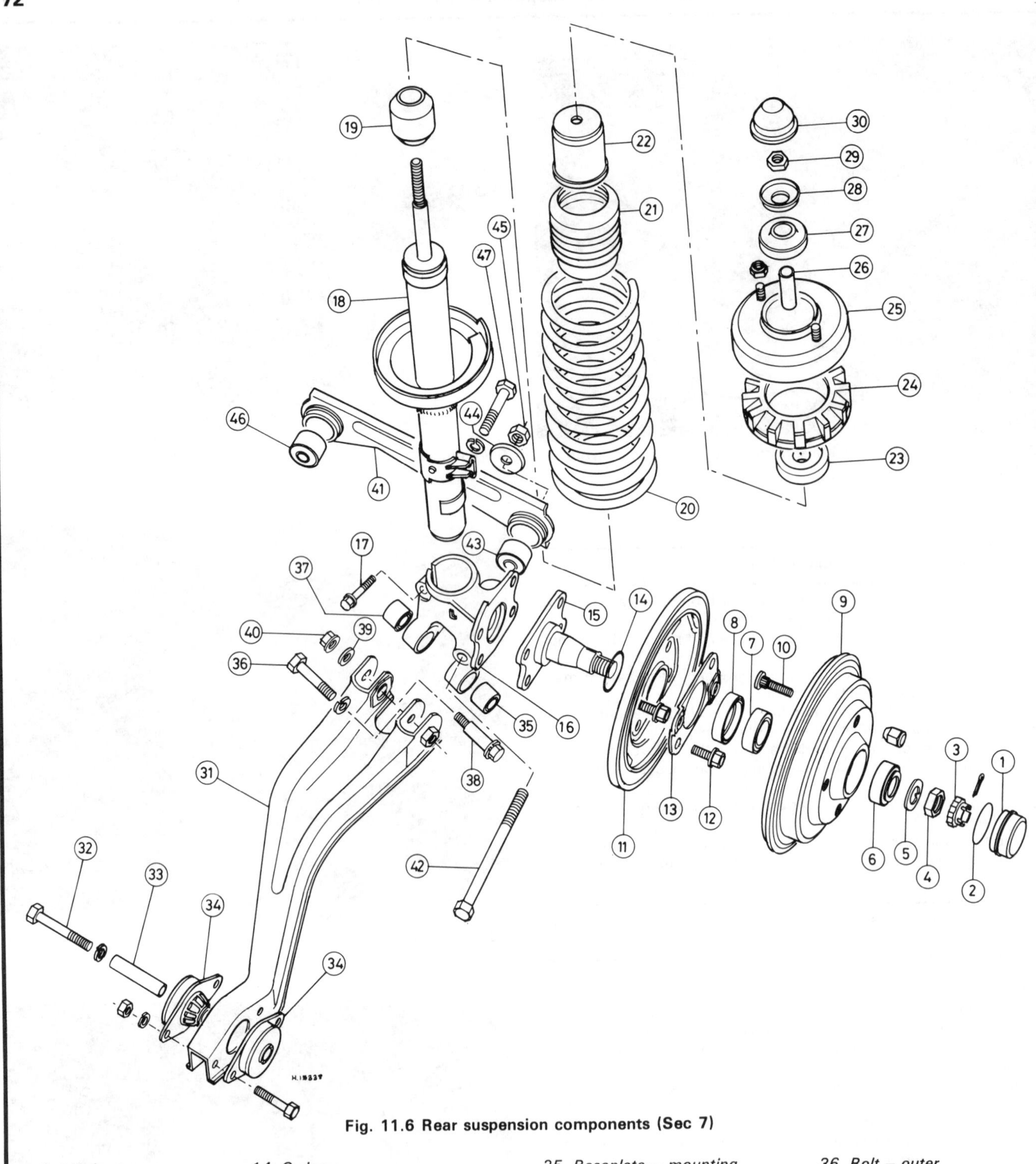

Fig. 11.6 Rear suspension components (Sec 7)

1 Hub cap
2 O-ring
3 Nut retainer
4 Hub nut
5 Hub washer
6 Bearing – outer
7 Bearing – inner
8 Seal
9 Brake drum
10 Wheel stud
11 Backplate
12 Bolt
13 Lockplate
14 O-ring
15 Stub axle
16 Hub carrier
17 Pinch-bolt
18 Shock absorber (suspension strut)
19 Bump stop
20 Coil spring
21 Dust cover
22 Dust sleeve
23 Mounting rubber – shock absorber
24 Mounting rubber – spring
25 Baseplate – mounting rubber
26 Spacer
27 Mounting rubber – shock absorber
28 Washer – dished
29 Locknut
30 Dust cap
31 Trailing arm
32 Pivot bolt
33 Spacer – inner sleeve
34 Front bush – pivot
35 Mounting bush – outer
36 Bolt – outer
37 Mounting bush – inner
38 Adjustment bolt – rear wheel alignment
39 Cam plate
40 Locknut
41 Lower arm
42 Mounting bolt
43 Mounting bush
44 Washer – dished
45 Locknut
46 Inner bush
47 Pivot bolt

11 Withdraw the coil spring together with the upper mounting plate and rubbers, dust sleeve, boot and bump stop. Carefully release the spring compressor, unless you are only renewing the shock absorber.
12 Clean all the components with paraffin and wipe dry, then examine them for wear, damage and deterioration. Check the operation of the shock absorber spindle through its full stroke, and renew it if there is any indication of seizure or uneven movement. Check that the coil spring free length is as given in the Specifications.
13 Reassembly and refitting are a reversal of dismantling and removal, but check that the coil spring is correctly located in the steps provided in the strut and upper mounting rubber. When assembling the bottom of the strut to the hub carrier, align the tab with the split in the carrier as shown in Fig. 11.7. Tighten all nuts and bolts to the specified torque, but delay final tightening of the lower arm and trailing arm pivot bolts until the weight of the car is on the suspension.
14 Remove the brake hose clamp or plastic sheeting from the fluid reservoir cap, then bleed the brake hydraulic system as described in Chapter 9.

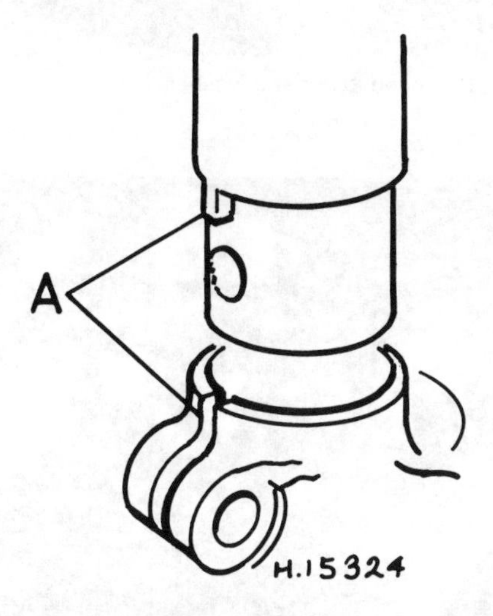

Fig. 11.7 Rear suspension strut alignment tab and slot (A) (Sec 7)

8 Rear wheel bearings – removal, refitting and adjustment

1 Chock the front wheels, then jack up the rear of the car and support it on axle stands. Remove the roadwheel.
2 Tap the hub cap from the brake drum/hub assembly and remove the O-ring (photo).
3 Extract the split pin and remove the nut retainer.
4 Unscrew and remove the hub nut and washer (photo).
5 Withdraw the brake drum/hub from the stub axle and at the same time catch the outer bearing inner race and rollers (photos). If difficulty is experienced due to the drum fouling the brake shoes, prise the stop plate from the backplate in order to allow the brake shoes to retract further. See Chapter 9 for further details.
6 Prise the inner oil seal from the hub and remove the inner bearing inner race and rollers (photo).
7 Scoop the grease from inside the hub, then clean the inside of the hub, the bearings, and the stub axle with paraffin and wipe dry. Take care not to contaminate the brake shoe linings. Examine the bearings for excessive wear and pitting and if new bearings are required, drive the outer races evenly from the hub using a soft metal drift in the cut-outs provided inside the hub. If necessary, the wheel studs can be pressed from the brake drum and new studs fitted. Obtain a new oil seal and hub cap O-ring.
8 Drive the bearing outer races into the hub using a suitable metal tube,
9 Pack the inner cavity of the hub with a lithium-based grease, referring to Fig. 11.8.
10 Pack the inner bearing inner race and rollers with lithium-based grease and locate them in the outer race.
11 Insert the inner oil seal with the sealing lip facing into the hub, and drive it in squarely using a block of wood. Smear the sealing lip with grease.
12 Wipe clean the stub axle and oil seal bearing surface. Locate the brake drum/hub on the stub axle. Refit the handbrake stop plate if necessary.
13 Pack the outer bearing inner race and rollers with lithium-based grease and locate them in the outer race.
14 Refit the washer and hub nut and tighten the nut finger tight.

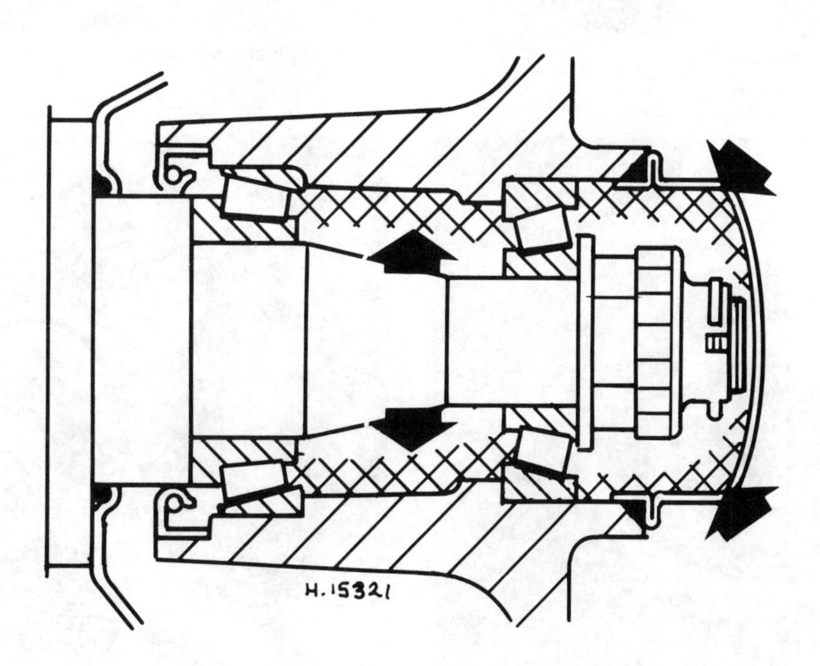

Fig. 11.8 Cross-section of the rear wheel bearings showing (arrowed) area to pack grease (Sec 8)

8.2 Removing the rear hub cap

8.4 Removing the rear hub nut and washer

8.5a Removing the rear hub outer bearing ...

8.5b ... and brake drum/hub

8.6 Rear hub inner oil seal

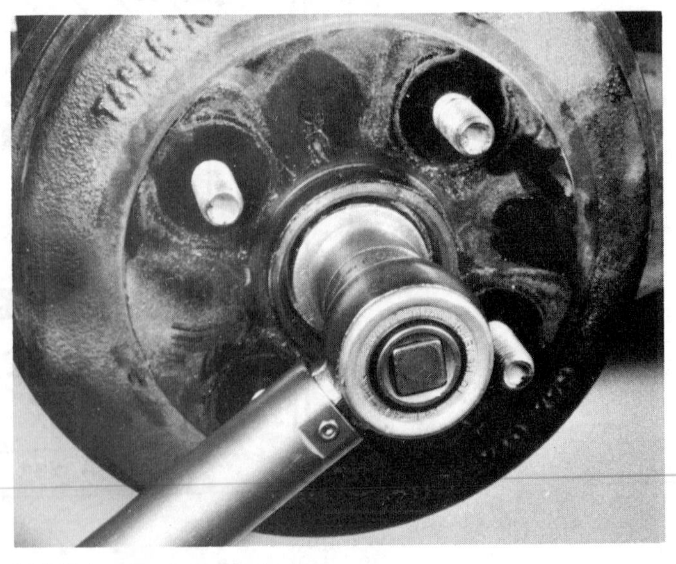

8.15 Tightening the rear hub nut

Adjustment

15 Tighten the hub nut to 18 lbf ft (25 Nm) while rotating the brake drum/hub (photo).

16 Loosen the hub nut, then retighten it to 3 lbf ft (5 Nm) while rotating the brake drum/hub. This torque can be approximately obtained by tightening the nut by hand as far as possible, using a socket only.

17 Locate the retainer on the nut so that the split pin holes align, then insert a new split pin and bend the legs circumferentially around the retainer.

18 Pack the hub cap with lithium-based grease, referring to Fig. 11.8. Locate the O-ring on its inner flange and tap it onto the brake drum/hub.

19 Refit the roadwheel and lower the car to the ground.

9 Rear stub axle and backplate – removal and refitting

1 Remove the rear brake shoes as described in Chapter 9.

2 Pinch the rear hydraulic hose with a brake hose clamp, or alternatively tighten the fluid reservoir cap onto a piece of plastic sheeting, in order to minimise the loss of fluid in the subsequent procedure.

3 Unscrew the brake pipe union nut from the wheel cylinder.

4 Unhook the handbrake cable from the brake shoe operating lever.

5 Bend the lockplate from the two retaining bolts, then unscrew all four bolts and withdraw the backplate, lockplate, and stub axle from the hub carrier (photo).

6 Separate the backplate from the stub axle and remove the O-ring.

7 Refitting is a reversal of removal, but use a new O-ring and lockplate. Tighten the bolts to the specified torque and use a cold chisel to bend the lockplate onto the bolt head flats. Refit the rear brake shoes and the brake drum and bleed the hydraulic system as described in Chapter 9.

8 Adjust the rear hub bearing as described in Section 8.

10 Rear lower arm – removal, overhaul and refitting

1 Chock the front wheels, then jack up the rear of the car and support it on axle stands. Remove the roadwheel.

2 Unscrew and remove the inner and outer pivot bolts together with the spring washer, dished washer and nut, and withdraw the lower arm from the car (photos).

3 Clean the lower arm and examine it for wear and damage. Check the bushes for wear and deterioration, and if necessary renew them using a long bolt, metal tube and washers.

4 Refitting is a reversal of removal, but finally tighten the pivot bolts to the specified torque with the weight of the car on the suspension.

9.5 The rear stub axle and backplate retaining bolts

10.2a Rear suspension lower arm outer pivot bolt

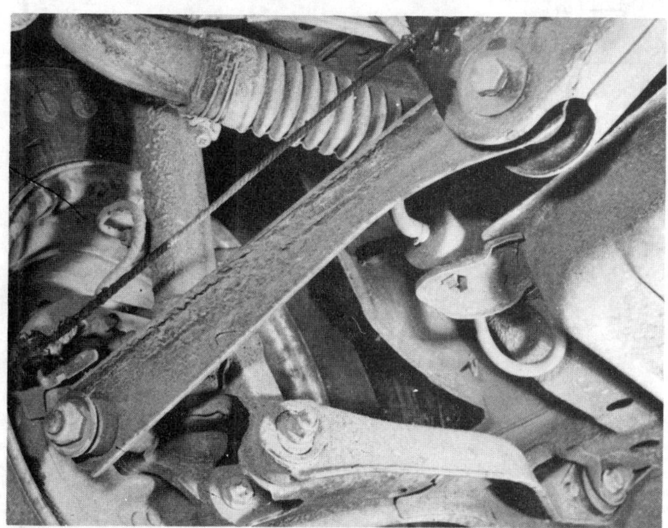

10.2b View of the rear suspension showing the lower arm and trailing arm

11.3 Rear suspension trailing arm front pivot bolt (arrowed)

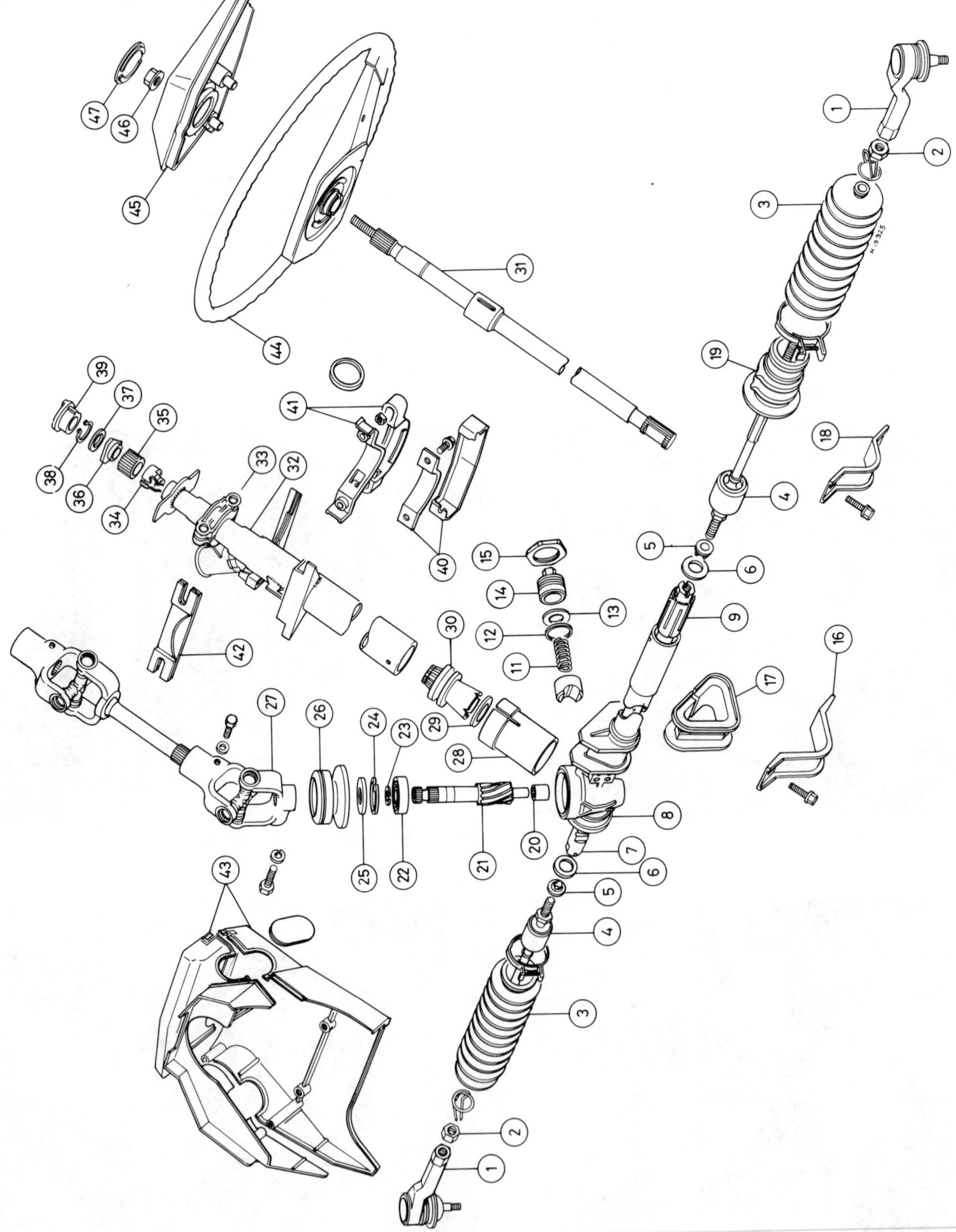
1
2
3
4
5
6
7
8
9
11
12
13
14
15
16
17
18
19
20
21
22
23
24
25
26
27
28
29
30
31
32
33
34
35
36
37
38
39
40
41
42
43
44
45
46
47

Fig. 11.9 Steering column and rack components (Secs 12 to 16)

1 Tie-rod ends
2 Locknuts
3 Bellows
4 Tie-rods
5 Lockwashers
6 Stop washers
7 Steering rack
8 Rack housing
9 Rack end bush
10 Damper
11 Pressure spring
12 Washer
13 Wavy washer
14 Guide screw
15 Locknut
16 Mounting bracket
17 Mounting rubber
18 Mounting bracket
19 Mounting rubber
20 Bearing – pinion spigot
21 Pinion
22 Bearing
23 Circlip
24 Snap-ring
25 Dust seal
26 Sealing grommet
27 Intermediate shaft
28 Column mounting collar
29 Washer
30 Bottom bush
31 Inner column
32 Steering column
33 Ignition switch and steering lock
34 Horn earth ring
35 Top bush
36 Thrust ring
37 Washer
38 Circlip
39 Cam – turn signal
40 Mounting bracket and cap
41 Mounting bracket and cap
42 Bending plate
43 Column shrouds
44 Steering wheel
45 Horn push
46 Nut
47 Centre pad

11 Rear trailing arm – removal, overhaul and refitting

1 Chock the front wheels, then jack up the rear of the car and support it on axle stands. Remove the roadwheel.
2 The inner pivot bolt connecting the trailing arm to the hub carrier incorporates an eccentric cam in order to adjust the rear wheel alignment. Before loosening the nut and bolt, scribe a line across the bolt head and the trailing arm, and another across the cam plate and the trailing arm, to ensure correct reassembly.
3 Unscrew and remove all three pivot bolts and withdraw the trailing arm from the car (photo).
4 Clean the trailing arm and examine it for wear and damage. Check the bushes in the trailing arm and hub carrier for wear and deterioration. Renewal of the hub carrier bushes is best achieved by removing the hub carrier from the strut and lower arm, removing the stub axle and backplate, and pressing out the bushes using a long bolt, metal tube, and washers. Press the new bushes centrally into the hub carrier.
5 To renew the front bushes, use a soft metal drift to remove the inner sleeve, then unscrew the bolts and remove the bushes and collar. Press the inner sleeve into the new bush so that it protrudes 8 mm (0.30 in) from the inner face. Fit both bushes and collar and tighten the bolts finger tight. Press the sleeve into the remaining bush so that it protrudes equally from each bush, then tighten the bolts.
6 Refitting is a reversal of removal, but make sure that the inner pivot bolt marks are aligned and finally tighten the bolts to the specified torque with the weight of the car on the suspension. The inner pivot bolt must not be moved when tightening its nut.
7 Check the rear wheel alignment as described in Section 17.

12 Steering wheel – removal and refitting

1 Set the front wheels in the straight-ahead position. Disconnect the battery earth lead.
2 Prise the cover from the centre of the steering wheel.
3 Mark the steering wheel and inner column in relation to each other, then unscrew and remove the retaining nut (photo).
4 Withdraw the steering wheel from the inner column splines using a rocking action (photo).
5 If necessary the horn push components can be dismantled by removing the cover screws and removing the springs, slip ring, and contact ring. Reassemble the steering wheel in the reverse order.
6 Refitting is a reversal of removal, but align the previously made marks and tighten the retaining nut to the specified torque.

13 Steering column – removal, overhaul and refitting

1 Remove the steering wheel as described in Section 12.
2 Extract the turn signal cancelling cam from the combination switch.
3 Prise out the fasteners and remove the cover from the bottom of the column.
4 Unscrew and remove the pinch-bolt securing the intermediate shaft to the inner column.
5 Disconnect the combination switch and ignition switch wiring connectors.
6 Unscrew the nuts from the upper mounting and the bolts from the lower mounting (photos).
7 Remove the mounting caps and seat and withdraw the steering column from the car.
8 Remove the combination switch as described in Chapter 10
9 Remove the rubber bands and the upper mounting bending plate and seat.
10 Extract the circlip and remove the washer from the top of the column.
11 Turn the ignition switch to position '1'.
12 Prise the plastic collar from the bottom of the column, followed by the washer and bottom bush.
13 Slide the inner column (steering shaft) from the bottom of the column.
14 Extract the thrust ring, top bush, and the horn earth ring from the top of the column.
15 Wash all components (except electrical switches) with paraffin

12.3 Unscrew the retaining nut ...

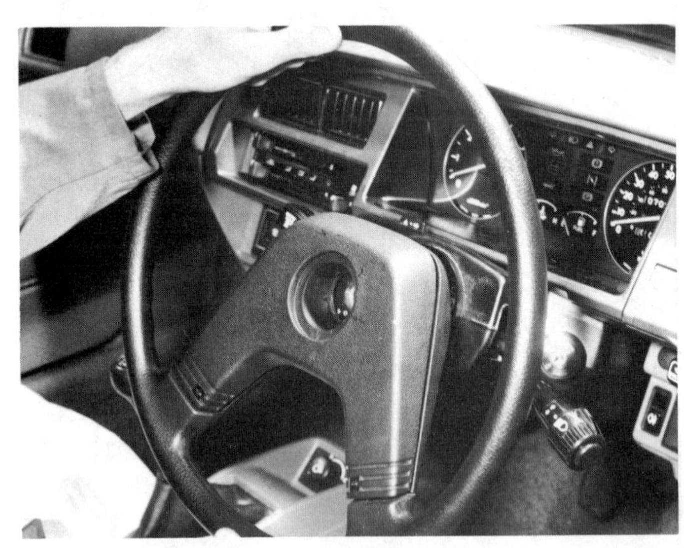

12.4 ... and remove the steering wheel

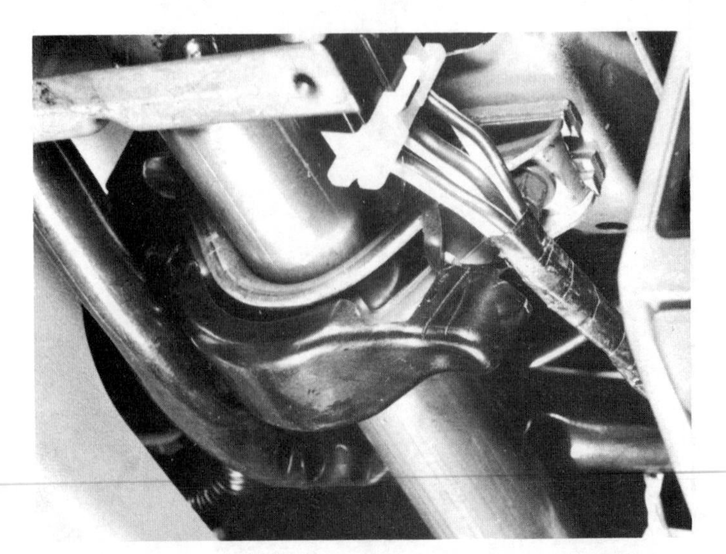

13.6a Remove the plastic cap ...

13.6b ... to gain access to the steering column upper mounting nuts (right-hand nut obscured by cable)

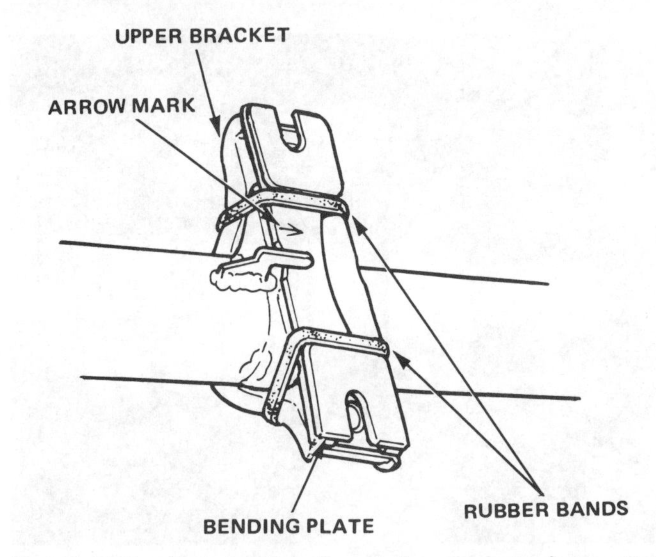

Fig. 11.10 Bending plate location on the steering column upper mounting – the arrow must face downwards (Sec 13)

and wipe dry. Examine them for wear and damage and renew them where necessary. Check the inner column for straightness by rolling it on a flat surface. Check that the bending plate is not distorted.
16 Reassembly is a reversal of dismantling, but lubricate the bushes with grease and lightly oil the inner column to prevent the formation of rust. Make sure that the round projection inside the plastic collar

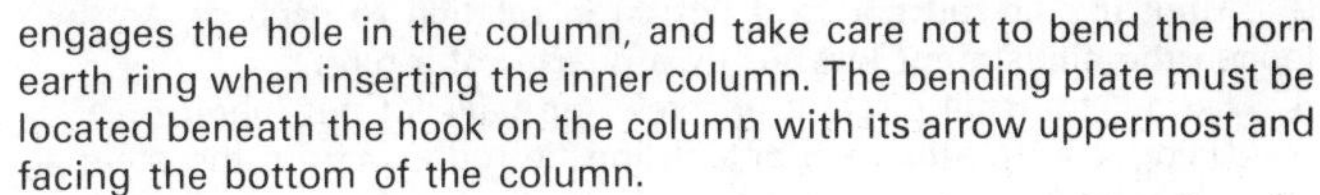

engages the hole in the column, and take care not to bend the horn earth ring when inserting the inner column. The bending plate must be located beneath the hook on the column with its arrow uppermost and facing the bottom of the column.
17 Refitting is a reversal of removal, but before tightening the intermediate shaft pinch-bolt, make sure that the shaft is pushed fully onto the inner column. Tighten all nuts and bolts to the specified torque.

14 Steering column lock/ignition switch – removal and refitting

1 Disconnect the battery negative lead.
2 Remove the cross-head screws and withdraw the lower shroud from the steering column. Remove the plastic cover.
3 Disconnect the ignition switch wiring connector.
4 Unscrew the sheer bolts retaining the lock/ignition switch to the column. To do this either drill off their heads or use a centre-punch to release them.
5 Remove the lock/ignition switch from the column and where necessary remove the remains of the shear bolts. If difficulty is experienced, drill them out using a 6 mm (0.25 in) twist drill, or use a stud extractor.
6 Refitting is a reversal of removal, but locate the lock/ignition switch on the column without inserting the key, and check the operation of the lock before finally tightening the shear bolt heads until they break off.

15 Intermediate steering shaft – removal and refitting

1 Prise out the fasteners and remove the cover from the bottom of the column.
2 Mark the intermediate shaft and the rack pinion in relation to each other.
3 Unscrew and remove the pinch-bolts securing the intermediate shaft to the inner steering column and rack pinion.
4 With the steering in the straight-ahead position, pull the intermediate shaft first from the inner column and then from the rack pinion.
5 Check the universal joints for excessive wear and if necessary renew the shaft.
6 Refitting is a reversal of removal, but align the previously made masks and also align the upper bolt hole with the flat on the inner column. Before tightening the upper bolt, press down on the steering wheel and at the same time press the shaft up to the column. Finally tighten the bottom bolt.

16 Tie-rod end and rack bellows – removal and refitting

Tie-rod end – removal

1 If the tie-rod end balljoint is worn excessively, free play is evident when attempting to move the tie-rod up and down. In this case the tie-rod end must be renewed.
2 Jack up the front of the car and support it on axle stands. Apply the handbrake and remove the roadwheel.

16.4 Tie-rod end balljoint

16.5 Using a separator tool to detach the tie-rod end from the steering knuckle

16.8 Steering rack bellows inner clip (right-hand side)

3 Mark the tie-rod end and tie-rod in relation to each other, then loosen the adjustment locknut by a quarter of a turn.
4 Extract the split pin and unscrew the balljoint nut (photo).
5 Using a separator tool, detach the tie-rod end from the steering knuckle (photo).
6 Unscrew the tie-rod end from the tie-rod, noting the exact number of turns necessary to remove it.

Rack bellows – removal

7 With the tie-rod end removed, unscrew the locknut from the tie-rod.
8 Remove the small clip from the bellows, then unscrew the large clip and release it from the other end of the bellows (photo).
9 Pull the bellows from the rack housing and tie-rod.

Refitting

10 Refitting is a reversal of removal, but before installing the bellows coat the inner surfaces with multi-purpose lithium-based grease. Also pack grease around the tie-rod inner joint.
11 When installing the tie-rod end, align the previously made marks and tighten the nuts to the specified torque. Always use a new split pin.
12 When completed, check the front wheel alignment as described in Section 17.

17 Wheel alignment – checking and adjusting

1 Accurate wheel alignment is essential for good steering and slow tyre wear, and in this context a good wheel alignment gauge must be used. If such a gauge is not available, have the alignment checked professionally.
2 Place the car on level ground with the wheels in the straight-ahead position. The car must be unladen and the tyres correctly inflated.
3 Rock the car from side to side, then roll it backwards 12 ft (4 metres) and forwards again in order to settle the suspension and steering.
4 Using a wheel alignment gauge, check that the front or rear wheel alignment is within the limits given in the Specifications.
5 If adjustment is necessary on the front wheels, loosen the tie-rod and locknuts on *both* tie-rods and release the bellows outer clips. Rotate each tie-rod by equal amounts until the alignment is correct. There must be equal amounts of visible thread on each tie-rod. Tighten the locknuts, make sure that the bellows are not twisted, then refit the outer clips.
6 If adjustment is necessary on the rear wheels, loosen the locknuts on *both* trailing arm inner pivot bolts while holding the three bolt heads stationary, then rotate each bolt head by equal amounts until the alignment is correct. With the spanner hanging down from the bolt head, move it forwards to increase the toe-in or rearwards to decrease the toe-in. Finally tighten the locknuts which holding the bolt heads stationary.
7 Camber and castor angles are preset and cannot be adjusted. However, if their accuracy is suspect, they can be checked by a suitably equipped garage.

18 Steering rack and pinion – removal, overhaul and refitting

1 Jack up the front of the car and support it on axle stands. Apply the handbrake and remove the roadwheels. Set the steering in the straight-ahead position.
2 Prise out the fasteners and remove the cover from the bottom of the steering column.
3 Mark the intermediate shaft and rack pinion in relation to each other, then remove the pinch-bolt and pull up the intermediate shaft as far as possible.
4 Remove the tie-rod ends as described in Section 16.
5 Unscrew the mounting bracket bolts and remove the bracket clamps (photos).
6 Lower the rack assembly and disconnect the pinion from the intermediate shaft, then rotate the assembly 180° and withdraw it from the right-hand side of the car.
7 Remove the pinion sealing grommet from the floor aperture.

18.5a Steering gear right-hand mounting bracket clamp

18.5b Steering gear left-hand mounting bracket clamp

8 Grip the rack assembly in a soft-jawed vice.
9 Remove the pinion end mounting rubber from the rack housing.
10 Unscrew the locknuts from the tie-rods. Remove the clips and pull off the bellows.
11 Straighten the tie-rod lockwashers, then unscrew the tie-rods while holding the rack stationary with a spanner. Remove the lockwashers and plain washers.
12 Loosen the rack damper locknut, unscrew the adjustment screw, and withdraw the washers, spring, and damper pad.
13 Prise out the pinion dust seal and extract the large snap-ring from the pinion bearing. Pull the pinion and bearing from the rack housing. Extract the small circlip and drive the pinion out of the bearing.
14 Slide the rack from the pinion end of the housing.
15 Slide the rubber mounting from the opposite end of the housing and extract the rack and bush.
16 Clean all components in paraffin and wipe dry. Examine them for wear and damage and renew them as necessary. In particular check the rack and pinion teeth for wear and pitting, the damper spring for correct free length (see Specifications), and the tie-rod balljoints for excessive wear. Before buying new components, compare their cost with that of a new or reconditioned unit.
17 Drive the bearing onto the pinion using a metal tube on the inner race – the shield end of the bearing must be uppermost. Pack grease into the bearing.

18 Smear the *inner* surface of the rack end bush with grease and slide it into the housing so that the projections engage the holes. **Do not** grease the outer surface, as this would restrict the air channels.
19 Slide the rubber mounting onto the housing, flush with the end face.
20 Grease the rack teeth and lightly smear grease on the rest of the rack surface, then insert the rack from the pinion end and centralize it.
21 Pack the pinion housing with 25 to 35 g (0.9 to 1.2 oz) of grease, then insert the pinion and bearing and fit the large snap-ring.
22 Press the pinion dust seal into the housing.
23 Grease the damper pad and install it together with the spring, washers, and adjustment screw, which should have sealing compound applied to its threads. Screw in the adjustment screw until it just touches the damper pad, then back it off one eighth of a turn. Fit and tighten the locknut.
24 Screw the tie-rods onto the rack together with new plain washers and lockwashers, making sure that the lockwasher tabs engage the slots in the rack.
25 Hold the rack stationary with a spanner and tighten the tie-rods to the specified torque. Bend the lockwashers onto one flat of the tie-rods.
26 Coat the inner surfaces of the bellows with grease and refit them to the housing, together with the clips. Screw the locknuts onto the tie-rods.
27 Fit the pinion and mounting rubber to the housing.
28 Refitting is a reversal of removal, but first centralize the rack within the housing and set the front roadwheels in the straight-ahead position. Tighten all nuts and bolts to the specified torque, and when completed check the front wheel alignment as described in Section 17.

19 Roadwheels and tyres – general

1 Clean the insides of the roadwheels whenever they are removed. If necessary, remove any rust and repaint them.
2 At the same time remove any flints or stones which may have become embedded in the tyres. Examine the tyres for damage and splits. Where the depth of tread is almost down to the legal minimum, renew them.
3 The wheels should be rebalanced half way through the life of the tyres to compensate for loss of rubber.
4 Check and adjust the tyre pressures regularly and make sure that the dust caps are correctly fitted. Remember to also check the spare tyre.
5 If it is wished to rotate the positions of the tyres to even out wear, note that tyres should only be moved from front to rear (and vice versa) on the same side of the vehicle, not from side to side.

20 Fault diagnosis – suspension and steering

Symptom	Reason(s)
Excessive play in steering	Worn rack and pinion or tie-rods Worn tie-rod end balljoints Worn suspension balljoints
Wanders or pulls to one side	Incorrect wheel alignment Worn tie-rod end balljoints Worn suspension balljoints Uneven tyre pressures Braking system fault
Heavy or stiff steering	Seized balljoint Incorrect wheel alignment Low tyre pressures Lack of lubricant in rack and pinion Incorrect adjustment of rack damper
Wheel wobble and vibration	Roadwheels out of balance Roadwheels damaged Worn shock absorbers Worn wheel bearings
Excessive tyre wear	Incorrect wheel alignment Worn shock absorbers Incorrect tyre pressures Roadwheels out of balance

Chapter 12 Bodywork and fittings

For modifications, and information applicable to later models, see Supplement at end of manual

Contents

1 General description

The bodyshell and underframe are of all-steel welded construction, being developed and assembled by the most modern methods. The side door apertures and rear panels are of one-piece construction for additional strength, and the front wings are of the bolt-on type for easy replacement.

The passenger compartment is of 'safety cell' design, where the bonnet and boot compartments absorb impact energy in the event of a collision. The floor is double-skinned in order to minimise engine and road noise.

The bodyshell is given several anti-corrosion treatments during manufacture, including a PVC underbody seal. Plastic liners are fitted to the front wheel arches.

2 Maintenance – bodywork and underframe

1 The general condition of a vehicle's bodywork is the one thing that significantly affects its value. Maintenance is easy but needs to be regular. Neglect, particularly after minor damage, can lead quickly to further deterioration and costly repair bills. It is important also to keep watch on those parts of the vehicle not immediately visible, for instance the underside, inside all the wheel arches and the lower part of the engine compartment.

2 The basic maintenance routine for the bodywork is washing – preferably with a lot of water, from a hose. This will remove all the loose solids which may have stuck to the vehicle. It is important to flush these off in such a way as to prevent grit from scratching the finish. The wheel arches and underframe need washing in the same way to remove any accumulated mud which will retain moisture and tend to encourage rust. Paradoxically enough, the best time to clean the underframe and wheel arches is in wet weather when the mud is thoroughly wet and soft. In very wet weather the underframe is usually cleaned of large accumulations automatically and this is a good time for inspection.

3 Periodically, except on vehicles with a wax-based underbody protective coating, it is a good idea to have the whole of the underframe of the vehicle steam cleaned, engine compartment included, so that a thorough inspection can be carried out to see what minor repairs and renovations are necessary. Steam cleaning is available at many garages and is necessary for removal of the accumulation of oily grime which sometimes is allowed to become thick in certain areas. If steam cleaning facilities are not available, there are one or two excellent grease solvents available, such as Holts Engine Cleaner or Holts Foambrite, which can be brush applied. The dirt can then be simply hosed off. Note that these methods should not be used on vehicles with wax-based underbody protective coating or the coating will be removed. Such vehicles should be inspected annually, preferably just prior to winter, when the underbody should be washed down and any damage to the wax coating repaired using Holts Undershield. Ideally, a completely fresh coat should be applied. It would also be worth considering the use of such wax-based protection for injection into door panels, sills, box sections, etc, as an additional safeguard against rust damage where such protection is not provided by the vehicle manufacturer.

4 After washing paintwork, wipe off with a chamois leather to give an unspotted clear finish. A coat of clear protective wax polish, like the many excellent Turtle Wax polishes, will give added protection against chemical pollutants in the air. If the paintwork sheen has dulled or oxidised, use a cleaner/polisher combination such as Turtle Extra to restore the brilliance of the shine. This requires a little effort, but such dulling is usually caused because regular washing has been neglected. Care needs to be taken with metallic paintwork, as special non-abrasive cleaner/polisher is required to avoid damage to the finish. Always check that the door and ventilator opening drain holes and pipes are completely clear so that water can be drained out (photos). Bright work should be treated in the same way as paint work. Windscreens and windows can be kept clear of the smeary film which often appears by the use of a proprietary glass cleaner like Holts Mixra. Never use any form of wax or other body or chromium polish on glass.

3 Maintenance – upholstery and carpets

Mats and carpets should be brushed or vacuum cleaned regularly to keep them free of grit. If they are badly stained remove them from the vehicle for scrubbing or sponging and make quite sure they are dry before refitting. Seats and interior trim panels can be kept clean by wiping with a damp cloth and Turtle Wax Carisma. If they do become stained (which can be more apparent on light coloured upholstery) use a little liquid detergent and a soft nail brush to scour the grime out of the grain of the material. Do not forget to keep the headlining clean in the same way as the upholstery. When using liquid cleaners inside the vehicle do not over-wet the surfaces being cleaned. Excessive damp could get into the seams and padded interior causing stains, offensive odours or even rot. If the inside of the vehicle gets wet accidentally it is worthwhile taking some trouble to dry it out properly, particularly where carpets are involved. *Do not leave oil or electric heaters inside the vehicle for this purpose.*

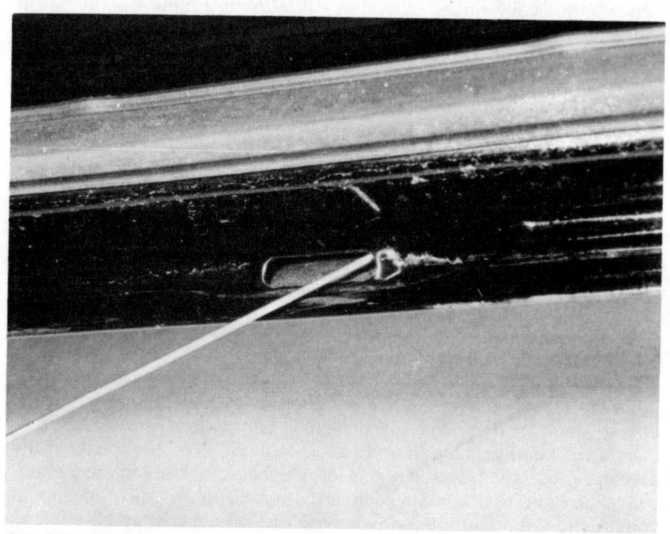
2.4a Clearing a door drain hole with a piece of wire

2.4b Clearing a sill drain hole with a piece of wire

4 Minor body damage - repair

The colour bodywork repair photographic sequences between pages 32 and 33 illustrate the operations detailed in the following sub-sections.

Note: *For more detailed information about bodywork repair, the Haynes Publishing Group publish a book by Lindsay Porter called The Car Bodywork Repair Manual. This incorporates information on such aspects as rust treatment, painting and glass fibre repairs, as well as details on more ambitious repairs involving welding and panel beating.*

Repair of minor scratches in bodywork

If the scratch is very superficial, and does not penetrate to the metal of the bodywork, repair is very simple. Lightly rub the area of the scratch with a paintwork renovator like Turtle Wax New Color Back, or a very fine cutting paste like Holts Body + Plus Rubbing Compound to remove loose paint from the scratch and to clear the surrounding bodywork of wax polish. Rinse the area with clean water.

Apply touch-up paint, such as Holts Dupli-Color Color Touch or a paint film like Holts Autofilm, to the scratch using a fine paint brush; continue to apply fine layers of paint until the surface of the paint in the scratch is level with the surrounding paintwork. Allow the new paint at least two weeks to harden: then blend it into the surrounding paintwork by rubbing the scratch area with a paintwork renovator or a very fine cutting paste, such as Holts Body + Plus Rubbing Compound or Turtle Wax New Color Back. Finally, apply wax polish from one of the Turtle Wax range of wax polishes.

Where the scratch has penetrated right through to the metal of the bodywork, causing the metal to rust, a different repair technique is required. Remove any loose rust from the bottom of the scratch with a penknife, then apply rust inhibiting paint, such as Turtle Wax Rust Master, to prevent the formation of rust in the future. Using a rubber or nylon applicator fill the scratch with bodystopper paste like Holts Body + Plus Knifing Putty. If required, this paste can be mixed with cellulose thinners, such as Holts Body + Plus Cellulose Thinners, to provide a very thin paste which is ideal for filling narrow scratches. Before the stopper-paste in the scratch hardens, wrap a piece of smooth cotton rag around the top of a finger. Dip the finger in cellulose thinners, such as Holts Body + Plus Cellulose Thinners, and then quickly sweep it across the surface of the stopper-paste in the scratch; this will ensure that the surface of the stopper-paste is slightly hollowed. The scratch can now be painted over as described earlier in this Section.

Repair of dents in bodywork

When deep denting of the vehicle's bodywork has taken place, the first task is to pull the dent out, until the affected bodywork almost attains its original shape. There is little point in trying to restore the original shape completely, as the metal in the damaged area will have stretched on impact and cannot be reshaped fully to its original contour. It is better to bring the level of the dent up to a point which is about $\frac{1}{8}$ in (3 mm) below the level of the surrounding bodywork. In cases where the dent is very shallow anyway, it is not worth trying to pull it out at all. If the underside of the dent is accessible, it can be hammered out gently from behind, using a mallet with a wooden or plastic head. Whilst doing this, hold a suitable block of wood firmly against the outside of the panel to absorb the impact from the hammer blows and thus prevent a large area of the bodywork from being 'belled-out'.

Should the dent be in a section of the bodywork which has a double skin or some other factor making it inaccessible from behind, a different technique is called for. Drill several small holes through the metal inside the area - particulary in the deeper section. Then screw long self-tapping screws into the holes just sufficiently for them to gain a good purchase in the metal. Now the dent can be pulled out by pulling on the protruding heads of the screws with a pair of pliers.

The next stage of the repair is the removal of the paint from the damaged area, and from an inch or so of the surrounding 'sound' bodywork. This is accomplished most easily by using a wire brush or abrasive pad on a power drill, although it can be done just as effectively by hand using sheets of abrasive paper. To complete the preparation for filling, score the surface of the bare metal with a screwdriver or the tang of a file, or alternatively, drill small holes in the affected area. This will provide a really good 'key' for the filler paste.

To complete the repair see the Section on filling and re-spraying.

Repair of rust holes or gashes in bodywork

Remove all paint from the affected area and from an inch or so of the surrounding 'sound' bodywork, using an abrasive pad or a wire brush on a power drill. If these are not available a few sheets of abrasive paper will do the job just as effectively. With the paint removed you will be able to gauge the severity of the corrosion and therefore decide whether to renew the whole panel (if this is possible) or to repair the affected area. New body panels are not as expensive as most people think and it is often quicker and more satisfactory to fit a new panel than to attempt to repair large areas of corrosion.

Remove all fittings from the affected area except those which will act as a guide to the original shape of the damaged bodywork (eg headlamp shells etc). Then, using tin snips or a hacksaw blade, remove all loose metal and any other metal badly affected by corrosion. Hammer the edges of the hole inwards in order to create a slight depression for the filler paste.

Wire brush the affected area to remove the powdery rust from the surface of the remaining metal. Paint the affected area with rust inhibiting paint like Turtle Rust Master; if the back of the rusted area is accessible treat this also.

Before filling can take place it will be necessary to block the hole in some way. This can be achieved by the use of aluminium or plastic mesh, or aluminium tape.

Aluminium or plastic mesh or glass fibre matting, such as the Holts

Body + Plus Glass Fibre Matting, is probably the best material to use for a large hole. Cut a piece to the approximate size and shape of the hole to be filled, then position it in the hole so that its edges are below the level of the surrounding bodywork. It can be retained in position by several blobs of filler paste around its periphery.

Aluminium tape should be used for small or very narrow holes. Pull a piece off the roll and trim it to the approximate size and shape required, then pull off the backing paper (if used) and stick the tape over the hole; it can be overlapped if the thickness of one piece is insufficient. Burnish down the edges of the tape with the handle of a screwdriver or similar, to ensure that the tape is securely attached to the metal underneath.

Bodywork repairs – filling and re-spraying

Before using this Section, see the Sections on dent, deep scratch, rust holes and gash repairs.

Many types of bodyfiller are available, but generally speaking those proprietary kits which contain a tin of filler paste and a tube of resin hardener are best for this type of repair, like Holts Body + Plus or Holts No Mix which can be used directly from the tube. A wide, flexible plastic or nylon applicator will be found invaluable for imparting a smooth and well contoured finish to the surface of the filler.

Mix up a little filler on a clean piece of card or board – measure the hardener carefully (follow the maker's instructions on the pack) otherwise the filler will set too rapidly or too slowly. Alternatively, Holts No Mix can be used straight from the tube without mixing, but daylight is required to cure it. Using the applicator apply the filler paste to the prepared area; draw the applicator across the surface of the filler to achieve the correct contour and to level the filler surface. As soon as a contour that approximates to the correct one is achieved, stop working the paste – if you carry on too long the paste will become sticky and begin to 'pick up' on the applicator. Continue to add thin layers of filler paste at twenty-minute intervals until the level of the filler is just proud of the surrounding bodywork.

Once the filler has hardened, excess can be removed using a metal plane or file. From then on, progressively finer grades of abrasive paper should be used, starting with a 40 grade production paper and finishing with 400 grade wet-and-dry paper. Always wrap the abrasive paper around a flat rubber, cork, or wooden block – otherwise the surface of the filler will not be completely flat. During the smoothing of the filler surface the wet-and-dry paper should be periodically rinsed in water. This will ensure tnat a very smooth finish is imparted to the filler at the final stage.

At this stage the 'dent' should be surrounded by a ring of bare metal, which in turn should be encircled by the finely 'feathered' edge of the good paintwork. Rinse the repair area with clean water, until all of the dust produced by the rubbing-down operation has gone.

Spray the whole repair area with a light coat of primer, either Holts Body + Plus Grey or Red Oxide Primer – this will show up any imperfections in the surface of the filler. Repair these imperfections with fresh filler paste or bodystopper, and once more smooth the surface with abrasive paper. If bodystopper is used, it can be mixed with cellulose thinners to form a really thin paste which is ideal for filling small holes. Repeat this spray and repair procedure until you are satisfied that the surface of the filler, and the feathered edge of the paintwork are perfect. Clean the repair area with clean water and allow to dry fully.

The repair area is now ready for final spraying. Paint spraying must be carried out in a warm, dry, windless and dust free atmosphere. This condition can be created artificially if you have access to a large indoor working area, but if you are forced to work in the open, you will have to pick your day very carefully. If you are working indoors, dousing the floor in the work area with water will help to settle the dust which would otherwise be in the atmosphere. If the repair area is confined to one body panel, mask off the surrounding panels; this will help to minimise the effects of a slight mis-match in paint colours. Bodywork fittings (eg chrome strips, door handles etc) will also need to be masked off. Use genuine masking tape and several thicknesses of newspaper for the masking operations.

Before commencing to spray, agitate the aerosol can thoroughly, then spray a test area (an old tin, or similar) until the technique is mastered. Cover the repair area with a thick coat of primer; the thickness should be built up using several thin layers of paint rather than one thick one. Using 400 grade wet-and-dry paper, rub down the surface of the primer until it is really smooth. While doing this, the work area should be thoroughly doused with water, and the wet-and-dry paper periodically rinsed in water. Allow to dry before spraying on more paint.

Spray on the top coat using Holts Dupli-Color Autospray, again building up the thickness by using several thin layers of paint. Start spraying in the centre of the repair area and then, with a single side-to-side motion, work outwards until the whole repair area and about 2 inches of the surrounding original paintwork is covered. Remove all masking material 10 to 15 minutes after spraying on the final coat of paint.

Allow the new paint at least two weeks to harden, then, using a paintwork renovator or a very fine cutting paste such as Turtle Wax New Color Back or Holts Body + Plus Rubbing Compound, blend the edges of the paint into the existing paintwork. Finally, apply wax polish.

5 Major body damage – repair

Where serious damage has occurred or large areas need renewal due to neglect, it means certainly that completely new sections or panels will need welding in and this is best left to professionals. If the damage is due to impact, it will also be necessary to completely check the alignment of the bodyshell structure. Due to the principle of construction, the strength and shape of the whole car can be affected by damage to one part. In such instances the services of a BL agent with specialist checking jigs are essential. If a body is left misaligned it is first of all dangerous as the car will not handle properly, and secondly uneven stresses will be imposed on the steering, engine and transmission, causing abnormal wear or complete failure. Tyre wear may also be excessive.

6 Maintenance – hinges and locks

1 Oil the hinges of the bonnet, boot lid and doors with a drop or two of light oil every 15 000 miles (24 000 km). Also oil the bonnet lock and release cable.

2 **Do not** attempt to lubricate the steering lock, as this would attract dust and dirt which would be detrimental to the lock mechanism. In addition, if oil penetrated the ignition switch this might cause it to malfunction.

7 Door rattles – tracing and rectification

1 Check first that the door is not loose at the hinges, and that the latch is holding the door firmly in position. Check also that the door lines up with the aperture in the body. If the door is out of alignment adjust it as described in Sections 17 and 19.

2 It the latch is holding the door in the correct position but the latch still rattles, the lock mechanism is worn and should be renewed.

3 Other rattles from the door could be caused by wear in the window operating mechanism, interior lock mechanism, or loose glass channels.

8 Bonnet – removal, refitting and adjustment

1 Remove the four radiator grille securing screws. Release the two grille clips by prying their tongues apart with the flat of a screwdriver. Pull the grille forward, unclipping its ends from the headlamp surrounds. To remove each headlamp surround, open the bonnet and remove the top securing screw (photo).

2 Mark the location of the hinges on the body using a pencil (photo).

3 Open the bonnet and rest it on the lock, then place some cardboard or rags between the bonnet and front panel.

4 Loosen the hinge bolts and extract the shims under each hinge, noting their location.

5 With the help of an assistant unscrew the bolts, and withdraw the bonnet from the car.

6 Refitting is a reversal of removal, but when the bonnet is shut, check that the front edge is level with the front wings. If not, loosen the hinge bolts, reposition the bonnet, and tighten the bolts. Check that the bonnet rear edge is level with the front wings and windscreen valance, and if necessary adjust the position of the bonnet lock (photo). Note that on models equipped with air conditioning the throttle boost solenoid must be removed. Finally check that the gaps on each side of the bonnet are equal; if necessary, alter the shim thickness at the hinges and reposition the lock.

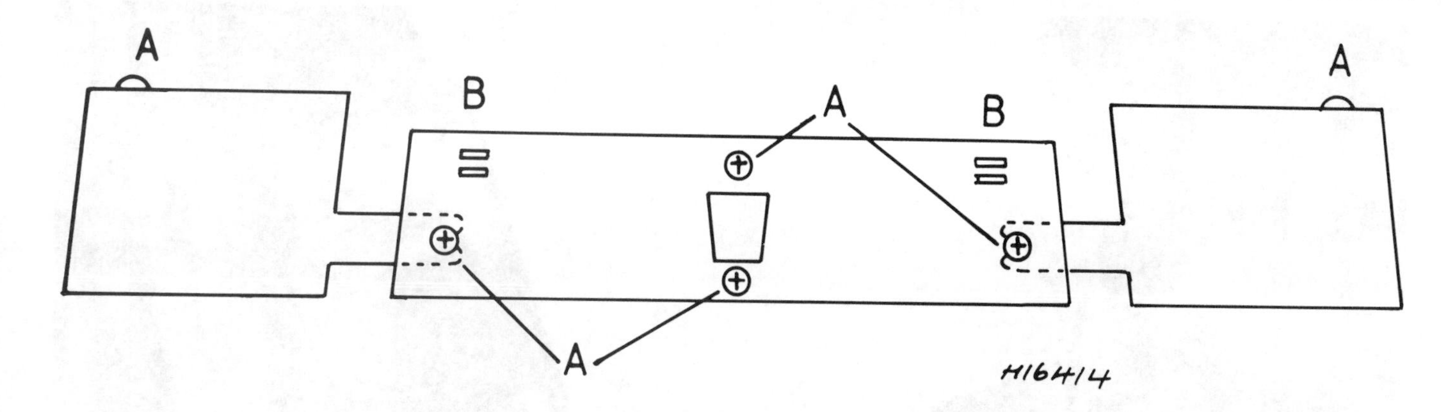

Fig. 12.1 Radiator grille and headlight surround attachments (Sec 8)

A Cross-head screws *B Clips*

8.1 Removing a radiator grille securing screw

8.2 A bonnet hinge

8.6 Bonnet lock – note cable routing

9 Front wing – removal and refitting

1 Disconnect the battery negative lead.
2 Prise the cap from the front bumper tailpiece, unscrew the two bolts, and withdraw the tailpiece.
3 Unscrew the bolts and remove the headlight shroud.
4 Disconnect the wiring and remove the side repeater lamp from the front wing.
5 Remove the rubbing strip and mud flap.
6 Unscrew the mounting bolts and withdraw the front wing from the car.
7 If necessary remove the plastic wheel arch liners.
8 Refitting is a reversal of removal. If a new wing is being fitted, paint it first.

10 Boot lid – removal, refitting and adjustment

1 Remove the boot lock as described in Section 13.
2 Disconnect the wiring from the number plate lamp, then remove the screws and prise off the hinge cover (photo).
3 Unclip and remove the wiring harness and release cable from the boot lid.
4 Mark the location of the hinges on the boot lid using a pencil.

10.2 Boot lid hinge arm and cover

10.7 Boot lid striker

5 Have an assistant support the boot lid in its open position, and place some cardboard or rags between the boot lid and the body.
6 Unscrew the hinge bolts and withdraw the boot lid from the car – note the location of any shims.
7 Refitting is a reversal of removal, but make sure that the wiring harness and release cable are not overstretched with the boot lid fully open. Check that the boot lid is level with the surrounding body and central in the aperture. If necessary, shims may be removed from or added to the hinges to alter the height. Fore-and-aft movement is possible by means of the elongated bolt holes. Adjustment is also possible on the striker (photo).

11 Bonnet release cable – removal and refitting

1 Open the bonnet and release the outer cable from the bonnet lock.
2 Disconnect the inner cable from the lock lever.
3 Working inside the car, remove the screws from the bonnet release handle bracket.
4 Prise out the rubber grommet and withdraw the cable through the bulkhead.
5 Refitting is a reversal of removal, but position the cable to avoid any sharp curves.

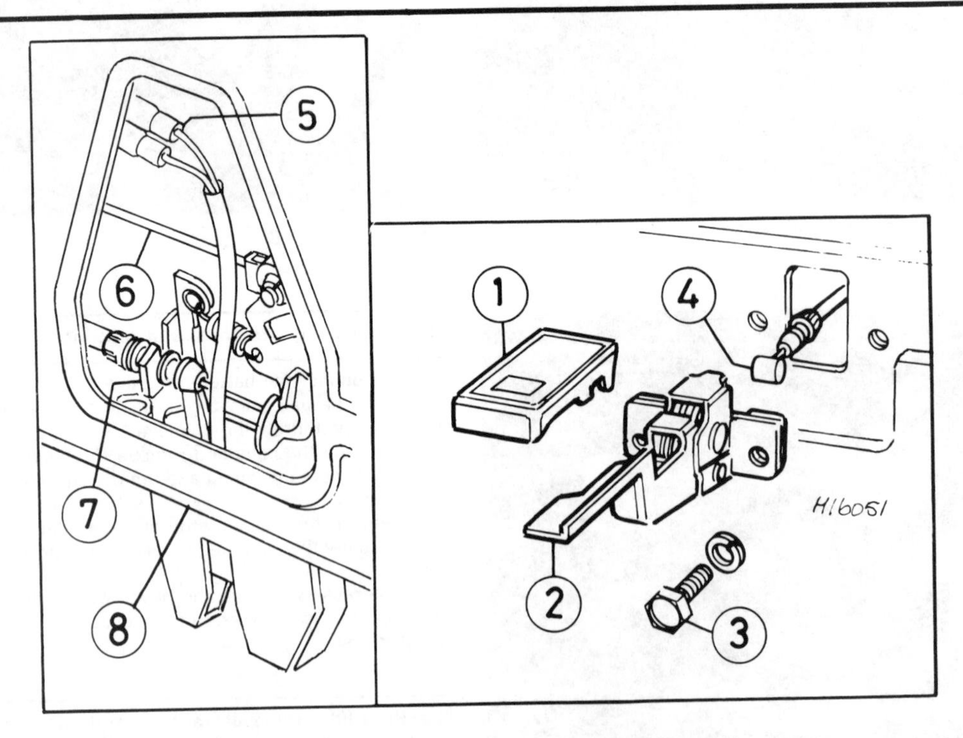

Fig. 12.2 Boot release cable components (Sec 12)

1 Knob
2 Release handle
3 Bolt
4 Cable
5 Number plate lamp leads
6 Private lock operating rod
7 Lock
8 Boot lid

13.5a Outer view of boot lock

13.5b Inner view of boot lock with cover removed

14.1 Boot private lock

12 Boot lid release cable – removal and refitting

1 Remove the driver's seat and the rear seat as described in Section 24. Open the boot lid.
2 Pull off the boot lid release knob, and (if fitted) the fuel filler release knob.
3 Prise out the clips and remove the front and rear inner sill mouldings.
4 Unscrew the release lever mounting bolts, withdraw the lever assembly, and disconnect the inner and outer cables for the boot lid release.
5 Remove the screw and withdraw the cover from the boot lid hinge.
6 Remove the boot lock as described in Section 13.
7 Release the cable from the retaining clips and withdraw it from the car.
8 Refitting is a reversal of removal. Note that the outer cable has three adjustment grooves at the boot lock end, and the cable should be positioned in the groove which gives the most satisfactory release action.

13 Boot lock – removal and refitting

1 Open the boot lid and prise out the lock access plate.
2 Disconnect the battery negative lead.
3 Disconnect the private lock operating rod from the boot lock.
4 Disconnect the number plate lamp wiring.
5 Unscrew the mounting bolts and withdraw the lock, then unhook the release cable and remove the lock (photos).
6 Refitting is a reversal of removal, but fit the outer release cable in the adjustment groove which gives the most satisfactory release action.

14 Boot private lock – removal and refitting

1 Open the boot lid and pull off the adhesive sheet at the back of the lock (photo).
2 Disconnect the operating rod from the lock.
3 Pull out the spring clip and withdraw the private lock and seal from the boot lid.
4 If necessary the lock barrel can be removed by extracting the circlip, removing the arm and spring, and pulling out the barrel with the key inserted.
5 Refitting is a reversal of removal, but renew the seal if necessary and make sure that the lock arm is fitted the correct way round.

15 Door trim pad – removal and refitting

1 Remove the screws and withdraw the armrest (photo).
2 Prise the square-headed retainer from the remote door handle trim plate and remove the trim plate (photos).
3 On models with manually-operated windows, extract the spring clip from the inner edge of the regulator handle and remove the handle and escutcheon (photo).
4 On the front doors, unscrew the nut and remove the escutcheon from the exterior mirror remote control (where applicable).
5 Using a wide-bladed screwdriver, release the trim pad retaining clips from the door inner panel, starting at the bottom corners. Pull off the locking button.
6 Withdraw the trim pad and, on models with electrically-operated windows, disconnect the multi-plug.
7 Refitting is a reversal of removal. On models with manually-operated windows, position the regulator handle pointing forwards and 45° upwards with the window shut.

16 Front door private lock – removal and refitting

1 Remove the door trim pad as described in Section 15.
2 Carefully pull off the polythene sheet.
3 Disconnect the operating rod (photo).
4 Pull out the spring clip and withdraw the private lock and seal from the door.

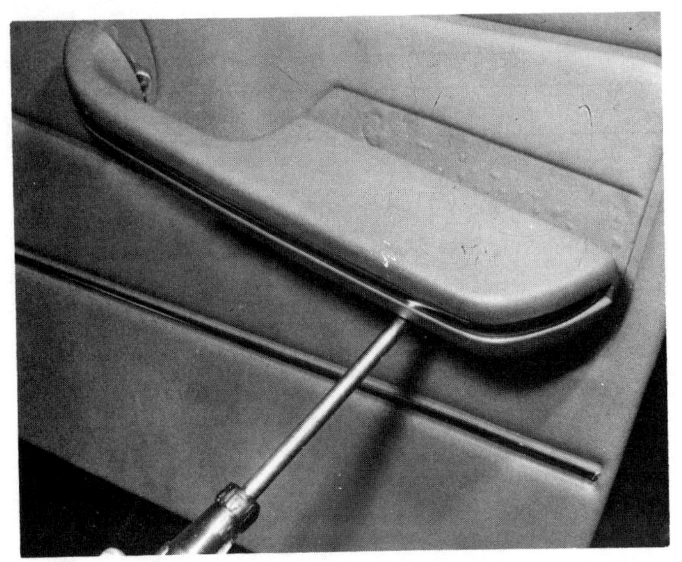

15.1 Removing the armrest

15.2a Prise out the retainer ...

15.2b ...and remove the trim plate from the remote door handle

15.3 Window regulator handle showing clip

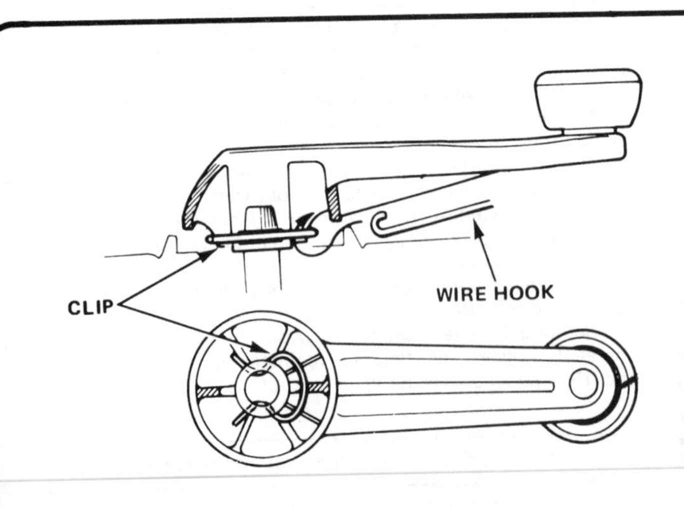

Fig. 12.3 Using a wire hook to remove the clip from the window regulator handle (Sec 15)

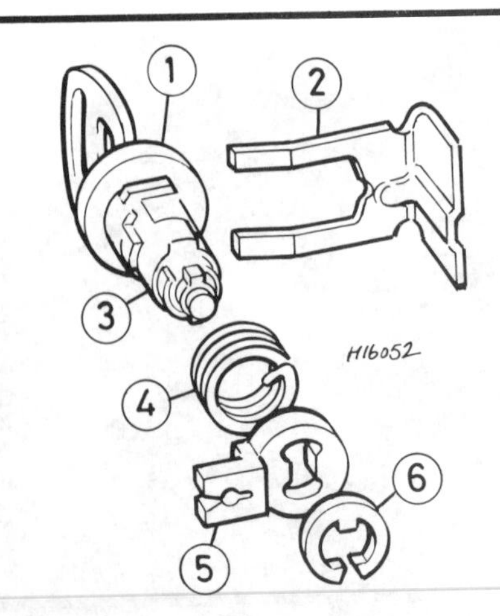

Fig. 12.4 Front door private lock components (Sec 16)

1 *Seal*
2 *Clip*
3 *Lock barrel*
4 *Spring*
5 *Arm*
6 *Circlip*

5 If necessary the lock barrel can be removed by extracting the circlip, removing the arm and spring, and pulling out the barrel with the key inserted.
6 Refitting is a reversal of removal, but renew the seal if necessary and make sure that the lock arm is fitted the correct way round (see Fig. 12.4).

17 Door – removal and refitting

1 Open the door and use a pencil to mark the hinge positions.
2 Drive out the check strap pin (photo).
3 On models with electrically-operated windows remove the door trim pad as described in Section 15, remove the polythene sheet, and disconnect the electric motor supply wires. Remove the wiring from the clips and grommet.
4 With the help of an assistant, support the door, unscrew the hinge-to-door bolts, and withdraw the door (photos).
5 Refitting is a reversal of removal, being sure to locate the hinges in their original positions. Check that the front edge of the door is slightly recessed relative to the front wing or front door as applicable, and if necessary reposition the hinges.

18 Front door remote control mirror – removal and refitting

1 Remove the door trim pad as described in Section 15. Remove the polythene sheet.
2 Prise out the retaining clip and push the remote control from the door inner panel. Pull the cable through the aperture ready for removal.
3 Extract the two caps, then remove the retaining screws and withdraw the mirror and control cable from the door together with the mounting pad.
4 Refitting is a reversal of removal.

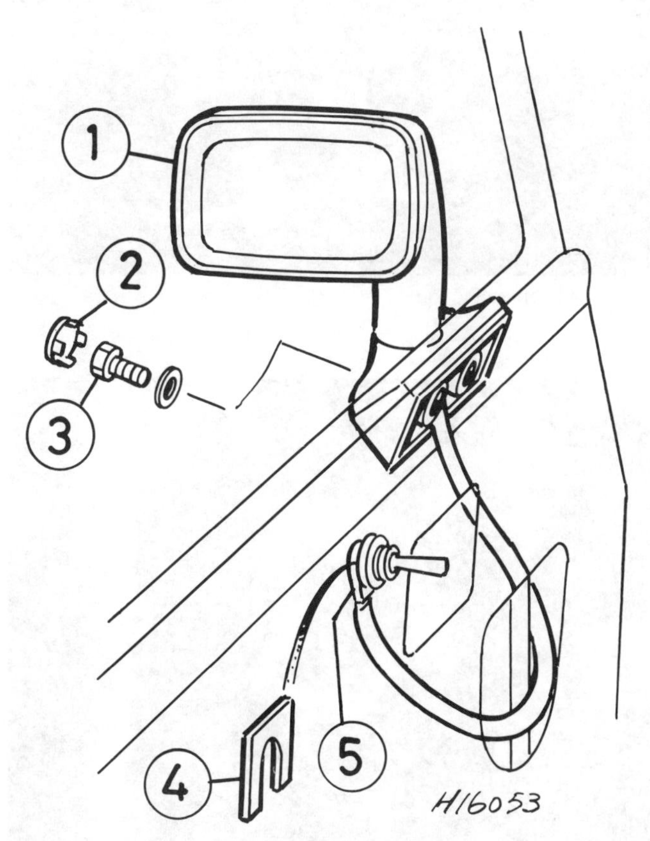

Fig. 12.5 Front door remote control mirror components (Sec 18)

1 Mirror
2 Cap
3 Screw
4 Clip
5 Control

16.3 Front door private lock

17.2 Door check strap and pin

17.4a Front door upper hinge

17.4b Front door lower hinge (note 'R' (arrowed) denoting right-hand)

19.2 Exterior handle operating rod

19.3a Interior remote door handle ...

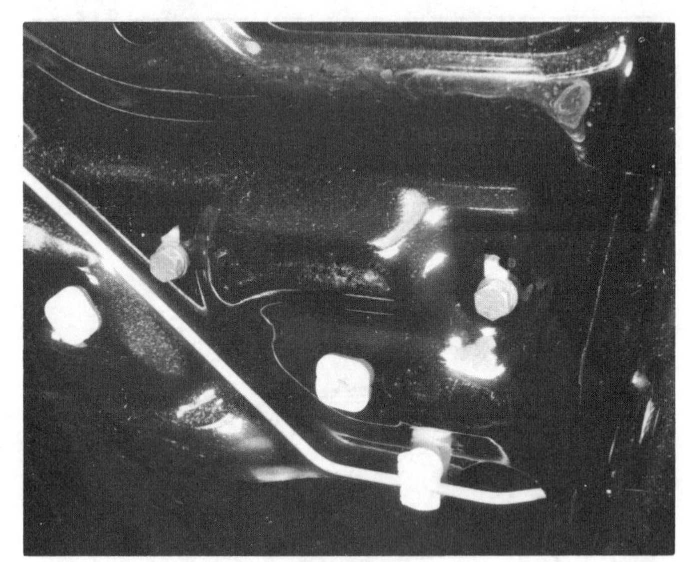

19.3b ... and operating rod

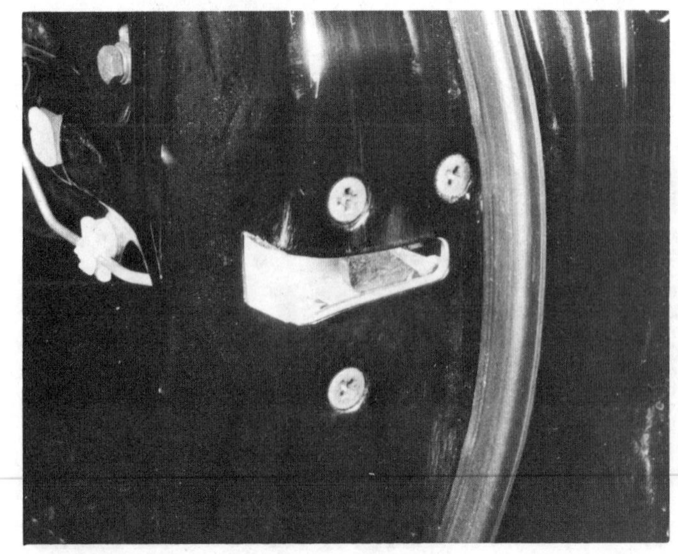

19.5 Door lock mounting screws

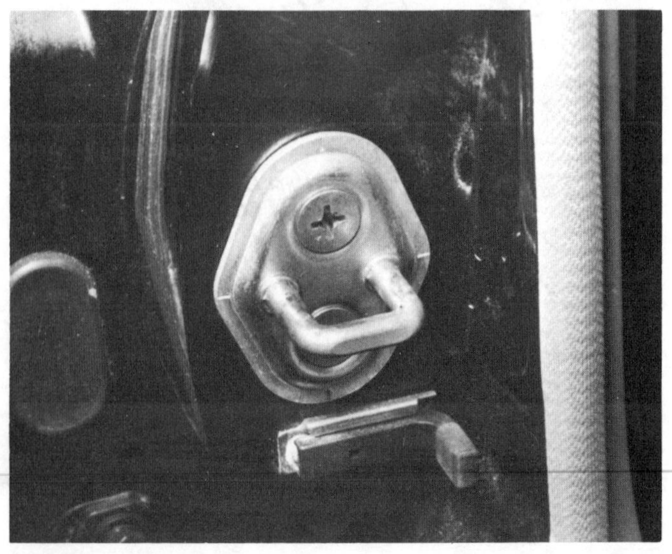

19.6 Door lock striker

19 Door lock – removal, refitting and adjustment

1 Fully close the window then remove the door trim pad as described in Section 15. Remove the polythene sheet.
2 Disconnect the operating rod from the outside handle (photo).
3 Remove the screws form the interior remote door handle assembly, release the operating rod from the guide, and disconnect the rod from the handle (photos).
4 On the front doors, disconnect the operating rod from the private lock.
5 Remove the mounting screws and withdraw the lock through the aperture in the door inner panel (photo). Note the location of the lock cover.
6 Refitting is a reversal of removal, but check that the lock operates smoothly and that the door is held firmly when shut. If necessary, loosen the striker screws and reposition the striker (photo).

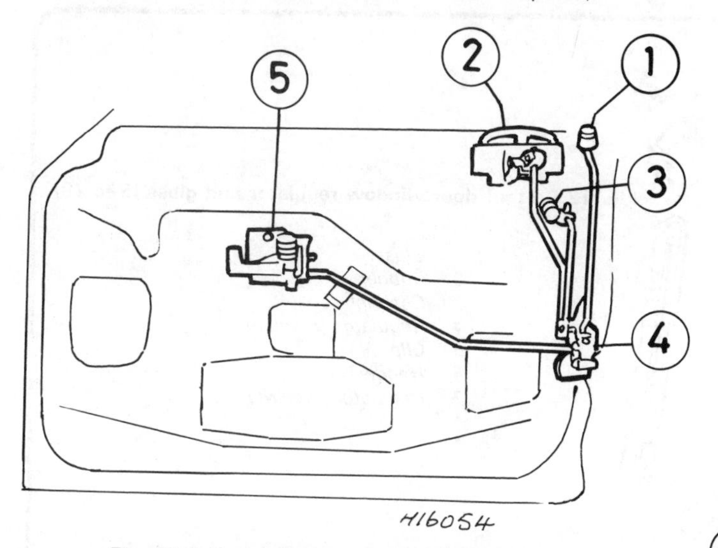

Fig. 12.6 Front door lock mechanism (Sec 19)

1 Locking button
2 Outer handle
3 Private lock
4 Lock
5 Interior door handle

20 Front door glass – removal and refitting

1 Remove the door trim pad as described in Section 15. Remove the polythene sheet.
2 Temporarily refit the window regulator handle and lower the window until the regulator arms are visible through the bottom aperture.
3 Support the window and remove the bolts securing the window bottom channel to the regulator (photo).
4 Lift the rear of the glass and tilt it forwards, then withdraw the window upwards through the slot to the outside of the door.
5 Carefully tap the bottom channel and rubber from the glass.
6 Dip the rubber in soapy water and locate it in the bottom channel, then carefully tap the channel onto the new glass with the rear mounting hole 40 mm (1.75 in) from the rear edge of the glass.
7 Lower the glass into the door and insert the bottom channel bolts loosely.
8 Loosen the front window channel bolts, then raise and lower the window several times and adjust the front channel so that the window moves smoothly (photo).
9 Tighten the bolts on the front and bottom channels.
10 Refit the polythene sheet and door trim pad with reference to Section 15.

21 Rear door glass – removal and refitting

1 Remove the door trim pad as described in Section 15. Remove the polythene sheet.

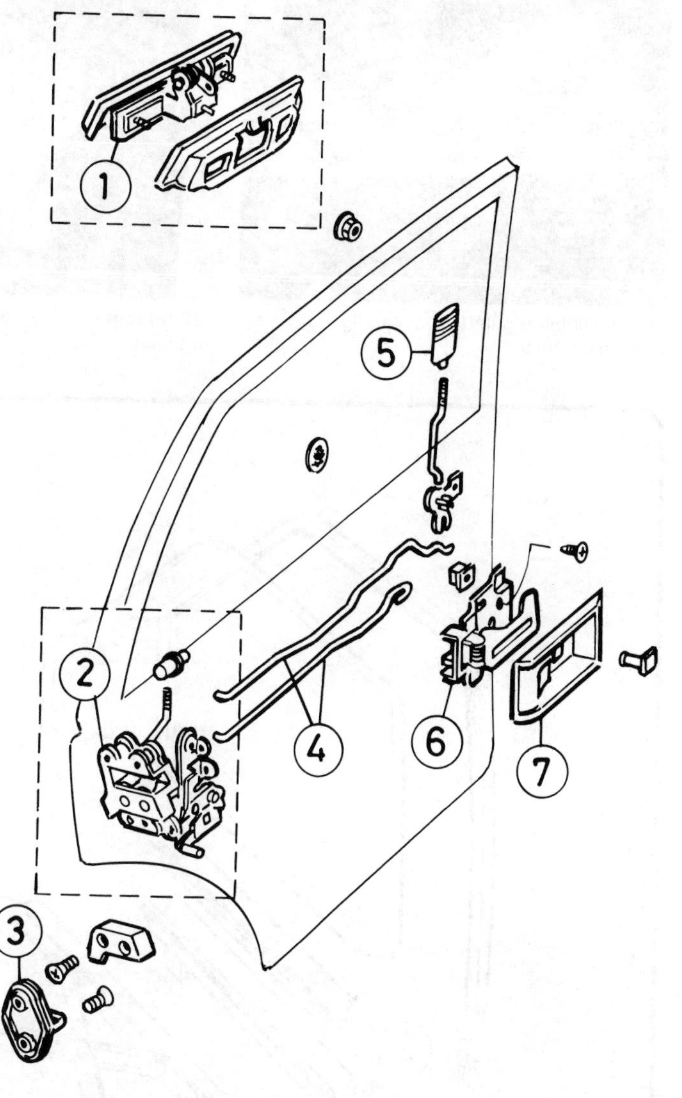

Fig. 12.7 Rear door lock components (Sec 19)

1 Exterior handle
2 Lock
3 Striker
4 Operating rods
5 Locking button
6 Interior handle
7 Trim plate

2 Temporarily refit the window regulator handle and fully lower the window.
3 Prise the outer glass seal from the door.
4 Lift the weatherstrip and remove the two screws securing the centre window channel to the top of the door (photo).
5 Remove the centre window channel lower mounting bolts.
6 Prise out and remove the felt channel section. Also remove the centre channel distance piece from the door inner panel.
7 Tilt the centre channel forwards, then remove the quarterlight from the door. Remove the channel.
8 Support the window and remove the bolts securing the window bottom channel to the regulator.
9 Withdraw the window upwards through the slot to the outside of the door.
10 Carefully tap the bottom channel and rubber from the glass.
11 Dip the rubber in soapy water and locate it in the bottom channel, then carefully tap the channel onto the new glass with the rear mounting hole 70 mm (2.76 in) from the rear edge of the glass.
12 Refitting is a reversal of removal, but do not fully tighten the channel bolts until the window has been raised and lowered several times to check that it moves smoothly.

20.3 Window regulator arms and glass bottom channel

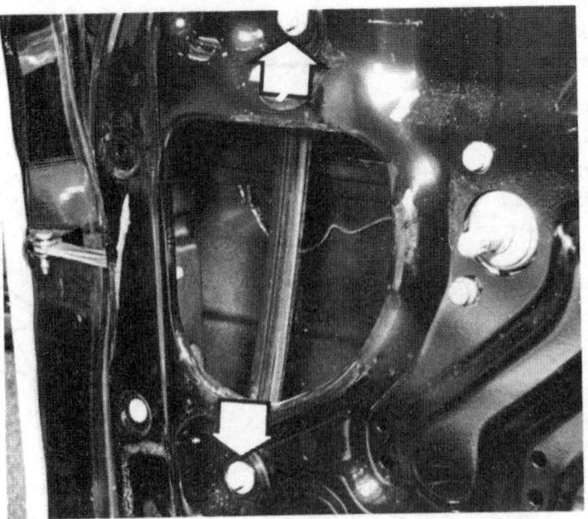
20.8 Front window channel and (arrowed) retaining bolts

21.4 Rear door centre window channel screw location

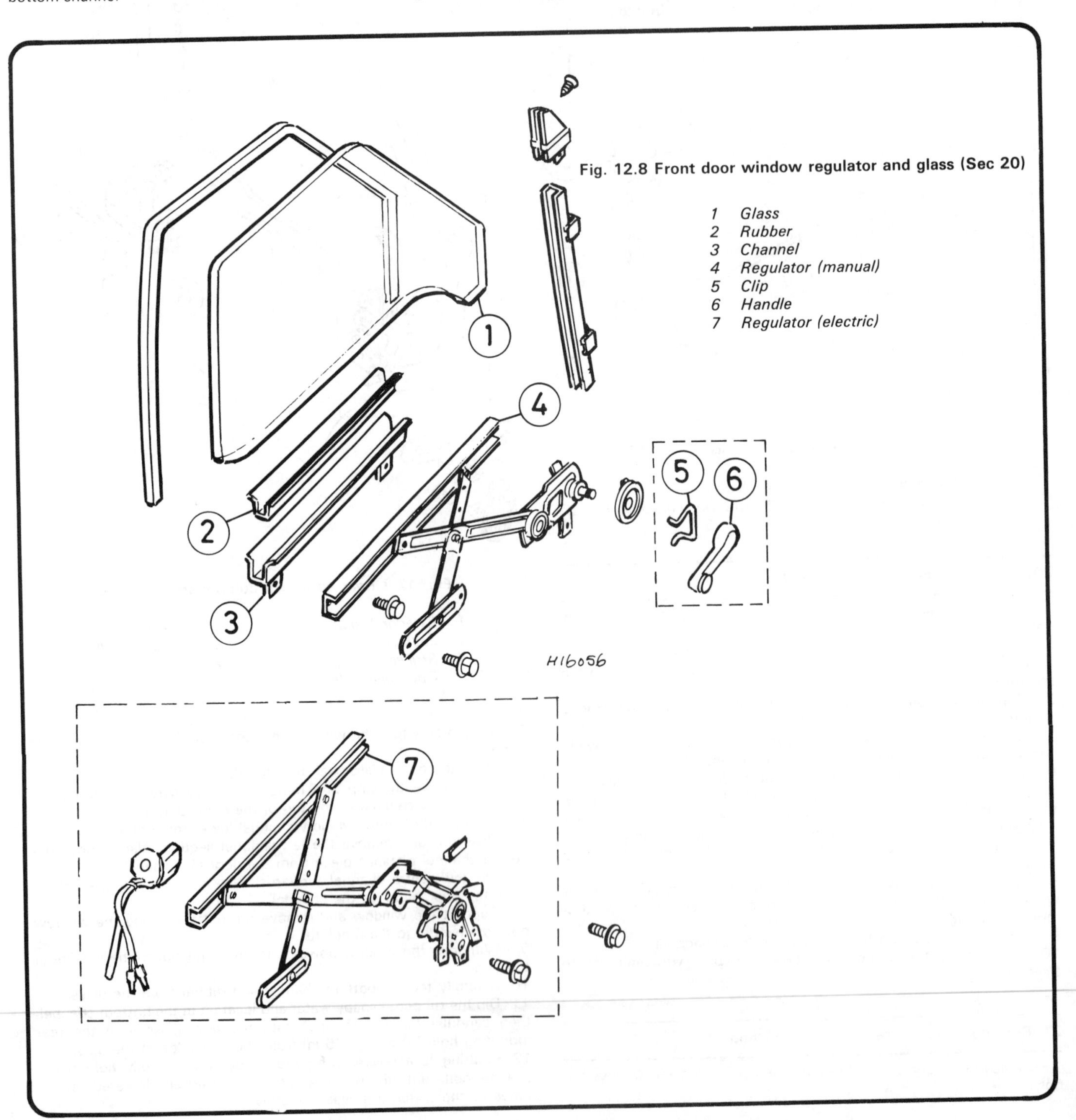

Fig. 12.8 Front door window regulator and glass (Sec 20)

1 *Glass*
2 *Rubber*
3 *Channel*
4 *Regulator (manual)*
5 *Clip*
6 *Handle*
7 *Regulator (electric)*

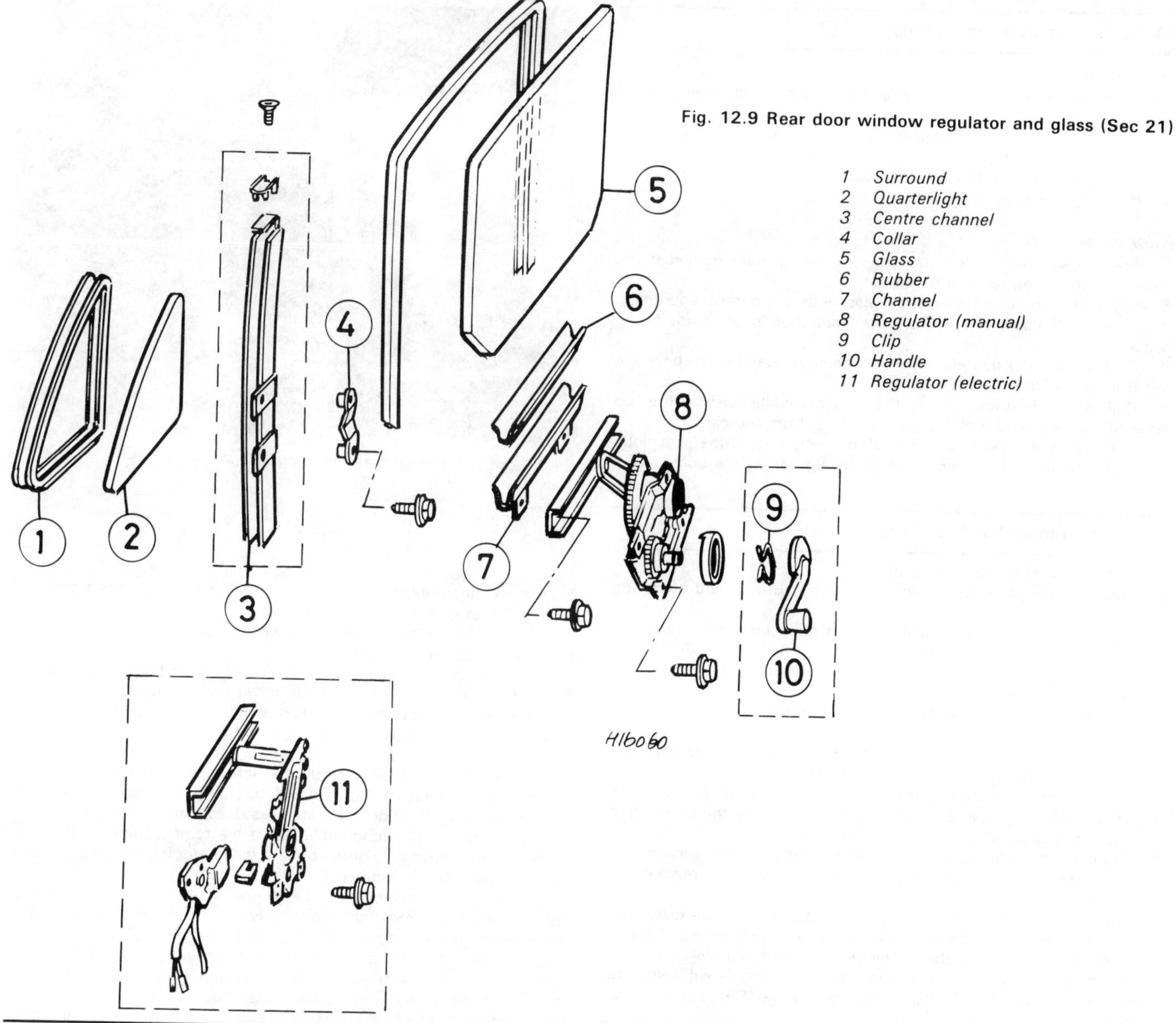

Fig. 12.9 Rear door window regulator and glass (Sec 21)

1 Surround
2 Quarterlight
3 Centre channel
4 Collar
5 Glass
6 Rubber
7 Channel
8 Regulator (manual)
9 Clip
10 Handle
11 Regulator (electric)

22 Windscreen and rear window – removal and refitting

Windscreen or rear window renewal is one job which the average DIY owner is advised to leave to the experts. The fitting charge made by a specialist is less than the expense of an accidentally broken new windscreen!

1 If the glass has shattered, cover the facia panel and air vents or rear seat with a large sheet of polythene to catch the pieces of glass. If available, adhesive sheeting will facilitate the removal. Remove all of the glass.

2 Remove the windscreen wiper arms or disconnect the rear window heater wires (as applicable).

3 If the glass is to be removed intact, release the rubber surround from the bodywork with a blunt screwdriver, taking care not to damage the paintwork.

4 Have an assistant support the glass, then, starting at a top corner, push the glass and rubber from the aperture using the feet (suitably padded) from inside the car.

5 Remove the finishers from the rubber surround and remove the surround from the glass.

6 Examine the rubber surround for damage or deterioration and renew it if necessary. Clean the surround channels and the body aperture, and repair any damage or distortion of the aperture flange.

7 Lubricate the rubber surround with soapy water and fit it to the glass. Where applicable, the joint must be at the bottom.

8 Fit the finishers to the surround.

9 Obtain a length of strong cord and insert it into the flange groove of the rubber surround with the free ends overlapping at the bottom.

10 Locate the glass on the aperture and have an assistant press gently from the outside.

11 From inside the car, pull each end of the cord in turn to locate the rubber surround on the flange. Tap the glass with the palm of the hand to make sure that it is fully seated.

12 Refit the windscreen wiper arms or reconnect the rear window heater wires (as applicable).

23 Fuel filler flap release cable – removal and refitting

1 Remove the driver's seat and the rear seat as described in Section 24.

2 Pull off the boot lid and fuel filler flap release handle knobs.

3 Prise out the clips and remove the front and rear inner sill mouldings.

4 Unscrew the release lever mounting bolts, withdraw the lever assembly, and disconnect the filler flap inner and outer cables.

5 Remove the rear bulkhead liner from the boot compartment.

6 Open the fuel filler flap and pull out the cable retaining clip.

7 Release the clips and withdraw the cable from the car.

8 Refitting is a reversal of removal.

24 Seats – removal and refitting

Front seat

1 Move the seat fully to the rear, then unscrew the runner front mounting bolts.
2 Move the seat fully forwards and unscrew the runner rear mounting bolts (photo).
3 Withdraw the seat through the door aperture.
4 Refitting is a reversal of removal.

Rear seat

5 Press down the centre rear edge of the cushion to reveal the mounting bolt, then remove the bolt.
6 Lift the rear of the cushion and release it from the front mountings.
7 Unscrew the seat belt anchor bolts located under each side of the backrest.
8 On HLS and CD models, prise out the stud retaining the backrest panel apron behind the backrest.
9 Pull up the bottom edge of the backrest while pushing the top edge to the rear, and withdraw the backrest from the car.
10 Refitting is a reversal of removal, but when fitted the seat belts should be positioned 45° upwards before tightening the bolts.

24.2 Front seat runner rear mounting bolt

25 Facia – removal and refitting

1 Disconnect the battery negative lead.
2 Unscrew the steering column mounting cap nuts and bolts and remove the caps and seats.
3 Disconnect the ignition switch wiring connector, and lower the steering column onto the front seat.
4 Detach the fusebox from the facia with reference to Chapter 10.
5 Remove the coin tray and ventilator.
6 Pull off the heater control knobs and prise the heater control panel from the facia (photo).
7 Disconnect the wiring from the blower switch, then remove the screws and withdraw the bracket and panel (photo).
8 Remove the instrument panel described in Chapter 10.
9 Open the glovebox and remove it (photo). Remove the screws and withdraw the catch and support bracket.
10 Remove the radio speaker and the left-hand air vent (photos).
11 Disconnect the air distribution and choke cables, and remove the lower facia panel.
12 Disconnect the wiring harness multi-plugs, the courtesy light leads, the choke warning lamp leads, the radio supply wire and aerial, and (where fitted) the left-hand electric window multi-plug.
13 Unscrew the mounting bolts and withdraw the facia sufficiently to release the heater control bracket and radio aerial. Remove the facia from the car.
14 Refitting is a reversal of removal, but make sure that the cables and wiring are correctly routed before locating the facia on the guide pin.

26 Bumpers – removal and refitting

1 Prise the caps from the corner bumpers, then unscrew the top and bottom corner bumper bolts (photo).
2 Move each corner bumper from the centre section, swivel them down, and remove them from the mounting clips.
3 Disconnect the wiring from the lamps mounted in the bumper.
4 Unscrew the mounting bolts and withdraw the bumper from the car (photo).
5 Refitting is a reversal of removal.

27 Heater unit – removal and refitting

1 Disconnect the battery negative lead.
2 Drain the cooling system as described in Chapter 2.
3 Remove the facia as described in Section 25.
4 Disconnect the heater hoses at the bulkhead (photo).
5 Unscrew the heater lower mounting nut and move the heater valve to one side.
6 On models equipped with air conditioning, loosen the band and detach the evaporator from the heater.
7 On models without air conditioning, unscrew the studs and remove the air duct (photo).
8 Disconnect the wiring and control cable from the heater (photo).
9 Remove the heater valve cable cover and the hose clamp.
10 Unscrew the mounting bolts and withdraw the heater from the car (photo). As coolant may spill from the heater, place polythene sheeting and rags beneath it to protect the matting and interior upholstery. Note that the earth lead is fitted to the top left-hand mounting bolt.
11 Refitting is a reversal of removal, but adjust the control cables as follows and refill the cooling system as described in Chapter 2.
12 To adjust the air blend cable, move the temperature control fully to the left and move the control arm on the heater fully rearwards, then fit the outer cable in the clip.
13 To adjust the heater valve cable, move the temperature control fully to the left and move the heater valve arm fully towards the engine rear torque rod, then fit the outer cable in the clip.
14 To adjust the air distribution cable, move the air distribution control fully to the right and move the control arm on the heater fully forwards, then fit the outer cable in the clip.
15 To adjust the fresh air cable, move the air distribution control fully to the left and move the control arm on the heater fully forwards, then fit the outer cable in the clip.
16 To adjust the air recirculation cable, move the air distribution control fully to the left and also pull out the 'REC' control, then move the outer cable to take up the slack in the sliding link and fit it in the clip.

28 Heater motor – removal and refitting

1 Disconnect the battery negative lead and remove the glovebox.
2 On models equipped with air conditioning, remove the left-hand radio speaker, unclip the wiring loom and remove the glovebox hinge rail. Release the band securing the blower unit to the evaporator.
3 On models without air conditioning, loosen the studs and remove the heater duct.
4 Unscrew the mounting bolts and lower the blower unit to the floor. Disconnect the control cables and multi-plugs, unclip the wiring loom and withdraw the blower unit from the car.
5 Remove the screws and withdraw the heater motor and fan from the blower unit together with the gasket (photo). If necessary, the fan can be removed from the motor by unscrewing the nut and tapping the motor shaft.
6 Refitting is a reversal of removal, but use a new gasket and adjust the control cables with reference to Section 27.

25.6a Pull off the knobs ...

25.6b ... and remove the heater control panel

25.7 Withdrawing the heater control bracket

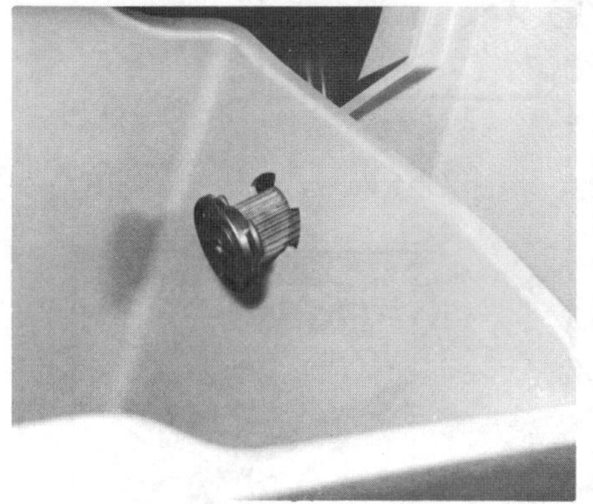

25.9 Removing the glovebox stops

25.10a Removing the left-hand air vent ...

25.10b ... and radio speaker

26.1 Bumper corner bolt

26.4 Bumper mounting bolt

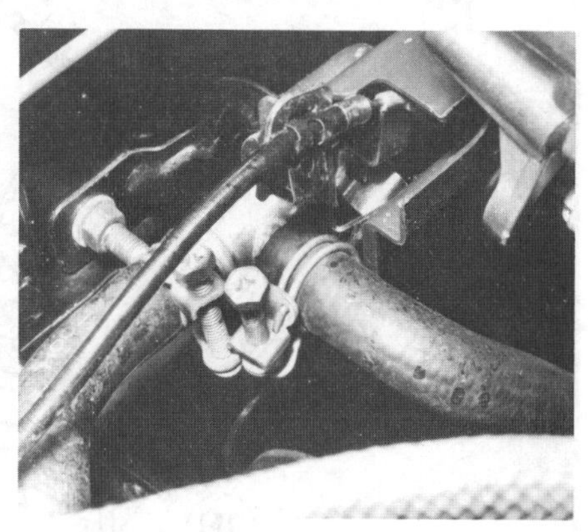

27.4 Heater valve located on the bulkhead

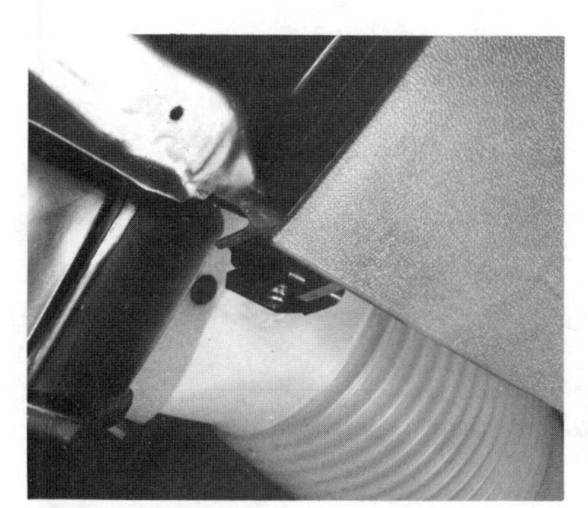

27.7 Heater air duct

27.8 Right-hand view of the heater

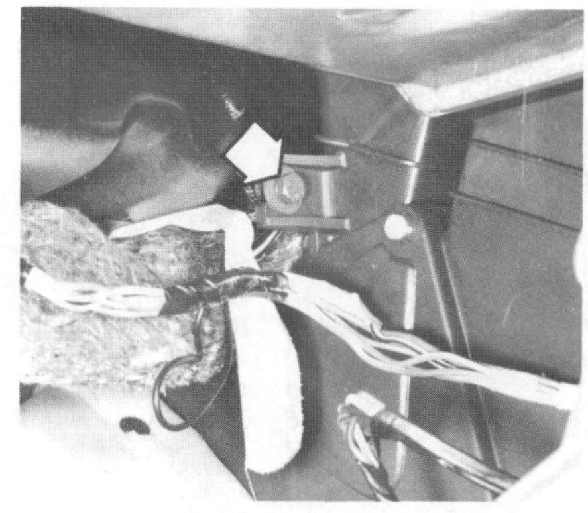

27.10 Heater left-hand mounting bolt (arrowed)

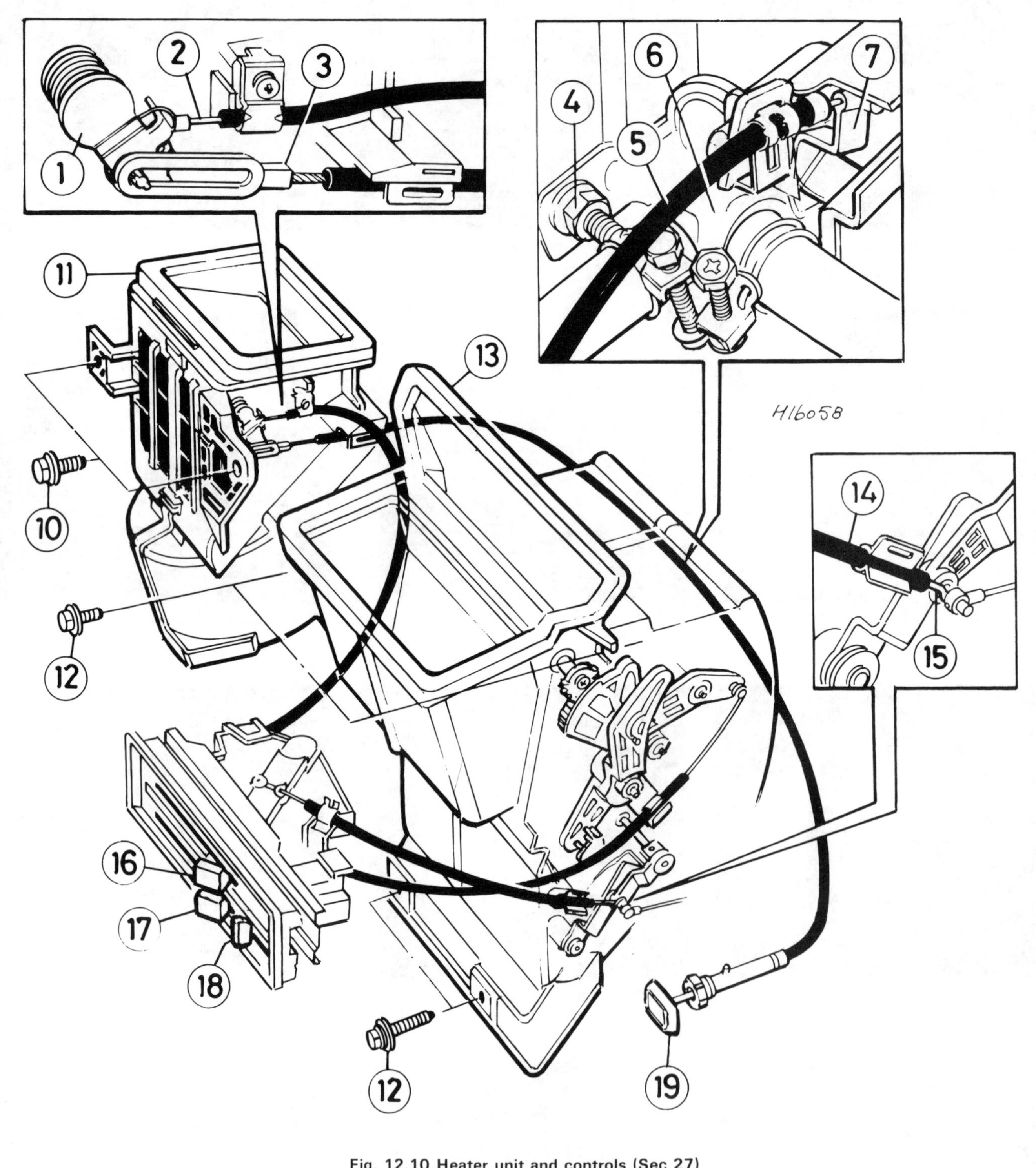

Fig. 12.10 Heater unit and controls (Sec 27)

1 Fresh air arm
2 Fresh air cable
3 Recirculation cable
4 Heater mounting nut
5 Heater valve cable
6 Heater valve
7 Heater valve arm
8 Distribution cable
9 Distribution control arm
10 Blower mounting bolts
11 Blower unit
12 Heater mounting bolts
13 Heater
14 Air blend cable
15 Air blend arm
16 Temperature control
17 Distribution control
18 Blower switch
19 Recirculation control

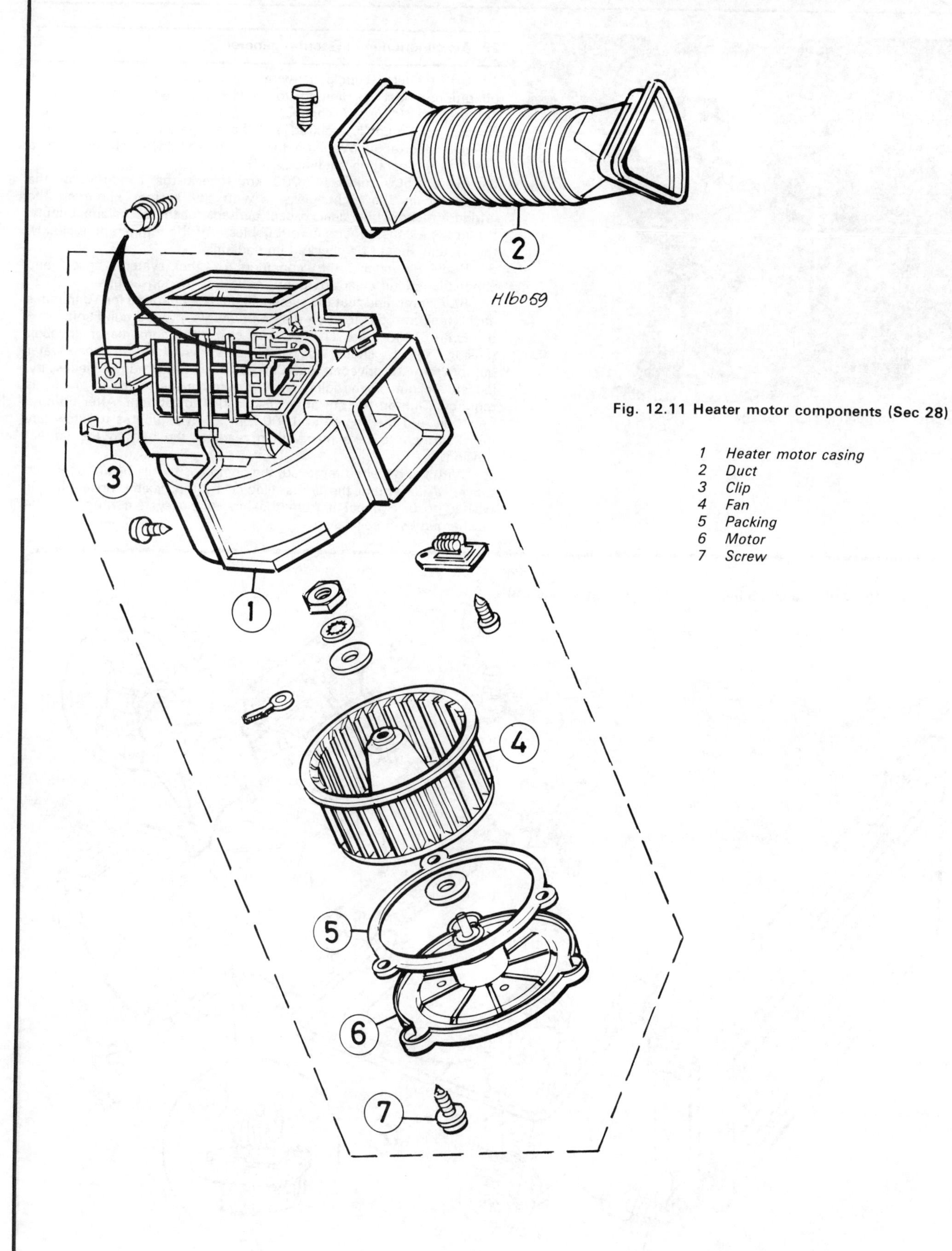

Fig. 12.11 Heater motor components (Sec 28)

1 Heater motor casing
2 Duct
3 Clip
4 Fan
5 Packing
6 Motor
7 Screw

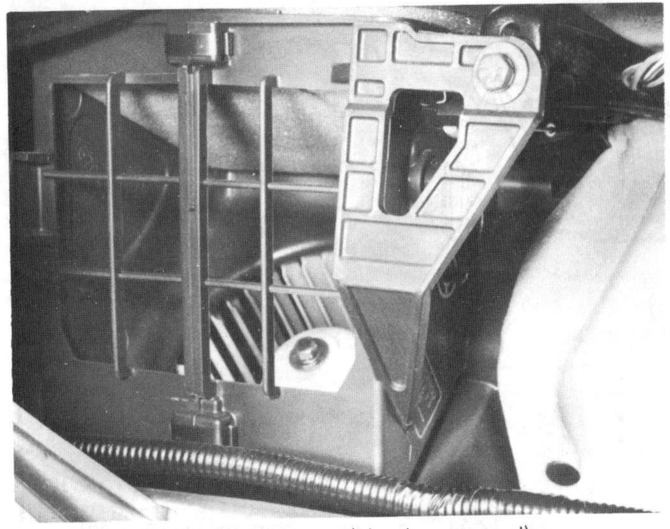

28.5 Heater motor and fan location (glovebox removed)

29 Air conditioning system – general

1 On models equipped with air conditioning, maintenance operations must be limited to those described in the following paragraphs. *Do not disconnect any part of the refrigerant circuit.* Special equipment is required and the refrigerant can be harmful if handled incorrectly. Work on the system should be entrusted to a qualified refrigeration engineer.
2 Every 7500 miles (12 000 km) check the condition of the refrigerant in the sight glass – with the system operating the refrigerant should be clear, except perhaps for the occasional bubble. If there is a constant stream of bubbles or if the refrigerant is cloudy, the system should be checked immediately.
3 Regularly check the condition of the system hoses and connections, and clear any debris from the condenser fins.
4 BL recommend that the system should be operated for 10 minutes each week in order to keep the components in good condition.
5 Every 7500 miles (12 000 km) check the compressor drivebelt tension, which should be the same as that for the water pump/alternator drivebelt (see Chapter 2). If adjustment is necessary, loosen the nut on the idler pulley and move the pulley in or out as required. Tighten the nut after making the adjustment. After fitting a new belt, run the engine at 1000 rpm for five minutes to allow any initial stretch to take place, then readjust the belt to the correct tension.
6 With the drivebelt removed, the compressor may be unbolted and moved aside within the limits allowed by the flexible hoses. If it is wished to disconnect it from the hoses, the system **must** first be discharged by a specialist.

Fig. 12.12 Air conditioning system components (Sec 29)

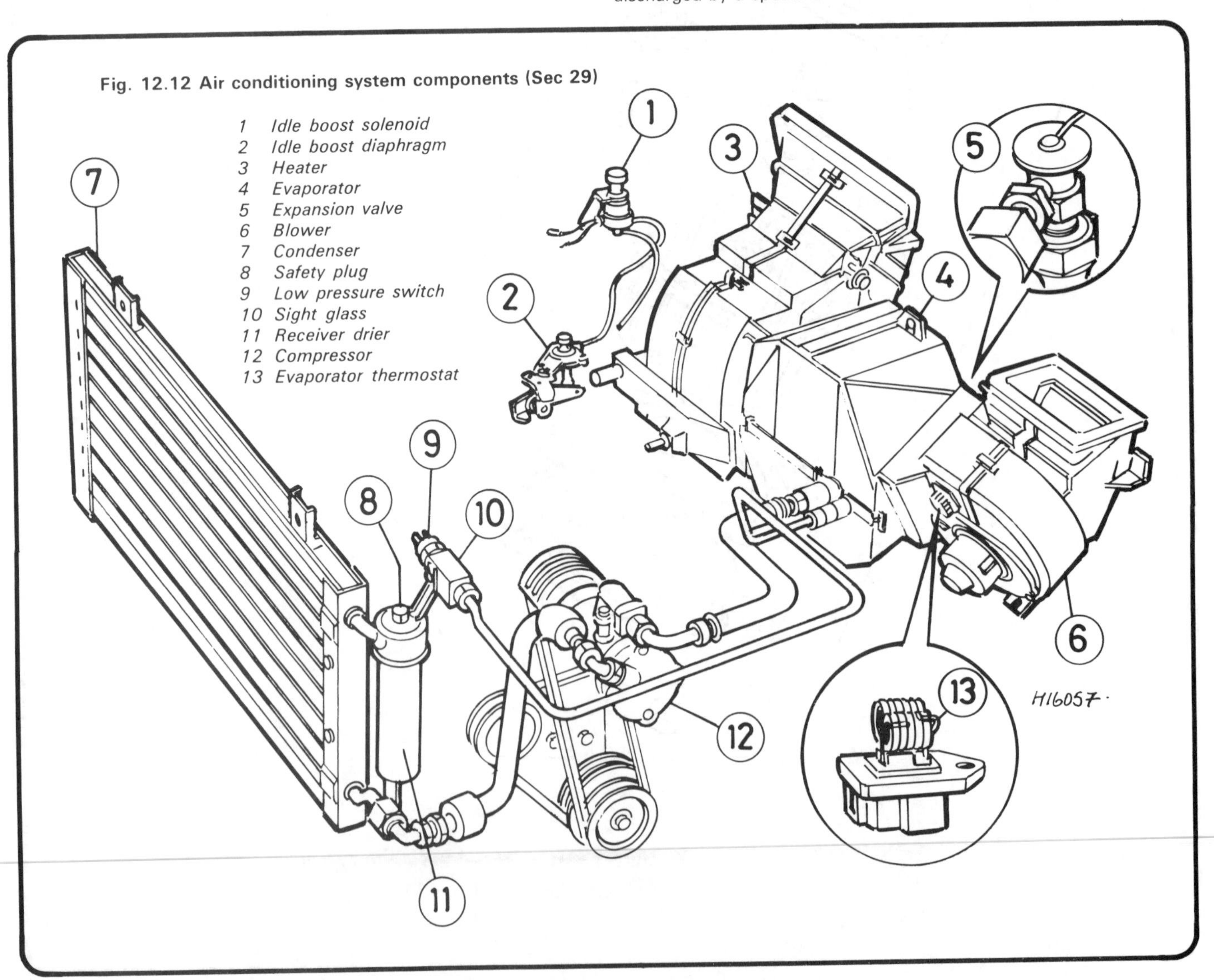

Chapter 13 Supplement: Revisions and information on later models

Contents

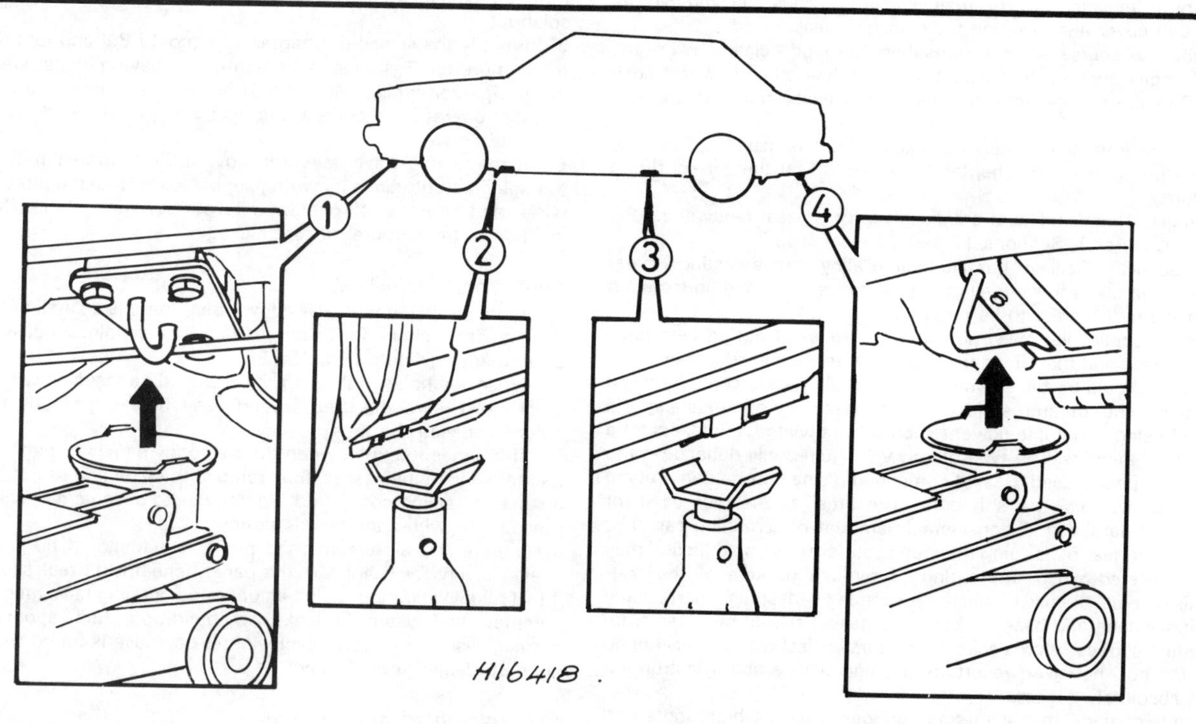

Fig. 13.1 Jacking points (Sec 2)

1 Front towing/lashing eye (trolley jack)
2 Front support and jacking point
3 Rear support and jacking point
4 Rear towing/lashing eye (trolley jack)

1 Introduction

This Chapter contains information which has become available since the manual was first written. It is suggested that, before undertaking a particular job, reference be made first to this Supplement for the latest information, then to the appropriate Chapter earlier in the book. In this way, any revisions can be noted before the job begins.

2 Jacking

The instructions on the car jack may be misunderstood, and the body shell lifting brackets mistaken for the jacking points. If damage to the floor panel is to be avoided, then the jacks or supports must be positioned as shown in the accompanying figure (Fig. 13.1).

3 Engine

Cylinder head retaining bolt threads

1 If, during examination of the cylinder block, it is found that the threads for the head retaining bolts are damaged or overworn, then refer the problem to your BL dealer or a competent engineering firm who will be able to advise on thread renovation and carry out the work involved.

2 The most satisfactory method of repair is by the fitting of a Helicoil thread insert which will allow the original size of bolt to be reused. If trouble is experienced in obtaining the correct size of insert (10 mm x 1.25 mm pitch) then contact BL for the address of a reliable supplier.

3 Helicoil inserts can of course be used to repair any damaged thread.

Oil leak detection and prevention

4 Where excessive oil consumption is experienced and subsequent investigation shows oil contamination around the pulley end of the sump, then do not immediately suspect the sump or crankshaft seals of failure. If leakage from these seals is not obvious then remove the timing belt cover and examine the camshaft seal.

5 If the leak source is not obvious then thoroughly clean and dry the area of engine around the suspect seal and dust it lightly with french chalk. Run the engine until oil staining the chalk indicates the leak source.

6 Leakage from the sump-to-crankcase joint is usually caused by incorrect fitting. Refer to Chapter 1, Section 33 for the correct fitting procedure.

7 Details of camshaft and crankshaft front oil seal renewal can be found in Chapter 1, Sections 17 and 18 respectively.

8 Because the Acclaim has aluminium alloy engine castings, great care must be taken to keep all mating surfaces clean and undamaged if oil or water leaks are to be prevented.

9 Where applicable, make sure that all traces of old gaskets have been removed and that the mating surfaces are clean and undamaged. Great care should be taken when removing old gasket compound not to damage the mating surface. Most gasket compounds can be softened using a suitable solvent such as methylated spirits, acetone or cellulose thinners. The type of solvent required will depend on the type of compound used. Gasket compound of the non-hardening type can be removed using a soft brass-wire brush of the type used for cleaning suede shoes. A considerable amount of scrubbing can take place without fear of harming the mating surfaces. Some difficulty may be encountered when attempting to remove gaskets of the self-vulcanising type, the use of which is becoming widespread, particularly as cylinder head and base gaskets. The gasket should be pared from the mating surface using a scalpel or a small chisel with a finely honed edge. Do not, however, resort to scraping with a sharp instrument unless absolutely necessary.

10 Slight damage to the mating surfaces, such as high spots and burrs, can be removed by careful use of a fine oilstone. Care must be taken to keep the affected surface flat. Degrease all surfaces before assembly.

Valve assembly noise

11 It should be noted that a slight tapping or knocking noise emitting from the valve assembly after starting with the engine cold is quite normal and cannot be eliminated. This noise should only last for up to one or two minutes and will be more prevalent in cold weather.

4 Cooling system

Oil cooler hoses – warning

1 On vehicles equipped with Trio-matic semi-automatic transmission, it is necessary to take great care when disconnecting the oil cooler hoses from the radiator right-hand end tank (Chapter 2, Section 6).

2 Do not use excessive force, otherwise the hose ends will shear and damage the radiator, resulting in expensive repair or replacement. If seizure of the hose ends is suspected, then apply penetrating oil to the affected threads.

5 Fuel and exhaust systems

Carburettor fast idle adjustment – warning

1 If it is necessary to bend the forked extensions of the fast idle lever to alter engine speed (Chapter 3, Section 10) then take great care not to apply any side load to the lever, otherwise the boss to which it is attached may shear.

2 Increase the gap between the forked extensions by placing the flat of a wide-bladed screwdriver between them and carefully turning the screwdriver anti-clockwise. Use pliers to narrow the gap. Do not move the extensions any more than is absolutely necessary.

Engine idling problems

3 A fuel cut-off solenoid is mounted on the side of the right-hand carburettor, its purpose being to eliminate the possibility of the engine running on after ignition is switched off. It achieves this by extending a needle valve into the idling circuit thereby blocking the fuel supply.

4 If problems are experienced with engine idling and the engine runs, possibly with slight misfiring, at speeds above 1200 to 1500 rpm, but stalls or runs roughly at lower speeds, then suspect the solenoid.

5 Identify the solenoid (Chapter 3, photo 12.8e) and remove it from the carburettor. Test solenoid operation by having an assistant switch on the ignition whilst the solenoid body is held against a good earth point. If operation is correct, the needle valve will be drawn into the solenoid body.

6 If the needle valve does not move, do not immediately condemn the solenoid but check its wiring supply for corroded contacts, chafed wires and the like. If operation is correct then check the needle location in the carburettor for blockage.

Fuel smell inside car

7 If, when driven with a window open, there is a smell of fuel inside the car, then check for missing seals at the points indicated in the accompanying figure (Fig. 13.2).

8 Unsealed holes in the boot floor should be resealed with adhesive tape. Make sure the area around each hole is properly degreased before applying the tape.

9 If a gap is found between the two body panels through which the fuel tank filler pipe passes, then remove the pipe and seal the gap with a suitable sealing compound. Remember to observe all necessary fire precautions whilst the pipe is removed.

10 Where the aforementioned points are found to be sealed, then check for unsealed holes in the panel beneath the rear seat cushion.

11 If all investigation to find an unsealed opening fails, then check the complete fuel system for leaks. Any build-up of fuel vapour inside the car can result in a fire or explosion; if no cause is found then consult your BL dealer immediately.

Exhaust noise and smoke

12 It is usual for white smoke to be emitted from the exhaust pipe for a few seconds immediately after starting the engine. The smoke does not indicate that engine oil consumption is excessive.

13 The exhaust system may emit sharp 'cracking' noises for some considerable time after the engine is turned off. This is due to the system contracting as it cools.

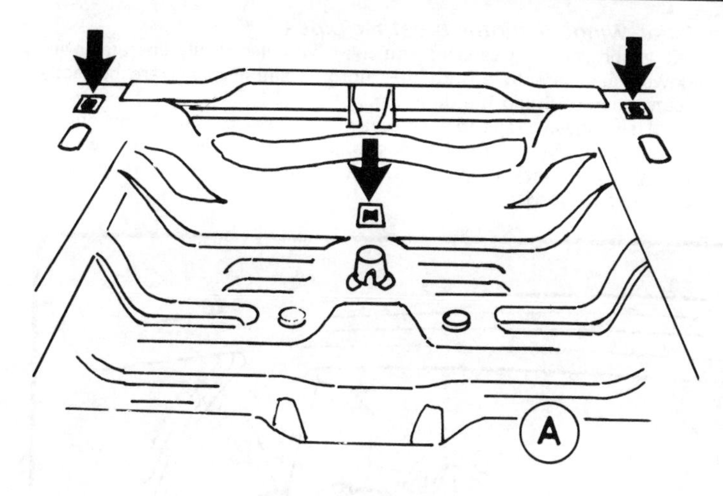

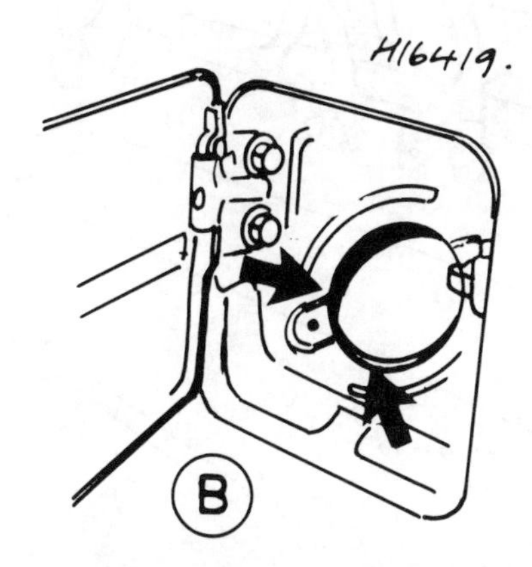

Fig. 13.2 Fuel vapour sealing points (Sec 5)

A Boot floor *B Fuel filler pipe*

6 Electrical system

Main fuse failure

1 It should be noted that blowing of the 55 amp main fusible link can be caused by electrical wiring becoming trapped between the floor panel and front seat runner. Check that all wires are taped well clear of the runner.

Headlamp alignment problems

2 Should it prove impossible to operate the headlamp levelling adjuster (Chapter 10, Section 28) then refer to the accompanying figure and check that the actuator piston end screws are correctly engaged with the headlamp lower brackets (Fig. 13.3).

3 To avoid jamming of a piston, its end screw must be located against the upper edge of the bracket slot. Each screw head can be viewed through the hole beneath the headlamp. To correctly position a screw, carefully press the lower section of the headlamp inwards and push the screw upwards into the slot.

7 Suspension and steering

Front suspension noise

1 It should be noted that, under certain driving conditions, the front shock absorbers may emit a dull 'knocking' noise. Whilst there is unfortunately no way of stopping this noise, the efficiency or safety of the vehicle is in no way impaired.

Steering lock – warning

2 Do not attempt to improve the efficiency of the steering lock by introducing oil into its mechanism. Oil finding its way into the ignition switch can create a fire hazard. Any oil in the mechanism will attract particles of dirt, thereby contributing to inefficient operation.

8 Bodywork and fittings

Front seat rearward adjustment

1 It is possible to increase the amount of leg room in the front of the car by repositioning the runner assemblies on each seat frame.

2 Remove the appropriate seat (Chapter 12, Section 24) and remove the runner assemblies from it. Identify the alternative bolt holes in the seat frame which are positioned approximately 25 mm (1 in) in front of the used holes. Reposition the runners and refit the seat.

Front seat belt anchorage repositioning

3 It is possible to lower the standard seat belt anchorage so that the belt can be made to fit comfortably and safely.

4 On all except the earliest Acclaims, a second anchorage point is provided some 25 mm (1 in) below that used as standard. This point can be felt through the trim.

5 To lower the mounting some 60 mm (2.4 in) from standard, BL provide the kit shown in the accompanying figure (Fig. 13.4). More spacers and washers may be provided than are actually needed. If no instructions are provided, then follow the fitting sequence shown. Use the original setscrew to secure the bracket to the body and use the 22 mm (0.87 in) long screw provided to secure the belt to the bracket.

6 Fitting the lowering kit to the lower mounting will, of course, lower the belt height by some 85 mm (3.4 in).

Rear seat belt fitting

7 The fitting of rear seat belts in any car will greatly reduce the risk of passenger injury in an accident. To make the fitting of belts relatively easy, BL provide anchorage points which take the form of nuts welded to the body panels beneath the rear seat cushions.

8 Provision is made for the fitting of three belts. The accompanying figure clearly shows the anchorage points and the position of male and

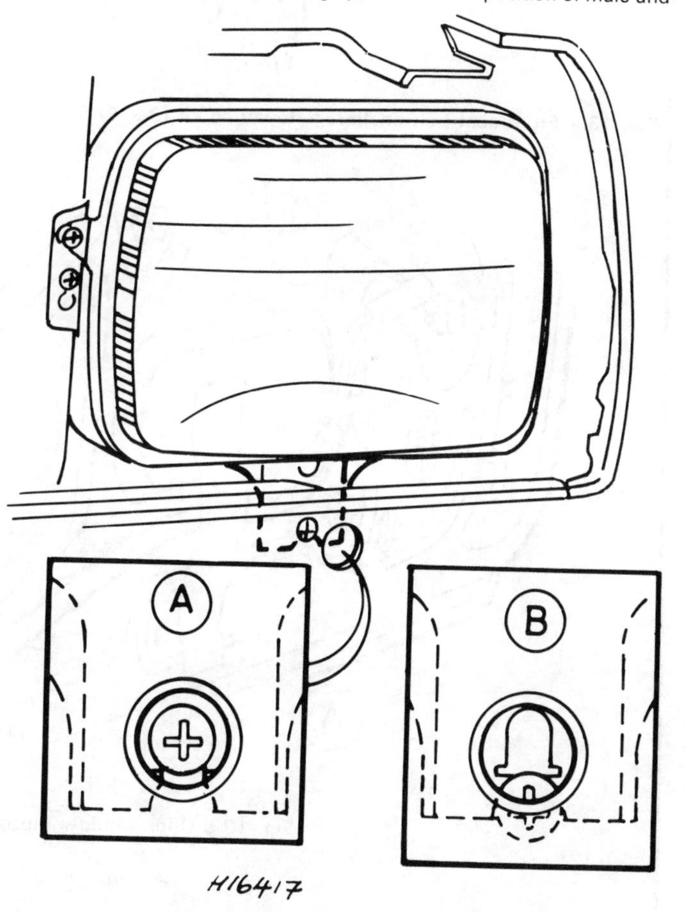

Fig. 13.3 Headlamp actuator piston end screw location (Sec 6)

A Correct *B Piston jammed*

female buckles on each belt (Fig. 13.5). Check all belt securing screws are properly tightened before refitting the seat cushions.

Sunroof – warning

9 BL advise against the fitting of any type of sunroof. The roof panel of the Acclaim is braced and stiffened by crossmembers which run through it and the cutting or removal of these members will seriously weaken the roof structure.

Door window motor breather pipes

10 When servicing vehicles equipped with electrically-operated windows, take care to ensure the motor breather pipes are correctly routed before fitting the door trim.

11 Use adhesive tape to secure each pipe as shown in the accompanying figure (Fig. 13.6). If a pipe is left to hang free inside the door cavity it may pick up water which will then enter the motor and decrease its service life.

Fig. 13.4 Front seat belt anchorage lowering kit (Sec 8)

Fig. 13.5 Rear seat belt anchorage points (Sec 8)

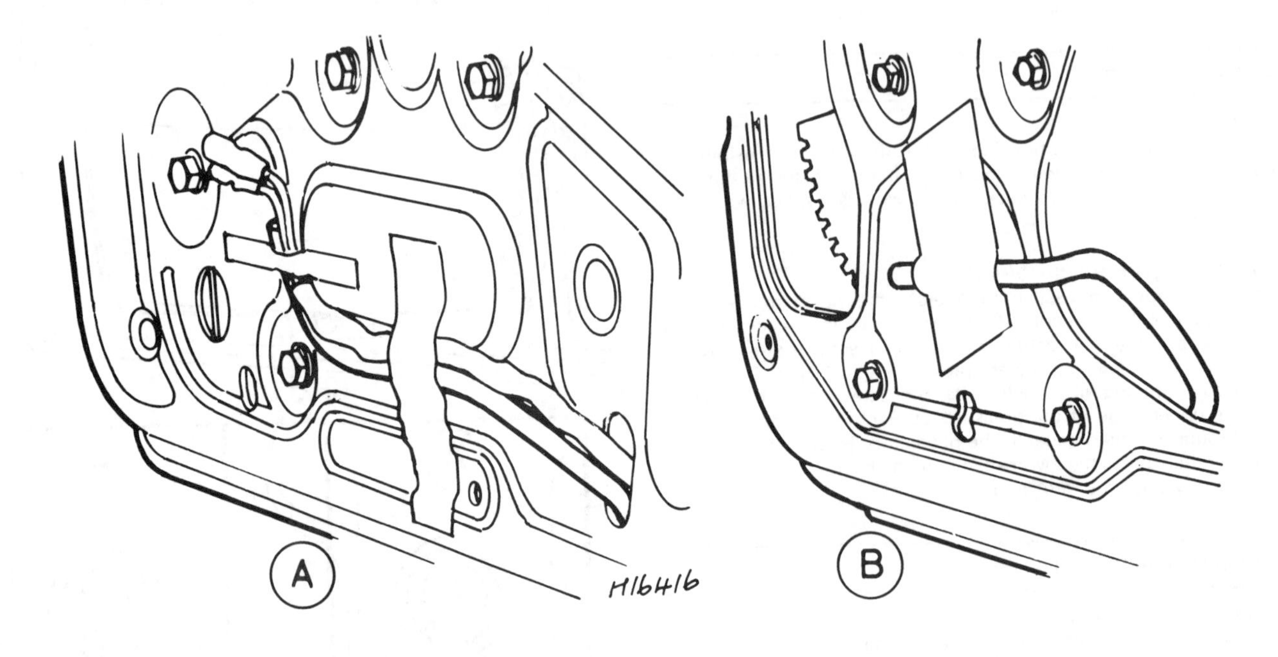

Fig. 13.6 Door window motor breather pipe location (Sec 8)

A Rear door *B Front door*

General repair procedures

Whenever servicing, repair or overhaul work is carried out on the car or its components, it is necessary to observe the following procedures and instructions. This will assist in carrying out the operation efficiently and to a professional standard of workmanship.

Joint mating faces and gaskets

Where a gasket is used between the mating faces of two components, ensure that it is renewed on reassembly, and fit it dry unless otherwise stated in the repair procedure. Make sure that the mating faces are clean and dry with all traces of old gasket removed. When cleaning a joint face, use a tool which is not likely to score or damage the face, and remove any burrs or nicks with an oilstone or fine file.

Make sure that tapped holes are cleaned with a pipe cleaner, and keep them free of jointing compound if this is being used unless specifically instructed otherwise.

Ensure that all orifices, channels or pipes are clear and blow through them, preferably using compressed air.

Oil seals

Whenever an oil seal is removed from its working location, either individually or as part of an assembly, it should be renewed.

The very fine sealing lip of the seal is easily damaged and will not seal if the surface it contacts is not completely clean and free from scratches, nicks or grooves. If the original sealing surface of the component cannot be restored, the component should be renewed.

Protect the lips of the seal from any surface which may damage them in the course of fitting. Use tape or a conical sleeve where possible. Lubricate the seal lips with oil before fitting and, on dual lipped seals, fill the space between the lips with grease.

Unless otherwise stated, oil seals must be fitted with their sealing lips toward the lubricant to be sealed.

Use a tubular drift or block of wood of the appropriate size to install the seal and, if the seal housing is shouldered, drive the seal down to the shoulder. If the seal housing is unshouldered, the seal should be fitted with its face flush with the housing top face.

Screw threads and fastenings

Always ensure that a blind tapped hole is completely free from oil, grease, water or other fluid before installing the bolt or stud. Failure to do this could cause the housing to crack due to the hydraulic action of the bolt or stud as it is screwed in.

When tightening a castellated nut to accept a split pin, tighten the nut to the specified torque, where applicable, and then tighten further to the next split pin hole. Never slacken the nut to align a split pin hole unless stated in the repair procedure.

When checking or retightening a nut or bolt to a specified torque setting, slacken the nut or bolt by a quarter of a turn, and then retighten to the specified setting.

Locknuts, locktabs and washers

Any fastening which will rotate against a component or housing in the course of tightening should always have a washer between it and the relevant component or housing.

Spring or split washers should always be renewed when they are used to lock a critical component such as a big-end bearing retaining nut or bolt.

Locktabs which are folded over to retain a nut or bolt should always be renewed.

Self-locking nuts can be reused in non-critical areas, providing resistance can be felt when the locking portion passes over the bolt or stud thread.

Split pins must always be replaced with new ones of the correct size for the hole.

Special tools

Some repair procedures in this manual entail the use of special tools such as a press, two or three-legged pullers, spring compressors etc. Wherever possible, suitable readily available alternatives to the manufacturer's special tools are described, and are shown in use. In some instances, where no alternative is possible, it has been necessary to resort to the use of a manufacturer's tool and this has been done for reasons of safety as well as the efficient completion of the repair operation. Unless you are highly skilled and have a thorough understanding of the procedure described, never attempt to bypass the use of any special tool when the procedure described specifies its use. Not only is there a very great risk of personal injury, but expensive damage could be caused to the components involved.

Conversion factors

Length (distance)

Inches (in)	X 25.4	= Millimetres (mm)	X 0.0394	= Inches (in)
Feet (ft)	X 0.305	= Metres (m)	X 3.281	= Feet (ft)
Miles	X 1.609	= Kilometres (km)	X 0.621	= Miles

Volume (capacity)

Cubic inches (cu in; in^3)	X 16.387	= Cubic centimetres (cc; cm^3)	X 0.061	= Cubic inches (cu in; in^3)
Imperial pints (Imp pt)	X 0.568	= Litres (l)	X 1.76	= Imperial pints (Imp pt)
Imperial quarts (Imp qt)	X 1.137	= Litres (l)	X 0.88	= Imperial quarts (Imp qt)
Imperial quarts (Imp qt)	X 1.201	= US quarts (US qt)	X 0.833	= Imperial quarts (Imp qt)
US quarts (US qt)	X 0.946	= Litres (l)	X 1.057	= US quarts (US qt)
Imperial gallons (Imp gal)	X 4.546	= Litres (l)	X 0.22	= Imperial gallons (Imp gal)
Imperial gallons (Imp gal)	X 1.201	= US gallons (US gal)	X 0.833	= Imperial gallons (Imp gal)
US gallons (US gal)	X 3.785	= Litres (l)	X 0.264	= US gallons (US gal)

Mass (weight)

Ounces (oz)	X 28.35	= Grams (g)	X 0.035	= Ounces (oz)
Pounds (lb)	X 0.454	= Kilograms (kg)	X 2.205	= Pounds (lb)

Force

Ounces-force (ozf; oz)	X 0.278	= Newtons (N)	X 3.6	= Ounces-force (ozf; oz)
Pounds-force (lbf; lb)	X 4.448	= Newtons (N)	X 0.225	= Pounds-force (lbf; lb)
Newtons (N)	X 0.1	= Kilograms-force (kgf; kg)	X 9.81	= Newtons (N)

Pressure

Pounds-force per square inch (psi; lbf/in^2; lb/in^2)	X 0.070	= Kilograms-force per square centimetre (kgf/cm^2; kg/cm^2)	X 14.223	= Pounds-force per square inch (psi; lbf/in^2; lb/in^2)
Pounds-force per square inch (psi; lbf/in^2; lb/in^2)	X 0.068	= Atmospheres (atm)	X 14.696	= Pounds-force per square inch (psi; lbf/in^2; lb/in^2)
Pounds-force per square inch (psi; lbf/in^2; lb/in^2)	X 0.069	= Bars	X 14.5	= Pounds-force per square inch (psi; lbf/in^2; lb/in^2)
Pounds-force per square inch (psi; lbf/in^2; lb/in^2)	X 6.895	= Kilopascals (kPa)	X 0.145	= Pounds-force per square inch (psi; lbf/in^2; lb/in^2)
Kilopascals (kPa)	X 0.01	= Kilograms-force per square centimetre (kgf/cm^2; kg/cm^2)	X 98.1	= Kilopascals (kPa)
Millibar (mbar)	X 100	= Pascals (Pa)	X 0.01	= Millibar (mbar)
Millibar (mbar)	X 0.0145	= Pounds-force per square inch (psi; lbf/in^2; lb/in^2)	X 68.947	= Millibar (mbar)
Millibar (mbar)	X 0.75	= Millimetres of mercury (mmHg)	X 1.333	= Millibar (mbar)
Millibar (mbar)	X 0.401	= Inches of water (inH_2O)	X 2.491	= Millibar (mbar)
Millimetres of mercury (mmHg)	X 0.535	= Inches of water (inH_2O)	X 1.868	= Millimetres of mercury (mmHg)
Inches of water (inH_2O)	X 0.036	= Pounds-force per square inch (psi; lbf/in^2; lb/in^2)	X 27.68	= Inches of water (inH_2O)

Torque (moment of force)

Pounds-force inches (lbf in; lb in)	X 1.152	= Kilograms-force centimetre (kgf cm; kg cm)	X 0.868	= Pounds-force inches (lbf in; lb in)
Pounds-force inches (lbf in; lb in)	X 0.113	= Newton metres (Nm)	X 8.85	= Pounds-force inches (lbf in; lb in)
Pounds-force inches (lbf in; lb in)	X 0.083	= Pounds-force feet (lbf ft; lb ft)	X 12	= Pounds-force inches (lbf in; lb in)
Pounds-force feet (lbf ft; lb ft)	X 0.138	= Kilograms-force metres (kgf m; kg m)	X 7.233	= Pounds-force feet (lbf ft; lb ft)
Pounds-force feet (lbf ft; lb ft)	X 1.356	= Newton metres (Nm)	X 0.738	= Pounds-force feet (lbf ft; lb ft)
Newton metres (Nm)	X 0.102	= Kilograms-force metres (kgf m; kg m)	X 9.804	= Newton metres (Nm)

Power

Horsepower (hp)	X 745.7	= Watts (W)	X 0.0013	= Horsepower (hp)

Velocity (speed)

Miles per hour (miles/hr; mph)	X 1.609	= Kilometres per hour (km/hr; kph)	X 0.621	= Miles per hour (miles/hr; mph)

*Fuel consumption**

Miles per gallon, Imperial (mpg)	X 0.354	= Kilometres per litre (km/l)	X 2.825	= Miles per gallon, Imperial (mpg)
Miles per gallon, US (mpg)	X 0.425	= Kilometres per litre (km/l)	X 2.352	= Miles per gallon, US (mpg)

Temperature

Degrees Fahrenheit = (°C x 1.8) + 32

Degrees Celsius (Degrees Centigrade; °C) = (°F - 32) x 0.56

**It is common practice to convert from miles per gallon (mpg) to litres/100 kilometres (l/100km), where mpg (Imperial) x l/100 km = 282 and mpg (US) x l/100 km = 235*

Index